DEMOCRACY'S FOOT SOLDIERS

Democracy's Foot Soldiers

WORLD WAR I AND
THE POLITICS OF EMPIRE
IN THE GREATER CARIBBEAN

Reena N. Goldthree

PRINCETON UNIVERSITY PRESS

PRINCETON & OXFORD

Copyright © 2025 by Princeton University Press

Princeton University Press is committed to the protection of copyright and the intellectual property our authors entrust to us. Copyright promotes the progress and integrity of knowledge created by humans. By engaging with an authorized copy of this work, you are supporting creators and the global exchange of ideas. As this work is protected by copyright, any reproduction or distribution of it in any form for any purpose requires permission; permission requests should be sent to permissions@press.princeton.edu. Ingestion of any IP for any AI purposes is strictly prohibited.

Published by Princeton University Press
41 William Street, Princeton, New Jersey 08540
99 Banbury Road, Oxford OX2 6JX

press.princeton.edu

GPSR Authorized Representative: Easy Access System Europe - Mustamäe tee 50, 10621 Tallinn, Estonia, gpsr.requests@easproject.com

All Rights Reserved

Library of Congress Control Number 2025942153

ISBN 9780691272511
ISBN (e-book) 9780691272535

British Library Cataloging-in-Publication Data is available

Portions of chapter two were previously published in the article "'A Greater Enterprise than the Panama Canal': Migrant Labor and Military Recruitment in the World War I–Era Circum-Caribbean." Copyright © 2016 Labor and Working-Class History Association. This article first appeared in *Labor: Studies in Working-Class History of the Americas*, Volume 13, Numbers 3–4, December 2016. Published with permission by Duke University Press.

Portions of chapter three were previously published in the article "'Vive La France!': British Caribbean Soldiers and Interracial Intimacies on the Western Front." Copyright © 2016 Reena N. Goldthree and The Johns Hopkins University Press. This article first appeared in *Journal of Colonialism and Colonial History*, Volume 17, Number 3, Winter 2016. Published with permission by Johns Hopkins University Press.

Editorial: Priya Nelson, Emma Wagh
Production Editorial: Elizabeth Byrd
Production: Erin Suydam
Publicity: William Pagdatoon
Copyeditor: Sherry Howard Salois

Jacket Credit: Contingent of British West Indian troops on parade. Granada (Windward Islands). Courtesy of the Colonial Office Collection at the Imperial War Museums, London.

Printed in the United States of America

10 9 8 7 6 5 4 3 2 1

To my parents and grandparents

with eternal love and gratitude

From the four corners of the world they come—
White, Brown, Black men of every hue and clime,
The children of the Empire in their prime.

—JOSEPH RUHOMAN, "FOR ENGLAND,"
DAILY ARGOSY, JUNE 29, 1915

England! That loved us with enticing show
Sweet adulation, and a broad decree
That all thy children should forever know
Justice alike, and Truth, and Liberty.
How has thy promise too oft proved unkept;
While we, forsaken, inward groaned and wept?

For faith unbroken, succor undenied
For silent sufferance both in peace and war,
For sacred hopes to loyalty allied
We are the outcast whom thou dost abhor.
O England! England! 'twas a manlier grace
Which kept thee free, and not a fairer face!

By all the dangers of the cannon's breath
Each deed of ours that kept our flag on high,
Our choice for THEE of victory or death,
By God Himself to whom all negroes cry,
Before unblinded eyes our need is set;
Who will may forgive; they sleep who forget.

—NIGER, "TO ENGLAND," *BARBADOS WEEKLY*
HERALD, AUGUST 23, 1919

CONTENTS

Illustrations · xi
Abbreviations · xiii

	Introduction	1
PART I	**HOMEFRONT MOBILIZATIONS**	17
CHAPTER 1	The "Color Question": War and the Racial Fault Lines of Imperial Belonging	19
CHAPTER 2	"Every True Son of the Empire": Martial Masculinity, Transnational Migration, and the Politics of Recruitment	51
PART II	**THE SOLDIER'S LIFE**	105
CHAPTER 3	"Humiliations and Disillusion": Military Labor and Wartime Interracial Encounters	107
CHAPTER 4	An "Insubordinate Spirit Prevailed": Rights, Respectability, and the Battle Against Discrimination in the British Army	137
PART III	**POSTWAR RECKONINGS**	173
CHAPTER 5	"Serious Discontent": Emigration, Rebellion, and Negotiation in the War's Aftermath	175
CHAPTER 6	"Equal Reward for Equal Service": Veterans' Politics in Postwar Trinidad	205
	Epilogue	241

[ix]

[X] CONTENTS

Acknowledgments · 253
Notes · 259
Bibliography · 327
Index · 355

ILLUSTRATIONS

0.1.	BWIR soldiers on parade in Grenada	3
0.2.	BWIR soldiers stacking shells in Ypres, Belgium	5
0.3.	Medal card for Tubal Uriah "Buz" Butler	8
0.4.	BWIR soldiers training in British Honduras	14
1.1.	Marcus Mosiah Garvey	21
1.2.	Arthur Andrew Cipriani	22
1.3.	"Shoulder to Shoulder," political cartoon	35
2.1.	BWIR recruitment rally in Port of Spain, Trinidad	65
2.2.	"Guiana's Sons," political cartoon	68
2.3.	"Young Man!" recruitment poster for the BWIR	70
2.4.	"Young Men of the Bahamas" recruitment poster for the BWIR	71
2.5.	Recruitment ad for the BWIR in Panama	78
2.6.	BWIR Enlistment by Territory (1915–18)	80
2.7.	Officers of the 1st Jamaica War Contingent of the BWIR	82
3.1.	Etienne Dupuch with family members	108
3.2.	Clennell Wilsden Wickham	110
3.3.	BWIR soldiers with Salvation Army members in France	128
4.1.	BWIR soldiers in the Middle East	140
4.2.	BWIR sergeant in uniform	142
5.1.	Return of the British Honduras Contingent of the BWIR	188
5.2.	Samuel Alfred Haynes	200
6.1.	Letterhead of the Returned Soldiers' and Sailors' Council	207
6.2.	Letterhead of the British West Indies World War Veterans' Association, Inc.	207
6.3.	Algernon Burkett	222
6.4.	Advertisement for Returned Soldiers' and Sailors' Council public meeting in Port of Spain, Trinidad	224
7.1.	Dedication of the Jamaica War Memorial	243
7.2.	Disabled veterans at the dedication of the Jamaica War Memorial	247

[xi]

[xii] ILLUSTRATIONS

7.3. "Leading in the Winner," political cartoon   248

7.4. Twenty-five-year reunion of Jamaica's 1st BWIR contingent   249

7.5. Jamaica War Memorial in National Heroes' Park   251

Maps

1. The Greater Caribbean, ca. 1914   xiv

2. The Eastern Caribbean, ca. 1914   xv

3. Selected Work Sites of the BWIR in France and
   Belgium during World War I   129

ABBREVIATIONS

ANZAC Australian and New Zealand Army Corps

BHCC British Honduras Contingent Committee

BWIR British West Indies Regiment

CSAC Central Supplementary Allowance Committee (Jamaica)

DSCA Discharged Soldiers Central Authority (Trinidad and Tobago)

JFL Jamaica Federation of Labour

RSSC Returned Soldiers' and Sailors' Council (Trinidad and Tobago)

SSU Soldiers and Sailors Union (Trinidad and Tobago)

TWA Trinidad Workingmen's Association

UNIA Universal Negro Improvement Association
and African Communities League

WIC West India Committee

WIR West India Regiment

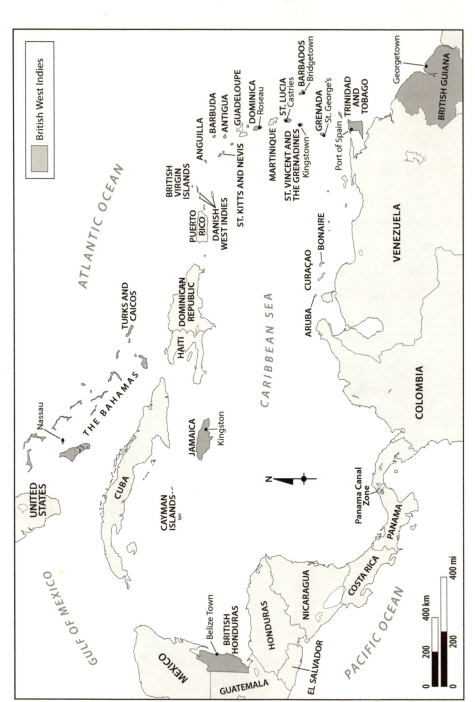

MAP 1. The Greater Caribbean, ca. 1914. Map by Ronald Draddy.

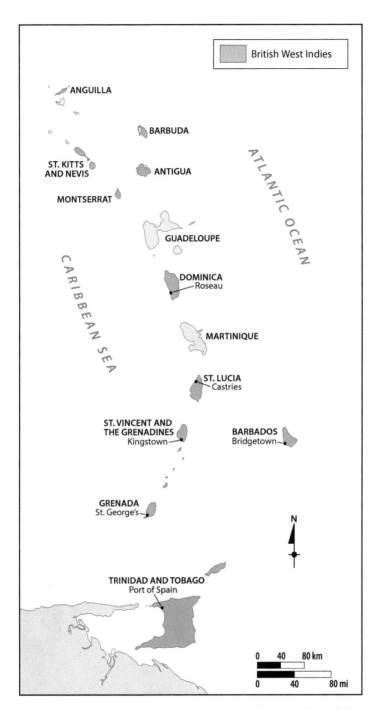

MAP 2. The Eastern Caribbean, ca. 1914. Map by Ronald Draddy.

Introduction

We are a new people, born out of a new day and a new circumstance.
We are born out of the bloody wa[r] of 1914–18.

—MARCUS GARVEY

A detailed history of the B. W. I. Regiment in the War will be told some day.

—C. L. R. JAMES

TUBAL URIAH "BUZ" Butler convened the first mass meeting of the Grenada Union of Returned Soldiers on September 11, 1919, less than three months after he was discharged from the British West Indies Regiment (BWIR).[1] That Thursday afternoon, a large crowd of spectators, including over one hundred ex-soldiers, gathered in St. George's, Grenada, to listen as the twenty-two-year-old ex-private announced his bold plan for the colony's first veterans' union. Standing atop the platform in Market Square, Butler recalled the triumphs and hardships Grenadian soldiers had endured during World War I and celebrated their contributions to the Allies' victory. "It is no boast when I say—our comrades of other islands heard it over and over from the mouths of high officers—that Grenadians were the brain, the flower of the British West Indies Regiment," he proclaimed. "The large number of Grenadians who wore stripes and were put in power of discipline over others," he added, "proves that we tried hard to merit your hopes for us, and that our efforts had been recognised by those in command."[2]

Yet Butler also alleged that in the aftermath of the war, colonial authorities in Grenada disregarded veterans' sacrifices and offered them only meager financial support. Expressing the anger of many, he railed against the government's parsimony, characterizing the low scale of gratuities awarded to ex-soldiers as "very ridiculous." "We take no pleasure in grumbling or in talking about what good we have done, but this is rendered necessary since those who should know, and feel, and act seem not be aware of these things," Butler asserted. "We did not expect to return to Grenada to be governors," he lamented, "but we did really expect to return to a grateful Government and people moved to help us resettle in civil life as comfortable citizens."[3] The state's refusal to provide adequate financial support to veterans, Butler concluded, was both a shocking act of ingratitude and a painful demonstration of imperial neglect.

Even as Butler publicly castigated colonial authorities, he advised veterans to respect the rule of law. The Grenada Union of Returned Soldiers was "not anti-Government or anti-law and order," he declared, and its members would seek redress solely through negotiation and other nonviolent tactics. "We are not going to fight the Government, except as we may in a constitutional way," he stressed. To secure support from civilians and garner their "minds and influences" for the union, Butler counseled that veterans must restrict their protests to respectable, sanctioned forms of dissent, taking great care not to behave in a "drunken and 'Tommified' way." The union's provisional president—pioneering black journalist and newspaper editor T. A. Marryshow—affirmed and echoed Butler's moderate stance. In an article about the new union published one day after the mass meeting, Marryshow stated plainly: "The Society has no desire to be anti-British, anti-Government, or anti-anything that may be rated disloyal or stupid."[4]

Butler's work to establish the Grenada Union of Returned Soldiers launched his remarkable, decades-long activist career as a trade unionist, politician, and preacher; while he asserted that he was not anti-government, colonial officials increasingly saw Butler as a threat to the colonial order. The same year that he founded the veterans' union, he also joined the Grenada Representative Government Movement, linking the fight for ex-soldiers to the campaign for voting rights and democratic governance. Two years later, in 1921, Butler migrated south to Trinidad, securing jobs in the colony's oilfields as a pipefitter, rig man, and pumpman.[5] Faced with stagnant wages and poor working conditions, he joined the Trinidad Workingmen's Association, a group led by fellow BWIR veteran Arthur Andrew Cipriani.[6] By the 1930s, Butler was the most influential working-class activist in Trinidad and head of his own political party, the British Empire Workers and Citizens Home Rule Party. Surveilled and persecuted by the colonial government, he endured years of imprisonment after being charged with inciting a riot and sedition in 1937.[7] Following his

FIGURE 0.1. BWIR soldiers on parade in Grenada. © Imperial War Museum (Q 17129)

release from prison, colonial officials detained him again, this time insisting that Butler posed an imminent security risk. The decorated BWIR veteran, who had fought to defend the British Empire during World War I, would spend the entirety of World War II at a makeshift detention center on Nelson Island off the coast of Trinidad.[8]

World War I—for Butler, Cipriani, and other BWIR soldiers—was a period of revelation and reckoning. The war and its turbulent aftermath prompted soldiers to interrogate their status as British colonial subjects and fueled heightened and, at times, contentious encounters with the colonial state. *Democracy's Foot Soldiers* investigates how the war shaped West Indians' understandings of and engagements with the British Empire. It addresses pivotal questions about the war's reverberations in the Caribbean, a region that remains understudied in the vast scholarship on World War I. Through analysis of archival, literary, and ethnographic sources—alongside materials from the circum-Caribbean press—it foregrounds the social, political, and geographic trajectories of BWIR soldiers and their civilian kin from the outbreak of hostilities in 1914 to the popular upheavals of the postwar period.

The British West Indies Regiment was a unique experiment in colonial military mobilization. Established in 1915, the regiment welcomed men from every British colony in the Caribbean, as well as thousands of West Indians who enlisted while living overseas. In a sharp departure from many colonial units and the metropolitan British Army after 1916, the BWIR was an all-volunteer force, recruiting soldiers through material incentives, patriotic rhetoric, and gendered appeals rather than conscription or impressment.[9] As one newspaper proudly affirmed, West Indians "rushed forward" to enlist, driven by "love and not by the lash!"[10] At its height, the BWIR swelled to include 15,601 soldiers organized into twelve battalions, making it the largest military force in the World War I-era British Caribbean. Most men who served in the regiment were not professional career soldiers; instead, they were first-time enlistees who pledged to serve for "the duration of the war," with the explicit expectation of returning to civilian life after hostilities ended.

Through universalist language, local recruiters mobilized a discourse that I describe as "martial interracialism," presenting soldiering as a crucial opportunity for West Indians to demonstrate masculine valor unencumbered by racial oppression.[11] They touted the BWIR as a model of racial equality, proclaiming insistently that men "irrespective of class, colour, or creed" could join in the empire's defense.[12] According to the recruiters, military service was the duty of all adult men, uniting subjects in the colonies with those in the metropole through shared sacrifice. As one Trinidadian recruiter declared to a crowd of potential volunteers, "There was no . . . colour distinction . . . in His Majesty's army. . . . Lord Kitchener welcomed everybody connected to the Empire no matter whether he was black, white, or green."[13] Yet, as this book reveals, martial interracialism was a pernicious myth.

Like other discourses of racial harmony in Latin America and the Caribbean, celebrations of martial interracialism during World War I sought to obscure structural inequalities and practices of exclusion that disadvantaged people of African descent.[14] In reality, soldiers of African descent—whether black or colored—were relegated to the BWIR's enlisted ranks, while only white men with "unmixed European blood" could lead in the regiment as commissioned officers. Military officials subjected BWIR enlistees to other forms of racial discrimination as well. The regiment's black and colored soldiers were often assigned to dilapidated housing, prohibited from recreational spaces reserved for British troops, and denied supplemental proficiency pay. In a major slight, the regiment was also barred from engaging in combat in Europe, meaning that most BWIR soldiers spent the war drudging as manual laborers rather than battling the Central Powers. Military service thus presented a path toward *unequal inclusion* in the British armed forces for black and colored BWIR volunteers. Furthermore, because enlistment policies restricted most Caribbean men of Indian and Chinese descent from joining the BWIR, the region's

FIGURE 0.2. BWIR soldiers stacking shells in Ypres, Belgium. © Imperial War Museum (E(AUS) 2078)

growing Asian communities were generally excluded from military service and the intense political struggles that it engendered.

Military deployment brought BWIR soldiers into contact with people from around the world—and across the color line. They experienced the global nature of the "world war" firsthand through daily encounters with civilians, military laborers, and servicemen from distant lands and diverse cultures. Trekking between theaters of war in Europe, Africa, India, and the Middle East, they served alongside soldiers from the British Isles and every corner of the British Empire while also interacting with troops from France and its empire, the United States, and other Allied nations. They observed contract laborers from China and the Middle East toiling away at military worksites, and they traded candies and played games with curious local children. They socialized with women at cafés, shops, homes, and brothels. Racial inequalities often, but not always, pervaded these encounters, as scholars have conclusively demonstrated.[15] Black and colored BWIR troops faced particularly intense hostility from their supposed comrades—white British soldiers. "The English Tommies do everything to cause us to lose control of our tempers," a Grenadian soldier detailed in an anguished letter. "Nigger, nigger, what you've come for. Bloke, see a monkey in Khaki. These are common insults of every day." Capturing the sentiment of many BWIR soldiers, he added: "But words are nothing. There is, moreover, a hostile spirit of unkindness toward us."[16]

Determined to expose the injustice and humiliation that BWIR soldiers endured, the generation of radical Caribbean writers and activists who came of age during World War I emphasized the war's transformative effect on black servicemen. Jamaican writer Claude McKay, after meeting with demobilized black servicemen in London in 1919, reported that their "grievance against things British" was "rapidly growing greater." In a blistering exposé published in the *Negro World*, McKay proclaimed: "We should rejoice that Germany so blundered, so that Negroes from all parts of the world were drawn to England to see the Lion, afraid and trembling, hiding in cellars, and the British ruling class revealed to them in all of its rottenness and hypocrisy."[17] Likewise, militant trade union organizer and black nationalist Eduardo Morales asserted that black soldiers had been "baptized with the baptism of fire" and "washed in the blood of sacrifice" on the "battlefields of Europe and Africa," transforming them into men ready to lead the fight for "an everlasting Negro Democracy." In a public letter to BWIR soldiers in Panama, Morales insisted that black veterans emerged from the war as new creatures: "You have descended into hell in order to bury the 'Old Negro' and have now returned to us as a 'New Negro,' holding high the standard of our racial purity in the face of the entire world, demanding equal rights for the members of your race."[18] The Trinidadian journalist George Padmore, in an article published in *The Crisis*, argued that the war "marked a definite turning point in West Indian ideology." "Most of the men who served abroad came back more racially and politically conscious, stimulated no doubt by the Wilsonian slogans of 'Democracy and Self-determination' for oppressed peoples and races," he explained. "It is therefore not surprising that the most militant and articulate post-war leaders among the common people of the islands are ex-service men."[19]

Based on these early and insistent pronouncements, I journeyed into the archive eager to reconstruct how BWIR soldiers battled against British rule in the Caribbean. Yet, as I pored over the vast archival traces left by soldiers, a more complicated story surfaced. This book, the result of my explorations, argues that many West Indian servicemen who experienced racism and discrimination during the war did not dismiss the empire entirely; rather, they made heightened claims to the imperial state. BWIR soldiers embarked on their own "war for democracy" by demanding racial equality, fair compensation, and the power to shape veterans' policies.

My contention here deviates from the conclusions of prior scholarship, which suggest that the degradations of the war years drove "black soldiers away from their connection to the British Empire" and prompted them to "fight for the end of the British Empire, independence for their islands, and for black people to govern themselves."[20] Instead, as I will show, many disaffected soldiers articulated their grievances through the reformist language of imperial patriotism, clamoring for redress by positioning themselves as loyal subjects of the Crown who had risked their lives to defend "King and Country." They insisted that the state had an inviolable obligation to care for soldiers and their families and demanded compensation on the same scale granted to white servicemen in the metropole. In their appeals, BWIR soldiers called for substantive reforms to British colonial policy in the Caribbean *rather than an end to colonialism itself.* Reformist veterans sought to amplify—not disavow—their status as faithful soldiers and subjects as a strategy to secure pecuniary and political benefits. And they conspired to expose, discredit, and marginalize more militant BWIR soldiers and civilians who did seek redress through violence and mass uprisings.

Studying War

Based on research in nineteen archives in six countries, *Democracy's Foot Soldiers* brings together previously untapped archival, newspaper, literary, visual, and ethnographic sources from Barbados, Belize, England, Jamaica, Trinidad and Tobago, and the United States, along with selected press sources from Grenada, Guyana, Panama, and the Bahamas. To situate BWIR soldiers in the rapidly changing social, cultural, and political dynamics of the wartime British Caribbean, it analyzes information gleaned from colonial government reports, military documents, police surveillance accounts, consular files, and newspaper articles alongside heretofore uncited soldiers' letters, petitions, memoirs, oral histories, photographs, and declassified correspondence. Given that no stark boundary existed between the civilian and military worlds, this book is especially attuned to the transnational circulation of ideas, policies, and people within the British Empire and beyond during the war years.

Civil and military authorities produced voluminous records about the BWIR—tracking soldiers through attestation forms, nominal rolls, court-martial files, medical reports, pension records, photographs, regimental war diaries, and police surveillance accounts—during and after World War I. "British colonial regimes," as anthropologist Karin Barber asserts,

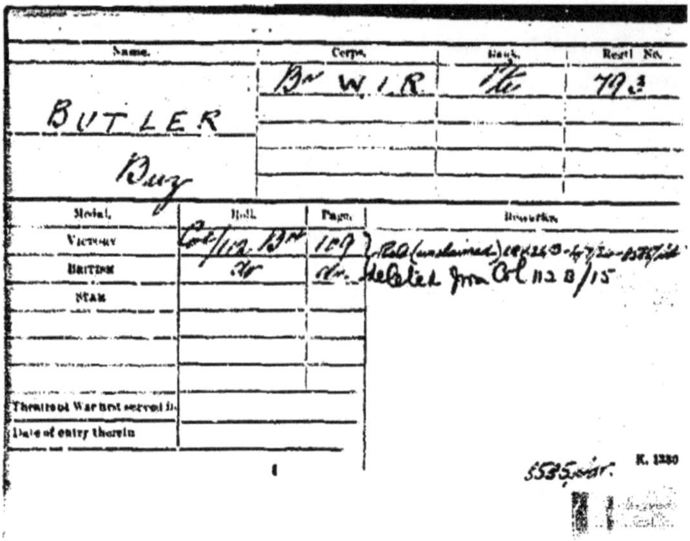

[8] DEMOCRACY'S FOOT SOLDIERS

FIGURE 0.3. Medal card for Tubal Uriah "Buz" Butler. National Archives of the United Kingdom.

"made extensive use of documentary forms of domination" to monitor and regulate subject populations.[21] This was especially true for the British armed forces, where every soldier completed a detailed attestation form at enlistment, received a unique regimental number, and was issued a medal card that recorded their rank, service unit, and medals received, along with the theaters of war where they served (see fig. 0.3). Soldiers' service papers and other military records offer an important, albeit partial, window into the mundane and extraordinary aspects of military life, while also betraying the bureaucratic imperatives and deep-seated prejudices of their authors.

But it is the writings and recollections of British Caribbeans that anchor this book, shaping the narrative and arguments that unfold in the pages that follow. Armed with paper and pen, BWIR soldiers and their supporters also produced their own rich documentary record. Volunteers for the regiment, unlike other non-white colonial troops, were initially required to pass a literacy test prior to enlistment, ensuring that most BWIR soldiers could read and write in English.[22] Literacy levels in the BWIR, according to some observers, surpassed even those of white regiments in the British Army.[23] And literacy would quickly become BWIR soldiers' most potent weapon. Servicemen meticulously recorded their experiences, grievances, and demands through multiple forms of writing.

They dispatched letters to the editors of Caribbean periodicals, wrote to loved ones back home, authored journalistic accounts of military life, and even published memoirs. They used creative genres like poetry, too, producing introspective reflections on race, masculinity, empire, and war. And servicemen inundated authorities on both sides of the Atlantic with hundreds of letters and petitions demanding redress. By placing documents from Britain's extensive colonial archive in dialogue with sources generated by British Caribbean colonial subjects, *Democracy's Foot Soldiers* chronicles wartime political currents from above *and* from below.

War, as historian Thavolia Glymph reminds us, "exposes in fine detail the politics of the most powerful and the smoldering demands of the most vulnerable and exploited."[24] This book illuminates BWIR soldiers' claims-making practices while also attending to transatlantic debates about race, military labor, and imperial loyalty among officials in Britain, the Caribbean, and the battlefields of Europe, Africa, and the Middle East. It contributes to scholarly dialogues on the World War I era in three broad fields: Caribbean social and political history, labor and migration studies, and African diaspora studies.

Democracy's Foot Soldiers offers a novel approach for understanding imperial patriotism, an ideology that affirmed the shared historical, cultural, and political bonds between colony and metropole and stressed personal allegiance to the empire. Since at least the mid-twentieth century, nationalist activists and historians have increasingly insisted that the symbols, rituals, and rhetoric of imperial patriotism expressed by West Indians illustrated colonial subjects' enthusiasm for Britain's colonizing and civilizing missions in the region. According to political scientist Gordon K. Lewis, for example, "Colonialism generated in the Caribbean mentality a divisive loyalty to the metropolitan culture that explains the historical tardiness of the final arrival of national independence." The "continuing dependency of thought and sentiment," Lewis insists, "also explains why, ironically, the British West Indies were the first to join the British Empire and the last to leave it."[25] Lamentably, this perspective effaces how colonial subjects reinterpreted, refashioned, and redeployed the discourse of imperial patriotism to critique racial inequality and demand economic and political reforms in the British Empire.

Democracy's Foot Soldiers instead understands imperial patriotism as part of a dynamic political language deployed by elite as well as subaltern groups. The rhetoric of empire, as literary scholars and historians have shown, provided malleable language for black colonial subjects to articulate their own conceptions of sovereignty and community.[26] As literary scholar Faith Smith writes, "imperial power provides the vocabulary through which people . . . imagine power or freedom" in the British Caribbean.[27] Building on these insights, as well as historian Gregory Mann's groundbreaking work on colonial armies in French West Africa, I posit that the language of imperial patriotism provided a common set of "words, images, ideas, and expressions of sentiment" through which individuals with deeply unequal access to power could articulate claims for political rights and social and economic privileges.[28] By reading declarations of imperial loyalty as strategic political maneuvers instead of transparent expressions of personal sentiment, I question the modernist "assumption of an inherent opposition between national consciousness and imperial loyalty" that marks historical scholarship on the origins of nationalism.[29] Rather than pitting imperial patriotism against protonational patriotism, *Democracy's Foot Soldiers* uncovers how British Caribbeans' nested local, regional, and diasporic identities coexisted with notions of imperial belonging.

My approach to analyzing expressions of imperial patriotism as a strategic political language follows the methodological shift pioneered by scholars of subaltern politics, including political anthropologist James Scott and historian Robin D. G. Kelley.[30] In his classic study of domination and resistance, Scott contends that "most of the political life of subordinate groups is to be found neither in overt collective defiance of powerholders nor in complete hegemonic compliance but in the vast territory between these two polar opposites."[31] This insight is particularly relevant for highly undemocratic, colonial societies like the World War I-era British Caribbean, where the realm of formal electoral politics was governed by patron-client ties and extremely limited in size and scope. Under Crown colony rule, most colonies in the region were administered by a governor who was appointed by the Crown and answered to the Colonial Office in London.[32] In Trinidad, for example, every member of the local Legislative Council was nominated by the governor, and the popularly elected Port of Spain Borough Council was abolished from 1898 to 1917 after its members had the temerity to question local fiscal policies.[33] In Jamaica, only 3 percent of the population met the qualifications to vote, and most of the members of the island's Legislative Council were nominated rather than elected.[34] Even in Barbados, which operated under the old representative system of government and had a fully elected House of Assembly, only a "small percentage" of the laboring class met the income qualifications to vote.[35] Thus, social and cultural histories of politics during this period must be attentive to the range of strategies that colonial subjects employed to advance their interests with the exceedingly small cadre of decision-makers. We must also consider how British ideals of patriotism, justice, fair play, and loyalty provided a shared vocabulary for women and men with a dizzying array of political agendas.

The history of the British West Indies Regiment must also be understood in the context of the growing urbanization and transnational labor migration of the early decades of the twentieth century. During this period, the fluctuating price of tropical staples, the concentration of desirable lands hoarded by multinational corporations (such as the United Fruit Company), stagnant wages, and the over-taxation of smallholders pushed many working men and women to seek better fortunes overseas or in the cities.[36] Between 1881 and 1921, approximately 146,000 Jamaicans migrated to the Spanish-speaking circum-Caribbean and the United States, while others moved to Kingston in order to escape a declining agricultural economy.[37] Over twenty thousand Barbadian men departed for Panama under contract with the Isthmian Canal Commission, while another forty thousand women and men journeyed from Barbados to Panama on their own without labor contracts.[38] Other Barbadians, Grenadians, and Vincentians migrated south to Trinidad and British Guiana.[39] Islanders also set sail for Brazil and Venezuela or ventured northward to the United States and Canada.[40] "Migration," as Smith and others have established, "was the great feature of anglophone Caribbean life in the later nineteenth and early twentieth centuries."[41] Military mobilization during World War I would draw upon and reconfigure circum-Caribbean migratory networks, propelling itinerant workingmen eastward across the Atlantic in defense of the British Empire.

By demonstrating that BWIR servicemen were also part of a highly mobile working class, I contribute to a growing scholarly literature that reconceptualizes soldiers as transnational laborers.[42] *Democracy's Foot Soldiers* moves beyond local studies of World War I colonial troops to situate the mobilization for war as part of what historian Lara Putnam defines as "the circum-Caribbean migratory sphere."[43] Among the volunteers for the BWIR were sojourners who had already left home and were residing far beyond the borders of the British Empire. Islanders working in the rainforests of northern Brazil, on the Caribbean coasts of Nicaragua and Costa Rica, and in the US-controlled Canal Zone in Panama, all clamored to enlist during the war years.[44] In this book, I map the transnational networks that yielded thousands of soldiers for the BWIR, including over 2,100 men who enlisted in Panama alone. I also expose how colonial officials helped to facilitate emigration after the war to rid the islands of discharged veterans. Between 1919 and 1920, over 4,700 ex-soldiers—approximately one-third of the BWIR—traveled to Cuba to work in the sugar industry. Other veterans departed for Venezuela, Panama, Colombia, Canada, and the United States, underscoring the continuing importance of overseas labor migration in the wake of demobilization.

Finally, I place the experiences of Afro-Caribbean soldiers in dialogue with African, African American, and African Canadian troops.[45] Studying the trajectories of black soldiers reshapes our understanding of the formation of the modern African diaspora, uncovering the role of the military in organizing the migration of millions of black soldiers and civilians during the twentieth century. World War I, as historian Chad Williams notes, "set . . . descendant Africans in motion through the demands of combat and labor, bringing them into contact with one another and fundamentally transforming the demographic, ideological, and imaginative contours of the diaspora."[46] During the war years, military bases in Belgium, France, and the Middle East became vibrant nodal points in the diaspora, connecting black servicemen from Africa and the Americas. As the editors of the Panama *Workman* explained in 1919, the mobilization for war had ignited a heightened diasporic identity among Afro-descendants: "The spirit of insularity and provincialism is dying out. We are fast approaching the time of intercolonial and international fraternization. All colored people are beginning to feel that they are related in aims, aspirations, demands, and interests. The accident of geographical conditions is becoming a diminutive proposition."[47] Similarly, in a 1928 essay, Martinican writer Jane Nardal suggested that the travails of the war years had helped to unify black people across the diaspora. The "sufferings of the war" and "similar infelicities of the postwar period," she argued, contributed to the rise of black internationalism.[48] This book explores how BWIR soldiers navigated their encounters with black soldiers from around the world and considers how these experiences spurred new understandings of the global color line and the racial stakes of the war.

Despite the massive mobilization of black soldiers during the two World Wars, scholarly accounts of twentieth-century black transnationalism rarely acknowledge the military as a central actor in the modern dispersal and resettlement of peoples of African descent. The unwillingness to grapple with soldiers as a particular class of diasporic subjects is surprising given the litany of black activists whose experiences as soldiers transformed their political imaginary. As my work demonstrates, attention to the roots and routes of black soldiers helps us to understand the working-class origins of black cosmopolitanism and transnational black politics in the World War I era. Furthermore, attention to the trajectories of black servicemen reveals new migratory circuits within the African diaspora, pushing us beyond New York, Paris, and London to rugged military outposts, where working-class visions of New Negro modernity were also being forged.

Capturing the complexities of black soldiers' wartime experiences requires that we also interrogate the gendered expectations that shaped military service. In response to the exegesis of war, military recruiters and civilian commentators in the British Caribbean valorized men who possessed the qualities of a modern soldier: physical fitness, self-discipline, bravery, and an indefatigable work ethic. Constructions of martial masculinity differed from both prevailing working-class understandings of masculine reputation and middle-class definitions of gendered respectability.[49] Instead, wartime conceptions of manhood in the British Caribbean emphasized physical traits such as muscular strength as well as ideological ones such as fidelity to the empire and strict obedience to authority. Local women played a significant role in disseminating and policing these masculine ideals, as recent work by historian Dalea Bean has shown.[50] Despite their status as civilians, women organized military recruitment rallies in communities across the British Caribbean and even established their own recruiting committees, ultimately serving as "intermediaries between men's bodies and the Empire's needs."[51] Female speakers at recruitment rallies often pressured men to enlist by questioning their manhood and publicly taunted those who refused to join the BWIR by confronting them with skirts and handkerchiefs. Women also affirmed martial conceptions of masculinity by writing poetry and patriotic songs that linked soldiering to the defense of the family and home front.

For black men who enlisted in the BWIR, soldiering came with the additional burden of battling racist stereotypes about black manhood. In the Caribbean, white planters, colonial officials, and other elites routinely disparaged black men as indolent, irrational, untrustworthy, hypersexual, and irresponsible. In London, officials in the War Office questioned West Indians' military fitness, suggesting that black volunteers lacked self-discipline, physical stamina, and courage. White officers and military physicians at times also echoed these racist assessments, portraying black BWIR troops as disorderly and prone to contract venereal diseases. In the face of these pervasive and pernicious stereotypes, BWIR soldiers and their allies in the colonies insisted that black volunteers were dutiful "sons of the Empire" *and* valiant representatives of the race.

FIGURE 0.4. BWIR soldiers training in British Honduras. Courtesy of the Belize Archives and Records Service.

Organization of the Book

Democracy's Foot Soldiers unfolds in six chronological chapters. Like the itinerant soldiers it studies, the book traverses a vast and varied geographical terrain, moving from the Caribbean to military sites in Western Europe, North Africa, and the Middle East and back again. In chapter 1, I reconstruct the protracted debates about British Caribbean military service following the outbreak of war in Europe in 1914. Then, in chapter 2, I examine the official recruitment campaign for the BWIR, uncovering the discourses and practices that shaped recruitment in the Caribbean colonies and Panama.

Chapter 3 considers BWIR soldiers' wartime interracial encounters, following the men as they moved between military work camps and sites of leisure. The first contingents of BWIR soldiers arrived in England in the fall of 1915, training at camps near Seaford and Plymouth before deploying to distant theaters of war. Although officially classified as infantry soldiers, British Caribbean servicemen were often relegated to noncombatant duties because of the British Army's policy of banning black colonials from combat against white enemies. In chapter 4, I analyze BWIR soldiers' transnational campaign against discrimination in the British Army during their final year of military service.

After the signing of the Armistice on November 11, 1918, BWIR soldiers and colonial authorities prepared for demobilization. In chapter 5, I explore the fraught homecoming of nearly fourteen thousand BWIR veterans as former comrades battled with colonial officials—and one another—in search of redress. Chapter 6 scrutinizes competing efforts in postwar Trinidad to establish autonomous veterans' organizations and the rising calls for participatory democracy in a Crown colony. The book concludes by demonstrating how the political debates over racial equality, imperial belonging, and democracy engendered by World War I reverberated in the British Caribbean during the postwar years.

"Black soldiers," historian Adrienne Lentz-Smith argues, "offer a way to see the interconnections of history between local, national, and global scales. They are, after all, local people swimming in the currents of international affairs."[52] In the pages that follow, *Democracy's Foot Soldiers* traces these currents through the Caribbean Sea, the Atlantic Ocean, and beyond, surfacing a new history of the BWIR and the ongoing fight for equality in societies forged through the violence of empire.[53]

Note on Racial Terminology

Racial terms pervade the pages of this book, yet racial terminology in the British Caribbean during the World War I era was neither uniform nor fixed. Official documents used a variety of terms to connote what present-day observers would describe as "race." In Jamaica, for example, census takers categorized the island's population into five "colours": white, colored, black, East Indian, and Chinese.[54] Meanwhile, in Barbados, the census sorted the population by "complexion" into three broad groups: white, mixed, and black.[55] In the Leeward Islands, census takers also labeled residents according to a tripartite system, employing the terms *white, coloured*, and *black*.[56] Census records in other British Caribbean colonies omitted racial demographic data entirely.

In this book, I use the term *black* to describe people of African descent. Many of the historical actors that I characterize as "black" would have described themselves as "Negro" or, less commonly, as members of "the African race." The terms *colored* and *brown* refer to people of mixed African and European ancestry. These individuals generally had lighter skin than their black counterparts and occupied an intermediary place in the colonial racial hierarchy. I use the term *white* to denote people of European ancestry, whether they were born in Europe or in the Caribbean.

The term *East Indian* refers to people from the Indian subcontinent who immigrated to the Caribbean and their descendants, while the term *Chinese* signals Chinese ancestry. Finally, I use *British Caribbeans* and *West Indians* as collective descriptors for all residents of Britain's Caribbean colonies, regardless of race or ethnicity.

PART I

Homefront Mobilizations

CHAPTER ONE

The "Color Question"

WAR AND THE RACIAL FAULT LINES
OF IMPERIAL BELONGING

... I had not the least idea there was any colour question in England.

—W. A. MOORE (1914)

ON THE EVENING of September 15, 1914, five weeks after the outbreak of
World War I, members of the Universal Negro Improvement Association
and African Communities League (UNIA) assembled at Collegiate Hall in
Kingston, Jamaica. Marcus Garvey, the fledgling association's president
and traveling commissioner, opened the weekly gathering with a speech
on the brotherhood of man and then trounced three fellow UNIA officers
in a spirited debate on the influence of religion and politics in the modern world. After his victory, the man destined to become the era's most
prominent black nationalist departed from the UNIA's standard program
of lectures, elocution contests, and musical performances to introduce two
special resolutions concerning the catastrophic conflict in Europe.[1]

One resolution, addressed to French President Raymond Poincaré,
expressed support for the French people while celebrating France's
"peaceful and civilizing influence on the world."[2] The second resolution,
dispatched to British Secretary of State for the Colonies Lewis Harcourt,
affirmed the UNIA's "loyalty and devotion to His Majesty the King and to
the Empire" and celebrated the "great protecting and civilizing nature of
the English nation and people ... and their justice to all men, especially
to their Negro Subjects scattered all over the world." Conveying words of
support for British soldiers deployed in Europe and Africa, the robustly
patriotic declaration "rejoice[d] in British victories and the suppression

[19]

of foes" and closed with "God Save the King! Long live the King and Empire."[3] In Garvey's letter of transmittal to the Secretary of State for the Colonies, he urged Harcourt to personally "convey the feeling of [the] resolution" to King George V. "Our love for and devotion to, His Majesty and the Empire, stands unrivalled and from the depths of our hearts we pray for the crowning victory of the British soldiers now at war."[4]

The proclamation of loyalty proved a public relations coup for an organization that was less than two months old. In the following weeks, the UNIA's resolution was reprinted in Jamaica's two major newspapers—the *Daily Gleaner* and the *Daily Chronicle*—as well as in the venerable London *Times*. It was also seized upon with alacrity by senior statesmen, colonial officials, and prominent reformers in both Jamaica and Britain, who dispatched personal notes of appreciation to Garvey while lavishly praising the UNIA's patriotism. Travers Buxton, Secretary of the London-based Anti-Slavery and Aborigines' Protection Society, applauded the UNIA for taking a public stance on the war, while Jamaica's Governor William Manning thanked Garvey for his "offers of readiness to serve in any way."[5] Conservative statesman Arthur Balfour, former prime minister of the United Kingdom, warmly acknowledged the resolution, noting that he read the document with the "greatest gratification."[6] The success of Garvey's declaration of loyalty was even felt at the Colonial Office in London, where a clerk in the West India Branch, in a handwritten endorsement on the official coversheet, wrote, "I blush to think that I once suggested to Mr. Marcus Garvey that he should go to the workhouse."[7]

Members of the UNIA were hardly alone in their expressions of imperial patriotism in response to Britain's entry into the war. White residents of the British Caribbean similarly rushed to proclaim their support of the "Mother Country," often linking imperial loyalty to calls for military mobilization in the colonies. One month after the UNIA's declaration, for example, Trinidadian cocoa planter Arthur Andrew Cipriani drafted his own declaration of loyalty and proposal for West Indian military recruitment from his home in Port of Spain. On October 12, 1914, Cipriani spotted a notice in the London *Times* stating that Arthur du Cros, a member of Parliament and honorary colonel in the Royal Warwickshire Fusiliers, was recruiting West Indian migrants in London for a new infantry battalion.[8] Inspired by du Cros's overture to West Indians in the metropole, Cipriani immediately contacted George Le Hunte, governor of Trinidad and Tobago, with a proposal to raise a contingent in Trinidad to fight alongside their fellow islanders in London. When Governor Le Hunte rejected his idea, Cipriani cabled du Cros directly and asked if he would accept men

FIGURE 1.1. Marcus Mosiah Garvey. Courtesy of the National Library of Jamaica.

residing in Trinidad for his nascent contingent. By the time his telegram reached du Cros, however, the London-based battalion was completely full. Undeterred, Cipriani appealed to du Cros once more, this time entreating him to use his influence to lobby on behalf of West Indians "bottled up" in the colonies who wanted to enlist. Men throughout the region, Cipriani explained, wanted to fight not only because of their loyalty to the Empire but also because of their pride as men. "West Indians have realized that it is a fight to a finish, that not only is the existence of the Mother Country at stake, but the very Empire that we are proud to be a part. We should not only feel isolated, but slighted, if our services are declined when men are still wanted to keep the flag flying," he declared.[9]

FIGURE 1.2. Arthur Andrew Cipriani. *Labour Leader*, January 14, 1925, 8.

Marcus Garvey and Arthur Cipriani inhabited radically different social spheres in colonial Caribbean society. Garvey, a black Jamaican printer, journalist, and activist with rural artisan roots, was an outspoken champion for "the race Afric," while Cipriani, a white member of the planter class, hailed from Trinidad's two most prominent French Creole families and served as secretary of the island's exclusive Breeders' and Trainers' Association.[10] What motivated islanders of various races, ethnicities, and classes to announce their support for the British war effort? What was at stake in their public declarations of loyalty? And how did conflicting notions of imperial belonging shape the transatlantic debate about mobilizing British Caribbean men for military duty?

This chapter chronicles the opening year of World War I in the British Caribbean, detailing how the mobilization for war in Britain sparked widespread debates about race, manhood, and imperial belonging in the colonies. I argue that West Indians employed the gendered language of imperial patriotism to assert publicly their full membership in the British Empire and to lay claim to a host of rights and privileges as British subjects. For Garvey, the members of the UNIA, and other black and colored reformers, the outbreak of war in Europe provided a dramatic opportunity to prepare the ground for demands for representative government, economic opportunity, and professional mobility that would be, they hoped, unhindered by the "color question." For white Creoles like Cipriani, as well as English expatriates who lived in the West Indies, the war offered myriad opportunities to affirm their elite social position, wealth, and ties to the "Mother Country."[11]

Although men from the British Caribbean had fought under the Union Jack since 1795, when enslaved Africans were impressed to defend British possessions during the French and Haitian Revolutions and Napoleonic Wars, the enlistment of thousands of civilians during World War I was one of the largest military mobilizations in the history of the English-speaking West Indies.[12] In the first half of this chapter, I uncover how the effort to raise a British Caribbean military force grew from a scattered, private campaign to sponsor a few hundred men into a publicly funded, regional movement that would garner over 15,600 volunteer soldiers by 1918. Departing from previous scholarship, I show that the earliest and most vocal proponents of the movement that would produce the British West Indies Regiment were well-connected, middle-aged white men like Cipriani rather than members of the black and colored majority. Envisioning military service as a vehicle for masculine self-assertion and regional advancement, white military boosters like Cipriani insisted that West Indians' martial labor would benefit the colonies as well as the metropole.

Wartime celebrations of military service were deeply informed by the discourse and the embodied practice of martial masculinity. Appeals to martial masculinity, as historian Kristin Hoganson argues, function simultaneously as a "motivating ideology and a political posture in debates over war and empire."[13] Bellicose commentators in the British Caribbean hoped that military service would solidify—and perhaps even advance—their standing in the British Empire, reversing the region's status as "the slums of the empire."[14] "If the West Indies [wants] a place in the sun," thundered Cipriani, "they must do their duty as a unit of the British Empire" by sending men to fight. Otherwise, the beleaguered region would remain "the weakest link in the grand chain of British imperialism."[15]

The second half of the chapter explores how the debate over military service exposed the fault lines of colonial society and amplified the racial anxieties of policymakers in Britain. The campaign to create a West Indian fighting force extended across the Atlantic to Whitehall, where officials at the Colonial and War Offices mulled over the possibility of mobilizing volunteers from the Caribbean, whether black, colored, white, or East Indian. Whereas the cadre of elites who marshaled the campaign for a regional fighting force imagined military service as a masculine right that (white) West Indians had earned through centuries of loyalty to Britain, officials in the metropole drew upon racialized hierarchies of martial fitness to disparage black West Indians' soldiering abilities and to rebuff their initial offers of service. Hence, as authorities in the Colonial and War Offices publicly celebrated West Indians' "patriotic spirit," they sought to maintain the established fiction of a color-blind empire while conspiring privately to keep black, colored, and East Indian volunteers from the battlefields of Europe. And, as we shall see, they even questioned the racial purity of white Creoles in the islands.[16]

"A Raw West Indian Negro Troop"

Jamaicans awoke on the morning of August 5, 1914, to the news that Britain had officially declared war on Germany. Before dawn, at 2:15 a.m., Governor Manning received an urgent telegram from the metropole "announcing the outbreak of hostilities with the German Empire."[17] Within hours, news of the war spread across the colony through telegrams, public notices, and informal networks of rumor and gossip. Describing the frenzied exchange of information during the first day of the war, Herbert de Lisser mused: "The telegraph wires hummed with the momentous tiding; sleepy telegraph clerks were startled into alert wakefulness as the significant message was spelled out by the tapping electrical instruments; on every public building, in the early hours of that sultry summer morning, the statement was displayed."[18] The prominent newspaper editor further recounted that "on the news being known, the streets of the city and the towns became filled with excited people who spoke and argued as if the next four-and-twenty hours would decide the fate of nations."[19] After weeks of nervous anticipation, the empire was finally at war.

Even before the official declaration of war, residents across the British Caribbean had followed the unfolding crisis in Europe, predicting how it would reverberate on both sides of the Atlantic. "All Jamaica, and particularly Kingston, has the 'war fever,'" the *Daily Gleaner* reported in early August, noting that there was "enormous demand" for newspapers as readers clamored for updates.[20] From his pulpit in Trinidad, Rev. E. W. Havelock, in an ominous assessment of the political landscape in Europe, pronounced: "Things have not looked so bad since the wars of Napolean."[21] The prominent Trinidadian planter and businessman Edgar Tripp likewise noted the rising apprehension in Port of Spain, as residents of the capital predicted that a German invasion was imminent. "All sorts of wild rumours are afloat, and believed in by the masses, as to the presence of hostile ships in the neighborhood," Tripp reported in a letter to the West India Committee in London. "There is a rumour . . . that the Government will not publish further telegrams [about the political crisis in Europe] for fear of exciting the people," he continued. Reassuring readers in London that West Indians would fully support the empire in its moment of crisis, Tripp averred that there was "no fear of dangerous excitement" in Trinidad. "The feeling [of imperial loyalty] is all one way, from Government House to negro hut—far more so than it was even during the Boer war," he proclaimed.[22]

Among the region's elite, Britain's entry into World War I triggered a flood of patriotic fundraising activity on behalf of the "Mother Country." In addition to establishing official war relief funds and making donations of tens of thousands of British pounds, local legislatures throughout Britain's "ancient and loyal" colonies in the Caribbean also offered gifts of tropical staples, cigarettes, and hand-sewn woolen wraps and uniforms to assist in the war effort.[23] Some black women, men, and children from the laboring classes contributed financially as well, denying themselves "the necessaries of life" to give to war charities. "There have been seamstresses and market women earning a few shillings a week insisting on giving either three or two shillings," the governor of the Bahamas boasted to imperial officials in London.[24] Those who dared to question the tremendous financial outlays to support the war effort, pointing to the widespread poverty and dilapidated infrastructure in rural communities across the Caribbean, faced accusations of disloyalty and withering criticism in the press.

Yet, for many members of the laboring classes, the hostilities in the metropole stoked fears of deepening hardship in the colonies. In the rural village of Christiana, Jamaica, residents worried that the local banana industry would be "crippled to a large extent" due to wartime trade disruptions.[25] Isedora Buckley, as a child in Whitfield Town, Jamaica, recalled walking home from primary school one afternoon when she overheard adults talking anxiously about the outbreak of war. Unsure of "what they ment [meant] when they spoke about war," the young Jamaican rushed home to query her parents. Their frank response was far from reassuring: "They told me that whenever war starts we are not going to get anything to eat and nothing to wear when those we had torn off," she remembered decades later. Shocked by her parents' dire predictions and overcome with tears, Buckley asked her mother if their family would "die for hunger and walk around naked" because of the war. Although her mother ultimately insisted that the "Lord will provide," her prediction that World War I would usher in a period of widespread deprivation and hardship underscored the profound fears of laboring peoples.[26]

As residents across the British Caribbean navigated a new and deeply uncertain wartime environment, some men in the colonies began lobbying local officials and authorities in Britain for the right to join "the splendid brotherhood [fighting] in the service of the Empire."[27] The discussion regarding West Indian wartime military service began in London on August 28, 1914, when officials at the Colonial Office dispatched an initial query to the War Office regarding Caribbean volunteers.[28] Before the War Office could reply, T. A. V. Best, Colonial Secretary of the Leeward Islands, telegraphed the Colonial Office on August 31, inquiring whether "coloured men" would be accepted as volunteers for military service.[29] Best's one-line missive prompted a lengthy exchange among the Colonial Office clerks, foreshadowing a debate that would eventually beset government officials and private citizens on both sides of the Atlantic.

A careful reading of the 1914 *Manual of Military Law* reveals that black and colored volunteers from the Caribbean colonies qualified for service in the British Army, even if under profoundly disadvantaged terms. According to the *Manual*, "negroes and inhabitants of Protectorates" could serve in British regiments but would be classified as "aliens" rather than British subjects. As "alien" servicemen, black and colored volunteers who enlisted in British regiments could not hold a rank higher than noncommissioned officer and were subject to restrictive enlistment quotas. Specifically, the *Manual* mandated that the "number of aliens serving together at any one time in any corps in the regular forces" could "not exceed the proportion of one alien to every fifty British subjects." Nevertheless, despite these discriminatory provisions, the *Manual* guaranteed that "any inhabitant of a British protectorate and any negro or person of colour" would be "entitled to all the privileges of a natural-born British subject" while on active duty.[30]

For the staff at the Colonial Office, however, the key issue was not the official policy as outlined in the *Manual of Military Law* but West Indians' martial fitness. In a handwritten minute, clerk R. A. Wiseman conceded that "some coloured W. Indians are men whom it would be a pity to discourage altogether," yet he doubted that most "negroes" possessed sufficient soldiering abilities. When compared to other nonwhite colonial soldiers, particularly those from the Indian subcontinent, Wiseman insisted that black West Indians simply did not measure up. "It is all very well to have Indian troops fighting in Europe, but to have negroes seems to me to be quite a different matter. Moreover, the Indian troops are part of a trained and efficient military machine whereas the West Indian troops would not be," he argued. Wiseman also claimed that local military corps in the Caribbean were woefully inefficient and, therefore, could never be "sent like the Indian army from the W. Indies to the theatre of operations."[31] In a slightly less disparaging assessment, clerk Gilbert Grindle suggested that black and colored West Indian soldiers might be utilized, but only to "set free better troops" for the frontlines.[32]

It is instructive that Wiseman justified the exclusion of black volunteers by referencing the fighting prowess of Indian soldiers. The same week that the Colonial Office took up the issue of black volunteers from the West Indies, the War Cabinet voted to deploy the Lahore and Meerut infantry divisions of the Indian Army in France, marking the first time that Britain mobilized nonwhite servicemen to fight in Europe.[33] Wiseman's predictions about the combat performance of black and Indian soldiers, like those of his superiors in the War Cabinet, drew upon theories about the inherent martial capacities of different races rather than systematic military evaluations. In the decades before World War I, British military elites increasingly embraced the idea that certain groups possessed a natural predisposition for armed combat. Drawing on late-nineteenth-century theories of race and human behavior, proponents of martial race theories posited that men from specific racial and ethnic groups were biologically and culturally inclined to be fierce and highly disciplined warriors.[34] Cold and temperate regions with rugged terrain, theorists argued, produced elite warriors, while tropical weather and urban living stifled physical development and masculine vigor.[35] Martial race theories had a tremendous impact in India, where General Frederick Roberts, Commander-in-Chief of the Indian Army and one of the most popular military heroes in late

Victorian Britain, reorganized the army to enlist more men from the Punjab, North-West Frontier, and Nepal. By 1914, 75 percent of soldiers in the Indian Army were from a handful of martial racial groups, and military leaders in India and Britain were championing the idea that the Indian Army was capable of fighting, and defeating, a European enemy.[36]

Whereas military officials and popular commentators in Britain valorized Indian soldiers as "high souled men of first-rate training," they largely ignored the long-standing military contributions of West Indian soldiers.[37] Indeed, during their extensive exchange, the Colonial Office staff failed to acknowledge that black soldiers from the West India Regiment (WIR) had fought and died at Britain's behest for nearly 120 years. The WIR, unlike earlier slave militias, was a standing unit commanded by officers from the British Army and was an official part of Britain's armed forces. WIR soldiers fought in several major campaigns during the French Revolution and Napoleonic Wars and helped suppress local uprisings in Barbados (1816), Demerara (1823), and Jamaica (1865).[38] Outside of the Caribbean, the WIR fought in West Africa in Gambia as well as in the Gold Coast.[39]

Despite its established record of military service, the Caribbean regiment never garnered the heroic reputation or popular esteem that other imperial regiments enjoyed in Britain. "The West India regiment is never seen in England," WIR officer A. B. Ellis lamented. "The British public knows nothing of such regiments, has no friends, relatives, or acquaintances in their ranks, and consequently takes no interest in them."[40] Ideas about martial fitness were also part of the problem. Ellis argued that Britons imagined black men as jovial, carefree dandies, not disciplined soldiers: "The popular idea in Great Britain of the negro is that he is a person who commonly wears a dilapidated tall hat, cotton garments of brilliant hue, carries a banjo or concertina, and indulges in extraordinary cachinnations at the smallest pretext."[41]

The question of West Indians' martial fitness, or lack thereof, was not the only problem for Colonial Office authorities debating a potential West Indian contingent. Domestic political and military considerations, particularly the problem of anti-black sentiment in the metropole, loomed large as well. Colonial Office functionaries anxiously pondered how a black contingent from the colonies would be greeted in Britain. Wiseman hinted that Britons in the metropole might not welcome black soldiers from the empire. "Is it likely that public opinion here would welcome a raw West Indian negro troop being sent over . . . to be trained alongside of the regiments in Lord Kitchener's new army?" he cautioned.[42] Although black

West Indian soldiers had fought in the Caribbean and West Africa, serving on European soil, shoulder to shoulder with white British servicemen, was quite a different matter.

If imperial officials were unwilling to raise "raw negro troop[s]" from the West Indies, they were also unsure about the utility of forming an all-white Caribbean contingent.[43] Clerk E. R. Darnley proposed that military officials in the West Indies form an elite "contingent of planters."[44] Unlike black civilians, Darnley argued, white West Indian planters had experience riding and shooting, and some had even served in the South African War.[45] But Darley's proposal failed to garner any support in the Colonial Office, as his colleagues insisted that the complex color-class hierarchy in the West Indies would make it challenging—both practically and politically—to create an all-white regional contingent. Wiseman warned that it would be "difficult if not impossible to discriminate between the pure white and the near white" volunteers, while Grindle insisted that any regional unit "would of course include black and coloured men."[46]

In short, imperial officials did not want to alienate black and colored West Indians by publicly acknowledging a color bar in the British Army. "On the whole," wrote Wiseman, "I think it should be our policy if possible to prevent any public discussion of the colour question in the West Indies, and I think that the only effective way to do this is to nip in the bud any attempt to raise local corps for service in Europe."[47] Grindle concurred, adding that military authorities in the colonies should not discourage black and colored men from volunteering for service, but rather should steer them toward local defense forces instead of the British Army.[48] To ensure that the War Office rejected the proposal for a West Indian contingent without provoking racial unrest, Wiseman directed his colleagues to inform the War Office that the Secretary of State for the Colonies would "depreciate the raising of the coloured question in the West Indies and would therefore propose to reply that local volunteers corps for service in Europe cannot be accepted."[49] Thus, Colonial Office officials not only devised their own strategy to derail attempts to form a West Indian contingent but also lobbied their colleagues in the War Office to adopt the same approach.

On September 2, 1914, B. B. Cubitt, Assistant Under-Secretary of State for the War Office, replied to the Colonial Office on behalf of the Army Council, the War Office's policy-making body. In the carefully worded letter, Cubitt diplomatically avoided any discussion of race and, instead, claimed that West Indian volunteers should focus on local defense efforts. Acknowledging West Indians' desire to serve, Cubitt stressed that the members of the Army Council applauded the "patriotic spirit which prompts the offer of a West Indian Contingent" but could not support the proposal to create a new unit for service in Europe. Instead, the Army Council suggested that "residents in the West Indies will be most usefully employed at present in denying supplies . . . to the enemy's commerce destroyers, and to maintain order, if necessary."[50] Pleased with the War Office's tactful rejection, the Colonial Office quickly dispatched a copy of the letter to the governors of Britain's Caribbean colonies on September 8.[51]

"Let Them Give Us a Chance"

It took nearly a month for the Colonial Office's September 8 missive to reach the West Indies.[52] As the confidential letter traveled westward across the Atlantic, Arthur Cipriani and other military boosters in the colonies—completely unaware that officials in the metropole had already decided to discourage volunteers from the Caribbean—launched an aggressive campaign for a West Indian fighting force. While historians have suggested that black West Indians eagerly "demanded the right to serve in a spirit of proud imperial patriotism," the earliest and most vocal proponents of the movement that would produce the BWIR were actually prominent whites.[53] In the metropole and in the Caribbean, white planters, businessmen, and professionals, occasionally joined by a small number of colored elites, spearheaded the drive for a British Caribbean military contingent. During a seven-week time span from late August to mid-October 1914, at least nine different plans for a military contingent emerged in Jamaica alone, while men from Trinidad to the Leeward Island presidency of Dominica likewise campaigned to serve alongside their fellow colonials in the British Army.[54] To make their case, these military boosters summoned familiar notions of loyalty and justice while also suggesting that the ties between Britain and her Caribbean colonies were anchored in reciprocity and mutual obligation.

Imperial patriotism provided a common lexicon for military enthusiasts, yet ideas about race exposed the fault lines in the pro-military camp. In Jamaica, in particular, the proposals for a military contingent laid bare racialized conceptions of martial fitness, as military enthusiasts not only lobbied for a publicly funded force but also debated which men should fill its ranks. Military boosters and potential volunteers waged a spirited campaign for a Jamaican contingent through the island's major newspapers, particularly the Kingston-based *Daily Gleaner* and *Jamaica*

Times. The opening salvo was fired in late August 1914 when an anonymous writer sent a brief missive to the *Gleaner*, the island's establishment paper, encouraging Governor William Manning to issue a public call for volunteers. The correspondent predicted that the island would quickly raise a draft of "sturdy young fellows" for combat in Europe.[55] Five days later, "Backwoodsman," a correspondent from Cambridge in the northwestern parish of Trelawny, offered his call for a contingent manned by Jamaica's rural majority. He urged the governor to form a regiment of two thousand rural recruits instead of expending hundreds of pounds on local defense efforts. Noting that there were many young men in his village who were "physically fit and accustomed to hardships," he suggested that 1,500 volunteers be deployed in Europe immediately, while the remaining five hundred volunteers function as a reserve regiment.[56]

Military enthusiasts also put forward plans to deploy soldiers and recently discharged veterans from the West India Regiment as combat troops in Europe. At its height in the nineteenth century, the WIR consisted of "twelve battalions of negro troops, raised exclusively for service in the West Indies."[57] By 1914, however, the once formidable regiment had been reduced to two understaffed battalions of black soldiers led by an all-white officer corps.[58] Yet several schemes to mobilize the regiment for combat duty once again were inspired by heroic tales of the WIR's distinguished past—including the fact that WIR soldiers Samuel Hodge (Tortola) and William James Gordon (Jamaica) were the first non-Europeans to win the Victoria Cross, Britain's highest military honor.[59]

On the same day that the *Gleaner* published the letter from "Backwoodsman," the paper also included a note from Charles Moulton, a "Jamaican and loyal British subject" in Ancón, Panama. Moulton was one of the eighty thousand Jamaicans who journeyed to the Isthmus between 1904 and 1914 to work as "silver roll" employees on the US-led canal construction project—or to labor informally as artisans, cooks, laundresses, and street vendors in the bustling Canal Zone. The vibrant, highly transient community of Caribbean migrants in Panama included black women and men from Barbados, Jamaica, and other British Caribbean colonies as well as from Curaçao, Martinique, and Guadeloupe.[60] Several hundred discharged soldiers from the WIR also made their way to Panama, looking to bolster their fortunes in the civilian world.[61] Yet, with the opening of the canal in August 1914, Caribbean migrants scrambled desperately to find new sources of employment as the Isthmian Canal Commission laid off nearly two thousand workers per month.[62] Writing in a climate of profound uncertainty and growing economic deprivation,

Moulton reported that there were many "military men" in Panama who were "qualified and . . . willing to go to the front." Although far from home, WIR veterans would, he predicted, eagerly "respond to the call and join the army" if the Jamaican government took the lead.[63]

The most publicized proposal to use the WIR in combat came from Major Edward T. Dixon, a member of the Legislative Council who represented the parish of St. Andrew. Born in Birmingham, England, in 1862, Dixon served in the Royal Field and Royal Horse Artillery before retiring from military life in 1889. He later relocated to Jamaica, where he purchased the Billy Dunn estate in Half Way Tree and then won a seat in the Legislative Council in July 1914.[64] Dixon proposed that the Second Battalion of the WIR, currently garrisoned at Up Park Camp in Jamaica, should be deployed on the battlefields of Europe. The professional soldiers of the WIR, he reasoned, were infinitely more fit than the British civilians flooding recruitment centers to join Kitchener's New Army. Dixon volunteered to recruit a local militia comprised of WIR veterans to serve as a local defense force once the active-duty WIR troops sailed for Europe. Using his platform as an elected member of the Legislative Council, Dixon presented his idea to the other elected members and garnered their unanimous support.[65] However, Governor Manning refused to back Dixon's proposal on both military and financial grounds, insisting that the plan would be too costly and would not contribute significantly to the war effort.[66] In June 1915, the Second Battalion of the WIR departed for Sierra Leone, and in 1916, the unit engaged in limited combat operations against German forces in East Africa.[67]

Whereas Major Dixon, Charles Moulton, and "Backwoodsman" envisioned Jamaica's black and colored majority representing the colony on the field of battle, there were other military boosters who argued from the outset that soldiering should be restricted to the "best classes," a euphemism for the island's white (and lightly colored) upper crust. These military enthusiasts championed an older, aristocratic model of military service that framed arms-bearing and other forms of martial labor as the preserve of cultured gentlemen.[68] In September 1914, S. C. Burke, the Assistant Resident Magistrate for Kingston, privately solicited Governor Manning's support to raise a contingent of three hundred men. Burke volunteered to organize a small, mounted unit, representing the "pick of the colony," which would train in Jamaica and then sail across the Atlantic with their personal horses and military supplies in tow. Confident that the unit would be a credit to the island, Burke insisted that the local government take on all of the group's expenses, including pre-deployment training, arms, equipment, uniforms, transportation, and soldiers' pay at the rate of 4s. per day, the maximum pay for noncommissioned officers in the British Army.[69] In a similar vein, Kingston-based solicitor J. H. Cargill formed his own private volunteer corps, which counted "quite a number of influential gentlemen" among its ranks. The exclusive group drilled three times a week in the hope of eventually serving overseas with the British Army. To restrict membership to the white elite, Cargill vetted all queries from prospective members in person and expected each corpsman to purchase his own military supplies, uniform, and other equipment.[70]

While Burke's and Cargill's proposals presented military service as a pastime for the island's most privileged men, more circumspect commentators sought similar regimental composition by counseling colonial authorities to screen all prospective volunteers based on their personal qualifications and military backgrounds. Cattle pen-keeper G. R. C. Heale, for instance, proposed that the local government sponsor only volunteers who could pass a thorough medical examination and shooting test as well as provide proof of previous military training. Given that the primary sources of military training for civilians in Jamaica were all-white private militias and rifle clubs, Heale's scheme effectively barred black, colored, and East Indian volunteers. Indeed, Heale flatly acknowledged that only "75 to 100 first class men" would be admitted to Jamaica's military contingent based on his criteria.[71]

As military-aged men and pro-enlistment voices flooded the local press with proposals, news that the War Office had declined the offer to raise a West Indian contingent came to light in late October 1914. On October 20, the *West Indian Committee Circular*, the official organ of the powerful, London-based West India Committee, addressed the "bitter disappointment" in the West Indies as word spread that the War Office had refused to raise a regional contingent. Rationalizing the unpopular decision in a front-page article, the editors posited that the number of volunteers from the West Indies "would not have been sufficiently strong numerically" to justify the formation of a new contingent. Furthermore, echoing the language of the War Office's letter, they insisted that any general campaign to mobilize West Indian men for overseas service would deplete local defense forces and make the islands more vulnerable to raiding parties from enemy ships.[72]

Like their colleagues in the metropole, some colonial officials in the British Caribbean also questioned the utility of mobilizing West Indian men for military service abroad. In a letter to Lewis Harcourt in October 1914, Governor William Manning reported that there had been "some agitation" in Jamaica to raise a "Mounted Force for Imperial Service" as well as "proposals to raise a corps to replace the West India Regiment for service in Europe." However, he refused to sanction either plan, asserting that the cost of raising troops for overseas service was prohibitive and could not be justified "from a Military point of view."[73] Likewise, military and colonial officials in Trinidad, including the colony's governor George Le Hunte, as Arthur Cipriani later recalled, dismissed the idea that a West Indian contingent could contribute to the war effort. "The idea that West Indian troops should be sent to help the Mother Country," Cipriani noted angrily, "was looked upon as absurd, preposterous, and unthinkable."[74]

Following the War Office's denial of their offers to serve, military enthusiasts expressed a mounting sense of frustration with both imperial and colonial authorities, insisting that patriotic West Indians had been robbed of their opportunity to demonstrate their manhood and loyalty in the crucible of war. For these would-be volunteers, martial labor functioned simultaneously as a public marker of imperial belonging and as a defining rite of passage for male citizens and subjects. Describing the intense desire to serve among those on the island, a writer from Barbados expressed his sadness in a letter to London. "We have put up sugar and money for the various subscriptions," he explained, "but that won't win our battles. It's lives we desire to give as it's for the Empire that the Motherland is fighting and it is only fair to give these colonies the opportunity of showing the true spirit of patriotism that they have always evinced in the past in a crisis of this kind." While the correspondent accused Barbados Governor Leslie Probyn of not advocating forcefully for a contingent, he also maintained that imperial authorities did not understand the pain Barbadians felt after being "slighted" once more by the War Office. Rejection of the offered contingent struck like a "cold water douche from the Government," dampening the spirits of young men throughout the island. "We are very much cut up about it," he lamented, "and are by no means satisfied that it should rest there." "I hope they will soon see their way to give our lads a chance of serving the Flag that they pride and honour, and so raise their spirits, which are at present very flat over the whole affair," he wrote. "If they could only realise at home what it means to a colony like Barbados, and the other West Indian colonies . . . to be able to hand down to posterity that their sons have fought and bled with the sons of the Motherland in the most critical period of her existence."[75]

As the Barbadian letter writer makes clear, elite calls for a West Indian combat force stemmed in part from deeply felt anxieties about the region's declining status in the empire and repeated public "slights" to

THE "COLOR QUESTION" [35]

SHOULDER TO SHOULDER

FIGURE 1.3. In the cartoon, each soldier is identified by the sash across his uniform and his distinctive dress. Soldiers from left to right: New Zealand, Canada, England, Australia, India, and Africa. Arch Dale, "Shoulder to Shoulder," *The Grain Growers' Guide*, November 14, 1914, 6.

the manhood of West Indians of all colors. Historians have documented how imperial interest in the Caribbean colonies declined significantly in the decades after emancipation in 1838 as the region's financial and strategic importance waned.[76] In fact, by the early twentieth century, recurring rumors that Britain might transfer its "ancient and loyal" West Indian colonies to the United States circulated throughout the region during periods of economic or social crisis in the metropole, heightening local anxieties about imperial belonging.[77]

The War Office's refusal to authorize a West Indian contingent, despite the region's past martial contributions, effectively relegated Britain's Caribbean colonies to the sidelines of the war, both literally and symbolically. This slight not only stymied efforts to solidify the ties between colony and metropole through martial sacrifice but also denied West Indians the social and political capital associated with arms-bearing. The intersection of martial masculinity and imperial belonging during the opening months of the war was powerfully illustrated in a political cartoon entitled "Shoulder to Shoulder," which was initially published in *The Grain Growers' Guide* in western Canada (see fig. 1.3).[78] Drawn by Scottish artist Archibald "Arch" Dale, the stirring image represented the British Empire as a military unit comprised of six male soldiers standing "shoulder to shoulder" in front of a large, billowing Union Jack. England—rendered as a stocky, middle-aged soldier reminiscent of John Bull—stands at the center, surrounded by armed soldiers representing New Zealand, Canada, Australia, India, and Africa. Conspicuously absent from the military unit is any figure representing the Caribbean; the cartoon thus excluded the West Indies from martial visions of the British Empire.

Like white military boosters, black and colored commentators also bemoaned the War Office's decision. W. H. Steele Mitchell, a colored planter in Grenada, eloquently expressed the profound sense of dejection other eager volunteers felt, writing that many military-aged men in the West Indies were "simply burning with desire to serve their King and country." These young men, particularly rural cocoa planters, were "accustomed to a hard, open-air life," Mitchell explained in a letter to officials in London, and would make fine soldiers if given the same opportunity as other colonials. Yet without a regional contingent, volunteers would have to pay the considerable sum of £25 to sail to England to enlist. Given that most cocoa planters in Grenada earned less than £200 per year—and rural wage laborers garnered far less—the fare to England was simply too great a cost to bear. To solve this problem, Mitchell proposed that the colony allocate part of its £50,000 reserve fund to send one hundred Grenadian volunteers to England. Mitchell framed military service as a way to show gratitude to the metropole, echoing earlier appeals by Arthur Cipriani and the correspondent from Barbados. "We think it very hard to remain here and not be able to do something in return for the protection given us by the [British] cruisers in these waters," he wrote.[79] For Mitchell, contributing to the war effort meant forsaking civilian life in the colonies to serve on the storied battlefields of Europe.

As disaffection mounted in the British Caribbean, a powerful new advocate for a West Indian contingent emerged in the metropole. Douglas Cochrane, the twelfth Earl of Dundonald, was a retired lieutenant general in the British Army and the former General Officer Commanding the Militia of Canada. His grandfather, the tenth Earl of Dundonald Admiral Thomas Cochrane, had served as the Commander of the North American station of the British Navy and published an early pamphlet outlining the commercial potential of Trinidadian asphalt. Like his grandfather, Dundonald invested in land in Trinidad—this time hoping to find oil instead of asphalt—and had visited Trinidad and Barbados during a tour of the West Indies from 1904 to 1905.[80] In November 1914, after hearing the plight of W. A. Moore, a dark-skinned black Trinidadian who was rejected when he tried to enlist in England, Dundonald wrote to Secretary of State Lewis Harcourt to lobby for the creation of a West Indian contingent. In his letter, Dundonald stressed that he was "strongly averse to the introduction of coloured people into British Regiments" on the grounds that racially integrated regiments would "be very detrimental to the Imperial connection." Yet, he acknowledged, "harm would be done to the Empire if we offended the susceptibilities of the loyal black population, for it is the black population and their loyalty to Great Britain which stands like a rock between any proposal to exchange the Stars and Stripes for the Union Jack." Therefore, he suggested that the Colonial Office organize a separate West Indian contingent that could serve in a warm climate, such as Egypt's.[81]

Dundonald detailed his ideas in a two-page memorandum entitled, "Proposed West Indian Contingent." He argued that imperial patriotism, as well as depressed economic conditions, made the British Caribbean a fertile ground for military recruiting. "The coloured population of the West Indies is intensely loyal, and Britain's war would be their war," he expounded, "but irrespective of sentiment the present time ought to be favourable for recruiting, as many thousands of West Indian labourers who have been employed in the construction of the Panama canal are, owing to the completion of the work, free for another opening." Moreover, he asserted, the "people of the West Indies are Christians," which made them less susceptible to German propaganda that sought to exploit tensions between Christians and Muslims in the British Empire. He estimated that the Caribbean colonies would be able to muster at least one division—approximately sixteen thousand troops—for service abroad and supply the necessary drafts to maintain the division in the field. In addition to mustering men with no previous military experience, Dundonald suggested recruiting veterans from the West India Regiment and local police forces to help "stiffen the ranks of the newly formed units." Since the rank and file of the new contingent would be black and colored men from the Caribbean colonies, he suggested that all of the senior noncommissioned officers and three-fourths of the commissioned officers should be from Britain, presumably to ensure that white men led the contingent. He also recommended that British officers and noncommissioned officers who had been injured at the front or were no longer fit to withstand the harsh winters in Europe could be used to train volunteers in the West Indies.[82]

Dundonald's modest proposal would have far-reaching consequences. Skillfully underscoring the stakes of the military question—by rejecting West Indians' aspirations to join the military, Dundonald warned, imperial officials were inadvertently provoking racial unrest and outright

[38] CHAPTER 1

disloyalty in the colonies—it reignited debate about West Indian military service at the Colonial Office.

Some remained unconvinced by Dundonald's argument. R. A. Wiseman reiterated his deep-seated concerns about the soldiering abilities of West Indian volunteers. "From the political point of view," Wiseman wrote in an internal minute, "I do not think the military value of the negro in the W. Indies is sufficient to make it necessary for us to press the W.O. [War Office] to modify their decision not to have anything to do with a W.I. [West Indian] contingent." Then he added, caustically, "What colony in the W.I. could raise a contingent sufficiently large to make any appreciable difference to the war?"[83]

Yet while Wiseman lampooned the idea of a West Indian contingent, characterizing Dundonald's plan as an effort to send "half fit soldiers to the West Indies to train negroes," other imperial officials increasingly emphasized the political value of permitting West Indians to serve in the military.[84] Although only a handful of black and colored West Indians had attempted to enlist, senior Colonial Office staffers reasoned that military service was a way to cement West Indian loyalty. "There is no doubt whatever that it is politically desirable to make some use of the black man, even if it only amounts to increasing the strength of the W. I. R. with a view to reinforcing the battalion in Sierra Leone," clerk Gilbert Grindle maintained.[85] Likewise, Under-Secretary of State for the Colonies G. V. Fiddes concurred with the plan to send West Indian volunteers to Egypt on the grounds that it was "very desirable to encourage loyalty in the West Indies."[86] And, in a remarkable volte-face, both Grindle and Fiddes insisted that black soldiers from the West India Regiment had served "with distinction" in previous conflicts and should have the opportunity to do so once again.[87]

On December 8, 1914, the Colonial Office endorsed a modified version of Dundonald's plan and forwarded his proposal to the War Office for the Army Council to review.[88] Three factors likely led to the Colonial Office's new stance on the question of West Indian military service. First, Dundonald's proposal sidestepped the volatile issue of black West Indians' status as "alien" military volunteers by proposing that Caribbean soldiers serve in their own contingent rather than with white troops in British regiments. Second, he recommended that the West Indian contingent should be stationed outside of Europe in Egypt or another country with a warm climate. Although the War Cabinet deployed Indian troops to fight in France, Secretary of State for the Colonies Lewis Harcourt insisted that the color question and other considerations made it utterly "impractical" to use

West Indian troops on the European continent. Third and most important, high-ranking imperial officials agreed with Dundonald's assertion that the military question could either weaken or strengthen West Indians' loyalty to the empire. In a letter to the War Office, Harcourt pressed the Army Council to consider "the political advantages to be gained by recognizing and encouraging the loyalty of the black and coloured population." To that end, he drafted a memo detailing how "to duplicate the present battalion of the West India Regiment in Jamaica and to form a service battalion for Egypt or some other warm country." If that was not possible, Harcourt proposed, "Contingents might be organized in the larger Colonies of Jamaica, Barbados, Trinidad and British Guiana" and deployed on the "lines of communication in Egypt."[89]

Policymakers at the War Office, though moved by the Colonial Office's political assessment of the military question, continued to doubt West Indians' martial abilities. Therefore, as a compromise, the Army Council agreed to raise a West Indian contingent, but insisted that the new contingent would not be "suitable" for combat duties in Egypt or East Africa. Instead, they offered to station the contingent in the former German colony of Cameroon and in other "Territories recently taken from the enemy in West Africa." Far from the battlefield, the new contingent would form part of the garrison of troops that would secure and hold newly acquired African territories.[90]

Harcourt swiftly rejected the plan to use West Indian volunteers for garrison duty, declaring that military-aged men were "so anxious to fight for the Empire" that they would "deeply resent" any proposal to serve as an occupying force in a West African backwater. Moreover, he argued, black West Indian troops would be susceptible to local illnesses, which would severely limit their effectiveness in West Africa.[91] Given that the West African Frontier Force was already in the area, Harcourt went on, it made little sense to raise a regiment of soldiers from the Caribbean when local recruits were readily available.

When the War Office proved unwilling to alter its stance, Harcourt wrote to Dundonald in late December 1914 to inform him that his proposal for a West Indian contingent had been rejected.[92] "The difficulties and disadvantages presented by this proposal are found to be too considerable to allow of it being adopted in any satisfactory form," Harcourt averred. "In the circumstances, therefore, it is feared that it will not be possible to employ West Indian troops for service outside the West Indian colonies."[93] For the second time since the outbreak of the war, officials at the War Office rebuffed the call to raise a West Indian fighting force. But this time, it disappointed not only military boosters but also the Colonial Office.

Confronting the Empire's "Nasty Cowardly Skin Prejudice"

As the threat of German invasion of the Caribbean dissipated by early 1915, colonial officials scrambled to come up with explanations for the War Office's intransigent position without publicly acknowledging the existence of a color bar in the British Army vis-à-vis West Indians.[94] Some local leaders suggested that men from tropical climates would never be able to withstand the harsh winters on the Western Front. The War Office's willingness to deploy thousands of Indian troops in France in September 1914 quickly belied that assertion, however. Others argued that the projected cost of raising and transporting publicly funded contingents was simply too great for the chronically cash-strapped colonies to bear. The most patently ridiculous excuse came from Barbados Governor Leslie Probyn, who claimed that black and colored volunteers' dark skin would make them dangerously "conspicuous" in a European conflict.[95]

Despite the plethora of justifications circulated by colonial bureaucrats in London and the Caribbean, military boosters and potential recruits increasingly challenged the War Office's rationale for excluding West Indian volunteers from the imperial armed forces. Evidence of the growing restiveness in the colonies abounded in the press in late 1914 and early 1915. In a published letter to the *West India Committee Circular*, Dr. A. A. Myers of Dominica insisted that the islands of the West Indies could easily produce enough men to send a contingent abroad while also maintaining a local defense force in each island. "It may interest you to know that, speaking for Dominica, there are good active men who would willingly give their service abroad," he wrote. Moreover, Myers attacked the Colonial Office's claim that West Indians should focus on local defense in order to prevent German ships from raiding coal and other vital supplies from the region's port cities. "As for preventing the enemy from obtaining supplies, surely sir, you cannot be serious," he wrote incredulously. "How can a handful of riflemen, however brave and well-trained stand up unsupported by artillery of any sort or kind, against quick-firing . . . guns of the modern cruiser?"[96]

Myers reported that in Dominica there was "much dissatisfaction at the prompt and unconditional rejection of our offer of service." The War Office, he reasoned, should have offered to review the proposal "later on" instead of curtly refusing to consider the possibility of a West Indian contingent. If accepted for service, West Indian soldiers could perform garrison duty in England or patrol communications lines in Belgium and on the Western Front, he suggested. Whatever the task, Myers stressed that West Indians had earned the right to serve the empire because of their loyalty and long-standing ties with Britain. "We are among the most ancient colonies of the Crown, and in loyalty hold ourselves second to none; we wish to do something more than we are doing for the King," he insisted. "Let them give us a chance, then."[97]

While Myers did not suggest that the "colour question" fueled the War Office's decision, other observers rightly guessed that racial concerns contributed to the office's intransigence. The editor of the Grenada *Federalist* condemned "the nasty cowardly skin prejudice characteristic of the empire," which prevented the recruitment of West Indians in a time of dire conflict. "The skin and colour prejudice which dominate the minds of the English authorities stand in the way of the utilisation of the services of the Coloured people for Imperial purposes," the editor alleged.[98] Likewise, in Barbados and Jamaica, many people believed that the imperial government was simply unwilling to arm black men, even to fight against a white enemy.[99] Remarkably, the most strident public rebuke of the War Office came from the pages of the British Honduras *Clarion*, the mouthpiece of the colony's conservative establishment. Redeploying the hyperbolic language of British war propaganda, the paper blasted the hypocrisy of those who demanded West Indians' unflinching loyalty while preventing them from demonstrating it through military service:

> Until the war is carried into Germany; until the Allied commanders sit in the imperial palace in Berlin, and dictate terms of peace; until the holocaust of blood, rapine and horror indescribable, offered in Belgium by Germany to her gods of demonical hate, arrogance and barbaric militarism has [been] avenged, the empire cannot dispense, unless she is obsessed with the spirit of self-destruction, with the services of her blackest and humblest citizen. Englishmen take long to learn their lessons. The killing of a German is an imperial duty of obligation, as the churchmen say; and god forbid that the complexion of the man who does the killing shall stand in the way of the victory, without which the England, which we all love, in spite of her many faults, shall stand humbled at the foot of an arrogant and despised conqueror.[100]

In other words, England's racist military policies not only kept her faithful "blackest and humblest" subjects from taking their rightful place on the field of battle but also made Englishmen more vulnerable to Germany's military might.[101]

As the region's pro-military businessmen and newspaper editors pressured the War Office to reconsider its stance on a West Indian contingent, a trickle of British expatriates and white Creoles sailed to England to enlist in Britain's burgeoning armed forces. These enlistees included junior civil servants, sons of planters and rural estate managers, constables, middling-level clerks and businessmen, prominent ministers, and a fair number of recent secondary school graduates who were driven to volunteer by a sense of manly duty, a thirst for adventure and fame, or simply boredom at home. E. P. Sibthorpe, the organist for Kingston Parish Church, joined the Eleventh Battalion of the Devonshire Regiment. While training for the front at Worgret Camp in Dorset, Sibthorpe sent home a striking self-portrait showcasing his new military uniform.[102] Twenty-one-year-old John Chandler of Claremont, Jamaica, resigned his position with the United Fruit Company in San Jose, Costa Rica, in May 1915 to enter the Inns of Court Officer Training Corps in England. Chandler was commissioned as a second lieutenant in the County of London Regiment.[103] The departure of the first group of white volunteers from Trinidad, as C. L. R. James later recalled, elicited the "most remarkable" celebrations "ever witnessed in the history of the colony."[104]

While taking in these white West Indian volunteers, Kitchener's New Army roundly discouraged black and colored West Indians from enlisting in its ranks. In a confidential memo circulated in November 1914, the Colonial Office instructed the region's governors to dissuade nonwhite would-be volunteers from sailing to England.[105] Three months later, in a secret letter to Governor Manning, Lewis Harcourt additionally insisted that "no candidate who is not of pure European descent should be recommended" for a commission in the "new Service Battalions of His Majesty's Army."[106] Yet determined black and colored professionals continued journeying across the Atlantic at their own expense to volunteer, only to then be victimized by the War Office's discriminatory policies. Dr. William Steele Mitchell, the acting resident surgeon of Grenada, applied for a position in the Royal Army Medical Corps in 1915 after reading about the desperate shortage of doctors in England. Despite the urgent need for trained physicians, the War Office decided that Mitchell—a "slightly coloured man" with "African wooly hair"—was "ineligible for such appointment" because he did not possess "pure European blood."[107] Mitchell's rejection initially touched off a firestorm of criticism in Grenada, but it failed to provoke any sustained protests.[108] Jamaican government veterinarian

THE "COLOR QUESTION" [43]

G. O. Rushdie-Gray was also rebuffed when he applied for a position in the Army Veterinary Corps, despite having previously served as a veterinarian to the WIR.[109] While continuing to insist that it did not maintain an "absolute bar against coloured men for commissions in the Vet. Corps," the War Office suggested that Rushdie-Gray's particularly dark skin color made his appointment impossible. This decision was seconded by officials in the Colonial Office, who expressed their shock that Jamaica's governor would have recommended a black man for a commission without mentioning Rushdie-Gray's complexion in his dispatch.[110] In an apologetic reply to the Colonial Office, Governor Manning promised to provide in the future the "required report" detailing a candidate's race if the "Officer applying for a Commission is not of pure European descent."[111]

Meanwhile, the manifest illogic of the War Office's position was made abundantly clear in the treatment of the small number of black and colored West Indians who had settled in England *before* the outbreak of the war since dozens of these men were allowed to enlist in British regiments. Jamaican leatherworker Egbert Watson was living in Camden Town in north London when the war began, and he enlisted in the Royal Garrison Artillery in January 1916. Watson fought as a gunner in France for two months before leaving the service because of myalgia and epilepsy.[112] Grenadian James Ernest Ross joined the Nineteenth London Regiment in 1914 and, like Watson, served as a machine gunner in combat. Captured by the Germans during the Battle of Cambrai, Ross was a prisoner of war for nearly six months before making a daring escape with nineteen other prisoners in 1918.[113] Alonzo Nathan, a Jamaican seaman in the bustling port city of Cardiff, initially served in the Army Service Corps although he would eventually be transferred to the BWIR once it was created.[114]

The most famous Jamaican volunteer was future Premier Norman Manley, who was in his first year at Oxford on a Rhodes scholarship when the war erupted. Postponing his studies, he enlisted in June 1915 along with his younger brother Roy, hoping initially to serve in the Royal Flying Corps; he ultimately settled on the Royal Field Artillery because of the prohibitively high cost of flight school.[115] In his memoirs, Manley noted that even "after the start of the first World War it was impossible to be in England and not be aware of the problems of colour. You were immediately aware in a thousand ways that you belonged elsewhere but not there."[116] Indeed when Roy Manley applied for admission to the Officer Training Corps in 1915, he was curtly rejected because of his racial heritage. Likewise, Norman Manley encountered such "violent colour prejudice" when he was promoted to corporal that he elected to revert to the rank of gunner and subsequently transferred to a new division.[117] In 1917, he was there to bury his twenty-one-year-old brother Roy after he was fatally struck in the heart by a shell-casing fragment while fighting in Ypres.[118]

As the colored planter Mitchell had noted, the steep cost of traveling to England to enlist, which ranged from £15 to £25 per person, effectively barred men of the laboring classes from joining the colors. Yet, a few were determined to do their bit for the empire in her hour of need. Some men sought out wealthy local patrons to sponsor their passage to England or joined the growing chorus of citizens lobbying for a publicly funded contingent. Others simply avoided paying the substantial cost of a ticket to England by stowing away on United Kingdom-bound ships. In May 1915, nine men from Barbados were discovered on the Royal Mail Steam Packet Company steamer SS *Danube*.[119] When questioned, the stowaways proudly asserted that they intended to go to England to join the army. When the *Danube* arrived in the metropole, the would-be soldiers were promptly arraigned at West Ham Police Court, where the magistrate informed them that they had little hope of being accepted in a British regiment. Undeterred, the men refused to return to Barbados, proclaiming that they had "come to fight and they were going to fight." Algernon Aspinall, the Secretary of the West India Committee, took an interest in the men's case and requested that the magistrate allow them to enlist in a battalion for colored men forming at Cardiff. The charges against the nine men were ultimately dismissed, and they were released into the care of the West India Committee.[120]

The logjam at the War Office came to an end only after the personal intervention of King George V finally compelled the office to accept a West Indian contingent. In April 1915, the king received a heartfelt appeal from a woman engaged in charitable work in the West Indies, who made the case for the creation of a combat regiment staffed by the region's men.[121] Moved by her petition, George V, through his Private Secretary Lord Stamfordham, wrote a letter to Lewis Harcourt informing him that it would be "very politic to gratify the wish of the West Indies to send a Regiment to the Front." Like Dundonald and other previous commentators, George V suggested that the regiment could be "usefully employed in Egypt."[122]

In a lengthy reply dispatched three days later, Harcourt blamed the War Office for declining two previous opportunities to raise a West Indian contingent, shrewdly minimizing the Colonial Office's role. Harcourt explained that the "question of meeting the natural and legitimate aspirations of the West Indies to take some action in the war" had been raised on several occasions since the beginning of hostilities and informed Stamfordham that the Colonial Office had discussed proposals for a West Indian contingent with the War Office in late August 1914 and again in December 1914. However, he insisted, the War Office flatly declined to authorize a contingent for service in a combat theater on both occasions. Harcourt admitted that it had been difficult for him to deal with the offers of service from the West Indies "owing to the colour question," since it was "not possible to enlist black or coloured men in British regiments." He went on to suggest that the formation of a West Indian force on the European front was "impracticable for various reasons, of which colour is only one." Yet, despite these difficulties, Harcourt acknowledged that he "had begun to feel some anxiety as to the possible effect of continued rejection of offers of service on the loyalty of the black population of the West Indies and on their existing attachment to the Empire." Thus, in December 1914, he had asked the Army Council to find some way to mobilize the "black population of the West Indies for the purposes of the war." However, the War Office failed to provide a mutually agreeable proposal, resulting in a four-month impasse.[123]

On April 22, 1915, Lord Stamforham notified Harcourt that George V had reviewed his letter and had spoken with Kitchener regarding the possibility of a West Indian contingent. Stamforham reported, "There is no recollection of the War Office having refused the offer of a West Indian Contingent" and that Kitchener "would be very glad to accept" a contingent as long as it was a "complete unit" and did not come with "any conditions as to where it should serve." Given the "political importance of not refusing the loyal offer of services from the West Indies," George V encouraged Harcourt to "make a proposal which would be acceptable to the War Office."[124] After a terse exchange between Harcourt and Kitchener, the War Office authorized the formation of a West Indian contingent, later officially deemed the British West Indies Regiment, on May 19, 1915.[125]

News that the British West Indies would have its own military contingent was greeted with enthusiasm throughout the region. In Jamaica, laborers and rural cultivators were said to have flooded the coffers of the War Contingent Fund, despite being squeezed to the breaking point by staggering wartime inflation. Workers at the Petersville Pen contributed £1 6s. 3d., while the Rose of the Isthmus Lodge of the British Independent Order of Good Samaritans and Daughters of Samaria collected £1 6d. from its working-class members for the effort.[126] Sad that he was too young to enlist, seven-year-old John Elliot McCrea Jr. of Port Antonio, Jamaica, decided to support the fledging contingent by collecting donations on Empire Day. His efforts netted an impressive ten shillings.[127] In

Trinidad, inveterate military booster Arthur Cipriani partnered with the *Port of Spain Gazette* to compile a roster of local men willing to enlist. On June 5, 1915, the *Gazette* published a rousing appeal to the "Men of Trinidad!," encouraging them to volunteer by sending their names to the paper's main office.[128] By month's end, 766 men had answered the call. Cipriani was listed as the very first volunteer.[129]

If the creation of the BWIR signaled that nonwhite colonials might also play a role in the imperial defense effort, George V's historic call for "men of all classes" to pick up arms in the service of the empire left little doubt that colonial subjects could also become British soldiers. George V's personal appeal for volunteers, published in late October 1915, issued a sweeping invitation to men in the empire to fight alongside their "brothers" in Britain. Weaving together powerful ideas about British justice, imperial fraternity, volunteerism, and righteous war, the sovereign's message invoked an egalitarian, color-blind "free Empire" sustained by the martial labor and voluntary sacrifice of both citizens and subjects. "In freely responding to my appeal," he wrote, "you will be giving your support to our brothers who, for long months, have nobly upheld Britain's past traditions, and the glory of her Arms." By soldiering on behalf of the empire, he suggested, colonial subjects could assume their "share of the fight" while honoring the sacrifices of their fellow Britishers.[130] Through his historic message, George V officially endorsed and broadcast the tenets of martial interracialism to subjects across Britain's vast empire.

The symbolic importance of "The Appeal"—which was read aloud in pulpits from Kingston to Castries and reprinted in all of the region's major newspapers—was tremendous.[131] Appropriating its language, military recruiters, journalists, black and colored reformers, and prospective soldiers would begin to offer their own visions of empire and mutual obligation as the war progressed. And, in an act that highlighted his personal commitment to colonial soldiers, George V officially endorsed the BWIR through a royal proclamation in *The London Gazette* on October 26, 1915, one day after circulating his stirring call throughout the empire.[132]

Race and the Rhetoric of Imperial Patriotism

Although whites spearheaded the transatlantic campaign that culminated in the creation of the BWIR, black and colored reformers in the British Caribbean celebrated the news of a regional contingent and recognized the opportunities that soldiering could enable. In Grenada, the editors of the *West Indian* rhapsodized about the historical significance of the BWIR for the region's black and colored majority: "The grand spectacle has been left for us—West Indians, most of us whom are descendants of slaves, fighting for human liberty together with the immediate sons of the Motherland in Europe's classic field of war made famous from ancient Grecian days to the days of Marlborough on Wellington. The bones of Clarkson and Wilberforce rattle in their graves today."[133] Similarly moved, Marcus Garvey invited military recruiters to UNIA meetings and gave a stirring address to the first contingent of soldiers to depart from Jamaica.[134]

Surprisingly, none of the region's leading black activists had put forward their own proposals for a military contingent during the first ten months of the war, even given the racial overtones of the military question as well as the increasingly high stakes of the debate. Published reports of the UNIA's meetings during this period do not include any references to the topic of military service, and Garvey's personal correspondence from August 1914 to May 1915 is conspicuously silent on the issue. Tellingly, the UNIA's celebrated loyalty resolution, with which this chapter opened, also neglected the larger question of West Indians serving "shoulder to shoulder" with Britons from the metropole. Likewise, colored Jamaican dentist Louis Meilke, the region's strongest proponent of a self-governing West Indian federation, did not chime in on the military question despite his previous support for universal military service. Grenadian editor and activist T. A. Marryshow also steered clear of the military question. Remarkably, none of Marryshow's early editorials in the *West Indian*, the progressive newspaper he co-founded in January 1915, called for the formation of a regional fighting force.

Instead, activists focused on how the dislocations of war could fundamentally reshape the social and political order in the British Caribbean. Capitalizing on the moment, they launched vibrant grassroots movements for political reform and racial equality. As the debate about a West Indian contingent raged in the press, black and colored middle-class reformers in Jamaica, Trinidad, Grenada, British Honduras, and elsewhere in the region challenged the legitimacy of Crown colony government, protested de facto racial discrimination, and advocated greater intra-regional and intra-racial cooperation. These educated men and women, based largely in the region's cosmopolitan capital cities, founded a host of new social and political groups during the first year of the war. In Kingston, Jamaica, for instance, two new organizations emerged in 1914 seeking to foster an appreciation of local history and culture while promoting a racially tinged West Indian identity. The Jamaica Patriotic League, established by colored musician Astley Clark, endeavored to advance the "spirit of patriotism, unity, mutual love, comradeship and citizenship" among the island's women, men, and youth. Guided by the nationalist motto "Jamaica's Welfare First," the League operated through a network of local chapters named after Jamaican historical figures and British patriots.[135] Clark also published a series of daily lessons for children in the *Gleaner* and *Jamaica Times*, which focused on moral uplift, social development, and local history.[136] In July 1914, Marcus Garvey and Amy Ashwood co-founded the UNIA, which Garvey officially registered two weeks later on Emancipation Day.[137] The new organization combined the pecuniary benefits of a fraternal society with the highbrow curricular offerings of a debating club and an explicit program for racial progress. Under the banner of "One God, One Aim, One Destiny," the association aspired to "establish a universal confraternity among the race, to promote the spirit of race pride and love, and to reclaim the fallen of the race." Unlike Clark, Garvey advanced an international vision of the struggle for black advancement in Jamaica, which he viewed as part and parcel of a global black movement that transcended imperial boundaries. Indeed, he boldly embraced transnationalism, positioning the UNIA as an advocate for "all Negroes, irrespective of nationality."[138]

As Garvey formulated his ambitious strategy to unify blacks in the Caribbean, United States, Brazil, and the African continent, colored doctor Louis Meikle led a regional crusade for a British West Indian federation from his home in Port of Spain, Trinidad. Born in the verdant coffee-growing parish of Manchester, Jamaica, in 1874, Meikle had traveled to the United States to study medicine and dentistry at Howard University. After graduation, he landed a position as a medical inspector with the U.S. Public Health Service and the Isthmian Canal Commission, working alongside fellow Caribbean migrants in the Canal Zone in Panama. By 1912, Meikle had relocated to Trinidad, where he published *Confederation of the British West Indies versus Annexation to the United States: A Political Discourse on the West Indies*, a book-length treatise that contrasted the promise of a West Indian federation to the perils of annexation to Canada or the United States. Lambasting British Crown colony rule as "autocratic in principle, and a gigantic farce," Meikle nevertheless argued that annexation to the United States would subject nonwhite West Indians to a virulently racist regime of legalized segregation and racial terror.[139] Unwilling to choose between the lynch law of the United States and the humiliations of Crown colony government, he instead proposed that the British colonies in the Caribbean form a political federation with Dominion status within the empire. Federation, he claimed, would "preserve the West Indies for the West Indians" and frustrate American aggression in the region.[140]

Central to Meikle's vision of a popularly governed "United West Indies" was compulsory male military service. As early as 1912, a full two years before the eruption of armed conflict in Europe, Meikle forewarned that Britain's defeat in an "approaching Anglo-German war" could force West Indians to become "subjects of the Kaiser."[141] To protect the scattered territories of the British Caribbean from foreign encroachment, he argued, the constitution of any future West Indian federation should require male citizens to serve in a local defense corps or the standing army. Drawing on his experiences in the fin de siècle United States, where secondary schools offered rudimentary military training and teenaged boys swelled the ranks of militarized cadet corps, Meikle concluded that martial labor instilled manly character, self-discipline, and physical strength. "The young men of to-day should be taught to handle the rifle at as early an age as is consistent with physical development," he wrote. "Judging from the signs of the time, education in these days must necessarily be extended farther than the use of the pen—it must also embody the use of the sword and rifle." With proper military training, he predicted optimistically, "a humped, slouchy-moving lump of humanity" is "transformed into a new creature." Meikle also included several references to soldiering in a public letter that his Trinidad-based West Indian Federation Committee circulated in August 1914.[142]

While Meikle relied on the region's elite-controlled press to publicize his federation proposals, other black and colored reformers founded their own progressive organs during the war years, independent papers that served the tripartite function of articulating demands for democratic political reform, promoting racial self-esteem, and informing local communities of the global struggle for black advancement. In British Honduras, middle-class activist Hubert Hill Cain established the *Belize Independent* in 1914.[143] The following year, journalist T. A. Marryshow and lawyer C. F. P. Renwick launched *The West Indian* in St. George's, Grenada. The masthead of the new paper contained a hand-drawn map of the Caribbean that boldly proclaimed the founders' regional vision by including the Spanish- and French-speaking isles as well as the Anglophone territories. And, it audaciously proclaimed the editors' nationalist mission: "The West Indies Must Be Westindian."

So why did the same cadre of leaders who had seemed relatively uninterested in the fevered debate over West Indian military participation readily embrace the British West Indies Regiment in the summer of 1915?

[50] CHAPTER 1

These men, I argue, realized that West Indians could leverage their overseas military service to call for social and political reforms on the home front. During the early months of the war, the debate over West Indian military service had been bound by the idea that a regional force would be limited in size and perhaps include only white men. Yet, the news that the War Office had authorized a regional contingent that would accept all men who met the standard requirements for a British soldier meant that military service could be used as a tool for local black and colored reformers to pursue enhanced social standing and a more democratic political culture.[144] Thus, in June 1915, the Grenada *Federalist* posited that the dislocations of war and black soldiers' performance on the battlefield would undermine deeply ingrained notions of white racial superiority that barred West Indians from the privilege of self-government. "We think the day is dawning," the editor predicted, "when the black man will be more fairly treated in the empire." But, in an implicit rebuke of imperial patriotism, the *Federalist* fearlessly proclaimed: "When that day comes we must thank Kaiser Wilhelm of Germany for it."[145]

CHAPTER TWO

"Every True Son of the Empire"

MARTIAL MASCULINITY,
TRANSNATIONAL MIGRATION,
AND THE POLITICS OF RECRUITMENT

*Mr. [Marcus] Garvey impressed on the men ... the duty of every true son
of the Empire to rally to the cause of the Motherland.*

—*JAMAICA TIMES* (1915)

*In the armed forces the Color Bar reigned supreme. It was carried to such
a ridiculous degree that the darker skin natives were segregated from the
lighter, as goats from sheep. The West Indian army was recruited strictly
on racial lines.*

—GEORGE PADMORE

SEVENTEEN-YEAR-OLD C. L. R. JAMES decided to abandon his final
year at Queen's Royal College, Trinidad's oldest and most esteemed boys'
secondary school, to attend to more urgent matters. Anxious to "see the
world," the restless teenager concluded that the "best way would be to go
to the war."[1] One morning in 1918, James skipped school and traveled to
an office where "one of the big merchants" in Port of Spain "examined the
would-be warriors." "Young man after young man went in, and I was not
obviously inferior to any of them in anything," he would later recall. "The
merchant talked to each [volunteer], asked for references and arranged
for further examination as the case may be." However, when James
approached the merchant's desk to enlist, he was rejected before receiving
an interview about his educational pedigree or even the required physical examination. "He took one look at me, saw my dark skin, and shaking

[51]

his head vigorously, motioned me violently away."[2] Even amid a global war for democracy, as James swiftly ascertained, Trinidad's colonial elite remained fiercely committed to the racial and socioeconomic order that secured white dominance.

James would never become a soldier despite being an accomplished athlete, "tall and very fit," and keen to enlist. Contemplating his failed plan decades later, James maintained that he was "not unduly disturbed" after being rejected for military service. Rather, he insisted that it was his white teachers at Queen's Royal College who were troubled by the overt racism that he experienced from recruiters. "When the masters heard what had happened to me some of them were angry, one or two ashamed, all were on my side," he wrote. "It didn't hurt for long because for so many years these crude intrusions from the world which surrounded us had been excluded. I had not even been wounded, for no scar was left."[3]

Tracing the countercurrents of inclusion and exclusion that marked the British Caribbean military recruitment campaign, this chapter presents a transnational history of military mobilization during World War I, with a particular focus on the political discourses, policies, and practices that shaped enlistment across the circum-Caribbean. By scrutinizing the regional dynamics of recruitment, rather than analyzing the recruitment process for each British Caribbean colony in isolation, the chapter demonstrates how the fevered drive to recruit men for the BWIR between 1915 and 1918 mobilized the imperial ideals of martial interracialism, mutual obligation, and devotion to the empire, while simultaneously rallying West Indians from diverse racial, color, and class backgrounds to support the war effort. Local commentators publicly celebrated men who volunteered for military service, hailing them as imperial patriots who answered "the Call for Conscience, not Conscription."[4] However, as this chapter argues, the experiences of overt racism that met C. L. R. James and countless others exposed the sharp disjuncture between the inclusive rhetoric of martial interracialism—as well as the recruits' optimistic hopes of what enlistment would bring—and the entrenched realities of racial discrimination and exclusion in the armed forces. As volunteers soon discovered, the racial, color, and class hierarchies within the British Army were even more rigid than those in the British Caribbean.

Reconstructing the regional dynamics of recruitment also reveals the dynamic interplay between military enlistment and labor migration in the circum-Caribbean. One in eight BWIR soldiers joined the regiment while living abroad, despite British officials' initial efforts to block West Indian migrants from volunteering. Panama became the second largest enlistment site for the BWIR, sending more men to the regiment than any circum-Caribbean territory except Jamaica. If "warfare migrates," as historian Vincent Brown contends, then scholars must consider how migratory journeys conditioned soldiers' lives—before, during, and after military deployment.[5] A careful analysis of the trajectories of BWIR volunteers demonstrates that thousands of enlistees had engaged previously in labor migration as an economic strategy *before* World War I. When recruitment began, they seized upon the opportunity to join the BWIR, as those who did not enlist faced mass layoffs and economic uncertainty in the Canal Zone.

Military recruitment for the BWIR was a decidedly civilian affair. Given the scant presence of the British Army in even the largest Caribbean colonies, the massive task of recruiting, training, and deploying thousands of men for overseas military service hinged on the unpaid labor of civilian women, men, and children. Throughout the region, estate laborers and cattle pen workers donated money from their paltry wages to buttress war relief funds. Primary school teachers offered free evening literacy classes for military-aged men. Red Cross nurses captivated audiences at recruitment rallies, while clergymen preached the gospel of military service. Local doctors performed free medical examinations of prospective enlistees, and women from all classes sewed clothing and other "comforts" for the volunteers. Thus, while imperial officials and colonial authorities defined the enlistment terms for the BWIR, the actual recruitment process was organized and directed by West Indian civilians in the islands, rimlands, and diaspora. By studying the social dynamics of the recruitment campaign, we can understand how military mobilization laid bare long-standing racial and class divisions while also holding out the promise of upward mobility to black men and women from the laboring classes.

The chapter begins with an analysis of the protracted negotiations to develop a framework for military mobilization. It then turns to the regional recruitment drive, interrogating the discourses that permeated BWIR recruitment rallies and spurred tens of thousands of men to answer the call to enlist. The final sections of the chapter expose both popular and elite resistance to the BWIR, including private efforts in British Honduras, Barbados, and Trinidad to create separate military contingents for volunteers from the "better classes" of whites and coloreds. Ultimately, this chapter reveals how recruiters, volunteers, war resisters, government officials, and military authorities engaged in a high-stakes battle over race, manhood, and the wartime obligation of military service.

[54] CHAPTER 2

"We Have to Face the Colour Difficulty": The Bureaucratic Battle Over Military Payments and Pensions

The War Office officially authorized the creation of a British Caribbean contingent in May 1915; however, the exact size, composition, and organization of His Majesty's new military unit remained undefined and open for negotiation.[6] Several vital questions about the nascent contingent had to be settled before recruitment could officially commence, despite an enthusiastic preliminary response. Would the BWIR include volunteers from every colony in the British Caribbean, or would the regiment welcome only men from the region's larger territories? Who would spearhead, finance, and administer the local recruitment process: colonial officials, private citizens, or military authorities? And most centrally, how many new soldiers did military boosters intend to recruit and what would be the criteria for serving?

During the latter half of 1915, metropolitan officials and administrators in the colonies sought to define the role West Indian troops would play in the imperial war effort and the specific terms that would dictate their participation. At stake in these bureaucratic wranglings was not only the military status of West Indian soldiers but also the social and economic rights afforded to colonials of color in the British Caribbean. Officials secretly contemplated whether volunteers from Jamaica, Trinidad, Barbados, and elsewhere in the region should enter the military under identical terms as white metropolitan troops or be relegated to colonial regiments. Officials also debated if the mothers, partners, and children of West Indian soldiers would receive financial support comparable to that afforded to white servicemen's families in the British Isles. These confidential negotiations took place in terse letters and private telegrams exchanged among a small cadre of British officials in London and the colonies. Military boosters, would-be volunteers, and local reformers in the West Indies were forced to wait for news rather than registering their own demands. Still, the incessant clamor for updates and action by the local press and interested observers created a charged atmosphere for bureaucratic debates within the colonial administration.

The negotiations to fix the terms of the BWIR reignited the tug-of-war among the Army Council, War Office, and Colonial Office, revealing the financial pressures and conflicting agendas that riddled the imperial bureaucracy. On one side, the Army Council and War Office maneuvered to minimize their financial and logistic contributions to the BWIR. In a letter to the Colonial Office, the Army Council endorsed the idea of forming a single West Indian contingent but stressed that the new regional unit would function as a "separate Contingent" rather than a regular British Army unit. By funneling West Indian volunteers into a colonial contingent instead of the British Army, explained clerk B. B. Cubitt candidly, the Army Council sought to prevent BWIR soldiers from claiming "all of the emoluments of a British soldier."[7] The Army Council further recommended that local governments in the colonies should provide funding for noneffective charges, such as soldiers' pensions and separation allowances (the financial support paid monthly to soldiers' dependents), as well as for each soldier's passage to England, including all meals during the voyage.[8] Finally, the Council proposed that BWIR soldiers should not be eligible for bonus proficiency pay, although they consented to compensating West Indian soldiers at "British rates" while on active duty.[9] Thus, in closed-door conversations, British defense officials readily jettisoned the principle of martial interracialism in order to curb the imperial government's expenditures on black and colored men.

On the other side, the Colonial Office pushed military authorities to use imperial funds to cover most expenses for the BWIR rather than draining the coffers of the colonies. In a letter to the War Office in early July 1915, Bonar Law, who had recently replaced Lewis Harcourt as Secretary of State for the Colonies, explained that he would feel "considerable difficulty" asking the colonies to assume full responsibility for separation allowances, pensions, and all other noneffective charges, given limited financial resources in the West Indies and the open-ended, "indefinite character" of such expenses. Moreover, he insisted emphatically that the BWIR "must be paid at British rates." However, as a compromise, Law stated he would be willing to ask the colonies to contribute a mutually agreed-upon proportion of the noneffective charges on an annual basis. All separation allowances and pensions for soldiers who resided in the West Indies, he further conceded, could be paid at the rate set for the West India Regiment, the colonial regiment that preceded the BWIR, instead of the higher scale for British soldiers. Still, Law repeated, "all other expenses in connection with the contingent should fall on Imperial funds," including the "cost of eventual repatriation to the respective Colonies of recruitment."[10]

Ultimately, the War and Colonial Offices consented to pay BWIR soldiers on the same scale as their British counterparts, with privates earning one shilling per day and noncommissioned officers receiving between 1s. 8d. and 4s. daily. Depending on their rank and years of service, commissioned officers in the BWIR could earn up to 16s. per day. After two years of service, soldiers would also qualify for proficiency pay in addition to their standard daily wage. Furthermore, in a July 17 letter to the Colonial Office, the War Office stated that disability pension rates for BWIR soldiers would be on par with those for European regiments and that widows of BWIR servicemen could claim a one-time payment equal to the deceased soldier's annual pay.

At the same time, BWIR soldiers would not receive all the material benefits provided to British Army troops. In keeping with Bonar Law's suggestion, the War Office mandated that separation allowances for the dependents of BWIR soldiers would be calculated using the lower rates for the West India Regiment instead of those for the British Army. Accordingly, the wife of a BWIR private would receive a separation allowance of only 11s. 1d. per week rather than the 12s. 6d. allotted to the wife of a British Army private.[11] Moreover, the War Office still insisted that colonial governments in the Caribbean pay the costs of travel to England for their respective contingents and a portion of the noneffective charges.[12] Once in England, however, imperial military authorities would assume all costs for the soldiers and combine the individual island contingents to form battalions of the BWIR.[13]

Officials at the Colonial Office were generally pleased with the terms outlined in the War Office's July 17 missive, yet at least one staff member fretted that the terms for the BWIR did not provide enough compensation for *white* volunteers and their kin. Clerk Gilbert Grindle, in a last-ditch effort to win more favorable pensions for white West Indians and their families, urged his colleagues to revise the regiment's pension provisions to ensure that the "widows of Europeans" who lived in the colonies would receive British Army pension rates, rather than the lower pension rates for BWIR soldiers. Grindle acknowledged that any effort to create a two-tiered pension system based on race might fuel "a little colour excitement" in the colonies, but he reasoned that the "general enthusiasm about the contingent" would mitigate widespread unrest. "We have to face the colour difficulty in the end and we had better face it boldly to begin with," Grindle argued in an internal minute. "We have done so over the commissioned ranks and so far no harm has ensued from the rejection of coloured applicants for commissions."[14]

If Grindle seemed remarkably cavalier about the potential fallout from his pension proposal, it may have been in part because prospective soldiers in the West Indies were losing patience with the pace of negotiations. "There is an idea" in the colonies, he reported, "that the delay is due to [a] reluctance to accept coloured men, and Jamaica is getting excited and the Barbados would-be recruits will soon be out of hand."[15] In fact, as Grindle predicted, increasing anger about the sluggish pace of military mobilization led to what one local paper in Jamaica described as a mood of "impulsive suspicion" throughout the island as local commentators stridently condemned the "alleged coldness of the Governor and the War Office towards the idea of our Contingent."[16] In Trinidad, military boosters directed their ire at the local government rather than imperial officials in London, accusing officials in Port of Spain of "bungling" the campaign to organize a West Indian contingent.[17] "There is no haggling over the statement that there is utter disgust and unfortunate lack of confidence in our government in regards to the vexed question of a contingent from Trinidad," one anonymous letter writer seethed. They added, "If the authorities are jealous of the bravery and willingness of our men, why do they not don uniform and go out to the firing line?"[18] Likewise, the editors of the *Port of Spain Gazette* reported that an unnamed "responsible citizen" in the colony predicted that local officials "would do their utmost to prevent a contingent being sent from Trinidad at all" in order to cover up their own mishandling of military recruitment.[19] Seeking to quell rising disaffection, at least two governors in the region, George Haddon-Smith of the Windward Islands and William Manning of Jamaica, wrote to the Colonial Office to demand that recruitment for the BWIR commence immediately.[20] In late July, imperial officials finally acceded to demands by local authorities and residents in the colonies to begin recruiting men for the BWIR, securing a hard-fought victory for West Indians who had argued for the right to enlist.

A "Fair Contribution": Contending Visions for the BWIR from Above and Below

The Colonial Office officially circulated the terms for the BWIR to governors in the colonies via telegram on July 21, 1915, and then turned its full attention to the question of recruitment.[21] In comparison to the tense exchange regarding the financial provision of the BWIR, there was little disagreement in official circles about the projected size of the regiment. Imperial authorities and government officials in the colonies all initially imagined the BWIR as a very modest unit of 950 to 1,500 servicemen. In June 1915, Governor William Manning estimated Jamaica could recruit up to five hundred volunteers for military service, while Barbados, Trinidad, and British Guiana would together supply another one thousand recruits.[22] That same month, the Combined Court of British Guiana, that colony's main legislative body, voted to recruit at least one hundred local men for military service, while Governor George Le Hunte affirmed during a special meeting of the Legislative Council that Trinidad could likely supply three hundred to four hundred soldiers.[23] The Colonial Office projected even lower totals, predicting that the BWIR's strength would be roughly 950 to 1,150 men, though it acknowledged that preliminary estimates "would probably be exceeded when recruiting started." However, unlike Manning, who proposed that the BWIR enlist only volunteers from the most populous British Caribbean colonies—Jamaica, Trinidad, Barbados, and British Guiana—the Colonial Office anticipated that at least fifty volunteers from the Windward Islands would sign on, too.[24]

The initial recruitment targets for the BWIR were markedly conservative, given that over two million people lived in the British Caribbean colonies in 1915.[25] The extremely modest recruitment goals underscored the fact that officials on both sides of the Atlantic doubted the martial fitness of black and colored West Indians and planned to consign them to a marginal role in the imperial war effort. Jamaica, Britain's most populous Caribbean colony, boasted over 830,000 residents, of whom roughly 433,000 were men, yet Governor Manning anticipated recruiting only five hundred volunteers.[26] Frustrated, the editors of the *Gleaner* reasoned that Jamaica should contribute at least one thousand soldiers to the BWIR since the island's population surpassed that of Trinidad, Barbados, and British Guiana combined. Moreover, to support their demand for more ambitious recruiting targets, they cited enlistment figures from the French Caribbean colonies to show that Martinique had supplied "between four to five thousand soldiers" for the French Army during the first year of the war from a local population of only 193,000 inhabitants. Even though the editors acknowledged that many Martinican soldiers were conscripts, they complained that the low recruitment targets for the BWIR caused the British Caribbean colonies to "show up somewhat poorly" compared to "the little French West Indian Island." In a rousing call for action, they declared, "It will thus be seen that Jamaica, from the point of view of population, ought to be able to contribute twice as many men as the other three colonies put together. . . . We have had no reason yet given why a thousand men should not go from Jamaica, and until that reason is given we shall continue to advocate [for] the sending of a thousand men."[27]

In Trinidad, the editors of the *Port of Spain Gazette* similarly questioned why a colony of over 300,000 should be expected to muster only 450 recruits. They urged the paper's readers to reassess the colony's contribution to the imperial war effort, declaring that "at least ten times the 450 men called for by the Government" should come forward. "The question may well be asked now," they wrote, "Have we lived up to what we should have done?"[28] For one well-connected Trinidadian commentator, the low recruitment targets for the BWIR reflected a lack of initiative by the colonial government rather than public indifference to the war. In his postwar history of the BWIR, Arthur Cipriani claimed that high-ranking members of the colonial administration—including the governor and the Inspector-General of the Constabulary—simply believed that local men "could not be got" for the contingent.[29]

While public commentators in the larger British Caribbean colonies lobbied for more ambitious recruitment targets, local leaders in smaller territories labored to convince imperial officials that they could successfully recruit, train, and mobilize any men at all for the BWIR. Remarkably, neither Governor Manning of Jamaica nor the Colonial Office included recruitment projections for the Bahamas, British Honduras, or the Leeward Islands in their proposals for the War Office, and Manning further ignored the Windward Islands as well. Not content to sit on the sidelines of the regional recruitment movement—and in the shadow of the larger colonies—colonial officials in the smaller islands submitted their own proposals to the War Office between July and September 1915 and won approval to contribute troops to the BWIR. After the War Office accepted Grenada's offer of men for the BWIR, the editors of the *West Indian* proclaimed, "We have clamoured for recognition. Our claims have been granted." They added, "We stand today charged with a great responsibility in the full gaze of other West Indian colonies who have in the past and in the present ignored our claims—and the West Indies stand in the full gaze of the self-governing colonies. It is ours now to prove that a worthy sister, a Dominion to be, is knocking at the door of Imperial Councils; it is ours to prove the sterling British ring of our natures."[30]

As the editorial in the *West Indian* reveals, the seemingly anodyne exchange about BWIR recruitment targets served as a proxy for more fractious debates regarding colonial standing and recognition. While the War Office was content to accept fifteen hundred soldiers from the West Indies—a symbolic yet militarily negligible contribution that could staff only one field battalion—military enthusiasts in the West Indies demanded to make a "fair contribution" to the war effort in "the shape of men to join the colours."[31] In doing so, they insisted that men in the British Caribbean, like fellow colonials in India, Australia, New Zealand, Newfoundland, Canada, and elsewhere, should be full and equal participants in the imperial war effort, including shouldering the responsibility of military service.

Amid their calls for full military mobilization, however, military boosters increasingly professed that only certain groups of men should enjoy the privilege of fighting for the empire. Specifically, they argued that the region's substantial population of Indian men should not be eligible for the BWIR. Local discussions about Indians' military fitness provide new evidence that metropolitan theories about martial races circulated to the far reaches of the empire, shaping how elites in the British Caribbean viewed local men of Indian ancestry. Although the region's newspapers frequently celebrated the battlefield exploits of Indian soldiers in the British Army, they contended that Indian immigrants and their descendants in the Caribbean lacked the martial abilities of other Indian "races."[32] In one particularly revealing editorial, published in Jamaica in June 1915, the *Gleaner* roundly discounted the soldering potential of Indo-Caribbean men and predicted that "very few [or] perhaps none" would be recruited for military service. Indian "coolies" in Trinidad, the editors charged, did "not belong to the fighting races of India" and lacked basic physical strength. They likewise concluded that none of Jamaica's twenty thousand Indians should be recruited for the BWIR, even though several Indian men had come forward to volunteer for the local defense force as early as August 1914. All seventy thousand Indians in British Guiana were also deemed unfit, along with the colony's indigenous Arawak and Carib peoples, who, the editors claimed, lived in a "primitive condition."[33]

Two months later, the War Office privately confirmed what the editors of the *Gleaner* had publicly speculated: Military officials would restrict Indians from joining the BWIR. In response to a query from the governor of British Guiana, War Office staffer B. B. Cubitt explained that Indian troops were "already so numerously represented in the fighting forces of the Empire" that the Army Council did not find it "desirable to make any special appeal or to encourage the enlistment of men of that race in a Contingent of West Indians."[34] The War Office's incongruous statement—namely that men of Indian descent in the Caribbean colonies should not be encouraged to enlist because of the abundance of Indian men serving in other units of the British armed forces—confused Colonial Office officials, who questioned whether the War Office had completely banned Indo-Caribbean volunteers or simply mandated that no further recruitment would be necessary. Hoping that Indian men who had already volunteered for the BWIR would be allowed to serve, clerk R. A. Wiseman shared a report from a visiting doctor who affirmed Indo-Caribbeans' potential as soldiers. Dr. Mirett not only "spoke highly of their physique," Wiseman reported, but also boasted that they were "fairly easy for white men to manage" and were "excellent material for soldiers."[35]

A clear statement of policy toward Indo-Caribbean volunteers would emerge only in October 1915, after Indian recruits from Trinidad sailed to England with the BWIR. Unsure of how to interpret the War Office's August 1915 statement on Indian recruitment, the Colonial Office had communicated the curious edict only to the governor of British Guiana. Military authorities in Trinidad remained completely unaware of the directive and enlisted thirty-eight men of Indian descent in their first contingent of BWIR soldiers. When the thirty-eight volunteers disembarked in England, military authorities in the metropole summarily discharged the soldiers, sending them home via Jamaica. After discharging the men, the War Office clarified its position on Indo-Caribbean recruitment in a second letter to the Colonial Office. Explaining the decision to discharge the Indian soldiers, the letter asserted that the men, all born in India, were "unsuitable and unlikely to become efficient soldiers, on account of their ignorance of the English language and of difficulties in connection with food." Yet, in a slight departure from the August directive, the War Office conceded it had "no objection to the inclusion of Creoles of East Indian descent" as long as they were "British subjects born in the Colonies, able to speak English, and prepared to accept the rations usually issued to British troops."[36] There is no evidence, however, that any British Caribbean colony accepted Indian volunteers after the thirty-eight recruits from Trinidad were rejected and shipped home. The War Office's decision effectively barred men of Indian descent from serving in the BWIR and excluded them from the financial and social rewards that black, colored, and white soldiers (and their families) garnered.

The War and Colonial Offices played a decisive role in defining the parameters of military mobilization in the British West Indies, but colonial governors ensured that the actual process of recruiting men for the BWIR remained firmly in local hands. During the latter half of 1915, governors throughout the region established local recruitment committees to administer and supervise official recruitment drives. With remarkable consistency, governors appointed members of the local white (and colored) upper classes to serve on these committees, solidifying elite control over the military mobilization effort. In Jamaica, for example, the inaugural nine-member War Contingent Committee included "well known gentlemen," such as businessman William Wilson, solicitor W. Baggett Gray, and journalist Michael de Cordova, as well as Brigadier General L. S. Blackden and Governor Manning.[37] Likewise, in Barbados, Governor Leslie Probyn handpicked wealthy Bridgetown merchants and high-ranking members of the colonial government to serve on the island's official recruiting committee.[38] The recruitment committees in Trinidad, British Honduras, and Grenada were also comprised primarily of merchants, planters, and military officials, but they included middle-class reformers, too. Governor Haddon-Smith appointed colored lawyer C. F. P. Renwick, co-founder of the progressive *West Indian* newspaper, to Grenada's eight-member recruitment committee, on which Renwick served as the group's inaugural Honorable Secretary. H. H. Vernon, a Creole member of the Belize Town Board and former member of the reformist People's Committee of 1907, served as the treasurer of the Contingent Committee in British Honduras. Most important, the acting governor of Trinidad appointed Arthur Cipriani, the indefatigable military booster, to the colony's four-member recruiting committee, a tacit acknowledgment of his crucial role in the year-long campaign for a British Caribbean military force.

Cipriani's appointment to Trinidad's official recruiting committee in 1915 was a risky decision for colonial authorities despite his elite pedigree, given that Cipriani's incessant activity on behalf of the war effort had already brought him into open conflict with local officials. To begin with, in December 1914, after introducing a Christmas sweepstakes that netted $1,725 for the Trinidad War Fund, Cipriani became the first person in the colony's history to be charged with organizing an illegal lottery. Forced to appear before the City Police Court, Cipriani pleaded guilty to the lesser offense of "publishing a proposal for a lottery" to avoid trial. The presiding magistrate, moved by the patriotic purposes that motivated the fundraising scheme, simply reprimanded the defendant and elected not to issue a fine. Buoyed by the judge's sympathetic ruling, Cipriani brazenly announced the results of the lottery to subscribers in Trinidad and Jamaica, submitting detailed reports of the winnings less than two weeks after leaving court.[39]

Cipriani's highly publicized brush with the law was a harbinger of his public skirmishes with colonial administrators during the first half of 1915. Two months after his court appearance, Cipriani condemned local officials for attempting to ban public Carnival festivities because of the war. He chastised elites for holding several weeks of private pre-Lenten celebrations while trying to stop members of the working class from masquerading on Carnival Monday and Tuesday. "'The man in the street' is not as unreasonable as the authorities evidently believe him to be; he is awaiting no opportunity to rebel or to massacre any European Exile,"

Cipriani huffed in a letter to the editor. "Had the government or clerical authorities appealed to his sense of loyalty—for he is as loyal as his lighter-hued compatriot—and informed him that on account of the war, Carnival would not be permitted this year," he continued, workingmen would have accepted the ban "without a murmur." "Let the better class show their sympathy with the Nation" by halting their nightly revelry, Cipriani proposed, and then "'the man in the street' will easily be convinced that he can . . . forgo Carnival."[40]

After temporarily silencing the anti-Carnival coterie, Cipriani focused his ire on the colonial government for its lethargic response to military mobilization. In a particularly scathing letter to the *Port of Spain Gazette*, published just weeks before his appointment to the official recruiting committee, Cipriani fumed: "Trinidad has been again forced into the humiliating position of 'follow my leader' by the local government and those responsible for the furthering of her interests."[41] He then urged the *Port of Spain Gazette* to compile a list of potential volunteers rather than waiting on the colonial government to spearhead the military mobilization effort. That same month, Cipriani launched an unauthorized, one-man campaign to recruit a contingent of Trinidadian Red Cross nurses for the front; however, he had to abandon the quixotic initiative when the War Office insisted it would accept only certified nurses with three years' experience.[42]

Despite his previous conflicts with the colonial government, Cipriani initially embraced his position on the local recruiting committee, describing the appointment as an "honor."[43] It is possible that the coveted appointment was a calculated move by Trinidad's acting governor to reign in an outspoken critic. Neither Cipriani nor local officials, however, could have predicted how Cipriani's role in the military mobilization effort would grow during the war, reverberating politically both in Trinidad and the wider British Caribbean in the years ahead.

"Missionaries of our Manhood":
The Gendered Politics of Recruitment

On August 30, 1915, ten months after he initially proposed the idea of a British Caribbean contingent in a letter to Colonel du Cros, Arthur Cipriani presided over Trinidad's first recruitment rally for the BWIR. [44] The momentous event, held at Port of Spain's Marine Square and attended by "thousands of all classes," offered a grand stage for Cipriani to position himself as the colony's chief recruiter. Speaking from a raised platform in the center of the square, he eagerly seized the moment. "I am one of the people," he proclaimed to thunderous applause. Distancing himself from the colony's white landowning planter class, he exclaimed: "I was born and bred in this colony, was reared in it from childhood to youth, and from youth to manhood. I have shared your sorrows and your joys, and I appeal to you today in the name of the King to enlist." Deploying the language of martial interracialism, Cipriani summoned all men—"irrespective of class, colour, or creed"—to step forward for military service.[45] He also implored women in the audience to "urge their sons, brothers, and sweethearts to do their duty," proposing that they should use their influence in the domestic sphere to aid the recruitment effort.

The response to Cipriani's appeal for volunteers was swift and wildly enthusiastic. "Several men leapt on the stage," the *Port of Spain Gazette* reported, "and [their] names and addresses were taken there." By the event's end, at least 250 volunteers had "enrolled on the spot." An elderly woman in the crowd, gripped by Cipriani's rousing speech, "ascended the platform" and gave impromptu remarks, imploring even more men to step forward. "If I was a man . . . I would certainly go and fight," she bellowed as applause rang out from the audience.[46] On the following day, Cipriani reported that over 450 men had volunteered. In less than twenty-four hours, Trinidad had met its BWIR recruitment target for the entire war.[47]

Throughout the British Caribbean and in British Caribbean migrant communities in Panama, BWIR recruitment rallies functioned as festive community events that combined the slogans and speakers of elite patriotic fundraisers with the boisterous atmosphere and lively call-and-response banter of a Caribbean market. Military boosters officially announced the location and date of upcoming rallies through newspaper advertisements, professionally printed circulars, and posted placards. Sunday sermons and circuits of neighborhood gossip carried the news to unlettered men, women, and children throughout the community.[48] Describing the circulation of up-to-date recruitment information through dense social networks and official public notices, one BWIR volunteer from rural Point Hill, Jamaica, insisted simply, "It was established[,] man. The war cry was established."[49]

Staged through communal labor, rallies drew upon the organizational acumen and social ties of local residents, offering a view into the underappreciated "war work" done by civilian women, children, and others who were not eligible for military service. On the day of the rally, local women painstakingly decorated rally venues with ribbons, bunting, banners, and

FIGURE 2.1. BWIR recruitment rally in Port of Spain, Trinidad, 1916.
© Imperial War Museum (Q 52436)

fresh flowers. When a rally was held on a weekday afternoon, teachers dismissed excited pupils at lunchtime, and local business owners shuttered their doors hours early in anticipation of the big event. At "monster recruiting rallies" with hundreds or thousands of attendees, the local militia or police band paraded near the rally site to drum up additional enthusiasm. By the time the scheduled speakers assembled on the wooden platform, the audience was brimming with men, women, and children from diverse class and racial backgrounds.

While charismatic male recruiters like Cipriani garnered significant public acclaim, BWIR recruitment depended largely on the unpaid labor and moral authority of women. In his journalistic account of Jamaica during the war, *Gleaner* editor Herbert de Lisser maintained that 1914 marked the first time in the history of the island that a large number of women "openly and gladly identified themselves with a public and patriotic movement."[50] Indeed, much of the responsibility for recruiting and mobilizing men for each colony's BWIR contingent fell on the shoulders of women—even as the initial campaign to garner the right to form a regional contingent was spearheaded by Cipriani and other elite men. As historian Dalea Bean has shown, elite and middle-class white women were pivotal in the planning, advertising, and staging of recruitment rallies.[51] In fact, two white women, Annie Douglas and Mrs. Trefusis, organized one of the region's first recruitment meetings, in Irish Town,

Jamaica, on October 14, 1914. Douglas and Trefusis later helped to establish an autonomous Women's Recruiting Committee to secure volunteers for the BWIR.[52]

In the British Caribbean, military officials and their civilian colleagues targeted women as vital allies in the effort to procure suitable soldiers, insisting that women performed a patriotic duty by pressuring reluctant sons and partners to enlist. Historian Nicoletta Gullace, in her study of wartime Britain, has demonstrated how gendered notions of patriotism "implicated women in defining the parameters of male citizenship, while endowing women's traditional domestic, maternal, and sexual roles with an openly expressed importance to the military state."[53] As military recruiters sought to garner new recruits through appeals to manhood and moral suasion, she argues, women's intimate relationships with male partners and the activities of the broader domestic sphere became matters of national security. The same was true in the British Caribbean. One zealous female speaker in Antigua commanded women to "inspire the men with a zeal that would make them wish to give their life's blood for their country!"[54] Jamaica's *Gleaner* editorialized that women had the power to make men "do almost any thing they please," and it was, therefore, their responsibility to "shame the men into greater patriotic activity."[55] The editors of the British Honduras *Clarion*, as historian Anne Macpherson reveals, explicitly targeted working-class women during the war years, using the recurring fictional character of Keziah Mimms.[56] Keziah, who wrote in the working-class Creole dialect of Belize Town, offered witty commentary on pressing issues of the day through a series of letters to her cousin Jane Biggs. In one letter, Keziah celebrates her son's new status as a soldier in the BWIR, boasting "Ah . . . tenk de Lawd dat me son is a man an not ah slacka."[57]

Red Cross nurses Annie Douglas and A. E. Briscoe were wildly popular—and highly effective—recruitment rally speakers because of their willingness to castigate and publicly shame men who did not embrace the tenets of martial masculinity. Douglas, in particular, was (in)famous for ridiculing men who would not enlist, referring to them as "ladies" and taunting them with items of women's clothing. At a recruiting meeting attended by thousands in Montego Bay, Jamaica, Douglas urged men in the audience to form a Cavell platoon in honor of the martyred British nurse Edith Cavell. She then announced, to great applause, that she had brought a dress for any "slackers and shirkers" who did not step forward to volunteer.[58] Speaking later that day at another rally in St. James Parish, Douglas revealed that she had brought a skirt to put on any man who refused to volunteer for the BWIR. She reportedly held up the skirt during her speech and asked men in the audience if they were prepared to don it, eliciting forceful shouts of "No!" and "Never!"[59] At a meeting in Old Harbour, a port town west of Kingston, she declared that men could either wave the Union Jack after enlisting or don a handkerchief and "play the part of an old woman."[60]

Female military recruiters not only chastised reluctant volunteers but also validated and affirmed the masculine virtue of men who did enlist. One particularly evocative image from British Guiana highlights how military recruiters invoked women's moral authority to sanction military service and masculine self-sacrifice (see fig. 2.2). In an illustration published in the *Daily Argosy*, the colony is rendered as an Indigenous woman who watches over her "sons" in the BWIR as they solemnly march off to war. In the foreground, a white uniformed soldier kneels before the towering barefoot woman who, on behalf of the colony, imparts her blessing on the volunteer. Inverting familiar representations of stoic departing soldiers surrounded by crying wives and mothers, the serene woman in the illustration comforts a prostrate, tearful serviceman. As the soldier weeps, the Indigenous woman touches his bowed head with her left hand while firmly holding a stalk of sugarcane, British Guiana's major export crop, with her right hand. Beneath the two figures, the artist included words of encouragement for BWIR troops, proclaiming, "Good Luck and God Bless You!"

Some women were undoubtedly motivated by the financial benefits that they could accrue if their male partner or relative enlisted. Military officers took great care to inform women about the financial support they would reap as the dependent of a male soldier. The wife of a BWIR private qualified for a separation allowance of 11s. 1d. per week, plus an additional 1s. 2d. per week for each dependent child. The spouse of a noncommissioned officer above the rank of corporal was entitled to even more, garnering 13s. 5d. per week. Soldiers' mothers and domestic partners could also petition for separation allowances as long as they proved that they had been financially dependent on the soldier for at least a year prior to his enlistment.[61] Given that most black women in the region eked out a living through domestic service or low-wage agricultural work, the promise of a weekly separation allowance for the duration of the war provided a compelling material reason to support mobilization. A humorist in Trinidad captured some women's economic motives for supporting the recruitment campaign in a piece published in the *Port of Spain Gazette*. In a sketch entitled "Inside the Recruiting Office," a sergeant asks a woman if

[68] CHAPTER 2

FIGURE 2.2. "Guiana's Sons" political cartoon. *Daily Argosy*, September 19, 1915, 5.

her husband wants to enlist. "*Want* to enlist! He's *got* to enlist," she quickly replies. Stating that she has four children to support, the woman asks the sergeant if she will receive a separation allowance. When the recruiter responds that she will garner 28s. 6d. per week, the woman exclaims: "Twenty-eight an' six a week! 'Nuff said. Rope him in."[62]

The Rhetoric and Symbols of Recruitment

Gendered appeals for military-aged men to volunteer to protect and provide for their mothers, wives, and sisters were eclipsed only by stirring calls to defend the "Mother Country" in her hour of need. The cult of monarchy and empire reached its apex during World War I, and as scholars have convincingly shown, bridged elite and popular cultures in the British Caribbean.[63] By visually constructing military service as an imperial duty and a personal demonstration of loyalty, military recruitment posters and patriotic banners appealed to recruits' pride in the empire and respect for the king. Banners proclaiming "Fear God and Honour the King" or "Long Live the King" often greeted recruitment rally attendees in Jamaica.[64] In the eastern Caribbean island of Dominica, one recruitment notice in the local newspaper boldly declared: "THE KING NEEDS YOU!"[65] When asked why he joined the BWIR, one Barbadian volunteer explained that the "island government told us that the king said all Englishmen must go to join the war."[66] Similarly, all of the surviving recruitment posters for the Bahamas Contingent of the BWIR prominently displayed the image or name of George V, forging a symbolic link between military service and respect for the sovereign (see fig. 2.3). These posters, printed by the Jamaican Gleaner Company between 1915 and 1917, featured new slogans, such as "Put yourself right with your King" as well as the more traditional invocation, "God Save the King." The sole poster without George V's portrait still referenced the king's celebrated October 1915 "Appeal," declaring that "HIS MOST GRACIOUS MAJESTY KING GEORGE has called on men of his Empire, MEN OF EVERY CLASS, CREED AND COLOUR, to COME FORWARD TO FIGHT that the Empire may be saved and the foe may be well beaten" (see fig. 2.4).

If loyalty to king and empire did not inspire potential recruits to take up arms, then military recruiters and their civilian allies invoked the dreaded prospect of German rule in the Caribbean. At a recruiting meeting in Ocho Rios, Jamaica, one speaker bluntly informed volunteers that they would be fighting not to save England but rather to "protect *their own homes* from German despotism."[67] During a special UNIA meeting for departing soldiers, Marcus Garvey recounted stories of German atrocities in Togoland, West Africa, and warned that Germany was plotting a global "war against the races." According to the UNIA president, German imperialists, unlike their British counterparts, willfully sought out every opportunity to oppress and degrade their African subjects.[68] The Grenada *Federalist* similarly called attention to the violence of German colonialism in Africa to emphasize the dangers of a German victory for colonials of

FIGURE 2.3. "Young Man!" recruitment poster for the Bahamas Contingent of the BWIR. Library of Congress, Prints and Photographs Division, LC-USZC4-11201.

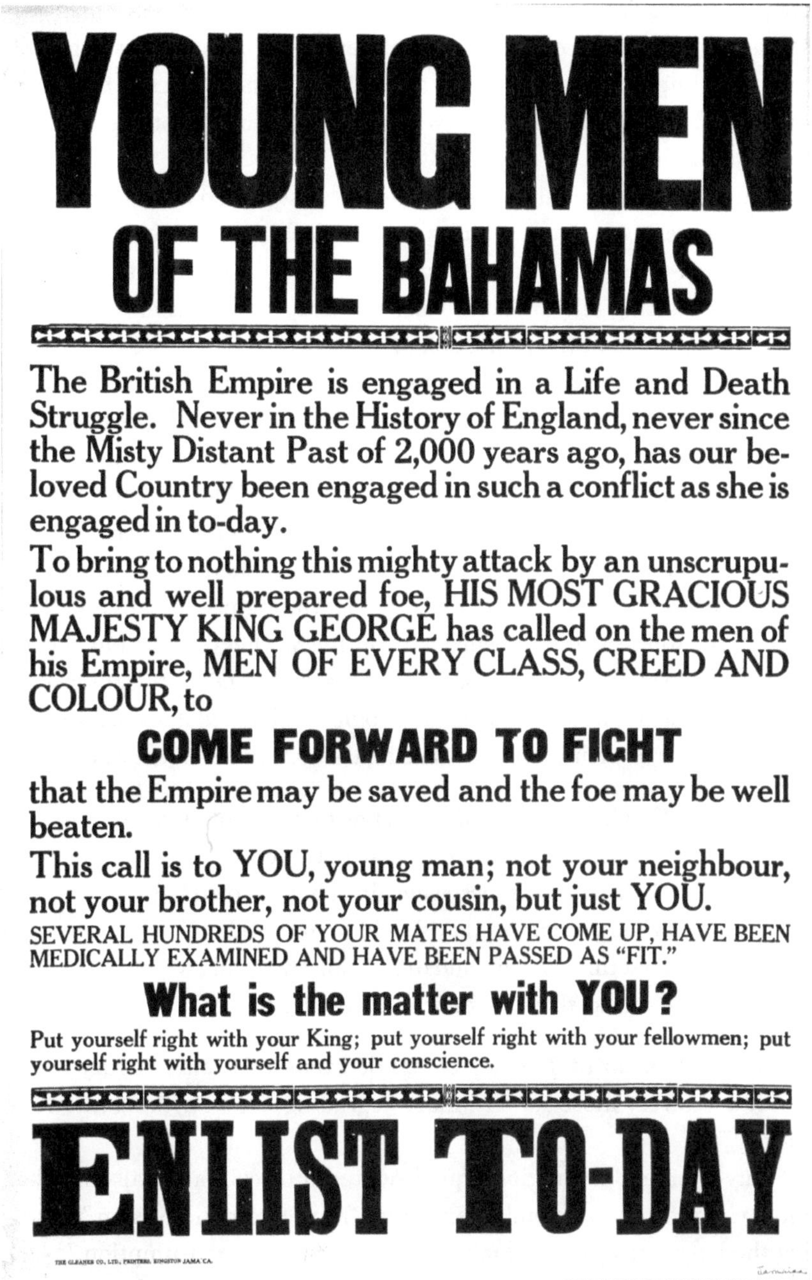

YOUNG MEN
OF THE BAHAMAS

The British Empire is engaged in a Life and Death Struggle. Never in the History of England, never since the Misty Distant Past of 2,000 years ago, has our beloved Country been engaged in such a conflict as she is engaged in to-day.

To bring to nothing this mighty attack by an unscrupulous and well prepared foe, HIS MOST GRACIOUS MAJESTY KING GEORGE has called on the men of his Empire, MEN OF EVERY CLASS, CREED AND COLOUR, to

COME FORWARD TO FIGHT

that the Empire may be saved and the foe may be well beaten.

This call is to YOU, young man; not your neighbour, not your brother, not your cousin, but just YOU.

SEVERAL HUNDREDS OF YOUR MATES HAVE COME UP, HAVE BEEN MEDICALLY EXAMINED AND HAVE BEEN PASSED AS "FIT."

What is the matter with YOU?

Put yourself right with your King; put yourself right with your fellowmen; put yourself right with yourself and your conscience.

ENLIST TO-DAY

THE GLEANER CO. LTD., PRINTERS, KINGSTON JAMAICA.

FIGURE 2.4. "Young Men of the Bahamas" recruitment poster for the Bahamas Contingent of the BWIR. Library of Congress, Prints and Photographs Division, LC-USZC4–11198.

color in the Caribbean. "Go to Africa and ask its smiling fields, its desert sands [,] what token of German love they of the darker races can give," the paper implored, "and they will show the whitened bones of butchered natives. They will tell that wherever German 'kultur' swept over Africa it left a desolation."[69]

The most sensationalist military boosters associated a German victory with the specter of slavery, crafting a particularly evocative image for men and women who were three generations removed from bondage. Speaking at a recruiting rally in Duan Vale, Jamaica, schoolmaster L. N. Welsh insisted that without the protection of the British navy, Jamaicans "would be more or less slaves" forced to live under a tyrannical German government.[70] At the same meeting, Rev. A. G. Eccleston ominously predicted that Jamaicans would suffer like the "Israelites of old in bondage in Egypt" if Germany triumphed over Britain.[71] The poem "The Motherland's Call" by Sydney Moxsy suggested that a German victory would result in complete devastation and slavery for the Caribbean. Published in the *Gleaner* in November 1915, the emotionally charged recruiting poem contended that England's ruthless foes threatened not only the Mother Country but her vulnerable subjects in the empire as well. If black men failed to demonstrate that "brave hearts may beat beneath a coloured skin," all Jamaicans would suffer because of their cowardice. The final stanza of the poem warned:

> That land is doomed which breeds a coward race,
> Who money seek, but never dare to face
> Their Country's foes; who fain at home would hide,
> When need arises they should stem the tide,
> That threats their land o'erwhelm, sweep all away,
> Or make them slaves beneath a foreign sway.[72]

Even the governor of Jamaica contended that a German victory would result in "slavery more serious, more degrading, than anything known to history."[73]

Calypsonians, the region's quick-witted musical bards, also mocked men who refused to defend their homes from "German invasion," retooling the language of martial masculinity for popular consumption.[74] One of the most popular calypsos during the war years humorously contrasted the bravery of Trinidadians who rallied to protect the island from German invaders with the cowardice of men who remained at home:

> When de rumour went roun' de town
> Dat de Germans were coming to blow de town
> Some, like cowards, remained at home

"EVERY TRUE SON OF THE EMPIRE" [73]

All de brave run down with stones
Some run with bottles, some run with bricks
Some run with bamboo, some run with sticks
Old Lady Semper run down with she old big po' chambe
[chamber pot]
Sans Humanité

Now listen to what I gotta say
Trinidadian boys gotta rule the day
Now listen to what I gotta say
Dey volunteered to fight fo' de King without anything
But listen boys, we got all de rum we need in dis colony
Sans Humanité[75]

Significantly, the calypsonian who penned this song not only celebrated the valor of Trinidadian military volunteers but also championed civilians who stood ready to repel an enemy incursion with stray bottles, felled bamboo, sharpened sticks, and handfuls of stones. If cowardly men refused to come forward, the calypsonian joked, then Old Lady Semper would battle in their place with her *po' chambe*.

Whereas calypsonians humorously implied that West Indian men "volunteered to fight fo' de King without anything," black and colored reformers envisioned soldiering as a route to postwar political gains and enhanced social standing. Fred Warner, a volunteer from Demerara, British Guiana, abandoned his plans to study music in the United States to serve in the BWIR. Explaining his decision, Warner boldly asserted: "I mean to win something in honour of my race."[76] For Barbadian recruit Douglas Haynes, battling the Germans and Turks on the other side of the Atlantic offered a powerful vehicle for contesting class and color discrimination at home. Instead of "patiently waiting for bones" in Barbados, he elected to join the colors to "prove himself as a man" in the crucible of war. After the Allies were victorious, Haynes announced he would return home to "claim [his rights] in the name of manhood."[77]

Local black newspapers upheld and amplified these claims. The Grenada *Federalist* forecast that black soldiers' performance on the battlefield would undermine the deeply engrained notions of white superiority that barred West Indians from self-government in the Caribbean. Yet, unlike Haynes, the *Federalist* pressed for a fundamental change in the *collective* political status of black and colored West Indians, writing:

As Colored people we will be fighting for something more, something inestimable to ourselves. We will be fighting to prove to Great Britain that we are not so vastly inferior to the whites that we should not be put on a level, at least, of political equality with them. We will be fighting to prove that the distinctions between God-made creatures of one Empire because of skin, color or complexional differences, should no longer exist, and that the same opportunities should be afforded the Colored subjects of the Empire as fall by right of race to its white citizens.

West Indians, the paper affirmed, were "not one whit behind the other races" of the British Empire and were prepared to defend the "sacred cause of Freedom" overseas *and* in the colonies. "We prophetise that while we help maintain the liberties of Europe, we shall gain and secure all those political rights and privileges for which the hearts of Colored British West Indians have so long yearned," the *Federalist* announced. [78]

The thrill of donning the king's uniform was a powerful inducement for some men to join the colors. Military uniforms function simultaneously as a tangible symbol of state power and as an embodied status marker, transforming civilians into military men worthy of both fear and esteem, as recent studies have documented.[79] Once in uniform, historian Heather Streets explains, soldiers take on a corporate martial identity that they perform for military and civilian audiences.[80] For colonial subjects and disenfranchised racial and ethnic minorities, wearing a military uniform often facilitated access to previously restricted social spaces, emboldened soldiers to assert their newfound authority over local law enforcement officials, and affirmed their claims to masculine virtue. African American soldiers during World War I, for example, strove "to make their character fit their uniform" by crafting an assertive masculinity that combined civic responsibility, racial uplift, and self-sufficiency with physical prowess, sexual vigor, and a confident swagger.[81] In his study of *tirailleurs Senegalais*, Gregory Mann found that West African colonial soldiers sported their uniform, especially the distinctive pants and red *chéchia*, for years after demobilization as a visual symbol of their ties to France and their superiority over the civilian population. These *anciens tirailleurs,* Mann argued, "used uniforms to appropriate, and not merely to reflect, the state's power" and insisted that their martial labor conferred lifelong social, economic, and political privileges.[82]

Colonial soldiers' "corporeal embodiment of authority" was instantiated and reinforced "through uniform wear, dress, and ceremony."[83] Jamaican Eugent Augustus Clarke recalled that "any man in a uniform was a Big Man" during the war years. Clarke was twenty-two years old and working as a gardener in Kingston when he first encountered soldiers from the BWIR. The sight of sharply dressed recruits drilling in tight formation outside the barracks at Up Park Camp impressed him, and he secretly enlisted shortly thereafter. Clarke's yearning for adventure and an independent life beyond the confines of his aunt's home also pulled him toward army life, in addition to his desire to assist the "Mother Country." "Me was enthusiastic to know England," he recounted years later. "Them say them a fight to defend England. Everything was England. Every man was loyal to England."[84]

Mobilizing West Indian Migrants: Recruitment Efforts in Central America

The recruitment campaign would eventually extend beyond the Caribbean colonies, tapping into well-established circuits of labor mobility that linked the islands to rimland migrant enclaves in Central America. As in the islands, enthusiasm preceded official recruitment efforts. New arrivals, English-language newspapers, and private letters carried information about the BWIR to the substantial British Caribbean population in Central America, where black migrants closely monitored the contingent movement and even offered their own proposals for a regional fighting force.[85] In June 1915, when British Caribbeans in Panama learned that a regional contingent would be allowed to serve in the war, the Panama *Star and Herald* reported that the news "threw the local West Indian colony into a fever of excitement" as *antillianos* in Colón and Bocas del Toro clamored to serve in the BWIR.[86] In the absence of a state-sponsored recruitment campaign, dozens of volunteers left Panama on their own to join the regiment in 1915 and 1916. A group of fifty-one West Indians in Bocas del Toro departed for Jamaica in December 1915, and a contingent of forty-eight men in Panama City followed suit two months later.[87] The *Gleaner* lauded islanders in Panama for their determination to enlist. "Throughout the Central American Republics there is a feeling of intense loyalty and patriotism on the part of the British subjects who are most anxious to see the Germans wiped out in the present conflict," the paper wrote approvingly.[88]

Most working-class black migrants, however, could not afford to travel home to "join the colours." One frustrated Trinidadian letter writer in Panama declared that there were "thousands of able-bodied West Indians" residing on the isthmus who were "burning with the desire to leave for the front and give their quota to help the cause." Yet, he claimed, "a great many" would-be soldiers in Panama lacked the money to sail home to enlist in the colonies. And even the handful of recruits who were "able to defray their own travelling expenses," he noted, "do not think it advisable to go through the sacrifice of relinquishing their remunerative posts, or throw up their old established clientele" without clear assurances that they would be accepted as soldiers.[89] W. A. Hume, a Jamaican living in the Canal Zone, questioned why military officials refused to recruit overseas for the BWIR. "Are the Jamaicans in foreign lands to have no part in the war? There are hundreds, if not thousands, of Jamaicans in the Central American republics, especially in the Republic of Panama, who would gladly go to Europe and fight for their King and the dear old flag." Citing the French government's mobilization of its colonial subjects working on the isthmus, Hume asked why British officials had not followed suit. "Could not the British or Jamaican Government send for us too? I appeal for myself and the rest. Let us have a chance. We can help in the making of history too."[90] These West Indian migrants were responding to the discourse of martial interracialism—and King George V's "Appeal" just the month before—which solicited men of every "class, creed, and colour" to defend the British Empire. But, to their great consternation, imperial authorities initially made no efforts to include them when they stepped forward to volunteer.

Some British officials in Central America scoffed at West Indians' attempts to join the BWIR.[91] After reading about the formation of the regiment, Jamaican men in Bluefields, Nicaragua, dispatched a letter to the local British consul asking for information about the enlistment process. To their "sad disappointment," the consul insisted that "they were not needed" and directed them to donate money to the war effort instead. Outraged by the consul's hostile response, a Jamaican writing from Bluefields fumed: "The men who applied to him . . . for the sole purpose of assisting the Mother Country are young, strong and robust. They have settled down and are making a fair living but are quite willing to sacrifice all for their King's benefit, but they receive no encouragement."[92]

Justifying their inaction, British officials in Central America stressed that Nicaragua, Panama, and Costa Rica were neutral states, which prevented any belligerent nation from formally recruiting men for the armed forces on their soil. Since the United States, also officially neutral until 1917, controlled the Panama Canal Zone, British authorities were prohibited from recruiting there, too. Would-be volunteers, however, accused the British consul in Panama of "frigid indifference" toward the imperial war effort and suggested that local British authorities intentionally stymied any recruitment efforts to appease US business interests. "It is whispered around that this evident lack of spirit for the cause on the part of His Majesty's Consuls is due to a fear of giving offense to the United States

"EVERY TRUE SON OF THE EMPIRE"   [77]

Government," a Trinidadian letter writer reported in November 1915, as it is "presumed in certain quarters that any attempt to recruit men on the Isthmus would result in a material reduction of the labour force of the Canal Zone." Although he quickly dismissed the rumor as "all bosh," the Trinidadian correspondent still stressed that any volunteers who abandoned their jobs in the Canal Zone to join the BWIR could be easily replaced "from the ranks of the unemployed."[93]

Geopolitical realignments ended the two-year stalemate over British military recruitment in Panama in April 1917, when the United States and Panama both declared war against Germany. With the legal hurdles now overcome and the War Office clamoring for additional volunteers to assist with noncombatant labor duties on the Western Front, British officials seized the opportunity to launch a recruitment drive in Panama, this time under the official auspices of the British Army. One month after Panama's declaration of war, Leslie W. Hitchens embarked for Central America to launch the first state-sponsored BWIR recruitment campaign outside of the West Indies.[94] Hailing from Canada, Hitchens held a commission as a second lieutenant in the British Army and was attached to the sixth contingent of volunteers from Jamaica. Significantly, the lieutenant's historic mission to Panama was not his first visit to the isthmus. According to a report in the local press, Hitchens had "worked for many years with the United Fruit Company in Bocas del Toro."[95]

While it is unclear if Hitchens exploited his ties to United Fruit in his newfound role as a military recruiter, it is apparent that he marshaled the support of British consul Claude Mallet and the local English-language press in Panama. Working with Mallet, "who gave his hearty co-operation," Hitchens established a recruiting office in the Panama City British Legation on May 11, 1917.[96] To garner volunteers, Mallet and Hitchens published advertisements in several US-owned English-language newspapers, including the *Panama Morning Journal* and the *Star & Herald* (see fig. 2.5).[97] Local West Indian newspaper editors—determined to assert their own stake in the recruitment drive—carefully monitored Hitchens's efforts. The *Central American Express*, founded by Jamaican J. A. Shaw Davis in Bocas del Toro, welcomed Hitchens to the isthmus with an open letter recounting the privately funded efforts to sponsor volunteers in 1915. Praising the state-sponsored enlistment campaign, the paper implored the lieutenant to recruit men on both sides of the isthmus. "As Britishers we demand our share in the privilege of having you here in your official capacity."[98]

Military boosters in Panama framed enlistment as a civic obligation for British subjects, particularly for colonials of color. "WEST INDIANS,

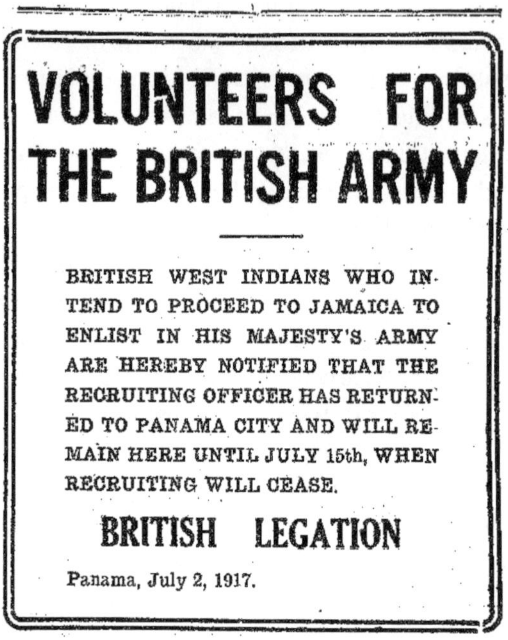

[78] CHAPTER 2

VOLUNTEERS FOR THE BRITISH ARMY

BRITISH WEST INDIANS WHO IN-
TEND TO PROCEED TO JAMAICA TO
ENLIST IN HIS MAJESTY'S ARMY
ARE HEREBY NOTIFIED THAT THE
RECRUITING OFFICER HAS RETURN-
ED TO PANAMA CITY AND WILL RE-
MAIN HERE UNTIL JULY 15th, WHEN
RECRUITING WILL CEASE.

BRITISH LEGATION

Panama, July 2, 1917.

FIGURE 2.5. Recruitment advertisement for the BWIR in Panama.
"Volunteers for the British Army." *Panama Morning Journal*, July 3, 1917, 7.

YOUR KING AND COUNTRY NEEDS YOU," announced one recruitment notice. By soldiering on behalf of England in the war, volunteers could secure the admiration of kith and kin for generations to come. "You will tell your children and they will tell their children that when the hour came along, you were not found waiting."[99] Some advocates for the BWIR further suggested that wartime military service was a means for colonials of color to repay a debt to England for the abolition of slavery. Soldiers in the BWIR, the *Panama Morning Journal* insisted, would have "the satisfaction of knowing that they have given all that is in them for the grand old country that was the first in the world to sever the chains of slavery, and that they have repaid the debt they owed the grand old flag that gave to their ancestors the full measure of liberty."[100]

Having waited more than two years to enlist, West Indian men in Panama rushed to join the BWIR—firm in the belief that serving in the military would grant them financial and social privileges otherwise denied them. Unlike the military recruitment efforts in Jamaica, Trinidad, and elsewhere in the Caribbean colonies, the state-sponsored enlistment campaign on the isthmus did not incite any public displays of resistance. In fact, in a report to the Foreign Office, Mallet bragged that his recruitment

"EVERY TRUE SON OF THE EMPIRE" [79]

efforts had "acted like magic." According to the British consul, "His Majesty's coloured subjects" displayed an "indescribable enthusiasm" for military service, and the recruiting office was "besieged with applicants."[101] On the first day of recruiting alone, over one hundred men came forward to volunteer. By the end of the second week, some 572 volunteers had been accepted for military duty.[102] In their extraordinary response to the call for volunteers, West Indians in Panama City alone had provided more BWIR recruits in a fortnight than the Bahamas, Leeward Islands, Grenada, St. Lucia, or St. Vincent mobilized during the entire course of the war.[103] By the end of the official recruitment drive in Panama in August 1917, over two thousand men had enlisted in the BWIR.[104]

"Answering the Call of the Motherland": A Collective Portrait of Those Who Enlisted

In the British Caribbean islands and rimlands, as in Panama, volunteers overwhelmed recruiters. Family members watched with a mixture of trepidation and pride as their sons, brothers, and husbands headed off to enlist. Samuel Anderson, a father of five sons, watched as each one left their small village in the Jamaican countryside and joined the war effort. Sons Maxi and Leonard enlisted in the BWIR in Jamaica, while sons Arnold and Cornelius volunteered for the regiment from Panama. Meanwhile, their brother Edward, who was residing in New York, ultimately traveled north to enlist in the Canadian Expeditionary Force after he was unable to join the BWIR while in the United States.[105] Wartime military mobilization for Samuel Anderson's sons and thousands of other men would inaugurate new migratory journeys—this time as soldiers rather than civilians.

Between 1915 and 1918, 15,601 men enlisted in the BWIR, filling the ranks of twelve battalions (see figure 2.6).[106] Most servicemen—over 52 percent of the regiment—resided in Jamaica at the time of their enlistment. In total, the island contributed at least 8,180 men to the BWIR.[107] Trinidad and Tobago, the second most populous British colony in the region, mobilized just 1,400 servicemen, far less than Jamaica and Panama. British Guiana contributed only seven hundred servicemen from a population only slightly smaller than Trinidad's. The War Office's decision to restrict the recruitment of Indian men for the BWIR significantly narrowed the pool of potential volunteers in both Trinidad and British Guiana, hampering mobilization efforts. British Honduras, the Central American territory with a population of fewer than forty-two thousand inhabitants,

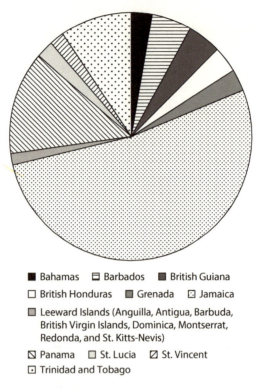

■ Bahamas ⊟ Barbados ■ British Guiana
☐ British Honduras ■ Grenada ⊡ Jamaica
▨ Leeward Islands (Anguilla, Antigua, Barbuda, British Virgin Islands, Dominica, Montserrat, Redonda, and St. Kitts-Nevis)
▨ Panama ☐ St. Lucia ⊘ St. Vincent
⊡ Trinidad and Tobago

FIGURE 2.6. BWIR Enlistment by Territory (1915–18). Chart by Max Burns.

enlisted BWIR soldiers at the highest rate per capita. As historian Nigel Bolland points out, British Honduras recruited 12.8 soldiers per thousand inhabitants, greatly exceeding the regional average of 4.9 men per thousand. In fact, by 1917, officials in British Honduras, after supplying 533 men to the BWIR, suspended military recruiting amid fears that further recruitment could deplete the local labor supply.[108] The BWIR also welcomed over seventy West Indian men who were already living in England when the regiment was established. These men enlisted in cities across England—including Bristol, Manchester, Hull, and Liverpool—or transferred into the regiment from other British Army units.[109]

Most men who aspired to join the BWIR began the uncertain journey from civilian to soldier at recruitment rallies or makeshift recruiting centers near their place of residence, where they completed an initial physical examination and literacy screening. Those who received preliminary approval then traveled to the nearest military barracks and submitted to a second, more invasive medical screening. To enlist, prospective servicemen

"EVERY TRUE SON OF THE EMPIRE" [81]

had to meet specific age, height, and weight guidelines, demonstrate "good character" and "intelligence," and possess a clean bill of health.[110] Furthermore, men who volunteered for the BWIR before November 1916 had to be able to read and write in English. In addition, some islands in the eastern Caribbean initially only accepted unmarried volunteers for military service.[111]

Colonial officials and local military boosters took great pains to characterize the regiment as "representative" of the region, insisting that the BWIR included volunteers from "practically every trade and industry and every walk of life in the West Indies."[112] Herbert de Lisser described the First Jamaica War Contingent as a "mixed lot" comprised of "clerks and artisans and labourers, boys who had served behind a counter and boys who had handled a hoe, young men who had sat on stools with the pen as their only instrument of labour, and young men who had wielded a pair of scissors or deftly manipulated an awl." Like other contemporary commentators, he also highlighted the interracial nature of the contingent, boasting that the new recruits ranged in skin tone from "white to black, including every shade of complexion known in the colour categories of a West Indian community."[113]

De Lisser's oft-cited description of the BWIR as an example of martial interracialism and cross-class camaraderie masked the profound hierarchies that existed within the regiment. In his journalistic history of the BWIR, published in 1917, de Lisser conveniently omits the fact that white men who enlisted in the regiment almost always served as officers, while black and colored volunteers typically served as enlisted men or, at best, noncommissioned officers. This inequality was not simply a reflection of class and color hierarchies in the Caribbean, but rather, was caused by the British Army's long-standing policy of banning nonwhites from holding the Sovereign's Commission.[114]

In keeping with the discriminatory policy of the British Army, the Army Council decreed in December 1915 that only recruits with "unmixed European blood" could be eligible for commissions in the BWIR.[115] Only a tiny number of men in the Caribbean colonies met this racist standard— in Jamaica, for example, white men comprised less than 1 percent of the total population. Thus, white men who volunteered for the BWIR were nearly guaranteed to become commissioned officers simply by virtue of their whiteness.[116] A photograph of the regiment's Jamaican officers illustrates the outcome of the Army Council's inequitable ruling. In the image, fourteen officers of the First Jamaica War Contingent, all white, pose in uniform (see fig. 2.7). The men are of varying ages and appear relaxed

FIGURE 2.7. Officers of the 1st Jamaica War Contingent of the BWIR. Jamaica Archives and Records Department, Orrett Photographs Collection, 7-130-1.

around each other. Given the small size and insularity of Jamaica's white elite, it is likely the officers already knew each other prior to enlisting and assuming command over hundreds of black and colored servicemen. Crucially, the race of prospective officers was more important than their military qualifications, as the War Office assured Caribbean governors that if recruiters in the colonies failed to mobilize enough local whites to staff the officer corps, it would supply "trained and partially trained officers" from Britain.[117] And, as we shall see, at least one prominent white man with no military background and well beyond the age limit for military service—Trinidadian Arthur Cipriani—also lobbied successfully for his inclusion as an officer in the BWIR.

In the absence of their official military attestation forms, it is possible to reconstruct only a tentative demographic sketch of the men who served in the regiment's rank and file.[118] Contemporary recruiting reports suggest that the initial wave of volunteers overwhelmingly resided in, or near, local capital cities. In Barbados, the chair of the Recruiting Committee noted that the first recruits came from St. Michael's and adjoining parishes while, in Trinidad, men from Port of Spain and surrounding communities comprised the earliest enlisted men.[119] In Jamaica, 13 percent of the first four thousand volunteers listed Kingston as their hometown, although the capital city was home to only 7 percent of the island's total population.[120] Sixty-two percent of the initial soldiers from Grenada hailed from St. George's, and a remarkable 76 percent of the men in the First Bahamas Contingent were from Nassau.[121] Unlike their rural compatriots, these urban denizens received frequent updates about the recruitment process and lived in proximity to the official enlistment centers, which were first opened in each capital city. Equally as important, urban residents had better access to the colony's medical and educational institutions, which might have allowed them to pass the required physical and literacy screenings at higher rates than the rural majority. However, as military recruiters increasingly ventured outside of the cities to rural settlements, mountain villages, and seaside fishing communities, the proportion of BWIR soldiers from these areas duly increased. By the end of recruiting in Jamaica, for example, the total number of volunteers from the rural parishes of St. Mary and St. Elizabeth surpassed the number of recruits from Kingston.

A significant percentage of the earliest volunteers had worked previously as constables or served in local militias, revealing how experience in colonial law enforcement provided a ready springboard to military service. One in three soldiers in the First British Guiana Contingent had cut his teeth in the constabulary, while eighteen of the first seventy-nine men to enlist in the Barbados Contingent were veterans of the local Police or Defense Forces.[122] The chair of the Barbados Recruiting Committee acknowledged that many more policemen "were anxious to join" the BWIR, but it was "inexpedient" to remove any more men from police duty.[123] In Jamaica, T. G. Beckford, a ten-year veteran of the Constabulary Force, enlisted in the regiment and convinced twenty of his friends and colleagues to volunteer as well.[124] Barbadian J. C. Hope had never worked as a constable, but he internalized the "soldierly spirit" after participating in a host of patriotic militia groups. During his days as a pupil at Barbados's Combermere School, Hope drilled with the school's Cadet Corps, joined the League of the Empire, and distinguished himself as the island's first King's Scout.[125] After graduation, Hope enlisted in the Barbados Contingent of the BWIR.

Whereas de Lisser maintained BWIR soldiers entered the military from a wide array of vocational backgrounds, other observers insisted the regiment's rank and file consisted of men from the working class.[126]

Indeed, C. L. R. James went even further, claiming that many recruits "for the first time wore shoes consistently" only after they enlisted in the BWIR.[127] Available evidence suggests that working-class men between the ages of eighteen and thirty did comprise the majority of BWIR volunteers. According to self-reported data from the first four thousand soldiers in Jamaica, 25 percent of men listed their previous occupation simply as "labourer." An additional 16 percent of soldiers, 657 men in total, stated that they worked as cultivators before enlisting. Over 30 percent of volunteers were skilled artisans who entered the military with valuable expertise in carpentry, coach building, masonry, plumbing, and boot making. In contrast, less than 10 percent of soldiers reported working in middle-income occupations such as clerks (6.2 percent), constables (1.1 percent), teachers (1 percent), chemists (.43 percent), and foremen and overseers (.43 percent) before enlisting.[128] Due to the British Army's racial restrictions on holding the Sovereign's Commission, race, color, and class hierarchies within the BWIR were even starker than those in British Caribbean societies, where highly educated, middle-class colored (and sometimes even black) men could secure respected leadership positions.

Facing Rejection

As impressive as the numbers of recruits were for the BWIR, the number of those who failed in their enlistment attempts was significantly higher. Most men who volunteered for the regiment experienced the sobering reality of rejection. Staggering rejection rates slowed military mobilization across the British Caribbean, with tens of thousands of men being classed as physically unfit or "not likely to become efficient soldiers."[129] In a letter to the Secretary of State for the Colonies, the governor of the Windward Islands lamented that local medical officers rejected over 25 percent of volunteers for the first contingent. Furthermore, military officials sent home another thirty recruits because they did not have sufficient accommodations for the would-be soldiers.[130] Fifty-seven percent of men who applied to join the First Bahamas Contingent were turned away, while an astonishing 71 percent of men who volunteered in British Guiana between 1915 and 1917 were rejected.[131] In Jamaica, the rejection rate climbed from 53 percent for the first contingent in 1915 to 66 percent for the fourth contingent sixteen months later.[132] As these statistics make clear, the rousing claim that "every mother's son" could be a soldier was contradicted by the pervasive reality of rejection across the British Caribbean.[133]

Arthur Cipriani experienced firsthand the bitter sting of rejection. After spearheading the campaign to mobilize volunteers for military service, Trinidad's premier military booster learned that he was too old to enlist.[134] Still determined to participate in the war effort, the forty-year-old recruited other men for Trinidad's first two BWIR contingents before attempting to enlist once again. In a reversal of his previous ruling, the Commandant of the Local Forces officially endorsed Cipriani's application for a commission in the BWIR in November 1915, noting that Cipriani had "taken a keen interest in recruiting" and was "most desirable as an officer" for the colony's contingent.[135] In January 1916, Cipriani entered the barracks to begin military training and ultimately departed with Trinidad's third BWIR contingent as a newly minted second lieutenant.[136] Cipriani's successful appeal is an illustration of how white men could wield their status during the recruitment campaign and how this unearned advantage permitted some to bypass enlistment criteria, gain prized commissions, and access the martial masculinity that would not be available to working-class black men who fell short of the recruitment standards.

Whereas Cipriani was eventually able to enlist, many rejected recruits wistfully remembered the disappointment of being turned away. In a letter to the *Daily Gleaner* in 1959, Joseph Campbell proudly recalled that he was the first man in his district to volunteer. Medical examiners in Jamaica declared him unfit, however, because he required heart medication for an unnamed ailment.[137] Another Jamaican man from St. Ann's parish, interviewed in the early 1970s, recalled that he had tried to join the contingent because all his close friends were "leaving out to the War." Yet when he attempted to enlist, a military official briskly rejected him, stating, "You too small, man, you too young."[138] Mr. Ferdinand, a fisherman and shopkeeper in Port Henderson, Jamaica, also vividly recounted the medical examination where a doctor disqualified him for military service. After watching Ferdinand complete a series of squats and examining his testicles, a military physician informed the teenaged volunteer that he had a "gentleman complaint" and could not enlist. "Man, I was vex!" Ferdinand explained in an interview decades later. "I didn't vex right off but I keep on telling him that is not so." When he eventually stormed out of the military barracks, a woman selling fruit nearby teased him, shouting: "Him vex, because him don't pass!"[139] It is unclear exactly why Ferdinand's testicles excluded him from soldiering, but ill health and disability were apparent in many volunteers of color, whose bodies bore the marks of backbreaking manual labor and colonial neglect.

Like Campbell and Ferdinand, the majority of BWIR volunteers were rejected for medical reasons. In Jamaica alone, over 26,600 prospective soldiers were examined at Up Park Camp military barracks between 1915 and 1918. Of these, 13,940 were rejected as medically unfit. The single most common cause for medical rejection was failure to meet the strict weight and/or chest width requirements for a soldier. Of the 13,940 men rejected from the Jamaica War Contingent, 27 percent were classed as "underdeveloped/underweight." Military authorities rejected an additional 1,280 recruits because of poor physique and 514 men for not meeting the minimum height requirement. Even men who met the height, weight, and chest requirements were often dismissed because of ailments caused by malnutrition and poor medical care, including rotten teeth, anemia, skin diseases, and hernias.[140] While physicians recorded this information as proof of the volunteers' ineligibility for service, these records are also a damning indictment of over two centuries of British rule in Jamaica.

In British Guiana, Britain's only colony on the South American mainland, mosquito-borne diseases stymied many volunteers' quests to enlist. Over 1,700 men were rejected because of filariasis, a parasitic disease that infects the lymphatic vessels and potentially causes swollen limbs, fever, and blindness.[141] George O. H. Easton, a thirty-year-old prospective soldier from Plantation Cane Grove in East Coast, Demerara, attempted to join the BWIR on two separate occasions but was rejected because of filarial glands. Challenging the diagnosis, Easton boasted that he was "strong as a lion" and could not recall the last time that he had suffered from any major ailment.[142] Rejected recruit Clarence Maynard likewise disputed the medical examiner's pronouncement that he was unfit due to filarial glands by insisting that he was "in the pink of condition to do any fighting." Maynard, in a letter to the editors of the *Daily Argosy*, explained, "The downfall of Britain would be a ruin to my race, and I feel I have as much right to serve my King and country to the end as a soldier."[143] Maynard's statement highlights the distress experienced by tens of thousands of men turned away from the BWIR. For those who embraced the messages of martial interracialism and martial masculinity and believed that it was their duty as colonial subjects to defend Britain, the inability to enlist also provoked racial and gendered anxieties about their standing as black men.

Rejected volunteers often reapplied for the military after receiving treatment for their disqualifying ailments or completing an exercise regime to increase their chest measurements, demonstrating a profound resolve to enlist.[144] After being turned away from the BWIR contingent

"EVERY TRUE SON OF THE EMPIRE" [87]

camp in Jamaica, Caleb Barrant and Charles Moore vowed to "get well in the next two or three weeks" and resume the enlistment process.[145] A fervent volunteer in Barbados elected to undergo an operation to correct the "internal trouble" that prevented him from enlisting.[146] Other men surreptitiously took advantage of the decentralized examination process, changed their names, and had a different physician complete the required examination. A troop of Boy Scouts in Port of Spain, Trinidad, satirized the plight of men who were repeatedly rejected on medical grounds through a humorous skit about an aspiring soldier named Luly. After visiting the military medical examiner, Luly discovers that he has a narrow chest and "too much belly" to enlist. Determined to don the king's uniform, he completes a strenuous exercise regime and then returns to the doctor. Unfortunately, however, the examiner informs Luly that his stomach has increased in size and his undersized chest has gotten even smaller. In a fit of desperation, Luly begs the doctor to "put him under some operation or to turn him upside down by means of which his chest would become belly and [his] belly chest."[147]

Meanwhile, the problem of venereal disease—particularly the "loathsome syphilis"—sidelined many other recruits.[148] In Jamaica alone, over 1,500 men were rejected because they were infected with a venereal disease—and this figure includes neither infected men who were treated and eventually allowed to enlist nor those who were turned away at the island's other recruitment sites.[149] Nearly 20 percent of recruits from Trelawny, a rural parish on Jamaica's northern coast, were declared unfit for service because of venereal disease. Volunteers from the rural parishes of Hanover, St. Mary, and St. Ann also had high rates of rejection.[150] In contrast, only 8 percent of recruits from the urban parishes of Kingston and St. Andrew were rejected due to venereal disease. The chair of Jamaica's Central Recruiting Committee speculated that the low venereal disease rates for urban recruits was due to their ability to access medical treatment facilities in the capital.

For J. Challenor Lynch, chair of the Recruiting Committee in Barbados and a member of the Legislative Council, the "frequent occurrence of venereal disease" among enlisted soldiers was an urgent matter of "grave concern." According to Lynch, at least 20 percent of recruits in Barbados developed a venereal disease after they began training, with fifty-one soldiers ultimately being discharged as medically unfit. Because the colony's military barracks were unenclosed and located near a public highway, military officials could not sequester newly enlisted soldiers from wives, girlfriends, and sex workers in Bridgetown or other nearby civilian populations. As a result, the regiment's medical officers struggled to manage an "enormously increased" caseload because of venereal disease, while military officials worried that infected soldiers would not be able to join their comrades overseas. In fact, after a raucous three-week stopover in Barbados, 20 percent of the soldiers in the Leeward Island Contingent were sent home with venereal disease.[151]

Lynch, echoing other commentators across the region, used a combination of moral and pragmatic language to describe venereal disease. "The existence of the evil has, no doubt, been long known, as it is also known that in the days when the ships of the Royal Navy cruised in these waters, this Port was regarded with ill favour by the Commanders, and shore leave was seldom accorded," he explained. "The existence of a body of men near Bridgetown, with regular pay and a good many hours of leisure," he went on, "has but served to bring it into the light." With public attention now firmly fixed on the problem of venereal disease among the colony's volunteers, Lynch called on the Legislative Council to give the issue "serious attention."[152]

Government officials in Barbados, Grenada, and Jamaica responded to public demands for action by unveiling new public health initiatives and enacting repressive legislation that targeted civilians. In August 1917, the Grenada Legislature passed an ordinance criminalizing the intentional transmission of a venereal disease. The new law required any adult suffering from venereal disease to seek treatment immediately and to register with local public health officials. The government offered monetary rewards to residents who reported an infected neighbor, while those who refused treatment for venereal disease were subject to prosecution and forced medical care.[153] In Jamaica, the Kingston Public Hospital opened an evening clinic to diagnose and treat venereal disease, and it served over 6,700 women and men between February 1917 and January 1918.[154] The Jamaica Legislative Council also passed a bill criminalizing the spread of venereal disease and imposed fines on herbalists and other traditional healers who treated venereal disease sufferers. These fines, as Glenford Howe contends, "were intended to have the double effect of encouraging infected persons to come forward, and more crucially, of asserting the hegemony of Western biomedicine over indigenous healing practices, which were regarded by the authorities as largely ineffective and obstructive."[155]

Illiteracy was another major cause for rejection, frustrating prospective soldiers and military boosters alike until November 1916, when the literacy requirement was quietly lifted. In Trinidad, the 1911 census reported that over half of the adult population could not read and write. The literacy rates among the island's sizable Indian community were even lower: only 11 percent could read and write in English.[156] Despite the tremendous expansion of primary education in Jamaica between 1867 and 1909, only one-quarter of school-age children attended classes regularly by the outbreak of the war.[157] As a result, over a third of the adult population was unlettered. After a series of rallies for the Jamaica BWIR Contingent at Dry Harbour Mountains, the recruiting agent reluctantly "turn[ed] away a good many" of the fifty volunteers because they could not meet the literacy requirement.[158] Likewise, Dr. S. A. G. Johnson, Secretary of the Friendly Societies War Contingent Committee in Panama, reported that the majority of the 150 men who volunteered from Bocas del Toro were unable to read and write. Frustrated that numerous "able-bodied industrious men" could not enlist, Johnson confessed: "I was truly ashamed to have so many of my countrymen illiterate."[159]

Primary school teachers across the region held free educational courses at night for men who wanted to achieve basic literacy in order to enlist.[160] But instead of seizing the opportunity to advocate for increased educational opportunities, some commentators depicted unlettered men as more physically fit and adventurous than their literate peers. A correspondent for the *Gleaner* wrote: "It is noticed that the illiterate are physically a stronger class of men. They, for the most part, grow up in the mountains and sleep and live out on the wilds. They grow a lusty set of men, and the life they are accustomed to fits them more for the trenches than the men who can read and write."[161] This view perhaps contributed to the decision to withdraw the literacy requirement for the BWIR in November 1916, as more bodies were needed in the war effort.

A significant number of men were discharged from the BWIR *after* they had taken the oath of allegiance because they contracted an illness at training camp or failed to adapt to the stringent rules and regulations of military life. Indeed, 2,082 men were discharged from Jamaica's military barracks at Up Park Camp after serving in the BWIR for only a few weeks.[162] Once celebrated as heroic volunteers, these men were summarily dismissed without pay and given a one-way train ticket home. To make matters worse, their names were sometimes printed in the local newspaper, along with the reason for their dismissal.

These dismissed soldiers responded in a variety of ways. One rejected volunteer became a recruiter himself and published a poem entitled "To Those Who Have Not Enlisted" in the *Port of Spain Gazette*.[163] Other would-be soldiers refused to relinquish their newfound status as military men. Felix George Brown enlisted in the BWIR in Jamaica but was sub-sequently discharged from the regiment in November 1915.[164] Instead of leaving the contingent camp, he secretly stole a khaki uniform and two officer stripes and pretended to be a newly commissioned corporal. For two weeks, he moved about the camp, bossing around new recruits before he was detected by police. Arrested for impersonating a soldier, Brown was charged with "habitually abstaining from labour" under Jamaica's Vagrancy Law and sentenced to two months in prison.[165]

"Why Should I Go to the Front? The War Is No Concern of Mine"

Colonial authorities and local military officers praised West Indians for their support of the empire, yet undercurrents of discontent swirled throughout the recruitment process. Enlisted soldiers sometimes faced taunts from unpatriotic civilians, and other men refused to volunteer at all. On September 2, 1915, a group of soldiers from the Trinidad Con-tingent of the BWIR encountered harassment on two occasions. During the day, as they paraded through the streets of Port of Spain on a training march, a group of boys assailed them, shouting, "Look at the German tar-gets!"[166] Later on that evening, civilians Alexander Morris and Anthony Graves spotted the humiliated soldiers downtown and bombarded them with a hail of rocks and sticks. When a constable attempted to arrest Mor-ris and Graves for their unprovoked attack, their female companion urged the men to resist arrest, proclaiming defiantly that they had done nothing wrong.[167]

The *Port of Spain Gazette* demonized the hecklers as unpatriotic, unmanly, and unworthy of British citizenship while simultaneously goad-ing the "enraged public" to retaliate on behalf of the island's soldiers. Dismissing Morris and Graves as "people who are of no consequence whatever in the colony," the paper insisted that such men lacked the patri-otic feeling and moral decency of true Britishers. "They are men with-out country; men whose souls have died within them, and they are of no use to this or any other land." The paper intimated that men who taunted BWIR volunteers were shirkers plagued by guilt because of their own fear of military service. Instead of becoming soldiers of the king, this band of resisters represented a contemptible "Cold Feet Brigade." Anyone guilty of disparaging servicemen, the paper argued, should be "placed in the dock" or banished from Trinidad altogether.[168] While BWIR soldiers were touted as respectable men worthy of a place in the British Empire, the hecklers—according to the *Port of Spain Gazette*—should not even be permitted to reside in Trinidad. In other words, men who dismissed their duty and criticized the BWIR had no home in the West Indies.

Like their beleaguered comrades in Trinidad, recruits in Jamaica faced public taunts from onlookers who cast doubt on their masculinity and soldiering skills. "Miss B," a Jamaican septuagenarian interviewed at her home in the 1970s, described how people in Kingston would assemble during the war to watch BWIR troops march through the city. As the men of the "conteegent" marched "round the town," the newly minted soldiers would jubilantly sing:

> Them going to fight the Kaiser
> If we only get a chance
> We are going to fight the Kaiser
> If we only get a chance
> It will be a hip hip hooray[169]

But in response to the soldiers' celebration of martial masculinity, some spectators would command the servicemen to "bow, boi, bow" and mock new recruits' ill-fitting uniforms and uncoordinated marching by singing:

> Lef' conteegent lef'
> Boot ah nuh fi you
> Hat ah nuh fi you
> Lef' conteegent lef'[170]

These public displays and other acts of resistance during the recruitment campaign belie the claim that West Indians were either "highly supportive or indifferent to the war."[171] They also show that some men openly rejected recruiting appeals that sutured manhood to military service and were unmoved by the rhetoric of martial interracialism.

Unlike the eager volunteers described earlier in this chapter, some West Indians did everything in their power to avoid military service. Some men escaped military service by feigning a medical condition or lying about their age. During the mandatory military registration period in Jamaica in 1917, for instance, one man reportedly insisted that he was prone to spontaneous fits and, therefore, unfit for duty. When the registrar responded that she would record his name anyway, he lamented, "Ah me Missus! Ah me Missus, me n' want fe fight!"[172] Similarly, one woman alleged that "some men drink soap sud, some hid their ages" to avoid joining the Jamaica Contingent.[173]

Marronage provided another tactic to avoid enlistment. Newspapers reported with alarm that groups of military-aged men were fleeing their homes en masse. In New Amsterdam, British Guiana, "bus loads" of men left town on the day that a recruiter for the BWIR was scheduled to visit after hearing a rumor that they would be impressed into service.[174] A similar rumor nearly derailed a major recruiting meeting in Gayle, Jamaica, when "some mischievous persons" suggested that the governor was going to compel every eligible man in the town to join the colors.[175] Even five decades after the war, rumors about forced impressments to fill the ranks of the BWIR still lingered in Jamaica. During an interview, "Miss B" insisted that military recruiters used to "walk and pick up men, whether you willing or not, to carry dem to a foreign."[176] While "Miss B" claimed that soldiers in the older West India Regiment voluntarily enlisted, she declared that soldiers in Jamaica's BWIR contingent were compelled to serve. "But when the war did get hot, deh walk and take men, young strong men—fe go fight," she maintained, "whether fe fight or watch or fe carr' things me no know."[177]

While men were not actually drafted into the BWIR, rumors warning of this possibility were not outrageous. Conscription began in England, Scotland, and Wales in 1916, and France had already implemented conscription in the metropole and its colonies. During the war, conscription was also introduced in the British Dominions of Canada and New Zealand, and powerful advocates for conscription would emerge in the Caribbean, too. As colonial subjects living under Crown colony rule, black West Indians understood all too well that their labor autonomy could be disrupted at any time by British officials in the colonies or in London.

Of course, not all black and colored men fled upon hearing about a recruiter's visit; some volunteered for the BWIR but then refused to take the oath of allegiance once they passed the final medical examination, backing out in the last stage of the recruitment process. While it is unclear why these recruits ultimately decided to forgo military service, their unwillingness to accept the rigors of military life implicitly challenged romantic portrayals of soldiering. In Jamaica, at least thirteen volunteers declined to sign the official enlistment agreement and were summarily dismissed from the barracks at Up Park Camp.[178] Recruits in Grenada likewise fled the barracks after being cleared for military duty. Grenada's governor angrily ridiculed volunteers who "jibbed" military authorities by refusing to complete the enlistment process. In a speech before the Legislative Council in 1915, he announced that any men who stepped forward

"EVERY TRUE SON OF THE EMPIRE" [93]

for the BWIR but then refused to serve would be transferred to the "Cold Feet Brigade," where they would receive medals for "sitting down and looking at the women make guava jelly."[179] Like many other commentators, the governor publicly impugned the manhood of men who failed to perform martial labor by comparing them unfavorably to women.

Some resisters, indifferent to the rhetoric of imperial patriotism and martial interracialism, simply felt no connection to a conflict being fought thousands of miles away on the other side of the Atlantic. The *Port of Spain Gazette* complained that many young men cared more about football than the violent conflict in Europe: "They are too inclined to regard the matter in no serious light and take very little or no interest whatever in trying to understand the perilous times which the British empire is at present experiencing. You speak to them of the retreat from Warsaw and they alter the conversation to football! You ask whether they have read the telegrams and their reply is that 'we don't bother to read the telegrams'!"[180] The chair of the Barbados Recruiting Committee admitted that many men and women who resided outside of St. Michael's parish initially took little interest in the war and felt no need to support local patriotic efforts.[181] He gladly noted, however, that they gradually started to embrace the recruitment campaign after recruiters repeatedly visited their communities. In British Honduras, protestors ripped down a copy of King George V's "Appeal." In its place, they wrote brazenly: "What the hell have we got to do with the war?"[182]

The notion that there was no place for black soldiers in the British Army led some men to rebuff calls to join the BWIR. During the early months of recruiting, the *Gleaner* fiercely contested accusations that Britain would never deploy "a single black soldier" by reminding readers that black troops were already fighting under the Union Jack in campaigns across the African continent.[183] The editors of the Barbados *Globe* likewise trumpeted the supposedly "mixed" nature of the imperial armed forces, dismissing "talk of colour prejudice" as "pure unadulterated bunkum."[184] Black journalists also challenged the assertion that the war was "a white man's quarrel" and argued that the conflict should concern all West Indians—"black and brown, and yellow equally as the white."[185] Nonetheless, some military-aged men questioned why black and colored West Indians should fight on behalf of the British Empire when Englishmen did not view them as equals. When asked why he ignored the call to enlist, one young Trinidadian retorted that Englishmen did not appreciate the support of black colonial subjects. "The coloured man has no right to interfere in this war," he insisted, "because the English snubbed an African chief who offered a contingent by telling him that this was a white man's war and they did not want Africans to assist."[186]

Others flatly rebuked the idea of imperial patriotism, stating that they had no obligation to defend the empire when British rule in the Caribbean was authoritarian and racist. War recruiter A. E. Briscoe was horrified when a Jamaican man remarked that he saw no reason to fight to preserve British justice when "he didn't see much liberty" in his own country. Scandalized by his "ingratitude," Briscoe quipped that the resister should move to Germany to gain a proper appreciation for the "gifts of liberty, freedom, and justice" in the British Empire.[187] Another critic of the war effort chastised BWIR soldiers training in Seaford, England, for fighting in a conflict between European elites. In a stinging rebuke of dominant narratives about the "German menace," he declared: "Look at your King, he's a German, and so are all the rest of the family, [so] why don't you lay down your arms and do no fighting."[188] Unwilling to tolerate such public affronts to the king and his soldiers, English officials swiftly charged the outspoken critic with "making remarks likely to jeopardize recruiting" and sentenced him to six months in prison with hard labor.[189]

As the war bore on, debates over conscription brought questions of racial and class injustice, mutual obligation, and imperial loyalty to the forefront of public discussion. Talk of conscription first emerged in Jamaica in October 1916, nine months after compulsory service was implemented in England. Governor Manning and his allies in the business community, however, roundly condemned any plans to introduce conscription on the grounds that it would disrupt the colony's labor supply.[190] Five months later, legislators H. A. L. Simpson and E. F. H. Cox once again proposed that Jamaica should implement conscription to fill the ranks of the BWIR. After receiving tacit support from Manning and the Colonial Office, Simpson and Cox introduced the Military Service Bill in the Legislative Council on March 6, 1917.

While some conscriptionists maintained that compulsory military service would compel Jamaicans of all classes to serve in the war, anti-conscription forces warned that the proposed law would disproportionately target the black working class. The *Gleaner* tried to reassure the public that conscription would not result in the mass impressment of black peasants and workers but would instead guarantee that men from all social strata enlisted "on the basis of equality."[191] "Compulsion does not mean that you are to seize any man and hustle him up to Camp," the editors reminded readers; "this is not Germany, it is part of the British Empire."[192] Other commentators wondered how conscription would impact the colony's Chinese and Indian men. In a letter to the editor, W. Clarke MacCalla of Kingston questioned whether the conscription bill would be "strictly confined to the natives of Jamaica" or if men from Asian immigrant communities would also be allowed to "share some of the glory" of military service.[193] While MacCalla celebrated "stalwart" men from the colony's Chinese and Indian communities, James Sawers of Port Maria urged military authorities not to conscript British subjects from Jamaica because the island was "already quite overrun with Chinese, East Indians, and others."[194]

Anti-conscriptionists, led by former Legislative Council member Alexander Dixon, held a public rally in Kingston on April 2, 1917, and dispatched a resolution protesting compulsory service to the Secretary of State for the Colonies.[195] Still, the Legislative Council ultimately passed the Military Service Bill, with twenty-one of the twenty-five legislators voting in favor of the law. The bill, which took effect on June 1, required every male on the island between the ages of sixteen and forty-one to register with authorities in their home parish and made them liable for military service if sufficient numbers of volunteers did not come forward.[196] Middle-class female volunteers, in addition to their numerous other contributions to the recruitment campaign, performed nearly all of the clerical labor required to process the over 122,200 men who registered in accordance with the Military Service Law.

Not all local men complied with the mandate to register for military service, however. In September 1917, George Chin, president of the Chee Kung Tong Society in Kingston, forwarded a petition to the Chinese Minister in London protesting the Military Service Law. Writing on behalf of the colony's 1,700 Chinese male residents, Chin argued that Chinese men residing in Jamaica should not be compelled to fight on behalf of the British Empire.[197] In a letter to the Secretary of State for the Colonies, the acting governor of Jamaica echoed Chen's questionable claim that all Chinese residents in the colony were foreign subjects. According to the governor, Chinese men would not be liable for military service due to their "alien nationality" and were required only to complete the preliminary registration process along with all other male inhabitants. Furthermore, to reassure the anxious Chinese community, the governor dispatched a "prominent and respectable" Chinese merchant from Kingston to answer any further questions about the Military Service Law on behalf of the government.[198] By strategically invoking their familial and political ties to China, Chinese immigrants and their descendants in Jamaica rejected the politics of imperial patriotism and its attendant obligations.

The "Better Classes" of "(Practically) White Men": Elite Perspectives on Military Service

Throughout the war, military recruiters publicly lauded the BWIR for welcoming volunteers "irrespective of class, colour, or creed."[199] Yet, in private, many of the very same white and colored elites conspired to keep the "better class" of volunteers from serving alongside black artisans and laborers. The "better class"—those men "who prided themselves on superiority of lineage or education," as Cipriani explained—included British and locally born men who hailed from esteemed families and had studied at exclusive secondary schools.[200] This small but influential group, forged through local understandings of race, class, and status, included individuals of color who had attained prominence through education, wealth, or professional achievement as well as the white planter and merchant establishment; together, they waged a backroom campaign to shape military service and recruitment to best suit the region's most prominent sons.

Even before recruitment for the BWIR officially commenced, sugar estate owners in Trinidad and British Guiana flexed their muscle, warning Secretary of State for the Colonies Bonar Law that efforts to recruit large numbers of white plantation managers and overseers for military service "would be extremely prejudicial to the best interest" of the colonies. In a private letter sent by the West India Committee in June 1915, the estate proprietors stressed that colonial officials in Trinidad and British Guiana should avoid recruiting the "comparatively few white employees on the sugar estates" or risk a "serious state of affairs" on the colonies' rural plantations. Specifically, they claimed white military-aged men were needed to maintain production and order, explaining that the "labour on the sugar estates is . . . almost exclusively East Indian" and that it was "essential that such labour should be controlled by white managers and overseers who are indeed indispensable." Though the proprietors maintained that they had not hindered any white employees from volunteering for military service, they urged Bonar Law to take up the matter of white military recruitment with the governors of Trinidad and British Guiana.[201] The Secretary of State for the Colonies honored their request and reminded the governors of the two "coolie colonies" to be mindful of local estate proprietors' labor needs.[202]

Others from the "better classes" balked at the thought of serving alongside black working-class men in the BWIR. They desperately clung to older models of military mobilization in which propertied white and colored men served in exclusive local militias (or as officers in the British

Army) while men from the laboring classes endured the arduous life of professional soldiers in the West India Regiment. In British Honduras, the impulse to divide the colony's military volunteers by class and color came from the highest reaches of the colonial administration. After receiving authorization to recruit one hundred British Hondurans for military service, Governor Wilfred Collet privately lobbied the Colonial Office for permission to create one contingent of fifty working-class woodcutters and a second contingent of middle- and upper-class men drawn from the colony's Volunteer Force. Justifying his proposal for two contingents in a colony of only forty-two thousand inhabitants, the governor wrote that local woodcutters were "a very different class of men," who "for the most part . . . are of a lower grade of life." Such men, Collet reasoned, "would be exceedingly useful wherever a knowledge of bushwork is required" but should not serve in the same unit as British Honduras's elite.[203] When the Colonial Office rebuffed his idea, the governor renounced the tenets of martial interracialism, protesting that it was "not an easy matter to maintain discipline" in a contingent "consisting of men of different colours, ranging from pure white to almost pure black."[204]

Collet's campaign in British Honduras faltered quickly. However, in Trinidad and Barbados, local elites did manage to create private military contingents that accepted only white and lightly colored volunteers who desired to serve in metropolitan British Army regiments rather than the BWIR. In the Trinidadian case, three members of the colony's official BWIR Recruiting Committee—George F. Huggins, Enrique Prada, and A. S. Bowen—covertly conspired with merchant William G. Gordon to craft plans for a privately funded unit, tellingly named the Merchants' and Planters' Contingent. Rather than focusing on their appointed duty to recruit soldiers for the BWIR, Huggins, Prada, Bowen, and Gordon began contacting members of the colony's financial elite in August 1915 to raise funds for their private contingent. The four men kept local colonial officials "discreetly in the dark" about their plans as they solicited donations, fearing a backlash from the governor and the Commandant of the Local Forces.[205]

Huggins, Prada, and Bowen concealed their unauthorized recruiting activities equally from fellow BWIR recruiting committee member Arthur Cipriani. Narrating the history of the BWIR years later, Cipriani recalled that he initially sensed a "rift in the clouds of local recruiting" when men from the "better classes" refused to volunteer for Trinidad's first BWIR contingent. After discovering that Huggins and "his brother merchants" had established a private contingent for men who desired to enlist in the

British Army, Cipriani rebuked the colony's elite for inserting "the question of class" into the recruitment effort and denounced their plans in letters to the *Mirror* and *Port of Spain Gazette*.[206] "Our better class young men are shirking" their duty, Cipriani alleged in his letter to the *Mirror*, "because of the lamentable question of colour which lies at the bottom of everything in these parts."[207]

The editors of the *Port of Spain Gazette*, unwilling to expose the racist machinations of the local elite, refused to publish Cipriani's letter, instead accusing him of trying to "fan smoldering embers into flames" by publicly invoking the "colour question."[208] Undeterred, the outspoken recruiter took on the organizers of the Merchants' and Planters' Contingent and the press at a public recruiting meeting in late August 1915. "The game has not been played in many quarters, it was not being played now," Cipriani fumed before a large crowd. "The raising of a rival contingent, the boycott of this meeting by the *Port of Spain Gazette*, the miserable and unfortunate attitude of those who were able to enlist from the public service in the defense forces of this colony—all gave evidence that the game was not being played." Three days later, in a biting letter to the editors of the *Gazette*, Cipriani once again took aim at the hypocrisy and racism of the local elite. "Have the Colonials declined to do their duty to King and Country," he asked pointedly, "because of the presence of East Indians and Blacks?"[209]

Cipriani's unflinching rebuke of the Merchants' and Planters' Contingent highlighted an ideological chasm among members of Trinidad's white upper echelon. While historians rightly cite the creation of the Merchants' and Planters' Contingent as evidence of white elites' hollow commitment to the principle of martial interracialism, the intraracial debate over the private contingent also signals that some local whites did reject the movement to divide the colony's military volunteers by race, color, and class.[210] Reflecting on the controversy after the war, Cipriani would reiterate his strident condemnation of George Huggins and others, who coordinated the Merchants' and Planters' Contingent despite their official obligations to the BWIR. The members of the Recruiting Committee, Cipriani concluded, never possessed any "real sympathy" for the BWIR and "on every possible occasion ... did all in their power to recruit the best available material for the Merchants' Contingent." Yet, unable to stop the rival group or to compel men from the colony's "better classes" to enlist in the BWIR, Cipriani admitted that the Merchants' and Planters' Contingent was an "unfortunate compromise" that accommodated Trinidad's elite to avoid "friction between classes" or "any show of public indignation." Such

"EVERY TRUE SON OF THE EMPIRE" [99]

shortsighted concessions to conservative powerbrokers, he predicted ominously, would have a "baneful influence" on the colony.[211]

Officials at the Colonial Office were forced to consider the political implications of the Merchants' and Planters' Contingent after two representatives from the private unit requested a meeting with Bonar Law.[212] In November 1915, A. S. Bowen and George Huggins disembarked in London with the first cadre of volunteers from the Merchants' and Planters' Contingent—a group of 112 recruits whom Bowen candidly described as "(practically) white men."[213] The Colonial Office staff quickly determined that the Secretary of State for the Colonies could not meet with Huggins and Bowen "without exposing himself to the obligation of seeing representative of other contingents;" yet staff members were less clear on the level of support, if any, the Colonial Office should extend to the Merchants' and Planters' Contingent.[214] "Since these men have considered themselves too good for the [BWIR] contingent," clerk R. A. Wiseman argued, "I presume that we should not feel obliged to make any exceptional effort to help them."[215] Clerk C. A. Darley offered a more positive assessment of the private contingent, stating that the group was "likely to contain some very useful men" for the British Army. However, both Darley and Gilbert Grindle questioned whether it would be feasible to aid the volunteers since they would be "scattered over various Regiments" in the British Army after enlistment.[216]

In a pragmatic compromise, the Colonial Office sent Grindle to meet with the two representatives of the Merchants' and Planters' Contingent after Bonar Law diplomatically declined their invitation due to prior engagements. The frank exchange among Bowen, Huggins, and Grindle casts light on the racial prerogatives of Trinidad's conservative elite as well as the intraracial squabbles among whites in the colony over the Merchants' and Planters' Contingent. During the private summit, Bowen and Huggins assured Grindle that they had no intention of opposing the local government or the official recruitment effort for the BWIR by siphoning off qualified men for their own contingent. Rather, Bowen and Huggins insisted, they had established the private contingent because "white and the better class of coloured men will not serve with the blacks [and] want to join British regiments." But instead of being acknowledged for their efforts to mobilize the colony's elite sons, they complained, colonial officials in Trinidad had given their unit the "cold shoulder" and even refused to provide a police escort for the group during public events. One well-heeled subscriber to the Merchants' and Planters' Contingent Fund complained that his wife was "knocked about from pillar to post" by rowdy working-class spectators who assembled uninvited to view the group.[217] As a result, Bowen and Huggins sought official assurance from the Colonial Office that local authorities in Trinidad would not blacklist volunteers who resigned from their jobs in the civil service to join the Merchants' and Planters' Contingent.[218]

After Grindle's meeting with Bowen and Huggins, Bonar Law dispatched a brief missive to Huggins, offering his support for the recruiting effort. In a diplomatically worded letter written on Law's behalf, F. G. A. Butler reported that the Secretary of State for the Colonies was "very sorry" that his schedule prevented him from meeting with representatives from the Merchants' and Planters' Contingent and thanked Huggins for his "work in getting recruits for the Army." In addition, Law promised to ask Trinidad's governor, George Le Hunte, to "give all proper facilities to the Committee in its work of helping young Trinidadians who wish to come to England to join a British regiment."[219]

The Colonial Office's official sanction of the Merchants' and Planters' Contingent cooled the local row over the group's aims and purpose. The leaders of the private contingent ultimately recruited 276 volunteers for the British Army between 1915 and 1918 and raised over $61,000 in local currency to cover initial training and transportation costs.[220] Though Cipriani remained adamantly opposed to the rival contingent, two young Trinidadians who would rise to prominence as nationalist literary figures in the postwar years sought to serve with the group.

Alfred Hubert Mendes, the prolific Portuguese Creole writer best known for his work with the *Beacon* literary group in the 1930s, was seventeen years old and studying in England when war erupted in 1914. Hoping to protect his son from danger, Mendes's father brought him back to Trinidad in the summer of 1915.[221] Mendes soon grew restless at home and, in "quest of new experiences to fuel his writing," enlisted in the Merchants' and Planters' Contingent less than a year after returning to Trinidad.[222] He sailed across the Atlantic along with sixty-nine other volunteers in December 1915.

Ironically, once in Europe, Mendes served with the King's Royal Rifle Corps alongside working-class colliers from northern England and two fellow Merchants' and Planters' Contingent volunteers from Trinidad.[223] Deployed to Abbeville, France, the eighteen-year-old private spent his first months as a soldier in a muddy, rat-infested dugout twenty feet below ground. Mendes managed to endure the "hell of mud and death" on the Western Front, but his two Trinidadian companions broke under the strain of constant shelling, homesickness, and fatigue. Of one, Mendes later wrote: "He wept without shame, choking with self-pity, his manhood lacerated and shredded. Intoning as one haunted by horrors, 'Oh Holy Mary, Mother of God, have mercy on me and save me!' he fell back upon the mud floor whimpering like a baby, until beyond endurance, he lapsed into a deep sleep." Shortly thereafter, military officials declared both of Mendes's Trinidadian comrades "unfit for service" and sent them home less than eight months after enlistment.[224] Mendes, however, climbed his way through the ranks to become a sergeant and received the Military Medal for his "coolness" and "complete disregard for his personal safety" during the Battle of Poelcappelle in Flanders in 1917.[225]

In the years following World War I, Mendes chronicled his battlefield experiences in a host of semi-autobiographical poems and short stories, which were published in Trinidad's major literary journals. Describing the horrors of trench warfare on the Western Front in a poem published in 1933, he wrote:

> I remember the months I spent in the
> trenches with lice playing hide-and-seek about
> my body in the midst of mud and the stench
> of decomposed bodies.
> and I remember the futility
> and the wickedness
> and the beastliness of it all[226]

Although C. L. R. James was four years younger than Mendes, both teenagers had a passion for English literature and had been educated at Queen's Royal College, and James, like Mendes, approached the Merchants' and Planters' Contingent when he decided to enlist. Yet, James hailed from a black lower-middle-class family, a fact that almost certainly caused him to be rejected when he volunteered in 1918. Writing about the local military recruitment campaign decades later, James vividly described how class and color divided the colony's volunteers into two distinct military units. The Merchants' and Planters' Contingent, he recalled, was the private group comprised of "young men of the upper middle class" who were "sent direct to England to join English regiments and financed by the local merchants." He mused, "The rumour was, and the facts seemed to show that the merchants selected only white or brown people" for their contingent. In contrast, the colonial government recruited the BWIR "public contingent" from "among the masses of people." When "white boys" from Queen's Royal College elected to serve with the less-prestigious BWIR, James remembered, they immediately received commissions as officers and returned to school "with chests out and smart uniforms and shining buttons."[227]

James's fleeting anecdote highlights one of the central ironies of the recruitment campaign: While white volunteers who joined the BWIR secured coveted appointments as commissioned officers or NCOs, only 26 percent of men who joined the Merchants' and Planters' Contingent received commissions in the British Army. In fact, most men from the "better classes" who enlisted with the Merchants' and Planters' Contingent—over 60 percent in total—soldiered as lowly privates throughout the war.[228]

Following the example of their peers in Trinidad, members of Barbados's upper crust also formed their own private contingent for volunteers who wanted to serve in the British Army.[229] In November 1915, merchant D. G. Leacock founded the Barbados Citizens' Contingent along with nine other white supporters and issued a public call for "all good Citizens in Town and Country to come forward and help."[230] The group amassed nearly £2,000 in private donations during its first month in existence, garnering words of praise from the Trinidadian press as well as the local establishment.[231] One of the region's black newspapers, however, blasted the leaders of the private contingent for appropriating the language of citizenship to recruit white and colored elites for their exclusive unit. "Citizen's Contingent! What a name!" the Grenada *West Indian* fumed. "If there is a Citizen's Contingent," the paper asked, "what condition does the Barbados [BWIR] Public Contingent represent? Those who are not citizens?"[232]

Even after the creation of private contingents in Barbados and Trinidad, many middle- and upper-class men still refused to step forward for military service. In fact, only eighty-nine recruits enlisted in the Barbados Citizen's Contingent, falling far short of its goal of one hundred to two hundred men.[233] In Jamaica, one frustrated observer disparagingly referred to the colony's young elite as "gilded youth" and "carpet knights" and questioned their bravery by citing biblical verses on fear and cowardice from Psalms and Isaiah.[234] Likewise, when the recruitment effort in Retreat, Jamaica, stalled in November 1915, one resident blamed the local class of gentlemen who urged smallholders and artisans to enlist while their own sons stayed behind.[235] The *Gleaner* openly castigated the island's privileged youth who idled at home "living a life of ease" while local laborers volunteered for the army in droves. "Has position no obligations?" asked the editors. "Has it ceased to be the duty of Gentlemen to lead where danger lies?"[236]

As the war progressed, frustrated commentators issued increasingly strident calls for the "better class" of men to join the colors. Speaking at a rally in Linstead, Jamaica, in 1917, W. F. Bailey contrasted the bravery and patriotism of Jamaica's black workers with the unwillingness of the island's wealthy scions to don the king's uniform. Chiding men who boasted about their English lineage yet refused to serve during a time of unprecedented crisis, Bailey challenged the elite to demonstrate their loyalty on the battlefield. "The barefoot peasant, the illiterate negro has come forward boldly," he protested. "But the educated class has provided the slackers in this country. 'Tis sad to say it, but nevertheless, 'tis true."[237]

Some men from the region's educated colored and black middle classes, like their white counterparts, also chafed at the idea of serving alongside the "mixed class of men" in the BWIR. In a speech before the Legislative Council, the Administrator of Dominica applauded the patriotic spirit of the island's laboring men, while lamenting the lack of volunteers from the "more educated classes of . . . [the] creole population."[238] An observer in Antigua similarly noted that the island's white elites and black working men volunteered to serve in the BWIR while the "better class of coloured young men" rarely did so.[239] In a desperate attempt to recruit more men for military service, Governor Leslie Probyn embraced a proposal from the Barbados Recruiting Committee to create a separate regiment for "the better class of coloured men." Forwarding the proposal to the Secretary of State for the Colonies in July 1918, Probyn noted that middle-class colored men had little interest in soldiering alongside black working peoples in the BWIR.[240] At least for some potential soldiers, Probyn implicitly acknowledged, the prerogatives of class and status trumped any allegiance to "King and Country."

Conclusion

The belated effort to establish a distinct contingent for colored men never materialized due to the end of hostilities in Europe, yet Probyn's overtures to the Colonial Office underscore the persistent salience of race, class, and color divisions in the recruitment campaign. Despite the soaring rhetoric of martial interracialism and odes to imperial loyalty, military recruiters and volunteers in the British Caribbean confronted the thorny task of managing gendered anxieties and interracial and intraracial hierarchies throughout the war years. Across the Atlantic, in Europe, Africa, and the Middle East, BWIR soldiers would confront similar issues as they struggled to navigate racial discrimination in military barracks and under abusive commanding officers and faced unexpected challenges from the War Office to their standing as soldiers.

PART II

The Soldier's Life

CHAPTER THREE

"Humiliations and Disillusion"

MILITARY LABOR AND WARTIME INTERRACIAL ENCOUNTERS

There have been West Indians employed on various duties in France, Italy, Egypt, East Africa and Mesopotamia and whether one speaks to Officer, N. C. O. or man, it has always been the same tale of heart-breaking humiliations and disillusion.

—LIEUTENANT COLONEL CHARLES WOOD-HILL

SOMETIME BEFORE HE left for the war, Etienne Dupuch posed for a family portrait (see fig. 3.1). The photograph, taken by acclaimed Bahamian photographer James Osborne "Doc" Sands, captures Dupuch in a moment of liminality.[1] As a newly enlisted soldier, Dupuch was spending his final days at home before deploying overseas with the BWIR. Dupuch staged his transition from civilian to soldier through the "performative practice" of family photography.[2] Wearing an oversized military uniform, Dupuch sits in a large wicker chair with his legs crossed in the center of the frame. His expressionless face stares directly into the camera. He is flanked by his cousin William on the left and his older brother Gilbert on the right, both men hovering above him in relaxed poses. Dupuch's little brother Eugene sits next to him on a wicker footstool, holding a small decorative cane. Dupuch gently cradles the three-year-old with his left arm while using his right arm to clasp Eugene's hand. Dupuch's military cap and khakis stand in sharp contrast to the civilian dress worn by Gilbert, William, and Eugene, announcing his new status as a soldier. Yet, the photograph simultaneously showcases his respectability and familial ties, depicting him surrounded by the male relatives that he will soon leave behind.[3]

[107]

FIGURE 3.1. Etienne Dupuch (seated at center) with Gilbert Dupuch (right), Eugene Dupuch (center front), and William Farrington (left). From Sir Etienne Dupuch, *A Salute to Friend and Foe: My Battles, Sieges, and Fortunes* (Nassau, Bahamas: Tribune, 1982), 32.

Born in Nassau, Bahamas, in 1899 to a colored, middle-class family, Dupuch was only fifteen years old when the war erupted. Inspired by the protagonists in Alexandre Dumas's swashbuckling adventure novel, *The Three Musketeers*, he imagined military service as an act of masculine heroism and a route to explore the world beyond his island home. After the formation of the BWIR, he jumped at the opportunity to enlist. "I thought this was an answer to my dream of carving my name in glory by giving my life for a just and glorious cause," he later mused.[4] However, due to his youth and small stature, the Bahamian teenager was rejected when he first volunteered for military service in 1915. Undeterred, he attempted to enlist several more times until he was finally accepted at age seventeen. Soon after, Dupuch and other Bahamian enlistees sailed on a schooner from Nassau to Kingston, Jamaica, and then journeyed across the Atlantic on a troopship bound for the Middle East.[5]

Soldiering as a "lowly private" upended Dupuch's romantic ideas about military service and transformed his perspective on the status of colonials of color in the British Empire.[6] During his three years in the BWIR, Dupuch traveled thousands of miles and served in multiple theaters of war, deploying to Egypt, France, Belgium, and Italy. Other BWIR comrades were stationed in England, Mesopotamia, and East Africa. The peripatetic nature of military service for Dupuch and other BWIR troops contrasts sharply with prevailing depictions of World War I soldiers as battle-fatigued men mired in the trenches on the Western Front. Instead, military officials dispersed the BWIR's twelve battalions across three continents and assigned them primarily to noncombatant roles. Members of the regiment worked grueling hours and often performed backbreaking manual labor. As Barbadian soldier Clennell Wickham ruefully observed, "An army day consists for working purposes of twenty-four hours. You get full measure, pressed down and running over. The variety of the work, too, is staggering."[7] West Indians hauled ammunition and built and repaired fortifications. They guarded supply lines and unloaded trains and ships. They prepared food and cleaned kitchens. They worked as stretcher-bearers and buried the dead. A select few performed skilled labor as carpenters, blacksmiths, telephone operators, and motor-boat drivers. In these auxiliary roles, BWIR troops traipsed between battlefields and military installations to support combat operations while at times incurring enemy fire. Traveling by foot, truck, train, and boat, West Indian soldiers experienced the war as a series of migrations through unfamiliar terrain. Theirs was a war on the move.

Soldiers from the British Caribbean joined the massive multiracial, multiethnic, and multilingual force assembled to defend the British Empire. In addition to the 4.9 million men who enlisted in the British Isles, nearly three million men from the empire served as soldiers and laborers between 1914 and 1918.[8] The scale and scope of military mobilization

FIGURE 3.2. Clennell Wilsden Wickham. From Clennell Wilsden Wickham, *A Man with a Fountain Pen: Clennell Wilsden Wickham, 1895–1938* (Bridgetown, Barbados: Nation Publishing, 1995), 48.

were wholly unprecedented in the British Empire. While overseas, BWIR soldiers met English "Tommies," Irish soldiers, Indian fighters, ANZAC troops, Canadian servicemen, and military laborers from South Africa. They also interacted extensively with civilian women and men from across the empire. BWIR chaplain Alfred Horner, a white minister trained by the Church Missionary Society, predicted that these wartime encounters would strengthen the "Brotherhood of Empire," fostering bonds of "sympathy and affection" between West Indians and British subjects from around the world.[9]

Some BWIR soldiers echoed Horner's perspective, depicting their intra-imperial encounters in glowing terms, especially during the early months of their deployment. Many others, however, denounced their white British military counterparts as intensely hostile and racist. As one Trinidadian sergeant lamented, "There is hardly a Christian precept which has not been violated in the treatment meted out to us; our relations with other troops are just as strained as those between black and white in [the] U.S.A. with the difference that over there wrongs can be redressed while with us there is no redress, for us we have no rights or privileges." He continued, "We are treated neither as Christians nor British Citizens, but as West Indian 'Niggers,' without anybody to be interested in or look after us."[10] Etienne Dupuch also painfully recalled the racial discrimination that he endured as a BWIR soldier. "The army was a shock to me," he confessed. "Many were the humiliations loyal 'natives,' sons of the Crown, were obliged to endure while voluntarily offering up their lives in the cause of freedom."[11] For the BWIR's black and colored enlistees, the fiercest battles of World War I would be fought *within* the British Army.

Soldiers' daily lives while on active duty were governed by strict regulations regarding dress, conduct, and labor, which emphasized conformity and obedience to authority. Wartime deployment required BWIR troops to master a host of new rules and routines—or face stiff punishment.[12] "The first thing that strikes a newcomer in the army is his own appalling ignorance; then the fact that things are not what they seemed," Clennell Wickham explained. West Indian soldiers had to quickly "learn a new language [and] . . . understand that for 'the duration [of the war]' all personal ceremony is dispensed with, and in its place is substituted a Regimental ceremony too vast and incomprehensible for even the most war-hardened veteran," he added.[13] Soldiers accused of transgressing British Army regulations could face fines, reduction in rank, imprisonment, penal servitude, or execution.[14] As Etienne Dupuch recalled, some commanding officers in the BWIR openly warned that they would "break" any soldier who defied their authority.[15]

Desperate to escape the hierarchical and tightly regimented environment in military camps and depots, soldiers sought opportunities to explore neighboring towns and cities. Recreational travel—whether authorized through official leave passes or done surreptitiously without permission—provided a vital avenue for soldiers to ease the monotony and loneliness of military life. In their letters home, BWIR troops recounted trips to major cities in England and France, religious sites in the Holy Land, and markets, mosques, and pyramids in Egypt. Soldiers also readily socialized with civilians who lived and worked near British military installations, at times even joining them in their homes as guests. During brief sojourns away from camp, Etienne Dupuch visited bars and a brothel in Egypt, ate at local *estaminets* [small cafés that served food and alcohol] in France, and spent time with cousins in the English countryside.[16] Although British military officials often limited or even prohibited West Indians from taking leave, Dupuch and other BWIR soldiers found ways to escape guarded military compounds, using mobility to their own ends to secure a reprieve from the burdens of war.

This chapter details how BWIR soldiers navigated the strictures of military deployment and engaged with the heterogeneous populations they met while overseas. Beginning with soldiers' transatlantic voyages on troopships, it follows servicemen as they traveled to military installations, bustling work sites, and war-torn towns on the Western Front. As previous scholarship has shown, military authorities consigned BWIR troops to low status, noncombatant roles, lodged them in dilapidated housing, and failed to protect them from abusive white officers and servicemen.[17] Yet, we still know little about how BWIR troops conceptualized their identity as soldiers and assessed their status in the British Army. Through analysis of soldiers' letters, poems, photographs, and memoirs, this chapter argues that BWIR soldiers characterized the war years as a period of intense exploration *and* deep disillusionment. Faced with the reality of a racist army, BWIR soldiers emphasized their stoic resolve in the face of hardships, their physical prowess, their strong work ethic, and their decency to present themselves as worthy of respect. They insisted that racial discrimination violated the tenets of martial interracialism and undermined the imperial war effort. And, they carefully documented acts of cross-racial solidarity, acknowledging the white civilians and soldiers who treated them as comrades in the fight for democracy.

A "Cargo of Human Freight": Life and Death on the Troopships

Nearly every soldier who enlisted in the BWIR began his overseas deployment in the same way—by sailing across the Atlantic on a troopship.[18] The long ocean voyage introduced soldiers to both the camaraderie and the hardships of military life. Felix Toraille boarded the troopship *Verdala* in Port of Spain in September 1915.[19] The Trinidadian private was one of the first BWIR servicemen to make the trip to England. Eager to document his journey, Toraille recounted his experience on the *Verdala* in a detailed letter to a friend. "I must candidly say that we had a pleasant trip," he wrote; "very few of the Trinidad men felt any sort of unpleasantness although [it was] their first trip over the oceans." The *Verdala*, like other troopships, docked at several Caribbean ports before embarking on the transatlantic crossing. After leaving Trinidad, it stopped at St. George's, Grenada, where 150 soldiers came aboard. Next, it picked up sixty men in St. Vincent before sailing east to Barbados. On arrival in Bridgetown, "110 Brave and Gallant Sons of Bimshire" made their way to the ship. "The patriotic display and send off extended the Barbadians was all that could be expected from loyal Barbados," Toraille noted proudly.[20]

Troopships functioned as "sites of anticipation and expectation— of becoming rather than being."[21] On the *Verdala*, men recruited from multiple colonies began forging a new collective esprit de corps as members of the BWIR. During the sixteen-day voyage from Port of Spain to Plymouth, England, Toraille socialized for the first time with comrades from other islands, perhaps exchanging stories or sharing meals together below deck. Other soldiers passed the time on ships by playing card games like "blackjack and wappy all night long."[22] While Toraille praised most soldiers' behavior, he had little patience for the "few mal-contents . . . who grumbled very much about their grubs." Dismissing their complaints about the quality of food, Toraille declared that soldiers must "make the best" of their circumstances. The trip was "as good and pleasant as could be expected," he maintained.[23]

Other BWIR soldiers—the men whom Toraille disparaged as "malcontents"—offered less sanguine accounts of the transatlantic voyage. Accommodations on the troopships were often cramped, cold, and unsanitary. Thousands of BWIR soldiers made their initial oceanic crossing on the *Magdalena*, which frequently plied the waters between the Caribbean, Europe, and North Africa. Originally built as an ocean liner for the Royal Mail Steam Packet Company, the *Magdalena* was over twenty-five years old when the British Admiralty requisitioned the ship for military use in 1915. Arthur Cipriani would later describe the aging ship as "a veritable death-trap." The "Old Maggie," he claimed, was the "slowest, oldest, and dingiest transport in His Majesty's service."[24] Etienne Dupuch, who traveled on the *Magdalena* on a different voyage, characterized his sleeping quarters in the bowels of the ship as a "hell hole."[25] "We were lodged in the hold of the ship and slept in hammocks slung side by side," he recalled. "The place was like a scene in Dante's vision of hell. To add to our misery, the place was crawling with body lice left behind by previous troops transported on this ship."[26]

Illness spread rapidly on troopships. Outbreaks of influenza, rubella, mumps, meningitis, and other infectious diseases swept through the ranks.[27] Doctors attempted to treat sick soldiers, but they often lacked basic medical supplies. Dupuch noted that on the *Magdalena*, the ship's doctor "had no medicines, not even a bottle of aspirin!"[28] Dupuch also "discovered that the battalion had . . . no provision for hospitalization of men who took sick on the voyage."[29] Men who contracted serious illnesses, like pneumonia, often died. Cipriani recalled that three fellow servicemen, Trinidadian Leonard Crichlow and two Barbadians, died from pneumonia while on the troopship.[30] Dupuch, too, watched in horror as many comrades "went down with pneumonia."[31] Of the fifty soldiers diagnosed with pneumonia, fifteen perished on the ship.[32] According to one commanding officer, poor accommodations and inadequate clothing created a deadly environment at sea. "Many West Indians lost their lives from pneumonia on board ship[s] from the West Indies to England, and this was entirely due to the fact that they were unsuitably clothed—no warm underclothing, no overcoats and sick accommodations totally unsuitable," Lieutenant Colonel Charles Wood-Hill charged.[33] Sickness, often caused by military officials' misguided policies or outright negligence, debilitated West Indian soldiers on troopships and on the shore. Indeed, illness was the leading cause of death in the BWIR.[34]

On many transatlantic voyages, BWIR troops faced the somber task of burying dead comrades while unmoored from kith and kin. Unlike the communal, multiday rituals for the dead in Caribbean societies, the British Army's prescribed burial practices for soldiers offered little opportunity to exchange stories about the departed, publicly grieve their loss, or commune with their spirit through food, music, and dancing.[35] A soldier's corpse was quickly enclosed in army-issued canvas, "placed in a hollow shell covered with the Union Jack," and transported to the ship's main deck.[36] There was no wake. Clergymen performed funeral rites, generally following the Anglican service outlined in the *Book of Common Prayer*, as soldiers looked on. Then, the corpse was committed to the sea, weighed down to prevent it from floating back up to the water's surface. "Those who have witnessed burials at sea need no description," Arthur Cipriani lamented, "but it is the most weirdly depressing ceremony one can witness."[37] Jamaican soldier Vere Johns, horrified by the "grim ceremony" he witnessed aboard a troopship, recoiled at the "sickening splash" of a comrade's corpse landing in the Atlantic Ocean and "cursed and swore at the injustice of it all."[38] These morbid scenes en route to overseas theaters of war offered stark reminders about the deadly perils of military service and "the true meaning of war."[39]

The BWIR experienced one of its deadliest disasters of the war on the *Verdala*, less than seven months after Felix Toraille's initial voyage on the ship. In March 1916, over 1,110 Jamaican soldiers boarded the *Verdala* in Kingston harbor to begin their voyage to England.[40] Unbeknownst to the men, however, the British Admiralty had secretly ordered the *Verdala* to sail due north to join a British navy convoy departing from Halifax, Nova Scotia, fearing that the troopship might be attacked by German raiders.[41] Disaster did loom—but the real hazard was extreme cold in the North Atlantic, not an enemy attack. As the *Verdala* arrived at Halifax, temperatures plunged to seven degrees Fahrenheit, and a massive blizzard slammed into the city.[42] "It was the first time that we'd ever seen snow," one soldier recalled.[43] The *Verdala* was wholly unequipped for the freezing weather. According to the commanding officer, the troopship had "no heating appliances on board" and its water pipes froze after snow blanketed the decks.[44] Another military official later privately admitted that the *Verdala* was "not well suited to a voyage to a severe climate . . . or indeed for any long voyage with troops on board."[45] Lodged in frigid quarters and dressed in only lightweight khaki uniforms, Jamaican soldiers on the *Verdala* "bawled out" in agony as their limbs began to freeze.[46]

Private Noel Fulkes recounted the dire conditions on the *Verdala*. "Some days after leaving Jamaica, we ran into very cold weather which made us suffer greatly," he explained. "We had no warm socks or gloves and our hands and feet got frost bitten."[47] The first sign of frostbite, Fulkes noted, was the "ticklish cramped sensation" in his foot. Soon, the pain felt like "a sudden dart into the flesh as to be almost unbearable."[48] By the time the troopship finally docked in Halifax, Fulkes and hundreds of other Jamaican BWIR soldiers were suffering from frostbite and swollen feet. In the days that followed, over one hundred men had a limb, or in some cases multiple limbs, amputated.[49] Seven others died from pneumonia.[50] Those men deemed healthy enough to travel were dispatched to Bermuda, where they recuperated in warmer climes for several weeks before continuing their journey across the Atlantic to England.[51]

Survivors of the disastrous voyage praised Canadians for providing them with succor and relief. As soldiers emphasized, it was fellow colonial subjects—Canadian soldiers and civilians—who rescued them from the *Verdala* after the Admiralty's reckless decision. Canadian infantry troops trudged through snow and ice in Halifax to transport critically ill men from the *Verdala* to nearby hospitals. According to one Jamaican sergeant,

Canadian servicemen gave West Indians "a hearty welcome" and treated them as "brothers at arms."[52] Hospitalized soldiers likewise praised Canadians' thoughtfulness and generosity. "Simply written words cannot express the extent of their kindness," Fulkes wrote during his hospital stay in Halifax. "They are very sympathetic and do everything in their power to help us to forget and get rid of our pain," he added.[53] The local Red Cross Society supplied the BWIR with seven hundred pairs of warm socks, while hospital staff and local residents raised funds to purchase games, chocolates, cigarettes, and other treats for frostbitten soldiers.[54] The governor of Nova Scotia even visited the hospitalized Jamaicans, speaking with each soldier individually during his trip.[55] These acts of interracial solidarity provided BWIR soldiers with a temporary reprieve from the hazardous conditions on the troopship and buoyed hopes that West Indians would be embraced as comrades by fellow Allied troops during deployment.

When news about the BWIR's tragic trip to Halifax reached Jamaica, residents blasted military officials for sending soldiers to Canada without appropriate clothing or supplies. "Outspoken criticism against those responsible for sending peasants of a tropical country to Canada at such a bitter time of the year," Hebert de Lisser recalled, "was soon heard everywhere."[56] Brigadier-General L. S. Blackden, commander of the local forces, publicly lambasted the Admiralty's "stupid blunder."[57] Meanwhile, the governor of Jamaica swiftly distanced himself from the disaster, claiming that the Admiralty had not informed him about the *Verdala*'s planned route. Even the *Daily Gleaner*, the mouthpiece of Jamaica's conservative white elite, implored colonial authorities to provide robust aid to amputees and other disabled servicemen. "We cannot tolerate that those so wounded should be left to charity," the paper maintained. "Should they be permitted to sit at the corners of our streets begging for a livelihood it will be an eternal shame."[58]

In the wake of the disaster, military officials discharged nearly four hundred soldiers as medically unfit, severing their ties to the BWIR.[59] These disabled men concluded their military service by sailing back to Jamaica on hospital ships. Sergeant Fred Cole, one of the guards on duty the "fatal night" that the blizzard struck, had his left leg amputated. Before he sailed on the *Verdala*, Cole had been a decorated athlete, participating in intercolonial sporting events as a runner and long jumper. However, following the amputation, he could no longer serve in the military or take part in track and field competitions. Reflecting on his life-altering experience with the "ill-fated 3rd Battalion," Cole noted that his trip on the *Verdala* prematurely ended his sporting career. "My left leg that got frost bitten took me and [I] was invalided and send back home and suffered with that leg till I had to take it off," he wrote, "so that's the end of an athlect's [athlete's] life."[60]

Victor Gruber, a twenty-year-old Jamaican private, was another one of the disabled veterans discharged in the aftermath of the *Verdala* tragedy. A shipwright by trade, Gruber had enlisted to demonstrate his "true loyalty" to the empire. Yet, after surviving the "painful blizzard" at Halifax, he was "partially incapacitated" from "doing any arduous labour." Grueber received a lifetime disability pension of 14s. per week, but he argued that it was insufficient to support himself, his wife, and their three children in their "battle against starvation." In a letter to Jamaica's Colonial Secretary, he pleaded for further assistance. "Sir, I desire to direct your attention to the fact that I am a tradesman. If I had not entered the war [,] I might have been living a happy life," he explained. "Truly, I am not commenting with regret on my service to the British Empire—an Empire under which I shall ever be proud," he continued, "but from the fact that I am being tossed in the billows of life's ocean without any merciful assistance."[61] Despite Gruber's efforts to present himself as a respectable and loyal subject—a veteran, husband, father, and skilled tradesman—colonial officials refused to increase his disability pension and blamed him for his financial woes. "He appears to be a man incapable of settling down to regular employment," one official alleged, "and is probably suffering from too much education judging from the many exhibits we have of his letters."[62] Thus, as his former BWIR comrades began their deployment at military sites overseas, Gruber faced the difficult task of rebuilding his life in Jamaica after a devastating stint as a soldier.

"We Are All British": Race and Imperial Belonging in England

Having sailed "in fair weather across the Atlantic," Felix Toraille arrived in Plymouth, England, in early October 1915. During his first hours on shore, he marveled at the "gigantic Railway operation" in Plymouth and acknowledged the historic significance of the BWIR's transatlantic sojourn. "For the first time," he mused, "a good many West Indians . . . had a glimpse of England."[63] For Toraille and other BWIR soldiers, England was the "Mother Country," the storied metropole of the British Empire. "The educational system and the institutions of the British West Indies," as scholars have shown, "helped to forge in many people a strong sense of British empire loyalism."[64] Yet, England was also a wholly new environment—a place very few men who served in the BWIR had visited before 1915. Indeed, as one newspaper noted, the regiment was "drawn chiefly from classes untravelled and unfamiliar with the life of European communities."[65] As West Indians deployed to England in unprecedented numbers during World War I, their experiences revealed how racialized ideas about colonial difference existed *in tandem with* celebrations of imperial belonging. White civilians, fascinated by the arrival of over 2,500 black and colored servicemen from the colonies, greeted the BWIR with intense interest and, at times, thinly veiled hostility. While acknowledging West Indians as fellow British subjects, they simultaneously viewed black and colored servicemen through racist tropes that associated blackness with ignorance, backwardness, and physical brawn.[66] Cognizant of these stereotypes, BWIR soldiers emphasized their status as Britons and their willingness to defend the empire.[67] As one Trinidadian private announced, "We have left our homes and comforts because the call-to-arms is as much to us as it is to an Englishman. We are all British and are proud to be members of the Empire and we will shed our last drop of blood to uphold its integrity."[68]

At the time West Indian soldiers began arriving in England, the number of black residents in the metropole was remarkably small. The combined black population in the British Isles, in decline since the nineteenth century, was approximately fourteen thousand out of a total population of forty-six million. Most black people resided in major English port cities such as Liverpool, London, and Bristol, where seamen from West Africa and the British Caribbean found employment in the maritime trade.[69] The black population also included hundreds of performers as well as smaller numbers of domestics, university students, and middle-class professionals (generally British-educated lawyers, doctors, writers, and teachers).[70] Despite its size, however, the minority community of black Britons was highly visible. Several black activists from the Caribbean—including Marcus Garvey, Trinidadian lawyer Henry Sylvester Williams, and Trinidadian journalist F. E. M. Hercules—spent significant time in England before or during the war years, partnering with local black reformers to demand greater social and political rights for black people in the British Empire.[71] By the time BWIR soldiers deployed to England in the autumn of 1915, black Britons in the largest port cities had their own established organizations, newspapers, and local leaders.

Even so, military officials initially stationed the BWIR at a training camp on the outskirts of Seaford, a sleepy coastal town in Sussex. Seaford was far from England's long-standing black communities, and there were few, if any, local black residents. Located on the southern coast, the quaint town was home to fewer than four thousand people before the war.[72]

"HUMILIATIONS AND DISILLUSION" [119]

Between 1914 and 1918, it was transformed into a major training site for British troops, welcoming twenty-five thousand servicemen from across the empire, including troops from Ireland, Canada, and the Caribbean. Beginning in January 1916, smaller numbers of BWIR soldiers were also stationed at Crown Hill Barracks in Plymouth and at Withnoe Camp to the west of the city.[73]

BWIR soldiers and clergymen wrote glowing accounts about their first impressions of England, documenting the "very enthusiastic reception" they received from local civilians.[74] When the regiment disembarked in Plymouth, soldiers were greeted by crowds of cheering onlookers. "The people working around the wharves and railways, cheered us like mad, and when we got in town, the people in the street would wave their hands and the children and grown-ups too would come to the windows and wave flags," a Bahamian soldier recalled. "It made one feel proud, and realise that the sacrifice we had made was appreciated."[75] Private G. J. Dadd, in a letter to his family in Jamaica, praised local residents' hospitality. "The English people, I must say, are the finest and most courteous you can find, so loving and willing to do anything for you," he proclaimed.[76] Private Emanuel Billouin echoed Dadd's laudatory assessment. "We are all treated very nicely by the people of Seaford who are simply delighted with some of us," the Trinidadian soldier boasted.[77] Chaplain Alfred Horner, reflecting on his wartime service with the BWIR, also fondly recalled the regiment's brief stay in England. "One thing I shall always be thankful for, and that is the magnificent way in which we were received," Hormer declared. "People at the stations, at level crossings, in the streets as we passed, and from the houses as we walked, cheered us to the echo. Eager hands brought refreshments to us and many willing helpers tended to our wants."[78]

In their letters home, BWIR soldiers reported that they received an especially warm embrace from white English women. According to many servicemen, English women showered them with kisses and other public displays of affection, intimate acts that would have been deeply taboo in the colonies. According to Felix Toraille, "a few damsels" deluged him with kisses while he was eating lunch at a train station.[79] Another Trinidadian soldier claimed that women blew kisses at West Indian servicemen whenever they encountered the soldiers away from camp.[80] G. J. Dadd even suggested that English women in Seaford preferred dating West Indian soldiers over local civilian men. "Plenty of girls. They love the boys in khaki," he exclaimed. "They detest walking with civilians. They love the darkies!"[81]

[120]   CHAPTER 3

Initial accounts likewise offered idyllic portraits of Seaford and North Camp, the training base where the BWIR was stationed. The coastal hamlet, one local commenter reported, was "bathed in sunshine . . . and the weather could not have been more propitious for acclimating the newly arrived troops from the tropics."[82] Another writer praised military officials for stationing the BWIR near Seaford, insisting that they "could hardly have chosen a better place from the health point of view" for West Indian soldiers.[83] According to the West Indian Contingent Committee, which sent a delegation to tour North Camp in October 1915 to welcome BWIR troops, the soldiers bunked in clean, spacious wooden huts supplied with extra blankets and "rows of hot shower-baths."[84] The committee also claimed that West Indian soldiers enjoyed "far more substantial" meals in the military than they had consumed at home in the Caribbean. "A Chinaman from British Guiana," the committee noted, "assumed the duties of cook, in which capacity he was giving every satisfaction."[85] These favorable accounts, penned by soldiers and other observers in England, were selectively excerpted and republished in Caribbean newspapers and functioned as unofficial recruitment literature for the BWIR.[86]

The reality at North Camp was far more rigorous. The exacting training regimen was designed to transform BWIR soldiers, the vast majority of whom had no previous military experience, into disciplined troops. Once the men arrived, as one Jamaican serviceman recalled, they "started their 'breaking in' to the strict discipline and hard work of the Army."[87] The military socialization process emphasized obedience to commanding officers, physical fitness, uniformity, and unit cohesion. During the week, the reveille sounded before daybreak at 6 a.m. sharp. Soldiers began their day by cleaning their quarters for inspection. At 8 a.m., they ate breakfast and then drilled and paraded with their platoon or company until lunch at 1 p.m. In the afternoon, soldiers completed further drills, physical training, and route marches until evening tea at 5 p.m. Then, they enjoyed some leisure time before the "Last Post" bugle call signaled the end of the day at 10 p.m.[88]

The arduous drill and exercise regimen at North Camp taxed soldiers physically and mentally. During route marches, soldiers tramped nine miles or more through muddy terrain. They also completed rifle and bayonet training, participated in strenuous physical workouts, and attended lectures.[89] Reflecting on his first two months at North Camp, Sergeant J. A. Graham acknowledged the harsh nature of soldiering. "Since we have been over [in England], we quite see that the soldier life is not a light one, or one to be taken up lightly, but one that is a stern reality," he stressed.[90] Even BWIR soldiers who had previously served in local militias in the colonies found the training to be exhausting. In a letter to a friend, Emanuel Billouin stated that he was required to "work and work very hard" for up to sixteen hours per day at North Camp. Life as a private in the BWIR, he insisted, was much more demanding than his previous role as a gunner in the Trinidad Artillery Corps. "Soldiering out here is very different to what it is in Trinidad," he observed, "discipline is carried out to the hilt here, no joking and drilling very hard." Despite the rigors of military life, Billouin insisted that he and his BWIR comrades should demonstrate stoic resolve. As "a soldier you must not grumble," he maintained.[91]

Unlike Billouin, some BWIR soldiers did complain openly about the conditions at North Camp. In October 1915, a group of soldiers staged a brief strike after not receiving their pay. Led by Private Henry Somerset of British Guiana, the strikers wrote "no money, no work" in chalk and refused to parade with their company.[92] While the exact number of striking soldiers is unknown, the group included men from Trinidad as well as British Guiana. In response to the strike, Colonel A. E. Barchard accused Somerset of insubordination, confiscated his military uniform, and ordered that he be sent back to the colonies with a small group of other West Indian soldiers characterized as "undesirables." Somerset sailed to British Guiana under military guard and was officially discharged from the BWIR in November 1915. In an interview, Somerset defended his actions and accused military officials of targeting him because he "spoke for his rights."[93] Even after the strike, soldiers continued to experience significant delays in receiving their pay. In January 1916, a BWIR officer at North Camp reported that he and his men were "stony broke" because they still had not been paid.[94]

On the weekends, soldiers relished the opportunity to leave camp. Before departing, they had to report their travel plans and secure a pass from their commanding officer. Some BWIR troops took advantage of discounted train and bus fares for soldiers and journeyed to nearby towns. In a letter home, Private Egbert Regis explained that he received time off each week for "a walk and holiday" from Saturday at noon until Sunday at midnight. During that time, Regis traveled to the seaside resort town of Brighton, where he claimed that the local women were "awfully nice" to West Indian soldiers and hailed them as heroes.[95] Private Walter Douglas used his time off to explore Brighton and Newhaven. During his sojourns away from camp, Douglas interacted with many English civilians, who responded to him with a mix of curiosity and gratitude. According to the

Trinidadian soldier, English women gave him beer, cigarettes, and chocolates, while also "ask[ing] all sorts of questions" about his background and reasons for enlisting.[96] BWIR soldiers also participated in events organized by local friendly societies. For instance, West Indian servicemen who were members of the Ancient Order of Foresters attended meetings of the friendly society's branch in Seaford.[97] Other soldiers used their time away from camp to attend church. Dozens of men from the BWIR were confirmed in a special service led by the Bishop of Lewes in England. Praising the men as symbols of both religious and imperial virtue, a local newspaper declared that it was "inspiring to see the reverent attitude of the soldiers who, being 4,000 miles from home, discharge their duty to the Empire and found a warm welcome in their mother church."[98]

While BWIR soldiers often took solace in their interactions with English civilians, they also reported that some whites in the "Mother Country" harbored racist stereotypes about black colonials. During their encounters with BWIR troops, many whites were shocked that the men spoke English fluently. "That the West Indian was coal black and could speak English correctly was a great source of worry" to some English people, Arthur Cipriani noted.[99] Similarly, Egbert Regis claimed that "the ladies of Seaford" had been told that West Indians were "all savages."[100] Some white Britons also derisively referred to BWIR soldiers as "blackie" or "darkies."[101] Central to these stereotypes was the idea that black colonial subjects were intellectually and culturally inferior to white Englishmen and that the Caribbean colonies were marked by endemic poverty and disorder.[102] Thus, even when donning the King's uniform, West Indians in England confronted stigmas attached to blackness and colonial subjecthood.

BWIR soldiers faced other challenges in England, too. As winter approached, they endured freezing temperatures, torrential rain, and declining hours of daylight. The "hastily knocked up" wooden huts where BWIR soldiers lodged provided scant protection from the elements.[103] At North Camp, for example, each hut housed approximately 30 soldiers and was heated by a single wood stove.[104] Writing to a friend in November 1915, Sergeant Bernard Brown reported that soldiers at North Camp had been issued five blankets apiece to stave off the cold. Despite keeping the "fire lighted day and night" in his hut, Brown complained that it was so frigid inside that he could "hardly hold the pen" to finish drafting his letter.[105] According to G. J. Dadd, Seaford was "positively mid-night dark" by 4 p.m. "You are just freezing, your hands, feet, ears, and nose," he wrote, and "you cannot stand still for 2 minutes you have to be on the move so as to get a little warmth."[106] Like their comrades at North Camp, BWIR troops stationed at Withnoe Camp near Plymouth also faced "particularly trying" weather. According to one account, the camp was inundated with "incessant rain, accompanied by heavy squalls and piercing cold winds."[107] Some BWIR officers readily acknowledged the heavy toll that England's winter weather exacted on the regiment. After enduring a cold, rainy Christmas Day at North Camp, Captain John Tough confessed that the men's "thoughts went back to their sunny homes among their own people." According to Tough, BWIR soldiers were desperately "longing for a sight of the sun again and a little of its warmth."[108]

In England, as on the troopships, soldiers soon fell ill. The most common illnesses were respiratory infections such as pneumonia, influenza, and bronchitis. Documenting the spread of illness in the BWIR, a Jamaican officer blamed the poor weather in England for decimating the regiment. "The weather conditions are frightful, rain all day and tramping in mud and slush," he reported. "Owing to the weather conditions, nearly all men and others have been laid up with influenza and colds. Our sick parade consists of about three hundred men." Likewise, J. A. Graham bemoaned how the "cold pierces through one's bones" in England, causing frostbite and other ailments. "When it's muddy, I feel it much worse as sometimes we have to stand for half an hour at a time in the mud on parade," he wrote. "You must know how frozen feet feel. They burn as much as when fire touches them."[109] Outbreaks of the mumps, measles, and meningitis also sickened many soldiers.[110] Ultimately, while stationed at North Camp, at least nineteen BWIR soldiers died and many more were hospitalized.[111]

Poems written by soldiers at Surrey Convalescent Home in Seaford provide a rare glimpse into how West Indians navigated illness and hospitalization in the early years of the war.[112] While scholars have carefully analyzed BWIR soldiers' experiences in English hospitals during the war's final year—particularly the violent upheavals at Belmont Road Auxiliary Hospital in Liverpool in 1918—we know little about soldiers' experiences at military hospitals in Seaford.[113] In their poems, BWIR soldiers at Surrey Convalescent Home described the intense pain and disappointment they experienced when becoming sick, while also expressing gratitude to the English nurses and orderlies who cared for them. Writing from their hospital beds, the men continued to affirm their status as soldiers and the rhetoric of imperial patriotism, even as they reckoned with the physical costs of military service. Private Jacob Cunningham wrote several short poems reflecting on his hospitalization in England. In an untitled poem, he extols the kindness and expert care that he received from medical staff while undergoing treatment for pneumonia.

> The far off W. Indies my Home
> At my country's call I have come
> But an illness I didn't expect
> Introduced me to Dear Old Surrey Home
>
> October 30th was the day
> When pneumonia showed me the way
> How English hearts were kind
> The like I'll never find

In a second poem, "To Sister Burton," Cunningham praises a Red Cross nurse for attending to him when his body was overcome with pain. He simultaneously invokes the agony of illness and the relief that he experienced during his hospitalization.

> I'm only a West Indian Soldier
> And I was dying as fast as can be
> For my chest was racking with pain
> That I thought wasn't natural to man
> And though I can't find words to express it
> I'm trying these few words to tell
> About you, kind Sister of the Red Cross
> May God Bless, help and prosper you well.

Like Cunningham, Private Lionel French also credited the staff at Surrey Convalescent Home for helping him to recover. In an untitled poem, French commends the "careful lot of sisters" and devoted orderlies who attended to him while he was suffering from "fever and cold" and proclaims that he will remember their kindness for as long as he lives.[114]

Unable to participate in drill and route marches, some sick soldiers longed to reunite with their healthy comrades. In an untitled poem, Cunningham recounts the experience of watching BWIR troops on parade from his hospital room. He demands that the nurses place him near the window so that he can observe soldiers' march by.

> Take me to the window Sister fling it open wide
> Bring a slipper for my feet and pull the blind aside
> Don't say another word sister, I'll give you no reply

For I've ears and eyes for nothing else
When our lads are marching by

Hear our bugles blowing and our big drums roll
I have a queer sensation away down in my soul
Hear the street a-ringing with the trample of their feet
Oh, it's fine to see our soldiers a marching up a street[115]

Cunningham captures the visual and sonic spectacle of soldiers on the march, describing the sounds of drums, bugles, and marching feet alongside the phallic imagery of a "khaki column" of uniformed men. He contrasted his own condition as a "shill and useless" invalid with that of his "strong and straight" comrades. He concludes the poem by asserting his desire to rejoin his fellow soldiers on parade, declaring that the "queer sensation" he experiences by watching soldiers on the march has transformed his broken body and compelled him to "go straight to the war."[116]

Faced with widespread illness among the troops, BWIR officers lobbied the War Office to transfer the regiment from England to a more favorable climate. During a meeting in London in early 1916, Lieutenant Colonel Wood-Hill "implored" officials to relocate the BWIR "as soon as possible to some warmer place . . . where there would be less wastage from disease."[117] The War Office ultimately decided to move the three BWIR battalions stationed in England to Egypt. During the winter of 1916, BWIR soldiers departed North Camp and set sail for Alexandria. That spring and summer, BWIR soldiers at Withnoe Camp followed suit.[118] While small numbers of sick and disabled soldiers would remain in England for medical treatment, no BWIR battalions would be stationed in the metropole after 1916.[119] Instead, BWIR soldiers would spend the remainder of the war serving in foreign lands in Europe, the Middle East, and East Africa, fighting simultaneously for respect within the British Army and for the Allied cause.

"Le soldat noir aimable": The BWIR on the Western Front

Traveling on a military troopship to France, Etienne Dupuch learned a devastating lesson about race and rank in the British Army. On the ship, the Bahamian private encountered "a battalion of magnificent Sikhs" from India.[120] Awestruck by the turbaned soldiers, Dupuch marveled at the Sikhs' towering physique and dignified presence. "This was the first time I was brought into contact with Indian troops," he recalled. "I thought Sikhs were the handsomest men I had ever seen." Dupuch, who befriended several Sikh soldiers during the voyage, watched with disgust as English Tommies harassed and abused Sikh servicemen. After witnessing a white private physically assault a Sikh sergeant and escape punishment, Dupuch condemned the treatment of "native troops" in the British armed forces. "It was then for the first time that I realized that the lowest, dirtiest, scrubbiest Englishman was considered superior to the finest Indian," he wrote.[121]

Dupuch's fraught journey to France was a harbinger of his experiences on the Western Front. While deployed on French soil, Dupuch would meet more colonial subjects from throughout the British and French empires, forever broadening his understanding of race and colonialism. The teenaged private would enjoy moments of genuine camaraderie with fellow Allied soldiers as he navigated the cosmopolitan social worlds of the war, including forging friendships with white servicemen from France. Yet, like the Sikh sergeant he befriended aboard the ship, Dupuch would also confront "discrimination in many forms" and the stigma of being a noncombatant manual laborer in a combat zone.[122]

The Allied powers' wartime mobilization of non-European troops and laborers radically transformed the racial demographics of the French Republic. Before World War I, France's black population was even smaller than England's; approximately five thousand black people resided in France, mostly in Paris and Marseille.[123] Beginning in 1914, upward of 600,000 foreigners migrated to France to serve in the war effort, including 300,000 people from overseas.[124] Deployed to provincial towns as well as in urban communes, foreign soldiers and workers spread across the French countryside and integrated previously all-white areas. Civilian contract workers from Egypt, India, South Africa, and China toiled across France, performing myriad tasks to support combat operations. Volunteers from New Zealand's Māori Pioneer Battalion constructed trenches, roads, and light railways in northern France, while black Canadians worked as loggers in the remote Jura Mountains. Men from the Fijian Labour Corps mixed with African American soldiers on the docks in Marseille and other coastal cities.[125] And, in an unprecedented decision, France deployed 140,000 of its own *troupes indigènes* to the Western Front to defend the metropole.

Struck by the ethnic and racial heterogeneity in France, Alfred Horner marveled at the "curious medley of badges, uniforms and dialects" at St. Martin's Rest Camp in Boulogne. "English, Scotch, Irish and Welsh, they were all there, and Colonials by the score."[126] Military garrisons and work sites generated frequent (and at times fraught) interracial exchange, establishing militarized contact zones in the heart of Western Europe. In her foundational study of European travel writing, literary scholar Mary Louise Pratt advanced the term "contact zone" to "invoke the spatial and temporal copresence of subjects previously separated by geographic and historical disjunctions, and whose trajectories now intersect." Contact zones, Pratt observes, are marked by "copresence, interaction, interlocking understandings and practices, often within radically asymmetrical relations of power."[127] For West Indian troops, the extraordinarily cosmopolitan milieu of military encampments and work sites in France offered new forms of sociability, including sanctioned and illicit forays across the color line. Fraternization among the diverse military units on the Western Front comprised quotidian encounters at work, in the barracks, at sporting events, or in hospitals, as well as dramatic confrontations in response to perceived slights and acts of violence.

Race, colonial status, gender, and military rank structured how BWIR soldiers experienced France, foreclosing access to combat duty while generating exposure to a broad spectrum of servicemen and civilians. Used as a peripatetic labor force, West Indians traipsed back and forth across France between 1916 and 1918, working in over forty communes in addition to the cities of Arras, Marseille, Rouen, and Boulogne.[128] BWIR soldiers straddled the divide between infantry troops and labor corps, sometimes enjoying the privileges granted to Allied servicemen, such as service in French *estaminets*, but also facing the indignity of serving in auxiliary roles.

In all their interracial encounters, BWIR soldiers sought to capitalize on their unique status as literate, English-speaking soldiers—a rarity among nonwhite colonial British troops—to move between spaces reserved for Europeans and those relegated to "natives."[129] The writings of those who served in the regiment provide richly textured accounts of cross-racial contact on the Western Front, allowing us to map connections between groups of workers often studied in isolation. For instance, accounts by Etienne Dupuch and Alfred Horner suggest that West Indian troops interacted with the 140,000 Chinese civilian laborers who were stationed in France and Belgium. Chinese laborers, most of whom were peasants from the northern provinces of Shandong and Hebei, were recruited by France and Britain to perform noncombatant work on the docks, in munitions plants, and on road building and construction projects.[130] Whereas French and British military officials questioned the ability of black soldiers to withstand France's temperate climate, they insisted that Chinese workers could easily endure frigid European winters. "The coolie

FIGURE 3.3. BWIR soldiers with Salvation Army members in France. Social History Images/Alamy Stock Photo.

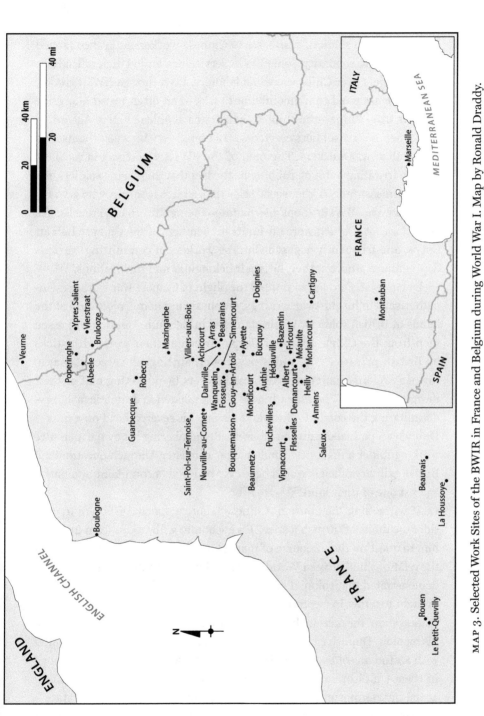

MAP 3. Selected Work Sites of the BWIR in France and Belgium during World War I. Map by Ronald Draddy.

is a splendid and versatile worker, inured to hardship and almost indifferent to the weather," one British officer confidently reported.[131]

West Indian soldiers' responses to Chinese workers in France ranged from disdain to solidarity. Some BWIR servicemen lorded their official status as soldiers over Chinese civilian laborers. Even though BWIR troops, also, were assigned to noncombatant tasks—and often toiled alongside workers from China—they touted their status as enlisted men. According to Horner, BWIR soldiers erected a strict boundary between themselves and civilian war workers. The men of the BWIR, the chaplain recalled, had "an irritating habit of 'rubbing in' the fact that they, being soldiers, are on an immeasurably higher social scale than a mere labourer, who is working for a wage." BWIR troops also flaunted their ability to use French cafés and *estaminets*, which were off-limits to members of the Chinese Labour Corps, and frequently accused Chinese workers of committing "various depredations amongst their kit, their belongings and their rations."[132]

By contrast, Dupuch recounted the plight of Chinese war workers sympathetically in his postwar writings, emphasizing their exploitation at the hands of British soldiers. While stationed in Belgium, Dupuch witnessed men from the Chinese Labour Corps "driven at their work with sticks by British privates." The unit's paymaster, an English sergeant major, further exploited unlettered Chinese laborers by pocketing half of their meager wages.[133] When the Chinese men retaliated in dramatic fashion— decapitating the corrupt officer and placing his severed head on a desk— Dupuch empathized with the laborers. Remembering his own experience working under a dishonest English quartermaster, Dupuch questioned if British military officials would have ever believed "a complaint by a native against one of their kind."[134]

If witnessing the abuse of Chinese laborers spurred Dupuch to consider the limits of "British justice," his encounter with troops from India led him to question the discourse of martial interracialism. Scholars studying the relationship between World War I and postwar anti-imperialism have demonstrated that colonial subjects from Africa, Asia, and the Caribbean, brought together in unprecedented numbers, were able to exchange information about the marginalization they faced in their respective homes.[135] In his memoir, Dupuch claimed that he was radicalized by a chance encounter with an Indian soldier on the Western Front. One night, while garrisoned in France, a disoriented Indian serviceman stumbled into Dupuch's tent at the quartermaster's store. Recognizing the soldier's distressed state— "hungry, dirty, [and] almost naked"—the BWIR private provided his unexpected visitor with food, clothing, and blankets. The two colonial soldiers "talked throughout the night," swapping stories about their experiences as British subjects. According to the BWIR private, he was horrified to learn about the oppression Indians endured under the British Raj. "He told me things about the inferior position held by Indians in their own country. It was a painful, almost unbelievable story," wrote Dupuch. "It was then that I began to dream of the time when I might be instrumental in helping to break down racial barriers in the Bahamas."[136]

"Just a Little Job to Help the Madame": Friendships and Erotic Intimacies Across the Color Line

The "stranger intimacy" engendered on the Western Front included not only interracial associations among nonwhite laborers and enlisted men but also relationships between BWIR soldiers and Frenchmen and women.[137] Reflecting on his wartime service with the BWIR, Horner fondly recalled the way in which French civilians embraced West Indian troops. It was "perfectly astonishing how our boys managed to wheedle themselves into the hearts and homes of the civil population," he mused. Following a long day's work, BWIR soldiers often ventured away from the military barracks to socialize with local villagers. "I remember well a little row of houses very close to our camp in every one of which, during the evening, B.W.I. boys might have been seen huddled round the stove . . . doing odd jobs for the lady of the house, regaling themselves with coffee," the chaplain remembered, "and so far as they were able carrying on conversation in which 'home'—so very different in every way from what they were experiencing—had a prominent place." When BWIR officers investigated these private nighttime gatherings between West Indian soldiers and French women, local villagers dispelled their fears, insisting that the men were "welcome guests, exceedingly polite and good mannered."[138] And, in the words of BWIR servicemen, their voluntary exploits in French homes were simply "just a little job to help the madame."[139]

BWIR soldiers also used their time in France to compare the treatment of black men under the tricolor with their treatment under British rule. With remarkable uniformity, West Indians portrayed their interactions with French *poilus* [infantrymen] as collegial and free from racial prejudice.[140] Sergeant Willie Jeffers, describing his wartime experiences, spoke with "the highest terms of respect for the French Nation, and their square deal to every man irrespective of nationality, creed, or color."[141] A group of BWIR soldiers from Jamaica offered a "chorus of praise" for "the kindness shown them by the French." French hospitality was "full, unwavering, and done with a most charming good fellowship," they asserted.[142] Like African American servicemen, who penned glowing and widely circulated accounts of French generosity, BWIR soldiers cherished the camaraderie of French troops.[143] "Everywhere as we met the soldiers of France our own men fraternised excellently," Horner reported. "They would join them in cafes, they would meet them in *estaminets* and they would compete with them in sports." Communicating through an "odd mixture of French and English," BWIR soldiers swapped war stories, exchanged cigarettes, and compared the "various merits of their respective countries, their rifles, [and] their equipment" with French servicemen.[144]

Horner rationalized the social bonds between BWIR soldiers and French citizens by invoking culturalist arguments about Frenchmen's "Latin temperament." Praising the "polite amiability and geniality" of French *poilus*, he credited French soldiers and civilians with turning West Indian servicemen into "society personages." According to the BWIR senior chaplain, the "innate charm and courtesy of the French character" had an "irresistible appeal to the West Indian." However, Horner quickly undermined his apparent celebration of French sociability by portraying Frenchmen and West Indians as "children of laughter" who are "happiest in a simple life."[145] Frenchmen's Latin temperament and willingness to socialize with black colonials, he further implied, ultimately weakened France's colonial prowess. In a revealing passage, the chaplain issued the following back-handed compliment: "The fact remains that although the French may not be the born colonizers the British are, they seem to possess in a wonderful fashion the happy knack of making other races feel at least very much at home with them."[146]

In the chaplain's narrative, interracial encounters between the BWIR and European troops reinforced stock racial stereotypes of black West Indians, offering proof that the dislocations of war did not undermine the established racial order. Amid the violent and disorienting upheavals of modern warfare, the trope of the ever-faithful and jovial black soldier offered a comforting counterpoint—and a compelling example of a united British Empire. Indeed, Horner omitted any references to interracial tension among troops, instead suggesting that both British and French servicemen embraced the men of the BWIR as sources of entertainment or as brown-skinned mascots. "If a canteen full of Tommies can only get our boys singing or dancing they are contented, and many a time . . . the role of society entertainer has fallen upon BWI boys," Horner boasted.[147] In another anecdote, the senior chaplain recounted a concert in a French village where BWIR soldiers "lustily caroled" a variety of "Jamaican and other West Indian tunes" before a rapt audience of white spectators. Even when hospitalized, the author insisted, a BWIR soldier served as "the pet and plaything" of the white staff and patients.[148] As Richard Smith observes, the trope of the "black soldier-entertainer" positioned West Indians as both "exotic and knowable" while simultaneously buttressing "imperial hierarchies of race."[149]

BWIR soldiers' most transgressive forays across the color line were their liaisons with white French women. The massive deployment of nonwhite colonial soldiers and laborers on the Western Front during World War I fueled fears of illicit interracial encounters, and panicked authorities across Western Europe feared that sexual liaisons between white women and men of African or Asian ancestry from the colonies would destabilize the bourgeois racial and sexual order that buttressed European imperialism.[150] Interracial sex on the Western Front, as historian Richard Fogarty suggests, dangerously reversed "the more frequent pairing of white men and indigenous women overseas."[151] Intimate relationships between white women and colonial subjects threatened to undermine "the prestige of the European woman," the purity of European racial stocks through the production of mixed-race offspring, and the socio-legal boundaries that separated subjects and citizens. Sex across the racial divide also placed white men in competition with black and Asian colonials for access to white women's bodies and reproductive labor. The competition over women among Europeans and nonwhite foreigners led to violent clashes, including incidences of murder, in wartime France.[152]

The state's "mobilization of femininity" in wartime France, as historian Margaret Darrow has detailed, urged women to serve the war effort through gender-specific roles as mothers, nurses, charity volunteers, and *marraines de guerre* [war godmothers].[153] "Feminine patriotism can be translated synthetically by the word, defense, and by extension, preservation, center, birth, giving life and protecting it," insisted journalist Marie de la Hire, "while the other, masculine patriotism has always meant conquest, attack, combat, vengeance, blood, and death."[154] Thus, French women were primarily viewed as patriotic care workers—despite the fact that 700,000 women were employed in the armaments industry by 1918—and their unpaid affective and reproductive labor took on heightened importance as public service to the nation.[155] Military propagandists applauded mothers who willingly sacrificed their sons on behalf of *la patrie*. The French press celebrated *marraines* who boosted troops' morale by writing to European and colonial soldiers at the front. And moralizing literature praised dutiful female volunteers who nursed wounded and convalescing servicemen.[156]

But French women's patriotic labor brought them into intimate contact with colonial troops of color as well as created new opportunities to contest bourgeois gender norms at home, work, and leisure. BWIR soldiers' encounters with French women occurred beyond the guarded confines of military camps, during evening excursions to neighboring towns, while in transit, or during furloughs. Whereas Horner was unwilling to broach the possibility of erotic encounters between French women and BWIR soldiers—emphasizing the "friendly" nature of West Indian troops' interactions with local women—Etienne Dupuch wrote candidly about his amorous trysts in France. In the Bahamian private's account, French women were cast both as surrogate mothers and as potential paramours. On the one hand, Dupuch recalled how French mothers rescued him during moments of difficulty, including one ill-fated route march where he fainted on a remote road in the countryside. In these renderings, French women's maternal devotion functioned as a feminized form of service to the war effort and allowed them to be seen as fictive kin for BWIR troops deployed far from home.

On the other hand, the Bahamian private also detailed his romantic encounters with French women as a defining aspect of his passage to adulthood. While stationed near the eastern city of Dijon, the teenaged soldier met a "beautiful young girl" at a local postcard store. Despite the obvious language barrier—Dupuch stressed that the young woman "didn't speak English" and that he could not speak French—they "carried on a delightful conversation" for several afternoons "with the aid of a pocket French-English dictionary." Although the young woman was unwilling to introduce Dupuch to her wealthy family because of his lowly standing as a private—and perhaps due to his status as a mixed-race colonial subject—Dupuch remained "moonstruck" by his French "dream girl." When the BWIR private ultimately received orders to leave Dijon after his unit was deployed to another town, he marched by his French "maiden" one final time, noting the tears "streaming down her cheeks." Reminiscing decades after the war, he opined, "Looking back I have often thought of our brief encounter as one of the pleasantest experiences of my army life."[157]

If metropolitan officials looked askance at interracial erotic liaisons, West Indian troops welcomed the companionship of local white women. Soldiers' erotic encounters with French women included flirtatious exchanges in local *estaminets*, illicit encounters with sex workers, and monogamous relationships. As Glenford Howe argues, partnerships with

European women constituted a "critical part" of soldiers' "responses to the problems of isolation, boredom and sexual deprivation."[158] One BWIR volunteer from British Honduras even publicly announced his intention to bring home a French wife after his tour of duty overseas.[159] Dupuch applauded French women's willingness to have sex with colonial soldiers, citing it as proof of their liberal sexual mores. "French women had the reputation of being always ready, able and willing to give glow to a passing moment in life," he enthused.

Yet, when analyzing French women's transgressive displays of erotic autonomy, he reverted to Victorian-era stereotypes of women as sentimental beings. In Dupuch's estimation, French women viewed sex as "something clean and precious" and, unlike their male partners, "remembered and cherished" every erotic encounter. Although "the average French woman seemed always accommodating in an intimate relationship," he reasoned, her "animal instinct" was ultimately tempered by her "precious spiritual side." And, to buttress his claims about French women's sexual propriety, Dupuch wrote approvingly of a French woman who kicked out her lover—an officer in the BWIR—after he showed her pornographic postcards.[160]

West Indian soldiers' celebratory accounts of friendships and sexual liaisons with French citizens buttressed the myth of French racial egalitarianism—and offered an implicit critique of racial discrimination in the British Empire. In their writings, BWIR troops contrasted the virulent and often violent racism of their white British counterparts with the friendliness of French *poilus* and civilians. "By contrast with the Anglo-Saxon race, the French had a good relationship with their African colonists," insisted Dupuch.[161] Like African American servicemen, whose laudatory descriptions of French colorblindness led many to believe that there was no racial discrimination in metropolitan France, BWIR servicemen did not acknowledge the plight of French colonial soldiers or the deep-seated antagonism toward civilian workers from the French Empire.[162] Instead, they composed sentimental accounts of French hospitality while carefully documenting acts of racial chauvinism by white British soldiers.

Conclusion

The racial climate in wartime France was far chillier than BWIR soldiers let on. France's "wartime experiment in multiculturalism," Tyler Stovall contends, "was undertaken reluctantly" and sparked fevered debate about the boundaries of French national identity.[163] While some French soldiers fully embraced nonwhite servicemen as comrades in arms, others reacted hostilely to the presence of colonial troops. French officers, for example, claimed that *troupes indigènes* were incapable of highly specialized technical work because of their supposedly innate mental inferiority.[164] Invoking racist and colonialist stereotypes to assess the fighting prowess of soldiers of color, these officers privately characterized West African troops as "savage" and "childlike" while noting Madagascans' supposed "physical frailty" and "lack of a warrior spirit."[165] More troublingly, some *poilus* physically assaulted colonials of color stationed in the metropole. French infantrymen and officers stationed in the Meuse region attacked Vietnamese troops on several occasions, including murdering two soldiers in 1917.[166] At times, French civilians also expressed fear and revulsion when black soldiers from the colonies encamped near their homes. Residents in the rural seaside village of Fréjus in southeastern France panicked when news spread that *tirailleurs* from West Africa would be stationed in their community for the winter. Vividly recalling the reactions of her neighbors, painter Lucie Cousturier wrote:

> What would happen to us? wailed the farm wives, we could no longer let our chickens roam near these thieves, or let our clothes dry outside or the fruit ripen on the trees. We could no longer let our little girls run along the roads among these savages. We ourselves would no longer dare go out alone to mow our lawns or gather firewood. Just imagine if one were captured by these gorillas.[167]

Therefore, instead of taking West Indian soldiers' narratives of French egalitarianism at face value, we might best understand these accounts as part of a strategic intervention to contest racism within the British armed forces and in the British Empire. Soldiers would tackle these issues with heightened focus and intensity in their final year of military service through their urgent writings and in militant mass protests.

CHAPTER FOUR

An "Insubordinate Spirit Prevailed"

RIGHTS, RESPECTABILITY, AND THE BATTLE AGAINST DISCRIMINATION IN THE BRITISH ARMY

WRITING FROM PALESTINE in the hot and dry summer months of 1918, a BWIR soldier secretly chronicled his wartime experiences. In an unsigned letter to his cousin in Trinidad, the private painted a harrowing portrait of military life: "We was simple cent away like a pack of cows to be sold to any purchaser. . . . It is true that soldiering is a hard thing, but with our unit it is twice as hard as it is with other units." Despite nearly three years of service in a combat zone, the soldier reported, his commanding officers insisted that West Indian servicemen had not "train[ed] enough for the firing line." Thus, instead of battling Turkish forces in Palestine, the soldier endured years of backbreaking manual labor, unremitting verbal assaults from his superiors, and an epidemic of influenza that sent his comrades "pouring into hospital by scores." After witnessing fellow soldiers "tied hands [and] feet" with rope for refusing to work, the beleaguered private questioned how supposedly civilized Englishmen could treat West Indian troops with such vicious disregard. "Do you think it right for such a thing to happen among a set of people who think they are the most civilised people in the world" and "who generally say England is fighting for civilization?" he asked caustically. Predicting that there was "going to be a mutiny" in his battalion due to the rampant discrimination and abuse they endured, the soldier implored his cousin to submit his account to the *Port of Spain Gazette*, Trinidad's most widely circulated

[137]

newspaper, so that civilians on the home front could know what was really happening to "their boys" in the BWIR.[1]

The young serviceman had been one of the earliest volunteers for the BWIR, joining the regiment during the fevered recruitment campaign in 1915. Yet, over the course of three years, his views of the war and West Indians' role in it had undergone a dramatic shift. "I now see that we were really not required out here, otherwise we would have been put into better uses as soldiers," he confessed. Angry that the "cold footed Englishmen" entrusted to lead his battalion refused to speak out on behalf of their men, the private mocked his superiors for "sheltering themself from bullets . . . instead of going [to] fight for their mother country." Unwilling to suffer further abuse, the soldier declared that he would have "preferred to die any sort of death rather than . . . undergoing what is happening at present" with his unit. Palestine, he concluded bitterly, was a "cursed country."[2]

The soldier's damning exposé never reached his cousin in Port of Spain or the Trinidadian press. Rather, military censors at British Army General Headquarters in Bir Salem, Palestine, intercepted and confiscated his letter less than a week after it was posted.[3] Citing the "nature of the letter" and the fact that it was "intended for publication in the press," military officials launched a wide-ranging investigation to uncover its author.[4] Postal officials used the army postmark on the envelope to trace the letter to the First Battalion of the BWIR; Lieutenant Colonel Charles Wood-Hill, the battalion's commanding officer, then conducted an internal probe to identify the letter writer.[5] When the colonel's investigation ended "without success," General Edmund Allenby, Commander-in-Chief of the Egyptian Expeditionary Force and the highest-ranking British officer in the Middle Eastern theater, took the extraordinary step of enlisting the assistance of Trinidad's governor, John Chancellor.[6] Working with the colony's Inspector General of the Constabulary, authorities in Trinidad ultimately identified the anonymous correspondent as Private Charles Roberts, an unmarried black soldier from the island of Tobago.[7]

While Private Roberts aimed to expose the indignities of military life through the press, higher-ranking BWIR servicemen, particularly the regiment's black and colored noncommissioned officers, generally elected to address their concerns through formal petitions to civil and military authorities. Grenadian sergeant W. E. Julien, who served alongside Roberts in Palestine in the First Battalion, risked his privileged standing by signing a petition that condemned the War Office's decision to exclude BWIR soldiers from the substantial pay increase mandated in Army Order No. 1 of 1918. The petition, dispatched to Barbados governor Charles

O'Brien in the autumn of 1918, was signed by forty-one other soldiers from the First and Second Battalions, thirty-eight of whom were noncommissioned officers.[8]

While chastising the War Office, Julien and his comrades took care to present themselves as respectable men: "taxpayers" and "loyal subjects of His Majesty." The petitioners appealed to O'Brien for his "co-operation" as a potential patron and ally and "respectfully beg[ged]" the governor to lobby the War Office on their behalf. They strategically sidestepped the contentious allegations of verbal abuse, dismal working conditions, and exclusion from combat that animated Private Roberts's searing personal account.[9] Rather, Sergeant Julien and his comrades articulated their grievances using the language of martial interracialism, noting that BWIR soldiers were "treated as British soldiers in equipment, training, and discipline" and had been "led to believe" that they would be "treated as Imperial Troops and receive any and all benefits accruing to such troops."[10]

The soldiers were similarly careful to frame their protest as a principled stance against discrimination in the military rather than a ploy for more money. "We would like it to be understood that the motive of this memorandum is not so much to get the pecuniary benefits from which we have been denied," they explained, "as to bring before His Excellency that we are alive to the fact that as West Indians we have been unfairly discriminated against." By accusing the War Office of violating the celebrated principles of martial interracialism and mutual obligation, the petitioners presented their protest as an extension of their patriotism rather than an act of disloyalty or greed.[11]

By reading these two accounts in dialogue with one another, we can begin to uncover the range of political perspectives and protest strategies that fueled BWIR soldiers' campaign against discrimination in the British armed forces. Roberts and Julien were part of a remarkable groundswell of activism that began during the last months of the war and crested after the Armistice. While individual West Indian soldiers had challenged discrimination, dire working conditions, and slights to their manhood from the very beginning of the war, soldiers' activism reached its peak intensity between July 1918 and March 1919. During the second half of 1918 alone, more than 220 BWIR soldiers signed petitions to British civilian and military authorities, while other servicemen echoed the call for equal treatment through individual (and often anonymous) letters of complaint. Most dramatically, BWIR soldiers stationed near the Mediterranean port city of Taranto, Italy, mutinied in December 1918, sparking the most violent protest in the regiment's history.

FIGURE 4.1. BWIR soldiers in the Middle East. Jamaica Archives and Records Department, Orrett Photographs Collection, 7-130-1.

Four interrelated grievances animated BWIR soldiers' battle against discrimination: the regiment's exclusion from Army Order No. 1, the prohibition against granting commissions to nonwhite soldiers, abusive treatment by commanding officers, and the practice of assigning BWIR units to sanitation and fatigue duties. Over the course of their yearlong drive to redress these grievances, soldiers forged new intraimperial alliances, experimented with various forms of collective protest, and mulled over the possibilities for equal treatment and opportunity inside the British Army and beyond.

This chapter excavates BWIR soldiers' multi-sited campaign against discrimination during the final year of their military service. It follows servicemen as they mobilized in two distinct geographic spheres—the Middle Eastern theater (Egypt, Palestine, and Mesopotamia) and the southern Italian coast—and participated in a transatlantic debate over race, status, and respectability in the British Empire. Most historical accounts of this watershed period focus on the fiery mutiny in Taranto, Italy, while obscuring the broader context of ferment. By analyzing the mutiny in isolation from other forms of protest, scholars have overlooked the ways in which soldiers set out strategically to cultivate and mobilize a network of allies across the British Empire to buttress their drive to be treated with dignity and compensated equitably. Through the exchange of letters and petitions, BWIR soldiers simultaneously invoked and substantiated their membership in Britain's imperial forces, insisting that West Indians constituted a special class within the empire.[12] The geographic scope and volume of soldiers' correspondence reveals previously unacknowledged intraimperial circuits during this period: noncommissioned officers in Egypt sent petitions to distant colonial administrators in Barbados, Dominica, and St. Lucia; soldiers in Mesopotamia wrote urgent pleas for assistance to military recruiters in British Honduras; servicemen in Europe reported fresh racial slights to sympathetic newspaper editors in Grenada and Trinidad; and soldiers in Italy relayed their grievances to retired civil servants in London. Their letters, in turn, were frequently forwarded (along with enthusiastic endorsements) to the Colonial Office or directly to the Secretary of State for the Colonies, validating soldiers' claims that discrimination against the BWIR was an "insult to the whole of the West Indies."[13]

Soldiers' protest strategies reflected their evolving understanding of military rules, regulations, and hierarchies, as well as their precarious status as subjects in a highly bureaucratic, global empire. Their use of petitions, letters to the press, and other written forms of protest was made possible by the nearly universal literacy rates in the BWIR, which distinguished West Indian soldiers from other nonwhite colonial troops.[14] When confronted with the intransigence of the War Office and their limited right of appeal in the military, BWIR soldiers redirected their efforts toward colonial officials in Britain and the Caribbean, deftly entangling civil authorities in a military dispute over pay and status.

Noncommissioned officers, the highest-ranking black and colored soldiers in the BWIR, were the fulcrums around which the yearlong campaign pivoted. Sergeants, corporals, and lance corporals used their military rank and other markers of respectability to demand equal treatment for the regiment. Drawing on their position of authority in the armed forces and their social and political networks in the colonies, noncommissioned officers nourished the movement as organizers and strategists. The BWIR sergeants' mess, a space where soldiers routinely gathered for "weighty discussion and learned discourses" before 1918, functioned as an intellectual and organizational hub for dissident servicemen throughout the protests.[15]

If the longstanding focus on the Taranto mutiny has obscured the dense networks that facilitated the transnational campaign for equality, it has also led many scholars to overstate soldiers' militancy, particularly the extent to which protesting servicemen articulated their grievances using

FIGURE 4.2. Portrait of a BWIR sergeant in uniform. The photograph was printed as a postcard and mailed in 1916. It likely depicts Christopher A. Foster of the British Honduras Contingent. Courtesy of the Belize Archives and Records Service.

anti-colonial rhetoric.[16] "The revolt at Taranto was . . . the beginning of the national liberation struggle leading to the demise of colonial rule in most of the British Caribbean," one historian proclaims, "and returning soldiers would play a large part in it."[17] Rather than viewing the mutiny as the defining act in this period of fevered mobilization, this chapter demonstrates that it was an exceptional moment of violence in a campaign overwhelmingly characterized by petitioning, letter writing, and other nonviolent forms of dissent. Both publicly and privately, soldiers couched their claims for equitable treatment in the language of martial interracialism and mutual obligation, presenting themselves as "loyal subjects" who sought racial equality in exchange for their voluntary service on behalf of the empire. They doggedly pursued and won the support of white allies and conscripted colonial authorities to act on their behalf by insisting that their military service should garner equitable recompense. Instead of positioning themselves at the vanguard of the "national liberation struggle" in the Caribbean, most BWIR servicemen vigorously pursued greater inclusion *in the empire* on the basis of genuine equality.[18]

Fighting for Army Order No. 1

Army Order No. 1 of 1918 was initially viewed as an unmitigated victory for British troops. On November 26, 1917, after sustained agitation by British servicemen and a statement of support from the Joint Committee of the House of Lords, the House of Commons, and the General Federation of Trade Unions, Chancellor of the Exchequer Bonar Law (formerly Secretary of State for the Colonies) announced before the House of Commons that the government had "decided to make certain further awards" to imperial soldiers and sailors.[19] Eight days later, on December 4, 1917, the sweeping new wage and benefits regulations were officially published as Army Order No. 1 of 1918. The order retroactively raised the minimum pay for privates from 1s. per day to 1s. 6d., a net increase of 50 percent.[20] Commissioned officers, NCOs, and enlisted men likewise received a major pay hike, though it was less generous than the unprecedented allotment for privates.[21] In addition to raising the minimum rate of pay, the order granted servicemen a bonus of 1d. per day for each full year of wartime military service. For soldiers who had served since the outbreak of war in 1914, for example, the "War Pay" provision increased their wages by 3d. per day or 1s. 9d. per week.[22] Furthermore, Army Order No. 1 drastically reduced the amount of time soldiers had to serve before they could qualify for additional proficiency pay and guaranteed that wounded soldiers would continue to draw their wages while hospitalized.[23] It also mandated that separation allowances for soldiers' dependents would be paid from public funds instead of being deducted from soldiers' personal wages.[24] Bonar Law predicted that taken together, the far-reaching financial provisions of Army Order No. 1 would cost the Treasury £65 million in the first year and at least £69 million in the following year.[25]

Not all soldiers serving under the Union Jack, however, qualified for the pecuniary entitlements of Army Order No. 1. Indeed, nearly all the provisions of the order—including those regarding soldiers' minimum daily pay, the "War Pay" bonus, and separation allowances—applied solely to soldiers who served in imperial units that maintained a depot "situated in the United Kingdom, Isle of Man, or the Channel Islands." Erecting a stark boundary between servicemen with roots in the metropole and those who enlisted in the empire, the order explicitly excluded all men who "enlisted for service in Colonial units or contingents" and soldiers who were paid at a colonial rate. Therefore, the 1.7 million soldiers who served in contingents raised in the self-governing Dominions of Australia, Canada, New Zealand, and Newfoundland were ineligible for the benefits of Army Order No. 1 and continued to draw their standard wages from their home governments.[26] Likewise, servicemen in the Indian Army, King's African Rifles, South African Native Labour Corps, East African Military Labour Corps, and similar regiments were disqualified due to their service in colonial contingents.[27] Finally, members of the Non-Combatant Corps, the labor unit comprised of British conscientious objectors, and all servicemen who labored in agricultural positions were excluded.[28] As a result, at least 2.6 million of the 8.5 million men who served in Britain's combined armed forces were legally barred from the benefits of Army Order No. 1.[29]

Although most non-European servicemen were prevented from enjoying the emoluments outlined in Army Order No. 1 because of their service in colonial units, the order did not make any explicit reference to race, color, or citizenship. As a result, Indian, black, and colored soldiers serving in regular British Army regiments—or in imperial units that met the strict criteria outlined in the order—qualified for the full benefits along with their counterparts in the metropole.[30]

By February 1918, two months after Army Order No. 1 was published, BWIR soldiers in Egypt began to make official inquiries about their standing under the new edict.[31] In keeping with military protocol, soldiers from the First, Second, and Fifth Battalions successfully secured the backing of their commanding officers, who, in turn, solicited the aid of

General Edmund Allenby, Commander-in-Chief of the Egyptian Expeditionary Force. The veteran general was an ideal patron for the BWIR, having recently led a string of decisive victories that drew international acclaim and climaxed in the capture of Beersheba, Gaza, and Jerusalem in the autumn of 1917.[32] A "physically large and confident" soldier who had served in the South African War (1899–1902) and on the Western Front (1914–17) before taking the helm of the Egyptian Expeditionary Force in June 1917, Allenby was known as a "bundle of contradictions."[33] On the one hand, his domineering presence, "brusque" manner, and frequent verbal tirades led his subordinates to nickname him the "Bloody Bull." On the other hand, Allenby exhibited an unusual willingness to interface with frontline troops and "took more personal interest in the rank and file than almost any modern British commander."[34] As one officer in the Egyptian Expeditionary Force later recalled, "There was scarcely a man in the force who did not feel that he was a matter of personal interest to the C in C [commander in chief] and the effect was miraculous."[35]

General Allenby wrote to the War Office on behalf of BWIR soldiers on February 6, 1918, to inquire about their standing relative to Army Order No. 1. In a succinct reply the following month, the War Office averred that the regiment was "not eligible for the benefits of Army Order No.1/1918"— except for the limited provisions regarding "Proficiency Pay and Hospital Stoppages"—because the BWIR did not meet the basic qualifications outlined in Articles 2, 3, 4, and 5. According to those articles, Assistant Financial Secretary G. F. Watterson explained in a letter dated March 27, 1918, only units with depots in "the United Kingdom, Channel Islands, or Isle of Man" qualified for the pay increase, subsidized separation allowance payments, and war service gratuity outlined in Army Order No. 1.[36]

Convinced that the BWIR should receive the full benefits of Army Order No. 1, Allenby dispatched a second personal note to the War Office in early May 1918, asking the Army Council to reconsider its position. For the bulk of the letter, Allenby skillfully outlined the regiment's history, emphasizing that the BWIR had formerly maintained a depot near Plymouth, England, and still operated a detail camp and pay office in the metropole.[37] He also took pains to stress the soldiers' respectability and class backgrounds, noting that many of the men held "first class positions in their Colony." Implicit in this seemingly quotidian claim was the idea that BWIR soldiers constituted a privileged class of colonial subjects: they were educated, responsible, and capable. By virtue of their educational and professional achievements, Allenby signaled, they were worthy of the basic rewards and privileges bestowed on servicemen in the British Army as a matter of course. This line of argument would reappear, in one guise or another, in nearly every favorable description of the BWIR during this period.[38] If loyalty and faithful service were not enough to secure the War Office's esteem, then BWIR soldiers and their advocates hoped that their respectability would carry weight.

The ideology of respectability constituted a double-edged sword for black and colored colonials in the British Empire. On the one hand, racialized and gendered notions of respectability exalted the anglophile culture of the ruling colonial oligarchy, positioning "cultured" white men as the rightful guardians of colonies with large black majorities. In the British Caribbean and elsewhere in the empire, respectability came to define the impermeable boundaries of Britishness and civilization, marking those who engaged in Afro-Creole religious, social, and cultural practices as backward, uncivilized, and utterly incapable of exercising the rights and privileges of citizenship. Yet, if the ideology of respectability buttressed white hegemony, it also provided a narrow opening for nonwhite colonials to achieve social mobility through educational attainment and Victorian social mores. In this patronizing logic, the "backward races" of the empire could aspire to hold positions of responsibility in the military, colonial service, and business world after a period of tutelage by their social betters. Ambitious black and colored West Indians took full advantage of the available educational and social opportunities to affirm their status as respectable men and women and to undermine notions of white superiority through individual achievement. For BWIR soldiers, rhetorical claims to respectability served as a means to transcend the racist strictures of the military and civilian worlds and as a declaration of racial equality.[39]

General Allenby's eloquent ode to respectability failed to move the War Office, however. In response to the general's second appeal, the War Office now insisted that the BWIR was ineligible because it was a "Native Unit."[40] Writing in June 1918, G. F. Watterson explained that "Native Units were excluded from the benefits of Army Order 1/1918 only after very careful consideration" and insisted that "no alternation in the decision" was possible.[41] Two months later, in response to a separate query, B. B. Cubitt, Assistant Secretary to the War Office, echoed Watterson's pronouncement, declaring that the BWIR was "definitely ineligible" for the benefits of the Army Order.[42]

The assertion that the BWIR was a "Native Unit" flew in the face of three years of precedent and policy and touched a raw nerve among West Indian servicemen. When word of the War Office's ruling spread among the ranks, historian Winston James argues, "The Rubicon was crossed, and a collective cry of outrage rang out."[43] For many BWIR soldiers, the term "native" was little more than derogatory shorthand for the uncivilized peoples of the empire, those backward men and women who could not speak the King's English, practiced non-Christian faiths, and were ignorant of British laws and customs. J. E. Lewis, a colored sergeant from British Honduras, captured the sentiment of many BWIR servicemen when he declared that he was a "Soldier of the King," and refused to be "bracketed with W. A. C. [West African Contingent], Chinese and Local Labourers, who are Arabs or Armenians, or Jews." The prospect of being lumped together with men of the West African Contingent—whom Sergeant Lewis described as "full-blooded Africans" who could "hardly speak English"—was unthinkable.[44]

More astute soldiers exposed the War Office's sleight of hand by rehearsing the institutional history of the BWIR instead of debating black and colored West Indians' status. They noted that the regiment had been established by a Royal Warrant issued in England, funded by the British Treasury, and governed by the rules and regulations of the British Army Act. Further, the War Office had consented to pay BWIR troops according to the ordinary rates of pay for the British Army and had faithfully done so since the BWIR was established in 1915, a clear signal that the regiment was a part of the imperial forces.[45] Any belated attempt to label the BWIR as a "Native Unit" and to exclude the regiment from Army Order No. 1 on those grounds, soldiers insisted indignantly, constituted a "manifold injustice."[46]

Even the most cursory examination of the language of Army Order No. 1 reveals that the War Office was on shaky ground. The text of the order did not include a single reference to "Native Units," much less a provision banning such units from the new regulations regarding pay and separation allowances. Moreover, the articles that specifically excluded "Colonial Units" clearly referred to regiments like the Australian and New Zealand Army Corps, Royal Newfoundland Regiment, and Canadian Expeditionary Force, which did not draw their pay from the imperial purse. Thus, when officials at the War Office blithely suggested that their ruling was simply meant to enforce existing policy, they were being disingenuous. Rather, the move to exclude BWIR soldiers from the full entitlements of Army Order No. 1 constituted a backdoor attempt to prevent the regiment from enjoying the full benefits allotted to imperial units *in violation of existing policy*. The War Office had repeatedly undermined the BWIR's official status as an infantry unit, derisively referring to the regiment as a "Service Battalion" and assigning most soldiers to labor duties. The ruling on Army Order No. 1 was yet another attack on the status of West Indian soldiers in the armed forces.

Rebuffed by military authorities, BWIR soldiers increasingly registered their discontent with allies in the civilian world. Most frequently, they solicited support from the West Indian Contingent Committee. As discussed in chapter 3, the London-based voluntary association initially directed most of its efforts toward providing entertainment, temporary lodging, warm clothing, and holiday gifts for soldiers.[47] By 1918, however, the committee increasingly mediated disputes between BWIR troops and the Colonial and War Offices and pressured officials in Britain to compensate aggrieved servicemen fairly. Well-heeled and very well-connected, the members of the Contingent Committee were particularly valuable advocates for BWIR soldiers because most of them had once held high-ranking posts in the colonial service. For example, several ex-governors of Caribbean colonies—including George Le Hunte, the recently retired governor of Trinidad and Tobago, and Sydney Olivier, the former governor of Jamaica—served on the committee. The group was chaired by veteran colonial administrator Everard im Thurn, who worked in British Guiana for over two decades before moving to the South Pacific to become Governor of Fiji. The prolific historian Algernon Aspinall served as the Contingent Committee's honorable secretary, while Princess Marie Louise served as the official patron of the group's Ladies Committee.[48]

During the final months of the war, BWIR soldiers inundated the Contingent Committee with messages protesting their exclusion from Army Order No. 1.[49] In response, the committee quietly launched an informal investigation of the pay dispute in June 1918. During a meeting on June 25, 1918, Algernon Aspinall read aloud portions of letters from frustrated BWIR soldiers who complained about Army Order No. 1, unpaid separation allowances, and a host of other financial discrepancies. Hoping to get to the root of the problem, Thurn directed Aspinall to get a copy of Army Order No. 1 since there was "much discontent at the BWIR not being entitled to the extra pay . . . granted to Imperial troops." He also instructed Aspinall to meet with the Command Paymaster to address soldiers' grievances about separation allowances.[50]

The Contingent Committee's fact-finding mission regarding Army Order No. 1 would meander through the summer and fall of 1918. As the committee slowly gathered information and reviewed soldiers' pleas for assistance, twelve Barbadian servicemen from the First Battalion secretly contacted J. Challenor Lynch, a member of the Barbados Legislative Council and chair of that island's BWIR Recruiting Committee, to express their simmering discontent. Writing from Egypt, the soldiers argued that the War Office's discriminatory policies were undermining their official standing as imperial soldiers. They relayed the crushing news that the BWIR had been excluded from Army Order No. 1, even though West Indian soldiers were paid through imperial funds and had always functioned as "Imperial troops." They also described how black and colored soldiers—"in spite of worthy recommendation"—were excluded from the Cadet System and systematically barred from gaining commissions. Frustrated at being denied the "privilege and advantage" afforded to "Tommies and White West Indians," the petitioners warned that they could no longer "uphold the honour and name of the West Indies" under the existing "adverse conditions and conflicting regulations." The exasperated soldiers were unwilling to endure further discrimination and sought immediate redress.[51]

These twelve Barbadian soldiers were well-educated men with ties to the island's most esteemed black and colored families. Petitioner E. F. Packer, for example, was the scion of a planter and the grandson of a judge. V. O. Thomas was part of a "middle-class and well-connected" family, and petitioner V. L. Talma's brother had studied at Oxford as the Barbados Scholar. Petitioner J. C. Hope was a celebrated King Scout and elementary school teacher before joining the BWIR, yet was forced to serve throughout the war as a lowly private.[52] Hope, like Sergeant W. E. Julien, ultimately received the Distinguished Conduct Medal for "conspicuous gallantry and devotion to duty" after he rescued a comrade and helped him return safely to camp.[53] For these middle-class soldiers, the British Army's discriminatory pay and promotion policies were particularly humiliating because they relegated all nonwhite servicemen—irrespective of educational attainment, class, or lineage—to a subordinate status in the armed forces. "It must be understood that the men of this regiment are like the men of all the new armies of the Empire, a different type to the old professional soldier," the Barbadian petitioners explained, "and there could never have been the response to the appeal made by the recruiting committees in the various islands but for the fact that we were made to understand that we would have been on an entirely different footing to the regular West Indian regiment, and that we would have enjoyed every privilege just as any other British soldier."[54]

Frustrated by the disjuncture between the promise of martial interracialism and the reality of endemic discrimination in the armed forces, the petitioners demanded that Lynch intervene on behalf of the men he had sent off to war. "We have been deceived," they wrote. "We like to think that the deception was not intentional. The fact remains that conditions are not as expected and it is to you and other gentlemen of like positions to whom we look" for redress. The petitioners did not specifically state which other gentlemen they expected to lobby on their behalf, but they did demand that Lynch formally present their petition to the colony's legislative body, the House of Assembly.[55]

At the same moment that the Barbadian soldiers prodded Lynch to take up their cause, soldiers from the eastern Caribbean islands of Dominica, St. Kitts and Nevis, and Montserrat each dispatched petitions to their respective colonial administrators. Like their comrades from Barbados, the Leeward Island soldiers condemned the War Office's decision to exclude the BWIR from Army Order No. 1 and protested the racist Cadet System, which kept them from advancing into the commissioned ranks.[56] The fact that these four groups of petitioners each elected to band together with other soldiers from their home island to petition the state—instead of drawing on pan-West Indian networks based on rank, unit, or political sensibility—complicates historian Glenford Howe's finding that petitioners usually collected signatures from "representatives from all of the colonies" and articulated their complaints in a pan-West Indian context.[57] In fact, BWIR servicemen employed a variety of organizational strategies during the yearlong campaign for equal pay and status, at times forming networks based on colony of origin while at others invoking pan-West Indian solidarities. Though we still know very little about how institutional constraints differed for soldiers stationed in the Middle East and in Western Europe—and how those constraints, in turn, impacted the ways in which dissident soldiers could articulate their grievances—it is clear that soldiers on all fronts functioned in overlapping networks based on rank, unit, class, and colony of origin and experimented with various organizational tactics to challenge discrimination in the armed forces.

J. Challenor Lynch never read the Barbadian soldiers' petition aloud in the chambers of the Legislative Council, but he did forward their petition to the governor along with a personal missive in support of the servicemen. In the past, Lynch, like most of his upper-class peers, had shown little concern for the travails of ordinary Barbadians.[58] However, as chair of the local recruiting committee, he was appalled by the soldiers' reports of rampant racial discrimination. In his letter to Governor O'Brien, Lynch stressed that the petitioners were among the very first volunteers from Barbados and were of "a different class" from the agricultural laborers who enlisted in later BWIR contingents.[59] "The first Contingents, the men who first responded to the call were, like their white brothers in England who first responded, some of the best," he explained, "and the Recruiting Committee feel that the claim to be put on the same footing as other combatant units of the British Army, is a just one. They joined with that understanding, they qualified, and they asked to be recognised as such."[60]

Further still, Lynch emphasized that the petitioners had selflessly come to the aid of the empire even though racist military officials in Britain had repeatedly rebuffed their attempts to enlist. They and scores of other West Indians had valiantly lobbied for the right to serve alongside their "white brothers," often at significant personal and professional expense. "West Indians were not content to look on when England needed man-power and other parts of the British Empire were making splendid efforts," Lynch reminded O'Brien. "Some paid their own expenses and joined in England, some had their expenses paid by subscription but for the great majority of the coloured men, entrance to the British Army was barred until the British West Indies Regiment was formed." With the formation of the BWIR, black and colored West Indians expected that they would serve in a combat unit and "would be treated in the same way as other British Regiments." To exclude BWIR soldiers from the entitlements of Army Order No. 1 clearly violated the terms under which the soldiers enlisted.[61]

Confident that O'Brien would see the merits of the soldiers' grievances, Lynch entrusted the governor to submit the soldiers' petition in a manner that would "win a favorable decision" for the troops.[62] At Government House, Charles O'Brien quickly realized the serious implications of the soldiers' complaints, but not for any of the reasons that Lynch had carefully laid out in his letter. If racial injustice and a sense of duty drove Lynch to support the petitioners, Governor O'Brien was motivated by more pragmatic concerns: the desire to maintain law and order. O'Brien, a retired lieutenant colonel in the British Army, worried that disaffected soldiers would wreak havoc in Barbados after the war. Therefore, attempting to stave off future confrontations, he forwarded the soldiers' petition and Lynch's letter of endorsement to Walter Long, Secretary of State for the Colonies, in October 1918. Writing in an apologetic tone, O'Brien acknowledged that the soldiers' petition was "irregular and contrary to Army Orders" because it had not been sent through the proper military channels. However, he stressed that the petitioners were men of "good character and standing" and that their appeal was "respectfully worded." O'Brien confided to Long that pragmatism, rather than a commitment to equality, fueled his concern about the aggrieved soldiers: "I am anxious that any representations of our men serving may be enquired into before their return" so that "the harmony of such a return may not be interfered with."

If O'Brien sympathized with the substance of the petitioners' grievances—namely that BWIR soldiers faced systemic discrimination relative to pay and promotion—he failed to express to Long his explicit support.[63]

By the time the petition reached the Colonial Office in late November 1918, nearly four months had passed since the twelve Barbadian servicemen penned their appeal for assistance. The soldiers' petition had traveled from a military outpost in the Egyptian desert to a British colony in the Caribbean and back across the Atlantic to the heart of Britain's imperial bureaucracy. In the intervening months, the sociopolitical landscape in Europe had changed dramatically. Two weeks before the soldiers' petition arrived in England, the war had abruptly ended with the signing of the Armistice between the Allies and Germany on November 11, 1918. As the focus shifted from winning the war to forging a lasting peace, the Colonial Office evinced little interest in lobbying the War Office on behalf of soldiers who would soon be demobilized and discharged. Thus, despite Lynch's robust endorsement of the petition and Governor O'Brien's tacit request for the appeasement of disgruntled BWIR soldiers, the clerks at the Colonial Office refused to challenge BWIR soldiers' exclusion from the benefits of Army Order No. 1. They also concluded that the War Office had agreed to grant commissions to "slightly coloured persons" in the BWIR at the discretion of their local governor. With that ruling in place, they considered the matter resolved.[64] Likewise, officials at the War Office continued to justify the regiment's exclusion from Army Order No. 1. When Sir John Butcher, MP for York, questioned Henry Forster, Financial Secretary to the War Office, in November 1918 regarding the BWIR's standing, Forester sidestepped the color question, and instead, claimed that the regiment was ineligible for Army Order No. 1 because it did not have a depot in the British Isles. Doubling down on the War Office's position, he insisted that the contentious ruling had "been made in strict accordance with the decision of the Government."[65]

"Increasingly Truculent" Behavior: Mutiny and Mass Mobilization at Taranto

The Armistice between the Allies and Germany on November 11, 1918, marked the end of fifty-two months of carnage stretching from northern Europe to southern Africa. The human toll of the war was staggering and unprecedented. Nearly sixteen million people lost their lives in the conflict, including 6.8 million civilians. More than 9.5 million servicemen died, which, according to one historian's grisly calculation, means 5,600

AN "INSUBORDINATE SPIRIT PREVAILED" [153]

soldiers perished on average each day of the war.[66] The war claimed the lives of over 1,200 BWIR soldiers, and another 2,500 were wounded while on active duty.[67] Despite their largely noncombatant role, one in thirteen BWIR soldiers met his end while serving overseas.[68]

Although the Armistice signaled the end of military hostilities, it only intensified BWIR soldiers' struggle for equal pay and status. With the dangers of war now squarely in the past, long-suppressed anger over Army Order No. 1 percolated to the surface rapidly and with tremendous intensity. Two weeks after the Armistice, Lieutenant Colonel Charles Wood-Hill, commander of the First Battalion of the BWIR, warned that a "very deep-seated feeling of dissatisfaction" existed among the troops stationed in Egypt. In an urgent letter to John Chancellor, Governor of Trinidad and Tobago, Wood-Hill confessed that the initial effort to secure the benefits of Army Order No. 1 for BWIR soldiers had faltered and that the War Office had flatly refused to reconsider its ruling. "At first the increased rate of pay was refused on the grounds that the British West Indies Regiment having no Depot in the United Kingdom could not be granted the additional rate of pay," he explained, "but when it was pointed out how absurd this ruling was, they dropped the question of a Depot and raised the question of being natives." Even though General Allenby had "done his best" to persuade the War Office to make an exception for the regiment, the soldiers were "classified as natives," and their claims to Army Order No. 1 were rebuffed.[69]

Unable to sway the War Office through direct appeals, Wood-Hill endeavored to recruit a network of allies who could pressure policymakers in Britain. In many respects, his tactics mirrored the protest strategies that black and colored BWIR soldiers had developed and tested in the final months of the war. He prodded colonial officials in the Caribbean to intervene on behalf of West Indian soldiers, writing personal appeals to Governor Chancellor as well as Governor George Haddon-Smith of the Windward Islands. And he reached out to Colonel L. S. Amery, a military insider who served as the Liaison Officer between the War Office and the War Cabinet, with the hope of influencing the Secretary of State for War. As Wood-Hill explained in his missive to Chancellor, the central hurdle in the BWIR's campaign for equality was not the intransigence of the War Office but rather the dearth of well-connected patrons. "The difficulty is, the West Indies not being federated, it is very hard to get combined action on their behalf as a whole, or to get anyone in England with sufficient influence to take the matter up," he explained. Thus, to overcome official indifference toward the regiment, Wood-Hill borrowed another aspect of

BWIR soldiers' protest strategy: he took pains to portray West Indian servicemen as members of the landowning and professional classes. Erasing the rural and working-class roots of most soldiers, he claimed that a "very large proportion" of men in the regiment had held "responsible Government positions in the West Indies" or were small landowners. Most others, he insisted with no further explanation, had "sacrificed a great deal to enlist." Thus, for Wood-Hill, the "very delicate question" of drawing the boundary between British and native troops necessitated that officials consider a soldier's class and comportment, not just his color.[70]

Before officials could respond to Wood-Hill's appeal, BWIR soldiers mutinied while stationed in Taranto, Italy. Led by soldiers from the Ninth Battalion, the mutiny demonstrated that some black and colored soldiers were prepared to seek redress for their grievances through physical confrontations rather than pleading their case through petitions. The men of the Ninth Battalion, Private Charles P. Coote acknowledged candidly, were a unit of "rough fellows."[71] The hardscrabble battalion was comprised primarily of peripatetic Jamaican and Barbadian migrants who, like Private Coote, had flocked to Panama before the war in search of work and then enlisted in the BWIR following the whirlwind recruitment drive on the Isthmus in 1917.[72] Under the command of Colonel Reginald E. Willis, the battalion had spent over a year hauling ammunition, building trenches, and performing a host of other backbreaking tasks as laborers in France.[73] Like most BWIR soldiers, the men of the Ninth Battalion never saw action on the front lines as combat troops; instead, they battled brutally cold winters, miserable working conditions, chronic illness, and a notoriously difficult commanding officer. Colonel Willis, as one soldier later recalled, "had the reputation of being a brute."[74] Once, when a frostbitten soldier failed to stand and salute, Willis angrily "dug his spurs" into the soldier's bandaged leg to force him to his feet. Afterward, the white Jamaican officer snarled, "When you write your mathi [mother] mountain back in Jamaica, tell the folks I'm turning Jesus Christ out here. I'm making the lame walk."[75] Despite the profound difficulties of the war years, however, the "rough fellows" of the Ninth Battalion showed little outward evidence of disaffection or rising resentment.[76] Rather, in the weeks following the Armistice, the battalion peacefully relocated to Cimino Camp on the outskirts of Taranto, Italy, to await demobilization.

Located on the southern coast of Italy near strategic ports in the Mediterranean Sea, Cimino Camp served as a major transportation hub for British soldiers who were traveling between Europe, the Middle East, and the Americas. In addition, the bustling base was home to corps of

AN "INSUBORDINATE SPIRIT PREVAILED" [155]

civilian contract laborers from Malta, Fiji, and Italy. After the Armistice, the eight BWIR battalions stationed in Western Europe congregated at Cimino Camp, marking the first time that all eight had assembled at the same base. Soldiers from the Eighth, Tenth, and Eleventh Battalions who had been stationed at Taranto before the Armistice were joined by the Third Battalion on November 10, 1918, and the Fourth Battalion two days later. The following day, on November 13, soldiers from the Ninth Battalion disembarked at Cimino Camp after traveling south from France. The Sixth and Seventh Battalions marched into the base on November 14, making Taranto home to over 7,500 BWIR soldiers.[77]

Less than a month after they arrived in Taranto, soldiers from the Ninth Battalion mutinied, sparking six days of unrest that marked the most serious breach of discipline in the BWIR's history. The mutiny erupted on Friday, December 6, 1918, after Colonel Willis commanded his men to clean the latrines of the Italian Labour Corps, a group of white civilian laborers.[78] In response to Willis's demeaning order, soldiers from the Ninth Battalion assaulted the colonel and then "danced, shouted, and poked holes in his tent with their bayonets."[79] Over the weekend, the protest gained momentum as soldiers from the Ninth and Tenth Battalions refused to work, and "disaffection and acts of insubordination" rapidly spread to other BWIR battalions as well. By the third day of the mutiny, the protests escalated sharply and claimed their first and only casualty. On Sunday, December 8, Acting Sergeant Robert Richards of the Seventh Battalion shot and killed Samuel Pinnock, a Jamaican private in his battalion, claiming self-defense. After the shooting, BWIR soldiers beat Richards in retaliation.[80]

Deeply rattled by the "increasingly truculent" behavior of BWIR troops, General J. H. V. Crowe, the base commandant at Taranto, dispatched a series of urgent telegrams to the War Office recommending that the Ninth and Tenth Battalions be "immediately embarked to Egypt, Malta, Salonika, or Marseilles."[81] If the War Office was unable or unwilling to transfer the troublesome units, Crowe insisted, then a "battalion of white troops [was] absolutely essential" to suppress the mutiny.[82] Before the War Office could dispatch reinforcements, the anxious general attempted to quell the protests on his own. On December 9, he made an example of the Ninth Battalion by temporarily disbanding the unit and scattering the officers and men among the seven remaining BWIR battalions at Taranto.[83] And to minimize any further violence, he punished the entire regiment by ordering all BWIR soldiers to turn in their rifles. Yet, even after the regiment was disarmed, the situation at Taranto remained tense and "unsettled."[84]

[156] CHAPTER 4

Determined to squash the mutiny once and for all, the British Army General Headquarters in Italy dispatched white soldiers from the Seventh Battalion of the Worcestershire Regiment and the Forty-Eighth Machine Gun Corps to Taranto.[85] If the infantry battalion and machine gunners were unable to stop the mutiny, British military authorities in Italy assured the War Office, a second battalion was "standing by," ready to be deployed.[86] The show of force worked. By December 12, six days after the initial protest commenced, the base commandant reported that there was "no further disturbance" at Taranto.[87] Lacking confidence in General Crowe's leadership, British military leaders in Italy sent Major-General Henry Thullier, head of the Army Chemical Warfare Department, and two other staff members to Taranto to maintain peace at the base.[88]

If the mutiny highlighted BWIR soldiers' growing willingness to buck authority and violently contest the terms of their labor, another collective protest spearheaded by BWIR soldiers at Taranto on December 6, 1918, revealed that more conservative notions of imperial patriotism and mutual obligation had not fully lost their sway. On the same day that the mutiny erupted, 180 BWIR sergeants at the base urgently petitioned Walter Long, Secretary of State for the Colonies, to lodge their grievances about discrimination in the British armed forces. The sergeants explained the purpose of their petition with remarkable diplomacy, writing that there were "certain circumstances" in the BWIR that did "not tend to engender the most cordial feelings for the Empire in the West Indies." Before disclosing their specific grievances, they reminded Long that West Indians had patriotically supported the war effort and had come forward "out of the keen spirit of loyalty" to fight for the empire. Black and colored West Indians who successfully enlisted in the metropole during the early months of the war, they noted with approval, "enjoyed all of the privileges and benefits" given to white British soldiers. "This clearly proves that, although they are West Indians, they are 'British', and we admit, is only just."[89]

Yet if West Indian recruits in Britain enjoyed the fruits of British justice, their compatriots who enlisted in the Caribbean were not so fortunate. Despite assurances that BWIR servicemen would receive "all of the privileges and benefits derivable from service in the British Army," the petitioners alleged soldiers who served in Italy and France were systematically barred from earning commissions or advancing beyond the rank of sergeant. To add insult to injury, they were denied the increase in separation allowances granted to British soldiers in 1917 and the pay raise awarded to British regiments in Army Order No. 1. Determined to have their grievances "settled on the basis of Justice," the sergeants urged the Secretary of State for the Colonies to "forcibly place" their petition before the War Office and His Majesty's Government. They also issued a searing indictment: "We feel we have been serving as Soldiers in the British Army, assisting in a World War for Justice and Freedom, yet we, ourselves have not derived the same benefits as those along with whom we have been doing our bit," the sergeants declared, "and that where any such benefits have been derived it has been on a one-sided basis."[90]

The 180 sergeants who accused the British Army of taking their labor without giving proper material and symbolic rewards in return were among the most senior black and colored soldiers in the BWIR. Of the 15,600 soldiers who served in the regiment, fewer than five hundred would ever don the three chevrons of a sergeant. As leaders in their respective battalions, the sergeants had successfully navigated the military hierarchy to become noncommissioned officers, a rank that imperialist poet Rudyard Kipling famously described as the "backbone of the Army."[91] Yet, they chafed under the same racist policies that excluded all BWIR soldiers— irrespective of rank, education, or achievement—from the social and financial benefits of soldiering. Having patiently endured the indignities of the war years, the sergeants exhorted colonial authorities to use all their influence to reverse the series of measures that relegated BWIR soldiers to second-class status.

Given the logistics of collecting 180 supporting signatures from soldiers in seven different battalions, it seems likely that the sergeants drafted the petition before the mutiny and decided to send it on December 6 after the mutiny erupted. However, it remains unclear whether the petitioners approved of the mutineers' confrontational tactics or directly participated in the uprising. Indeed, it is important to note that the sergeants' petition did not include any reference to the upheaval at Taranto or any explicit expression of solidarity with the striking soldiers. It also failed to mention the discriminatory labor assignments that fueled the initial confrontation between the Ninth Battalion and Colonel Willis. Thus, instead of assuming that the sergeants dispatched their petition on December 6 as a part of a coordinated campaign with the mutinous soldiers, we must consider the possibility that the sergeants hoped to present their grievances as separate and distinct from their subordinates' actions. The fact that the sole fatality of the mutiny occurred when a black sergeant took up arms against a mutinous black private suggests that noncommissioned officers and privates might have divided into opposing camps during the upheaval.[92]

[158] CHAPTER 4

In the wake of the mutiny, military and colonial officials pondered how to punish the rebellious soldiers. Fearful of additional unrest, British military authorities in Italy requested that all eight BWIR battalions be repatriated immediately and replaced by Italian and British labor corps. At the Colonial Office, however, former clerk Gilbert Grindle, in his new role as Assistant Under Secretary of State for the Colonies, suggested the insurgent soldiers should have additional time added to their tour of duty instead of being rewarded with an early trip home where they could stir up trouble in the colonies. "Other things being equal, these men ought to serve a further term for their misbehavior," Grindle argued. "If they are in a 'truculent' state, it would be better that they should be brought to their senses before they are let loose in the W. I. [West Indies]." Moreover, from a financial standpoint, it made little sense to replace black BWIR soldiers with European soldiers, given that BWIR soldiers were "cheap compared to white troops."[93] Ultimately, the plan to repatriate all eight BWIR battalions stalled when the War Office refused to provide replacement laborers at Taranto.

Unable to rid themselves of BWIR soldiers en masse, British military authorities in Italy hastily rounded up and arrested seventy-two soldiers, charging them with offenses ranging from mutiny to disobedience. Over half of the arrested servicemen—thirty-seven men in total—came from a single unit: the BWIR's Ninth Battalion. West Indian soldiers from the Fourth, Sixth, Seventh, Eighth, Tenth, and Eleventh Battalions were also arrested, although in much smaller numbers than the "rough fellows" of the Ninth. It is striking that sixty-seven of the apprehended servicemen were privates, and only five held the privileged rank of noncommissioned officer.[94]

The seventy-two accused mutineers faced field general courts-martial at Cimino Camp in Taranto between December 1918 and January 1919. Judged by a panel of three commissioned officers, fifty soldiers were convicted of disobeying a commanding officer and of mutiny, which was broadly defined as any act of "collective insubordination, or a combination of two or more persons to resist or induce others to resist lawful military authority."[95] Fifteen other soldiers were convicted of "conduct to the prejudice of good order and military discipline" or other lesser offenses, and seven men were acquitted of all charges. Although mutiny was a capital offense in the British Army, forty-five of the convicted servicemen received sentences ranging from three to five years' imprisonment.[96] Two other convicted mutineers—Privates E. Edwards and A. Marshall of the Ninth Battalion—were sentenced to eight years of penal servitude. The harshest sentences were meted out to three servicemen in the Ninth Battalion: Private D. Myers was sentenced to ten years in prison, Private J. Munroe received a twenty-year sentence for mutiny and for striking a commanding officer, and Private Arthur Sanches was initially sentenced to death, though the base commandant had his sentence commuted to twenty years in prison.[97] Instead of sailing home as war heroes, the Taranto mutineers traveled back to the West Indies in leg irons, guarded by white British soldiers and BWIR military police.[98]

The fact that all of the BWIR mutineers escaped with their lives, despite the seriousness of the charges they faced, reflects the British Army's anomalous stance toward mutiny. For reasons that are still poorly understood, British Army brass charged soldiers with mutiny much less frequently than their European peers and almost never executed convicted mutineers. Only 1,800 British servicemen were charged with mutiny between 1914 and 1920, compared to twenty-five thousand to forty thousand soldiers in the French Army.[99] And of the British soldiers charged with mutiny during the war, only three were executed.[100] Soldiers were much more likely to face the firing squad for desertion, cowardice, murder, or even quitting their posts than they were for mutiny.[101] Indeed, the four BWIR soldiers who were executed during the war lost their lives not because they had led collective protests against military authorities, but because of individual transgressions that included desertion and violence against their comrades.[102]

The Taranto mutiny made visible the depth of soldiers' discontent and heightened the stakes for subsequent confrontations. For Caribbeanist scholars, the mutiny serves as an example of the radicalization of BWIR soldiers and highlights their willingness to contest the "racist fetters imposed upon them by the War Office."[103] Yet, a panoramic view of this period reveals that the mutiny was part of a wave of collective protests launched by frustrated metropolitan and imperial soldiers in the wake of the Armistice, climaxing with the massive riot of Canadian servicemen at Kinmel Park Camp in March 1919.[104] These upheavals, as Cathryn Corns and John Hughes-Wilson rightly assert, "were much more in the nature of 'strikes' than 'mutinies' and were . . . more concerned with demobilization grievances than with refusing to fight."[105] While the Taranto mutiny would cast a long shadow over the BWIR, it was not nearly as violent or threatening as uprisings by white servicemen following the Armistice. Indeed, as Lieutenant Colonel Wood-Hill noted in an account written after the war, BWIR soldiers behaved with tremendous "restraint" compared with mutinous British and Dominion troops.[106]

From Repression to Representation: Imperial
Officials' Shifting Views of Dissident Soldiers

On the surface, an uneasy calm settled on Taranto in mid-December 1918. BWIR soldiers returned to their daily routine of fatigue duty and regimental parades, while the Worcestershire Regiment soldiers who had been dispatched to the base "with ammunition in their pouches" prepared for demobilization after the mutiny abruptly petered out.[107] However, under cover of darkness, a group of BWIR soldiers had begun gathering to share their common grievances and discuss the future of the West Indies. At an inaugural meeting held on the evening of December 17, 1918, the group of sergeants formalized their ties by establishing a secret association called the Caribbean League. The leaders of the new association, Sergeants H. L. Brown, C. Herbert Collman, and A. P. Jones, were all Jamaicans from the Third Battalion.[108] While it is unclear if Brown, Collman, and Jones were also involved in organizing the petition to the Secretary of State for the Colonies, the Caribbean League emerged from the same set of disappointments regarding pay, promotion, and regimental status that fueled that earlier effort. The three co-founders, like the previous petitioners, explicitly connected the plight of BWIR soldiers to the question of colonial governance in the West Indies. For these soldiers, the struggle for justice and equality in the British Army was inextricably linked to the fight for freedom on the home front.

Between December 1918 and January 1919, the Caribbean League met three times and grew to include noncommissioned officers from every BWIR battalion at Taranto. In scholarly accounts, historians often portray the league as an anti-colonial group, arguing that it represented a "landmark in Anglophone Caribbean nationalism."[109] Yet organizationally, the league most closely resembled a West Indian-friendly society or fraternal order. The stated purpose of the league was the "promotion of all matters conducive to the General Welfare of the islands constituting the British West Indies and the British Territories adjacent thereto." To fund the association's initiatives, prospective members were required to pay an "admission fee" of one shilling as well as a one-shilling annual "subscription." Despite its military origins, membership in the Caribbean League was open to "individuals of both sexes" who resided in the British Caribbean colonies or were children of West Indians. In keeping with the pan-West Indian ethos articulated in the league's purpose, the founders proposed that a "Committee of Management" govern the association with representatives from throughout the British Caribbean. Yet, they also proposed that the association's headquarters be in Kingston, Jamaica, leaving the other islands to make do with smaller suboffices to handle local affairs.[110]

It is significant that the founders of the Caribbean League elected to model their organization after the civilian voluntary associations that peppered West Indian communities instead of forming a veterans' association or military brotherhood. Scholars have richly documented how black West Indians created a vast network of voluntary associations in the early twentieth century that combined racial uplift, mutual aid, and political advocacy.[111] These trans-local associations connected West Indian men and women across the Greater Caribbean while also providing a training ground for a generation of new leaders. Not content to advocate on behalf of servicemen alone, the founders of the Caribbean League structured the association to foster broad civic engagement and a trans-local West Indian identity. At least one of the three co-founders, C. Herbert Collman, had garnered valuable organizational experience as a member of two fraternal orders in Jamaica prior to the war. Before joining the BWIR, Collman had led the drive to establish in Port Antonio, Jamaica, a court of the Ancient Order of Foresters, a popular fraternal order with lodges throughout the British Caribbean and Panama. Because of Collman's "untiring zeal and energy," the new court was established in June 1915 under the patronage of Governor William Manning.[112] Collman was an active Freemason as well.[113]

The sole surviving accounts of the league's meetings are from Sergeant Leon Pouchet, a Trinidadian soldier-turned-informant from the Eighth Battalion.[114] According to Pouchet, fifty to sixty soldiers attended the second meeting of the Caribbean League, which was held at the Tenth Battalion's sergeants' mess on December 20, 1918. While soldiers at the first meeting discussed the purpose of the league in largely apolitical terms, by the second gathering, some soldiers openly assailed British racism and imperialism and articulated a militant agenda for black self-determination. In a fiery speech, a soldier from the Third Battalion declared that "the black man should have freedom and govern himself in the West Indies and that force must be used, and if necessary bloodshed to attain that object." Pouchet reported that the majority of the audience "loudly applauded" the soldier's call for black social and political power in the British Caribbean. The meeting then evolved into a heated discussion of the "grievances of the black man against the white," as soldiers discussed the litany of racial slights they endured while serving under the Union Jack. Since the league was composed entirely of noncommissioned officers, the soldiers' most urgent complaint was that military authorities routinely undermined their leadership role in the BWIR by replacing black NCOs with white NCOs. As a result, the small cadre of black NCOs faced the constant threat of losing their hard-earned status if a white NCO transferred to their unit. Members of the Caribbean League responded by making "veiled threats" against any white NCOs who traveled to Jamaica during demobilization. In addition, the disaffected soldiers agreed to launch a general strike to secure better wages once they returned to the West Indies.[115]

Sergeant Pouchet's account of the first two clandestine meetings of the Caribbean League offers a rare glimpse into the ways in which BWIR soldiers expressed their frustrations among their comrades and away from the intense gaze of powerful colonial and military authorities. In their letters to British officials, BWIR soldiers buttressed their appeals for equal treatment by celebrating British justice and Britain's interracial empire. In private, however, some soldiers framed their misfortunes in stark racial terms, articulating their grievances as restive black men, not as loyal British subjects. They fumed that educated and experienced black soldiers had limited opportunities for advancement, even in an overwhelmingly black regiment like the BWIR. They condemned white minority rule in the Caribbean and issued demands for freedom in the postwar period. They discussed the chasm between the rhetoric of martial interracialism and the reality of racial discrimination in the British Army. Instead of waiting on the assistance of sympathetic white allies, the men challenged each other to carry the fight for self-determination back home to the colonies and to employ violence if necessary to obtain redress. Meetings of the Caribbean League, at least for a short time, provided a space where BWIR soldiers could collectively articulate an alternative language of protest and struggle.

Just as the members of the Caribbean League were beginning to formulate strategies to challenge their dual subjugation as soldiers and colonial subjects, increased surveillance and internecine conflict irrevocably splintered the group, and the underground movement to mobilize BWIR soldiers at Taranto faltered. Two soldiers who attended the meeting on December 20 reported the league's covert activities to military authorities later that month. Immediately after the league's second meeting, a sergeant from the Tenth Battalion notified his commanding officer about the association, and Sergeant Pouchet from the Eighth Battalion provided a detailed report about the league to his commanding officer, Major Maxwell Smith.[116] As news of the league spread throughout the military chain of command, commanding officers from several BWIR battalions confronted their men about their role in the association. Colonel A. E. Barchard, commanding officer of the Third Battalion, ordered the sergeants in his unit to submit an account of the inaugural meeting of the league and to reveal the association's purpose. While Barchard ultimately approved of the league after reading the soldiers' report, the commanding officer of the Tenth Battalion cautioned his men to be "very careful over the League business and [to] leave political matters alone." In a thinly veiled threat, Lieutenant-Colonel C. W. Long menacingly warned BWIR soldiers that West Indian troops could never "stand up against the British Tommy" as it was "the British Tommy who beat the Germans."[117] Yet, in an important concession, just three days after the league's second meeting, General Henry Thullier ordered that Italian civilian laborers replace BWIR soldiers for all "sanitary work" on the base, eliminating one of the soldiers' major grievances.[118]

Once the Caribbean League was exposed, attendance at the meetings declined significantly. Given the high stakes of participating in unsanctioned activities while on active duty, many soldiers elected to abandon the league instead of waiting for the likely backlash from military officials. As a result, only thirty soldiers attended the league's third meeting on January 3, 1919.[119] Most of the soldiers who remained involved came from the Third Battalion—home to the three co-founders of the league—or from the rebellious Ninth and Tenth Battalions, which had led the mutiny at Taranto. Their comrades from the Fourth, Sixth, Seventh, and Eleventh Battalions voted with their feet, fleeing the league en masse.

While the Caribbean League could perhaps have continued to exist in the face of growing external pressure and declining membership, internecine feuds over tactics and organizational structure sent the association into a precipitous decline. During the January 3 meeting, Sergeant Pouchet protested the plan to locate the league's headquarters in Jamaica, predicting that Jamaicans would perpetually monopolize the leadership positions. Not surprisingly, Pouchet garnered strong support from the non-Jamaican members of the league, while the Jamaican members rebuffed his claim.[120] Latent interisland rivalries were just the tip of the iceberg, however. During the same meeting, some soldiers proposed that the league should move beyond its base of noncommissioned officers and recruit rank-and-file BWIR soldiers; other members—perhaps thinking of the recent mutiny—warned that it was "rather risky" to recruit privates to join the league since they might "misunderstand" its purpose and "get excited." Moreover, members debated whether the league should take a strident anti-government stance or work with the colonial authorities to promote gradual reform. In a marked departure from the militant tone of the second meeting, several soldiers advocated cooperating with the colonial government and stressed the "peaceful purpose" of the league. Even those who embraced a more confrontational strategy cautioned that the league should wait for a more opportune moment. Sergeant Monte, a Jamaican soldier from the mutinous Ninth Battalion, counseled that the "best thing to do was not to pull against the government but to work in harmony with them for the present and then strike at the right moment." At least one soldier, a Vincentian sergeant from the Tenth Battalion, rejected any form of collective action at all. After listening to the debate over tactics, he remarked ruefully, "I do not intend to associate myself anymore with the league as I see it has taken a serious turn."[121]

The leaders of the Caribbean League scheduled an additional meeting for the following night, but there is no record that any gatherings took place after January 3, 1919. Despite the league's rapid collapse, General Thullier remained alert for signs of insurgency in the BWIR and personally interviewed Sergeant Pouchet to gather additional information about the league's covert activities. In a secret letter to the War Office, Thullier alleged that the Caribbean League was "formed ostensibly for industrial and reform purposes" but was actually "covering seditious designs for execution on return to the West Indies after demobilization." Intent on punishing the leaders of the league, Thullier initially considered charging the three co-founders with "conspiracy to cause sedition." However, he quickly concluded that it would be "useless and inadvisable" to court-martial the men because of the lack of corroborating witnesses. He also acknowledged that the defendants would likely produce their own witnesses, who would deny the seditious aims of the league. In the absence of a court-martial, Thullier urged the Colonial Office to inform all West Indian governors about the league and suggested that the Jamaican police monitor the activities of Sergeants Brown, Collman, and Jones when they returned home.[122]

Still reeling from the mutiny and faced now with reports of potentially seditious activities among the BWIR's black and colored NCOs, the Colonial Office embraced General Thullier's alarmist assessment of the Caribbean League. The clerks at the Colonial Office viewed the league as an ominous bellwether and feared that radicalized soldiers could stimulate anti-colonial sentiment, and perhaps even violent unrest, in the colonies once they returned from the war. "The League may confine itself to legitimate objects, or it may disappear; but there is undoubtedly great risk that it may give rise to some seditious movement which would be made much more dangerous by the knowledge of arms and discipline which has been acquired by the men of the Regiment," warned senior clerk E. R. Darnley. Since all three co-founders of the Caribbean League hailed from Jamaica, Darnley was particularly anxious that the league might "foment sedition and violence" in Britain's most populous and important Caribbean colony.[123] Gilbert Grindle, Assistant Under Secretary at the Colonial Office, offered a similarly dire assessment. Expressing his "considerable apprehensions" about demobilizing 7,500 BWIR servicemen in Jamaica, Grindle cautioned that the "mutinous state" of the soldiers would only worsen when they encountered poor economic conditions at home. The men, he lamented, would be "turned adrift" in an island plagued by chronic underemployment and few job prospects for returning veterans. "Some rioting seems inevitable," he concluded gravely.[124]

Ironically, the Colonial Office turned to Colonel R. E. Willis, the infamous officer whose abusive actions had sparked the mutiny in the Ninth Battalion, to devise a strategy to limit unrest during demobilization. In early January 1919, E. R. Darnley met with Colonel Willis in England to discuss the Caribbean League and craft a "scheme of demobilization" for the regiment. Instead of suppressing the remnants of the league outright, the men proposed that the governor of Jamaica should closely monitor the group's leaders and activities and "be prepared to take prompt action" at the earliest sign of unrest. In addition, Grindle urged Governor Probyn to "get on with his plan for providing employment" for returning servicemen, as the "problem of keeping order" was now his primary responsibility. After meeting with Willis, the Colonial Office staff relayed their instructions to Governor Probyn in a confidential letter and enclosed copies of the reports about the Caribbean League written by military officials in Italy and at the War Office.[125] On the same day, they also warned the governors of British Honduras, Trinidad, British Guiana, and the Bahamas about the Taranto mutiny and the formation of the Caribbean League.[126]

As Colonial Office staffers secretly instructed governors in the West Indies to prepare for the worst, they also belatedly began to evaluate soldiers' complaints of pay discrimination. Throughout 1918, Walter Long, Secretary of State for the Colonies, had adamantly refused to review BWIR soldiers' appeals for equal compensation. Instead, when pressed, Long simply repeated the War Office's paper-thin excuse that BWIR soldiers were ineligible for the imperial pay increase because they did not have a regimental depot in the British Isles. However, on January 10, 1919, Alfred Milner, a conservative statesman and veteran colonial administrator, replaced Long as Secretary of State for the Colonies. Unlike his predecessor, Milner had significant experience in both colonial governance and military affairs, and he had a particular interest in civil-military relations. Before assuming the helm of the Colonial Office, Milner had served as the Secretary of State for War from April 1918 to January 1919. He had also held a series of important positions in British southern Africa during the Second South African War (1899–1902) and likely coauthored the Balfour Declaration of 1917.[127] Having successfully presided over the War Office during the final months of World War I, Milner understood the politics of soldiers' compensation and immediately set out to tackle BWIR soldiers' grievances over Army Order No. 1.

By reviewing the pay dispute, Milner sought to appease disgruntled BWIR soldiers before a second round of disturbances erupted. He also aimed to mollify the growing chorus of white elites in the metropole as well as in the colonies who anticipated that the failure to compensate BWIR soldiers on par with their British counterparts could foment unrest. The most insistent call for action came from the West India Contingent Committee. Having read "numerous complaints" from dispirited BWIR soldiers and conducted their own informal investigation of Army Order No. 1 during the summer of 1918, the Contingent Committee formally petitioned the Colonial Office during the final weeks of 1918 to lobby colonial administrators to intervene on behalf of the regiment.[128] When Alfred Milner took over at the Colonial Office in early January 1919, the Contingent Committee welcomed him with a second call for action.[129]

The Contingent Committee's petitions to the Colonial Office in late 1918 and early 1919 highlight the mix of pragmatic and principled reasons that led white elites increasingly to support the BWIR. On one hand, the dispute over Army Order No. 1, with its strong racial overtones, was a budding public relations nightmare for colonial administrators and white business leaders. If official celebrations of interracial fraternity in the empire were shown to be little more than a myth, elites feared that there would be a virulent antiwhite backlash in the West Indies. Noting that the pay issue was "giving rise to very great dissatisfaction in all ranks of the British West Indies Regiment," the Contingent Committee foresaw that discrimination against the regiment would have a "serious effect on public opinion" in the colonies.[130] In a later letter, the Contingent Committee ominously reported that soldiers' anger about Army Order No. 1 had become "intense."[131]

On the other hand, the Contingent Committee reluctantly acknowledged that BWIR soldiers possessed a "legitimate grievance" against the War Office.[132] The all-white South African Overseas Contingent, which lacked the required depot in the British Isles, received the full benefits of Army Order No. 1, as did West Indians who served in British regiments.[133] BWIR soldiers, the Contingent Committee stressed, had willingly volunteered to fight in the war "in spite of the fact that their services were at first refused." If British soldiers who were drafted into service received the full entitlements of the Army Order, then it was a "manifest injustice" to deny the same rewards to the BWIR.[134]

The eighteen men who signed the Contingent Committee's petition wielded considerable political clout. Most were veterans of the colonial service and boasted extensive personal and professional ties to the Caribbean. The seven most prominent signatories—Francis Fleming, James Hayes-Saddler, Frederic M. Hodgeon, George Le Hunte, R. B. Llewelyn, Sydney Olivier, and William Grey Wilson—had all recently served as colonial governors in the region.[135] Given their ties to both the upper echelons of the colonial service and rank-and-file BWIR soldiers, the petitioners rightly assumed that their appeals would be reviewed with the utmost consideration.

Before Milner could placate the Contingent Committee, news arrived that colonial authorities in Barbados were preparing to settle the pay dispute with or without the endorsement of officials in Britain. In response to the flood of appeals by BWIR soldiers and their allies, F. J. Clarke, Speaker of the House of Assembly and chair of the local committee for returning soldiers, recommended that the local government use public funds to grant soldiers the raise mandated in Army Order No. 1. If the "Imperial Government" was not "disposed to grant equal pay," Governor O'Brien relayed in a brief telegram, then legislators in Barbados were poised to intervene in "accordance with [the] promise on enlistment that the men would receive equal treatment to British troops."[136] O'Brien assured Milner that he would keep the proposal in abeyance until he received instructions from the Colonial Office, yet the fact that the legislative body in Britain's most conservative Caribbean colony was prepared to affirm BWIR soldiers' right to the benefits of Army Order No. 1 jolted the Colonial Office staff. If Barbadian soldiers received the pay increase from local coffers, then soldiers from other West Indian colonies would likely press for similar concessions, setting off a new round of agitation and protest. "The political effect" of the House of Assembly's plan, Gilbert Grindle concluded, "would be deplorable."[137]

Under pressure from several quarters, Milner ordered his subordinates to prepare a memo assessing the row over Army Order No. 1. The resulting document, written in lucid, uncomplicated prose by Confidential

Clerk H. T. Allen, found that there was an "irresistible case" for awarding BWIR soldiers the disputed pay increase. Guided by a basic commitment to fairness and a keen awareness of the larger political stakes, Allen argued the War Office's ruling was neither politically savvy nor just. "Discrimination in the matter of pay on colour grounds seems unfair," he concluded after scrutinizing the telegrams that established the original rate of pay for BWIR soldiers. The War Office had promised volunteers "pay at British rates" and never suggested that their wages would be frozen if British soldiers received a raise. "Supposing it had been necessary to reduce the pay of British privates to 9d. a day, would the War Office or Treasury have interpreted the correspondence to mean that the privates of the British West Indies Regiment remained entitled to 1s. a day?" Allen asked incredulously. The War Office's backroom machinations, coupled with the racial overtones of the pay dispute, he warned, could fatally undermine West Indians' loyalty to the empire. "The West Indian negro is in general proud of his British nationality (even to the point of being obnoxious about it when abroad)," but "discrimination in the matter of pay based on colour grounds . . . is calculated to arouse, and has in fact already aroused, great resentment," Allen noted. There was already "reason to fear trouble" in Jamaica during demobilization, and the risk of unrest would be heightened if "any legitimate grievance in regard to pay remains unremedied," he predicted.[138]

The staff at the Colonial Office had less than a day to digest Allen's thoughtful memo before meeting with officials from the War Office. Having exchanged terse letters for months, representatives from the Colonial and War Offices finally met on January 31, 1919. If there had been any lingering debate, the meeting convinced officials at the Colonial Office that the extant ruling was completely untenable. When pressed to justify their decision, representatives from the War Office jettisoned the claim that the BWIR was a native regiment, maintaining instead that financial considerations spurred their ruling against West Indian troops. If the BWIR received the full benefits of the Army Order, then "coloured units" from Fiji, Bermuda, and South Africa would demand similar financial concessions as well.[139] Unimpressed by this latest excuse, officials from the Colonial Office retorted that a "clear line could be drawn" between the BWIR and the other units. And, as H. T. Allen had pointed out earlier, the estimated cost of granting the pay increase to all colored units was merely £500,000, equal to what the British Treasury spent on "two hours . . . of the war."[140] More to the point, they stressed that the fallout from further inaction could be dire. In a handwritten internal note after the meeting,

Grindle warned that the War Office remained blithely unaware of the "grave political issues" of their ruling. Grindle, however, possessed no such naivete: "If these men are discharged in the W. I. [West Indies] with a rankling sense of injustice due to their colour, I fear the British connection will be weakened just when we want the loyalty of the black man to hold out against American aggressiveness." Further still, predicted Grindle, if returning soldiers rioted during demobilization, the Colonial Office would reap the blame for the War Office's bungled ruling.[141]

Authorities at the Colonial Office, especially Alfred Milner, were determined not to take the fall for the War Office. In the wake of the meeting, Milner directed E. R. Darnley to draft a Cabinet memo outlining the Colonial Office's stance on the BWIR and Army Order No. 1 and stressed that the memo should be written "in the first person" and sent to the War Office over his signature to add heft.[142] The final document, collectively revised by several staff members with substantial input from Milner, emphatically argued that BWIR soldiers should receive the full benefits of Army Order No. 1. Milner pressed the War Office to reconsider its decision on two grounds—"that of immediate necessity and that of future political effect." Recapitulating H. T. Allen's earlier reading of the enlistment terms for the BWIR, he concluded the War Office had promised to pay West Indian volunteers at the same rate as their British counterparts. While it remained unclear if BWIR soldiers had also been guaranteed any future increases in pay, Milner insisted the exact wording of the original documents was irrelevant given the larger political stakes. "The fact is that, however the question may be argued here, nothing will ever convince either the men themselves or their friends at home that they have not been put off with a lower rate of pay purely on account of their colour," he explained. If the soldiers returned to the colonies "labouring under a grievance based on racial distinctions," they could incite political unrest across the West Indies. Any money saved by excluding BWIR soldiers from Army Order No. 1, Milner warned urgently, "will be most dearly bought."[143]

If these immediate political considerations were not sufficiently compelling, Milner entreated, the War Office should consider the long-term consequences of its ruling. Any hint of racial prejudice on the part of the imperial government, he maintained, would alienate black and colored West Indians and "prejudice the British connection for generations."[144] Given that black and colored West Indians were pivotal allies in the fight against U. S. expansion in the Caribbean, Milner went on, echoing Grindle's internal note, the War Office's decision could have major geo-political repercussions. "The coloured population of the West Indies has hitherto been more attached to the British connection than the white, and properly handled is our chief bulwark against American designs," Milner confessed. "If this question of pay is so handled as to leave behind a sense of injustice and a colour grievance the attachment of the negro population to the Empire will be seriously affected, and in addition to racial riots in the near future we shall incur a sensible weakening of our hold on the West Indian Islands."[145] With the first BWIR battalion scheduled to sail home in a matter of weeks and the threat of disturbances looming, Milner called on the War Office to act immediately to settle the dispute.

Besieged on all sides, the War Office finally relented. In February 1919, B. B. Cubitt, Assistant Secretary to the War Office, announced that the Army Council would grant all BWIR soldiers the "full terms" of Army Order No. 1, including over seventeen months of back pay at the increased rate.[146] Further still, the Council agreed to award BWIR servicemen the war gratuity outlined in Army Order No. 17 of 1919, to be paid as a lump sum upon demobilization.[147] Officials at the Colonial Office gushed over the hard-won victory. "The War Office have now given us all we asked in regard to pay, and more than we asked in regard to gratuity," a clerk boasted.[148] Alfred Milner quickly telegraphed the good news to the governors of the Caribbean colonies, and E. R. Darnley personally informed Contingent Committee chair Everard im Thurn.[149] After a year of vigorous petitioning, organizing, and protesting, BWIR soldiers had scored a significant victory in the fight for equality in the British imperial armed forces. Their transnational campaign not only forced the War Office to honor its original promises to the regiment but also led the Army Council to consider granting other "coloured units" the benefits of Army Order No. 1.[150]

Conclusion

Colonial Office functionaries attempted belatedly to claim credit for the War Office's revised ruling; however, BWIR soldiers were unquestionably the driving force behind the victorious campaign.[151] Their unlikely victory, which garnered significant material concessions and official recognition of the regiment as a unit in the imperial armed forces, highlights the political acumen and sheer determination of West Indian troops. When confronted with the intransigence of the War Office, BWIR soldiers strategically deployed the language of martial interracialism to add moral heft to their demands for equal treatment, castigating the War Office for both reneging on its promise and violating a central tenet of the empire. Soldiers' written overtures to far-flung colonial administrators, military officials, and

West Indian political elites map the multiple, overlapping networks that nourished the protest movement and demonstrate how soldiers moved adeptly between the civilian and military worlds. Their petitions and letters to colonial administrators, as historian Gregory Mann noted in his study of West African veterans, also illuminate the complex "process of creating and treating clients."[152] As this chapter has shown, the military and political elites who supported the BWIR's campaign nearly always imagined BWIR soldiers as loyal and respectable clients worthy of their benevolent patronage. Finally, the soldiers who rebelled in Taranto—and the noncommissioned officers who flirted with militant strategies during meetings of the Caribbean League—found collective action an appealing alternative to protracted lobbying.

BWIR soldiers faced a vicious backlash from senior military officials in Italy in the wake of the battle over Army Order No. 1. Brigadier-General Cyril Darcy Vivien Cary-Barnard, the new commandant at Taranto, confined the regiment to the base for the duration of their stay and instituted a host of discriminatory policies. He established a strict system of racial segregation, barring black and colored soldiers from British Expeditionary Force canteens, YMCA huts, and other recreational spaces for British units, in a departure from past practice.[153] He also relegated black and colored servicemen to inferior "native hospitals" where, according to one BWIR officer, sick servicemen "were starved and were not given sufficient blankets to keep warm."[154] On the one occasion when Cary-Barnard did permit BWIR soldiers to use the base's cinema, he allegedly demanded that the regiment fill every seat because he "would not allow British troops to sit down alongside niggers."[155]

Cary-Barnard also sought to undermine the crucial victories that BWIR soldiers had secured regarding their work assignments. Overturning the previous decision to remove the BWIR from fatigue duties and other sanitary work, the general stipulated that the regiment had to perform the same menial labor tasks that had sparked the mutiny. When Major J. B. Thursfield, commanding officer of the regiment's Fifth Battalion, confronted Cary-Barnard about assigning BWIR soldiers demeaning fatigue duties in violation of their official status as an infantry regiment, the irate general refused to rescind his order. Unleashing a verbal tirade, Cary-Barnard barked that he was "perfectly aware of the promise" made to BWIR soldiers, but he refused to honor it since the men were "only niggers and . . . no such treatment should ever have been promised to them." Furthermore, he claimed that BWIR servicemen were "better fed and treated better than any nigger had the right to expect" and insisted he would assign the men whatever jobs he saw fit. If any soldiers refused, Cary-Barnard threatened, he would "force them to do it."[156]

The indignities that the BWIR faced at Taranto threw into sharp relief black and colored soldiers' concerns about race, status, and belonging in the British armed forces and exposed the rhetoric of martial interracialism as an empty promise. Even after the successful campaign for Army Order No. 1, BWIR servicemen endured pervasive discrimination and violent threats from white commanding officers who, flouting official policy, insisted that black and colored men were unworthy of respect. Metropolitan allies in London and colonial officials in the West Indies ultimately failed to intervene as the regiment faced a torrent of racist abuse at Taranto, leaving BWIR troops to fend for themselves. When demobilization finally commenced in the spring of 1919, BWIR soldiers shifted their attention to the home front and began to imagine a new status for black and colored men in the postwar empire.

PART III

Postwar Reckonings

CHAPTER FIVE

"Serious Discontent"

EMIGRATION, REBELLION, AND
NEGOTIATION IN THE WAR'S AFTERMATH

We can provide against disorder, improve conditions, and be careful over questions of race but nothing we can do will alter the fact that the black man has begun to think and feel himself as good as the white.

—GILBERT GRINDLE (1919)

Thank heaven, the blacks are disillusioned.

—CLAUDE MCKAY (1920)

THREE MONTHS AFTER the Armistice, J. R. H. Homfray dispatched an ominous report to Maurice Hankey, secretary of the War Council.[1] As a lieutenant colonel in the Royal Marine Artillery, Homfray had visited every Caribbean colony during World War I as part of Britain's imperial defense effort. Now that hostilities had concluded, he sensed a "great deal of uneasiness" among colonial elites regarding the demobilization of the BWIR. Veterans, predicted Homfray, would return to the colonies "imbued with revolutionary ideas" and demand unreasonable compensation for their military service. "All the blacks" who have returned from the war, the lieutenant colonel claimed, "seem to imagine they are not going to work anymore" and will be "supported by a grateful country." If disaffected ex-soldiers revolted, as they had in Taranto, the small number of white volunteers in the British Caribbean would not be able to contain the unrest. Since colonial authorities could not depend on black volunteers to quell an insurrection—presumably because of their sympathies with BWIR soldiers—Homfray recommended that the War Office

[175]

dispatch Royal Marines armed with machine guns to Barbados, Trinidad, and Jamaica during demobilization. "At St. Kitts, Antigua, Dominica, and [St.] Lucia, I think there will not be very much trouble," he forecast, "but Demerara, Barbados, Trinidad, and Jamaica are decidedly pessimistic."[2]

Lord Hankey forwarded Homfray's dire assessment to Secretary of State for the Colonies Alfred Milner, instructing Milner that Homfray's opinion on the West Indies was "not one to be neglected."[3] Military officials in the metropole likewise advised the Colonial Office to expect trouble from returning West Indian servicemen. Colonel Piers W. North, commander of the Third Royal Berkshire Regiment, reported that West Indian volunteers who served in British regiments had gotten "hold of white women" and soldiered alongside white men. Having asserted their equality with whites on the battlefield and in the bedroom, black and colored veterans, North cautioned, would be "quite spoilt" when they returned to the colonies.[4]

Civilian observers on the home front confirmed military officials' worst fears about BWIR soldiers. In May 1919, Governor Leslie Probyn fretted that Jamaican veterans, inspired by the Russian Revolution of 1917, would bring home "a form of Russianised unrest."[5] The following month, Governor Charles O'Brien detected "considerable disaffection" among Barbadian veterans due to their "treatment at Taranto and during the war."[6] In his memoir, white Jamaican constable Herbert Thomas recalled that there was tremendous anxiety about the loyalty of BWIR servicemen since the men had mutinied while "quartered in idleness at Taranto."[7] Fellow white lawman Percy Fraser, Superintendent of Prisons in Trinidad, likewise described how veterans harbored a "high pitch of resentment" because of the racism they endured in the military. Angered by the "bad and unfair treatment" they received overseas, he explained, veterans had returned to Trinidad with a militant agenda to stamp out class and color inequalities.[8] "I have no hesitation in stating that this awful class feeling cropped up in full force," wrote Fraser, "on the return of the soldiers of the British West Indies Regiment from the First World War."[9]

This chapter examines the strategies veterans and their civilian allies employed in their attempts to wrest material, political, and symbolic rewards from the colonial state in the aftermath of the war. It chronicles the tense and volatile period from 1919 to 1920, when nearly fourteen thousand BWIR veterans returned to the colonies after serving in World War I, and revolutionary upheavals in Europe contributed to a mood of popular militancy in the British Caribbean. The chapter begins by situating elite anxieties about returning servicemen in the context of heightened claims-making by activists on the home front and the explosive growth of Marcus Garvey's Universal Negro Improvement Association. It then investigates colonial authorities' efforts in Jamaica and other colonies to forestall dissent through subsidized emigration initiatives and limited political concessions. Finally, narrowing the geographic frame, the chapter explores the politics of demobilization in British Honduras, the Central American outpost where an explosive rebellion led by returning black veterans erupted in the capital city in July 1919, contributing to the wave of uprisings by militant ex-servicemen in the Americas.

BWIR veterans and their civilian allies highlighted their wartime sacrifices to contend that Britain owed a debt to loyal West Indians. In contrast to veterans in the metropole, who increasingly turned to private charities and voluntary organizations to meet their needs after the Armistice, British Caribbean veterans directed their demands for recompense squarely at the colonial state.[10] Furthermore, they deliberately publicized their experiences of racism and discrimination in the British Army, citing each slight as proof that the "Mother Country" had violated the tenets of martial interracialism. Yet, during the dramatic rebellion in British Honduras in 1919, which pitted veterans who favored negotiation with the colonial state against those who sought change through popular revolt, reformist ex-soldiers ultimately prevailed. Their strategic use of the language of imperial patriotism and disavowal of violent protest tactics would have a moderating influence on the tone and trajectory of veterans' politics for years to come.

A "Great Deal of Uneasiness"

As 1919 dawned, metropolitan officials looked ahead with trepidation to the impending return of the BWIR.[11] Even before receiving Lieutenant-Colonel Homfray's urgent warning in February 1919, the Colonial Office had begun to request additional military support in anticipation of the return of West Indian troops.[12] Deeply rattled by the Taranto mutiny and the formation of the Caribbean League, Colonial Office staffers secretly asked the War Office to deploy a battalion of British infantry to Jamaica to maintain order during demobilization.[13] Nevertheless, in response to Homfray's call for heavily armed marines and military cruisers in Barbados, Jamaica, and Trinidad, the Colonial Office questioned the utility of such an overwhelming show of force. Dispatching three cruisers to the West Indies, clerk E. R. Darnley maintained, "would look like panic." Instead, Darnley proposed that the War Office station a single warship at

Jamaica since over 7,200 BWIR veterans, including the founders of the Caribbean League, would be demobilized there. In the other colonies, where smaller numbers of veterans would disembark, local authorities could recruit loyal BWIR ex-servicemen to serve alongside the standing police force if trouble arose.[14]

Unlike his subordinate, Alfred Milner was unwilling to disregard Homfray's proposal without first consulting authorities in the Caribbean. In a telegram to colonial governors on February 20, Milner instructed local officials to "take every precaution for the maintenance of order during demobilization," warning that there was still "serious discontent" in the BWIR despite the recent victory regarding Army Order No. 1.[15] Milner also asked the governors of Trinidad, Barbados, British Guiana, and the Windward and Leeward Islands if they would require a warship to render assistance when veterans returned. Since the British navy was stretched thin, he stressed, governors should only solicit additional assistance if it was absolutely necessary.[16]

At least two governors in the region, Charles O'Brien of Barbados and William Allardyce of the Bahamas, responded to Milner's telegram by requesting a strong naval presence during demobilization, demonstrating that anxieties about returning veterans permeated the region's smaller territories as well as Jamaica.[17] O'Brien, having previously served as acting commissioner of the Transvaal Town Police during the violent 1907 miners' strike in Witwatersrand, South Africa, had no qualms about using deadly force to suppress popular uprisings. Despite the relatively small number of BWIR veterans projected to return to Barbados, he requested that a warship dock at the colony during the entire period of demobilization. Additionally, he called for armed marines and sailors to be stationed in pickets throughout the capital in case of any unrest and ordered the Commandant of the Local Defense Force to post guards at the colony's armory. Justifying the need for such a substantial show of force, O'Brien alleged that BWIR soldiers had sent threatening letters to various individuals on the island. More ominously, he noted, returning servicemen were "trained to the use of arms" and knew the location of the colony's major stores of guns and ammunition.[18]

The specter of the Caribbean League spurred William Allardyce to request a gunboat to help maintain order in the Bahamas. Although the league disbanded in early January 1919, Allardyce remained deeply troubled by the "seditious movement." In a secret dispatch to Admiral Morgan Singer in late February 1919, the governor predicted that his island's small Defence Force would not be able to keep the peace when Bahamian veterans returned from overseas. Stressing that the Defence Force was "composed mainly of coloured persons," Allardyce echoed Homfray's earlier assertion that colonial authorities could not rely on black and colored militiamen to suppress an uprising by the BWIR.[19] Like many other white elites, Allardyce insisted that only white British troops could be trusted to suppress the nonwhite majority during a crisis.[20] The loyalty of black and colored lawmen, like that of BWIR veterans, was always suspect.

Meanwhile, many colonial subjects in the British Caribbean hoped to leverage the wartime sacrifices of returning soldiers to demand enhanced political privileges in the postwar era. Prominent black activist and solicitor Emanuel M'Zumbo Lazare expressed the hopes of many West Indian reformers in a public letter published in the *Argos*, Trinidad's laborite newspaper, in January 1919. A fierce opponent of Crown colony rule, Lazare had served as a lieutenant in the West India Regiment in the 1890s and even met Queen Victoria during the Diamond Jubilee celebrations in 1897. During a review of black colonial troops, Queen Victoria had reportedly leaned out of her carriage and asked the Trinidadian officer if he spoke English.[21] After returning to Trinidad, Lazare fought for constitutional reform through his work with the Ratepayers Association as well as the short-lived Pan African Association.[22] His letter to the *Argos* a decade later strategically invoked West Indians' role in the imperial war effort to reignite the regional struggle for representative government. Moved by "filial obligation," he wrote, military-aged men throughout the West Indies dutifully put aside their political grievances and answered the wartime call for volunteers. Likewise, civilians willingly donated money and agricultural produce to aid the metropole. On the battlefields of Europe, white, black, and colored Trinidadians gave their lives in the "greatest of all causes"—the fight for democracy. Now that the war was over, Lazare asked pointedly, would West Indians "be included in that great democratic circle, which is now encompassing the world? Shall we (the West Indian colonies) not be given a voice in the Congress of Nations?"[23]

According to Lazare, BWIR volunteers had "earned" the privilege of representative government for all West Indians through their martial labor. The noted activist urged the mayor of Port of Spain to gather the colony's "leading citizens" to petition the metropole for political reforms in anticipation of BWIR soldiers' impending return. "Preparations are now being made for the reception of our noble boys who have covered themselves with glory and won our political emancipation," he wrote. "Shall we be so inconsistent to ring out joy bells in honour of their home-coming after we shall have failed to reap the benefits of their glorious achievement?"

If the mayor and the Legislative Council refused to advocate for democracy, maintained Lazare, then the "people must rise to the occasion and be up and doing."[24]

Esteemed schoolmaster U. Theo McKay, elder brother and mentor of Jamaican poet Claude McKay, likewise used the language of mutual obligation to articulate the state's debt to BWIR veterans.[25] Yet, in contrast to Lazare's call for political concessions, McKay lobbied the colonial government in Jamaica to reward veterans materially with land grants and pensions. He recommended that returning soldiers receive well-paid jobs in recognition of their sacrifices on behalf of the empire, along with "a sum of money or a bit of land." Having seen the world and served in the British armed forces, he argued, veterans should not be expected to "go back to use the pick and shovel" at home. Decrying the low prewar wages on the island, the noted socialist and freethinker added that ex-soldiers, civil servants, and laborers must receive fair compensation if Jamaica hoped to advance in the postwar era. "The old order has passed, and passed forever," McKay maintained. "The cry is 'forward!' and any man who puts himself in the path of progress will find himself crushed to atoms."[26]

Lazare and McKay were part of a rising chorus of black activists whose demands for reform sparked the explosive postwar growth of the Universal Negro Improvement Association (UNIA). In the five years since the Kingston UNIA division had dispatched a loyalty petition to the Secretary of State for the Colonies, Marcus Garvey's organization had grown from a fledgling club in Jamaica to a massive transnational movement headquartered in Harlem.[27] Garvey himself, no longer content to negotiate with colonial authorities using the language of imperial patriotism, spoke with increasing militancy after his move to the United States in 1916. In response to the Armistice, the Jamaican black nationalist warned European statesmen to "be very just to all the people who may happen to come under their legislative control" in the postwar period. "The masses of the whole world have risen as one man to demand true equity and justice," Garvey declared in the pages of the *Negro World*, advising that black men and women would no longer tolerate the prewar status quo. "There will be no peace in the world until the white man confines himself politically to Europe, the yellow man to Asia and the black man to Africa," he insisted. And, in a clear warning to the world's colonial powers, the UNIA's president-general added that "anyone who dares to interfere with this division" of land would reap "trouble for himself."[28]

The *Negro World*, the UNIA's official organ, carried Garvey's message of African redemption and black empowerment throughout the Caribbean.

The motto emblazoned on the newspaper's masthead—"NEGROES GET READY"—rallied readers to prepare for a new sociopolitical order. Copies initially reached readers in the Caribbean via traveling sailors and international mail in late 1918. Shortly before the Armistice, Garvey mailed fifty copies of the newspaper to D. B. Lewis in Corozal, British Honduras, and promised to forward the same number of copies each week to raise awareness about the UNIA's program.[29] Around the same time, members of the British Caribbean diaspora in Panama first encountered the *Negro World* in the Canal Zone, where Japanese sailors reportedly distributed the periodical.[30] By February 1919, official representatives from the UNIA were selling copies of the *Negro World* in Trinidad and enrolling new members as well.[31] In the months that followed, officials in British Guiana and Barbados discovered that copies of Garvey's militant newspaper were circulating in their colonies, too.[32] And according to a leading historian of the UNIA, BWIR servicemen read the *Negro World* while stationed overseas and secretly brought copies home with them during demobilization.[33]

For West Indian readers, the *Negro World* offered an uncompromising call for "universal democracy." Four months after Garvey's controversial essay, W. A. Domingo published a trenchant editorial on the future of the British West Indies. Domingo, a Jamaican journalist who migrated to New York in 1910, cut his teeth as an officer in the National Club in Jamaica before reuniting with Garvey as the literary editor of the *Negro World*.[34] Like Garvey, Domingo hoped that the end of World War I would inaugurate a political "renaissance" for black men and women. Constructing a provocative counter-history of the war, the socialist writer argued that Britain had conscripted the Caribbean colonies into the war effort, denying the region's residents any voice in international affairs. "Too small and too weak to cherish any notion of aggression," the British Caribbean colonies reluctantly stumbled into the European conflict because of bellicose politicians in the "Mother Country." Despite this, Domingo claimed, colonial governments in the British Caribbean "went the limit" to demonstrate their loyalty, assuming financial burdens that would "impoverish them for generations." And West Indian men, like other subjects in the empire, voluntarily served in the war for democracy even though most lived under autocratic Crown colony governments at home.[35]

Yet "beneath the surface of their self-sacrificing patriotism," Domingo assured readers, lay "an ineradicable belief that their suffering and their participation in the war" would garner significant social and political rewards in the postwar period. Having soldiered in a war for democracy, BWIR veterans would no longer accept "economic serfdom or political slavery," Domingo proclaimed. "The British Empire cannot be half de[s]potic and half democratic. If oligarchical rule is not to be tolerated by Englishmen in England, it should not be tolerated by them in sections of their own empire," he continued. "If political freedom is good enough to be forced upon Germans, then it is certainly good enough for Jamaica, Trinidad, Barbados, St. Kitts and other islands of the Antilles."[36]

Already anxious about the impending return of BWIR veterans, colonial authorities moved rapidly to suppress the *Negro World*. In British Honduras, acting governor Robert Walter banned the importation and sale of the newspaper, writing that the *Negro World* would "incite racial hatred" and was probably funded by "German or Bolshiviki money." Walter's ban failed to stem the circulation of the *Negro World*, however, as copies were smuggled into British Honduras via Mexico and Guatemala.[37] Officials in Trinidad began surreptitiously intercepting copies of the *Negro World* in late February 1919, later justifying their illegal actions by insisting that the newspaper was "seditious and contrary to public policy."[38] The wartime postal censor in British Guiana started confiscating parcels of the *Negro World* in May 1919 after senior administrators in the colony declared that the paper "observe[d] a policy of antagonism to the white race." Casting a suspicious eye on all incoming African American periodicals, they likewise sought to restrict the circulation of *The Crusader*, the socialist magazine of Harlem's African Blood Brotherhood and even prohibited *The Christian Recorder*, the organ of the African Methodist Episcopal Church.[39]

Postwar Homecomings

After months of nervous anticipation and military buildup, BWIR veterans finally began to arrive in the colonies en masse in the spring of 1919. Colonial officials publicly celebrated returning soldiers as paragons of imperial loyalty while privately bracing for violent upheavals, public demonstrations, and the resurgence of the Caribbean League.[40] In Jamaica, constable Herbert Thomas remembered, colonial officials were especially tense. Shortly before the first group of veterans arrived in the colony, a local "scaremonger" had warned Governor Leslie Probyn that exservicemen would launch a "deliberately planned and organised rebellion" upon their return.[41] In response, the governor ordered all police officers to take special precautionary measures and assigned constables to guard the major demobilization hubs. In addition, when the first 1,200 Jamaican veterans disembarked on May 2, 1919, Probyn ensured that a warship was stationed near Kingston Harbor and sent a detachment of West India Regiment troops to stand guard near the ship. When residents condemned the brazen show of force, Jamaica Military Headquarters issued a public statement claiming that authorities had ordered the security measures to protect veterans from throngs of eager spectators.[42] Unconvinced, a group of BWIR sergeants drafted a letter to the governor protesting "the reception accorded to them on their return" and the "untrue statements" government officials circulated about their loyalty and behavior during the war.[43]

Authorities in Jamaica arranged for ex-servicemen to return to their home parishes within twenty-four hours of mustering out to minimize the threat of a large-scale veterans' protest in the capital.[44] After brief words of welcome by the governor and other leading officials, military authorities quickly shepherded veterans away from crowds of well-wishers and onto departing trains. Villages and towns across the island greeted "their sons" with home-cooked meals, cigarettes, and free entertainment in local community gatherings in lieu of a central homecoming celebration in Kingston.[45]

Once in their home communities, the men each collected a £2 advance on their final wages as soldiers. Like other British troops, BWIR veterans garnered a one-time war gratuity based on their length of military service as well as a demobilization allowance. Thus, within thirty days of demobilization, most former soldiers received a total of £20 to £25, a sum equal to approximately seven months' wages for a private.[46] Commentators warned that returned soldiers, without firm guidance, would spend their final pay recklessly. "From the rumshop, the gambling table, the pimps, the brothel, and from sharpers and charlatans, every good citizen should do his or her best to help returning soldiers to escape," the *Jamaica Times* declared. "Let him get his money into the bank, the Government Savings Bank. It will be safe there," the paper added, broadcasting a message about thrift and financial responsibility that soldiers across the Caribbean would hear repeatedly from colonial officials and black and colored reformers in the postwar years.[47]

War widows could apply for a one-time payment equal to a year of their spouses' military salary, but only if they proved that they had been financially dependent on a deceased soldier's earnings and were legally married at the time of his death.[48] Given that less than 40 percent of black and colored laboring people in the British Caribbean were formally married in the World War I era, many women were excluded from the benefits for war widows despite having lived in partnerships with BWIR soldiers.[49] Further still, many war widows who did meet the requirement of legal marriage would have had difficulty proving that they were dependent on their deceased husbands' wages. The "ideal of the dependent, non-wage earning housewife," as Rhoda Reddock and others have demonstrated, departed sharply from the reality of high rates of female wage labor in the West Indies.[50] In Trinidad and Tobago, for example, over 64 percent of women were classified as "gainfully employed" in 1911, and 62 percent of women held paying jobs in 1921 despite mounting unemployment in the postwar period.[51] In Barbados, over 82 percent of women performed remunerative labor outside of the home by 1921, highlighting the disjuncture between elite gender ideals and working-class families' dependence on female wage earners.[52]

Across the region, colonial authorities breathed a sigh of relief as the first days after demobilization passed without incident. Governor Charles O'Brien, commenting on the behavior of ex-soldiers, noted with pleasure that the men's conduct had been "quite correct" since their return to Barbados. Indeed, the governor went so far as to suggest that most veterans had "benefitted by the years under [military] discipline."[53] After talking with recently returned veterans in St. Elizabeth, Jamaica, constable Herbert Thomas similarly concluded that colonial officials' fears about ex-servicemen were overblown. BWIR veterans, he reckoned, had "nothing in their hearts but joy and pleasure at being once more at home."[54]

Indeed, some Jamaican veterans readily joined the empire-wide peace festivities in July 1919, positioning themselves as imperial patriots rather than dissidents. Demobilized soldiers marched through the streets of the capital along with members of the Jamaica Federation of Labour (JFL) in Kingston's Peace Day parade, symbolically linking their plight to the cause of organized labor.[55] Led by Alexander Bain Alves, a member of the island's colored middle class, the JFL functioned as an umbrella organization of skilled and unskilled workers, including longshoremen, hotel workers, coal heavers, banana carriers, and cigar makers.[56] Like many ex-soldiers, the leaders of the JFL articulated their calls on behalf of laboring peoples using the language of imperial patriotism rather than the rhetoric of revolutionary class struggle. In a commemorative Peace Day address to Secretary of State for the Colonies Alfred Milner and King George V, the JFL declared its "unswerving Loyalty and Allegiance" to the sovereign and the empire on behalf of the "workingmen of Jamaica." Citing their countrymen's military service, the JFL boasted that the "sons" of the island had upheld their vow to defend "the sacred person of His Majesty" and "His Imperial Interests." Indeed, the members of Jamaica's largest workers' organization requested that the Prince of Wales "pay a visit" to "His Majesty's most ancient and loyal" Caribbean colony as a "reward" for their wartime loyalty.[57] In response, George V's emissary reported that the King was "pleased" to receive the JFL's address and remained "well assured" of Jamaicans' loyalty.[58]

Meanwhile, colonial officials in Jamaica worked to secure veterans' quiescence through short-term political and economic concessions. These limited concessions, while not undermining white economic dominance or Crown colony rule, did provide substantive benefits to veterans that were not available to civilians from the black and colored laboring classes. On the political front, the Legislative Council voted to grant all returning servicemen the right to vote in the 1920 island-wide election, exempting ex-servicemen from the restrictive property and income qualifications for voters for one election cycle.[59] During the same session, the Council also enfranchised approximately three thousand propertied women, making Jamaica the second British Caribbean colony to grant some women the right to vote.[60] Taken together, these two measures expanded the Jamaican electorate by 25 percent, which offered an unprecedented opportunity for women and black and colored male veterans to register their concerns through formal politics. Yet, for reasons that remain unclear, ex-soldiers showed scant interest in exercising their newly acquired voting rights. Only 164 men, approximately 2 percent of the island's veterans, registered to vote in the 1920 election.[61] Similarly, propertied women in Jamaica, like their female counterparts in British Honduras, evinced minimal interest in electoral politics. Of those newly eligible, only 173 chose to register for the 1920 election.[62]

Within weeks of demobilization, local authorities also launched several economic initiatives for BWIR veterans. To help ex-servicemen reenter the civilian workforce, every parish established an employment committee that provided information about job openings, pay and pension benefits, and special training programs for disabled veterans. In addition, the Central Supplementary Allowance Committee (CSAC), the island-wide agency in charge of veterans' affairs, created a job registry in Kingston where over a thousand men applied for employment in 1919. The colonial government also offered a small number of educated former soldiers the opportunity to work as assistants and clerks in the civil service. Forty veterans took the required examination; twenty-one men ultimately passed and received jobs in the Government Service.[63] For veterans who sought to become smallholder farmers, the CSAC provided loans of up to £25 to purchase land, tools, or supplies to build a house. Between 1919 and 1920,

1,227 veterans applied for such loans, but only 213 were approved, leaving most men without the capital required to become independent farmers.[64]

Poor job prospects, soaring inflation, and insufficient government aid forced many ex-soldiers to travel overseas once again within months of demobilization. Indeed, the most popular economic initiatives for veterans in the immediate postwar period were emigration schemes, highlighting the centrality of migrant labor for many soldiers before, during, and after World War I. Acknowledging that the depressed local economy could not support 7,232 returning servicemen, Jamaica's CSAC provided informational leaflets and free work permits for veterans to migrate to Cuba. Arthur Herbert Pinnock, a member of the committee, also offered to help purchase the men's travel tickets to prevent any ex-soldier from "failing into the hands of dishonest agents who will fleece him of his money."[65] Over four thousand men, approximately 56 percent of BWIR veterans in the colony, participated in the migration initiative between June 1919 and March 1920.[66] In addition to encouraging migration to Cuba, Governor Probyn suggested that black and colored veterans might be willing to migrate as far as the South Pacific to perform agricultural labor. In a telegram to the Colonial Office, Probyn averred that ex-servicemen might pursue employment opportunities in Samoa if they received at least $1 per day in wages and free passage for their families, stressing that a land grant on the South Pacific island would offer a strong inducement to migration.[67] The Jamaican government also considered sending veterans to work for the United Fruit Company in Costa Rica, until West Indian banana workers in the Bocas Division launched large-scale strikes in 1919.[68]

Hundreds of returned BWIR soldiers from the eastern Caribbean islands likewise left their homes in search of employment, joining the tens of thousands of *antillanos* who entered Cuba in 1919 and 1920.[69] At least 422 ex-servicemen from Barbados, more than half of the colony's former BWIR soldiers, journeyed to Cuba after demobilization, with some men traveling "under the supervision" of ex-BWIR sergeant major Herbert Yearwood to work at the Cuban American Sugar Company's *Chaparra* mill in Oriente.[70] In St. Vincent, approximately one in three returned servicemen emigrated within a year of demobilization. According to a newspaper report, a group of 120 Vincentian veterans traveled together on a Cuba-bound schooner that was contracted by local authorities.[71] Dozens of ex-servicemen from St. Lucia and Dominica departed, too, for the "Queen of the Antilles" to work in the booming sugar industry.[72] Colonial authorities welcomed the mass exodus, viewing emigration as a remedy for unemployment *and* a means to rid the colonies of potential militants. Instead of providing sufficient funding for land settlement programs or robust vocational support, officials championed emigration as an expedient way to return to the prewar status quo.

If local authorities viewed emigration as the solution to the "returned soldiers' problem," their optimistic perceptions were irrevocably dashed when black veterans and civilians attacked whites in multiple colonies in July 1919. In Jamaica, on the night of July 18, a crowd of black ex-soldiers and sailors beat white seamen from HMS *Constance* in downtown Kingston. During the attack, the assailants reportedly shouted, "Kill the whites," as they slashed five to six visiting sailors with razors. One or two white civilians were also pummeled during the fracas. In response to the attack and the "open threats of the mob," the captain of the *Constance* landed a piquet of fifty armed marines, who patrolled Kingston for the remainder of the evening. The following day, the acting governor stationed guards from the WIR and HMS *Constance* throughout the capital to maintain order.[73] Similar incidents occurred in Port of Spain, sparking fear and anger in Trinidad's white community.[74] The upheavals in Jamaica and Trinidad, however, were soon overshadowed by a spectacular popular uprising in Belize Town, the remote colonial capital of British Honduras.

"We Are Going to Give Them Hell Tonight"

Veterans from the British Honduras Contingent of the BWIR returned home on July 8, 1919.[75] Sailing to Belize Town on the *Veronej*, the 339 officers and men were greeted aboard the ship by the commander of the local Territorial Force, Lieutenant-Colonel James Cran; nominated member of the Legislative Council and chair of the Returned Soldiers Welfare Committee Archibald Usher; and a throng of eager reporters. The veterans disembarked near Court House Wharf and paraded through the streets of the capital to Government House, the governor's stately residence on the shore of the Belize River. On the parade route, people from "all classes" showered returning servicemen with a "spontaneous outburst of welcome" and outpourings of joy.[76] "The royal reception accorded to us on our return here . . . filled us with pride and admiration," Corporal Samuel Haynes recalled. "We know for a fact and we are exceedingly proud," he boasted, that the welcome-home celebration in British Honduras was "the grandest and best yet given to returned soldiers throughout the West Indies."[77] At Government House, Governor Eyre Hutson praised BWIR soldiers for their role in the empire's "fight for freedom and justice" and congratulated

FIGURE 5.1 Return of the British Honduras Contingent of the BWIR. Courtesy of the Belize Archives and Records Service.

them on defeating "the King's enemies." He promised that, in recognition of their wartime sacrifices, all veterans would receive a "substantial" gratuity from the military, demobilization pay, and assistance finding civilian employment. Furthermore, during "a few days of holiday and rest," the men could enjoy free sporting events and entertainment along with their families and friends.[78]

While Governor Hutson celebrated the wartime exploits of BWIR soldiers, he also sought to limit veterans' financial demands on the colonial state. Inverting the language of mutual obligation, the governor insisted that the empire had fulfilled its debt to World War I veterans and that returning servicemen had a responsibility to reintegrate promptly into colonial society. He reminded ex-soldiers that the West Indian Contingent Committee in London and the Contingent Society in British Honduras had looked after their welfare and raised thousands of dollars for their families. He urged veterans to demonstrate their gratitude by returning to work quickly rather than waiting until their "money is exhausted." Advising former servicemen to embrace thrift and "honourable labour," the governor invited them to deposit their military gratuity, back pay, and any subsequent earnings in newly created savings accounts. By securing gainful employment and avoiding the "temptation to spend," he suggested, BWIR soldiers could contribute to British Honduras' postwar prosperity and honor their commanding officers. "I am confident that the good repu-

"SERIOUS DISCONTENT" [189]

tation which you have won while on active service will be jealously guarded by each one of you on your return to your native land," Hutson proclaimed, and that you will "resist any temptation to excesses" and "bear in mind the reputation you have earned" as a member of the British Army.[79]

Following his address, Governor Hutson shook hands with returning veterans and presented each man with a printed copy of his speech. Then, the men marched to Drill Hall, where they celebrated over "cold refreshments" and received $10 in local currency as an advance on their final pay. The ex-soldiers reassembled two days later to receive their final disbursement of £20. Heeding Governor Hutson's advice, "a considerable number" of former servicemen deposited part of their gratuity in the state-run Savings Bank, while others met with members of the newly established Employment Committee to begin searching for work.[80]

Colonial authorities in British Honduras, largely unaware of veterans' deeply demoralizing experiences overseas during the war, assumed that there was "no serious dissatisfaction" among ex-soldiers.[81] In fact, Superintendent of Police Robert Wyatt initially concluded that veterans had returned "considerably improved" after their stint in the army.[82] However, there was mounting evidence in Belize Town that neither veterans nor civilians were willing to accept the prewar status quo.[83] During a variety show and film screening for former servicemen on July 11, 1919, veterans and townspeople loudly applauded the French flag but sat defiantly silent when pictures of King George V and Queen Mary appeared.[84] According to one witness, the audience greeted an image of the Union Jack with even more hostility. When the flag of the British Empire flashed across the screen, Cyril Fuller later recalled, the audience at the theater groaned and made other "sounds of disapprobation."[85] And, in an explicit rebuke of imperial patriotism, some BWIR veterans in the theater openly declared that "the French flag was the only one that they would fight for" in the future.[86]

One day after the incident at the theater, a deputation of four demobilized soldiers met with Governor Hutson, having heard rumors that "a shipload" of white veterans from England had arrived in the colony to take well-paid jobs at local businesses.[87] Led by Sergeant H. H. H. Vernon, the group of non-commissioned officers complained that two prominent Belize Town firms had recently hired European immigrants for clerk positions while many qualified Creole men remained unemployed. Vernon argued that "men of the Colony," particularly returning BWIR veterans, should be given preference over European jobseekers and called on the governor to intervene. Despite his recent appeal for BWIR veterans to find employment as quickly as possible, Governor Hutson refused to condemn local merchants' discriminatory hiring practices, claiming he "could not possibly interfere in such a matter." Further still, the governor admonished ex-servicemen *not* to expect preferential treatment for the colony's black majority.[88]

Veterans' demand for preferential access to local jobs reflected the increasingly precarious financial position of Creole men and women. Between 1914 and 1919, the cost of living in British Honduras had increased 300–400 percent, leading laboring and middle-class residents to accuse merchants of wartime profiteering.[89] The price of vital foodstuffs, in particular, soared, as the colony had little domestic agriculture and depended overwhelmingly on imported food. Residents faced stiff hikes in the price of clothing as well, leading to "exceptionally bad" conditions in Belize Town.[90] Commenting on the extent of wartime inflation, barrister Frans Dragten declared, "I do not think there is anything that has not gone up in price" during the war.[91] To make matters worse, wages in the colony's vital forestry sector had declined almost 50 percent, and hiring for forestry jobs in the Belize District had fallen nearly 60 percent.[92] As economic conditions worsened, the *Clarion* noted, many parents in the colony could no longer afford to send their children to school.[93]

Laboring people confronted similarly staggering price inflation elsewhere in the Caribbean, though conditions were rarely as difficult as in British Honduras. In Trinidad, the price of consumer goods surged 126 percent in Port of Spain, 167 percent in San Fernando, and 140 percent in rural areas.[94] Officials in Jamaica reported that the cost of foodstuffs increased 145 percent while clothing prices jumped 350 percent.[95] Residents in Grenada grappled with a comparable rise in food costs while watching clothing prices increase as much as 500 percent.[96] Cost-of-living reports from authorities in St. Lucia and British Guiana likewise noted significant material privation due to skyrocketing housing, food, and clothing costs.[97] The editors of the *Barbados Weekly Herald*, sounding the alarm about food insecurity on the island, warned that a "square meal . . . is an impossibility for seven-tenths of our population."[98]

Hence, as Governor Hutson dismissed returning soldiers' requests as unreasonable, other local voices pressed veterans to demand more significant reforms as repayment for their wartime service. Creole activists, for example, urged returned soldiers to use the leadership skills and vocational experience they acquired overseas to spur political and economic development at home. The *Belize Independent,* edited by black activist

Hubert Hill Cain, dedicated nearly all of its July 16 edition to examining the role that veterans would play in the future of British Honduras.[99] In an editorial welcoming home ex-servicemen, the *Independent* proclaimed that the return of BWIR veterans inaugurated a "new era" in the colony's history. While the colonial government had been marred by "deadlock and stalemate" during the war, the dislocations of the global conflict had produced heightened demands for reform in the postwar period. "The masses throughout the length and breadth of the civilized world," the paper declared, "are determined that Liberty, Equality, and Fraternity shall no longer be mere catchwords; Democracy shall be no empty romance." Those who "went to fight and we who remained to pay," it warned, "are taking serious thoughts about it ourselves instead of . . . leaving it to others." As "true patriots" who had traveled abroad and served alongside soldiers from throughout the empire, BWIR veterans had a special obligation to challenge political oppression and exclusion on the home front. The *Independent* pressed veterans to "make their voices heard" in the fight against Crown colony rule, asserting that "no one is more qualified to determine the future of his own land than the soldier who risked his life blood." The paper reminded ex-servicemen of their obligation to their compatriots and asked, "Will men who travelled thousands of miles to protect the name of the Empire, refuse or neglect to perform a more sacred duty that lies right at hand?"[100]

A second article in the *Independent* linked wartime sacrifice and political privilege more explicitly, conscripting ex-soldiers into the battle for representative democracy. Writing under the moniker "Patriot," a correspondent argued that British Hondurans had earned the right to representative government and improved living conditions because of their contributions to the imperial war effort. "Patriot" insisted that British Hondurans' displays of loyalty to the empire should be repaid with substantive political and economic reforms. Describing how local women and men had voluntarily donated money and materials to the war effort despite their distance from the metropole, "Patriot" claimed that the colony's forty-one thousand British subjects now expected "better recognition" from local and metropolitan officials. "British Honduras has done her share in the great struggle and we are looking out for our reward," the correspondent insisted. "We want a voice in our affairs. We are entitled to it, and we must have it." Imagining veterans as the natural leaders of the reform movement, "Patriot" posited that ex-soldiers had "become used to modernism" abroad and could, therefore, spearhead development projects at home. After seeing "good roads and many other useful and necessary things" overseas, "Patriot" declared, veterans would accept nothing less in their own communities.[101]

While local reformers urged veterans to join the movement for political reform, ex-soldiers in British Honduras, like their comrades in Jamaica, largely focused their efforts on securing material concessions from the state. Between July 8 and 21, at least sixty former soldiers met with members of the state-sponsored Employment Committee to discuss their work history and prospects for future employment. The committee, chaired by Legislative Council member Sally Wolffsohn, identified suitable job openings and wrote letters of recommendation for ex-servicemen. Although veterans initially established a good rapport with the committee, relations soured when the group secured jobs for only one or two men.[102] During a tense meeting on July 21, veterans' frustration with the lack of employment reached a tipping point. "The demeanor of the ex-soldiers at the meeting," committee member and *Clarion* editor Phillip Woods later testified, was "aggressive and ugly."[103] Unwilling to work for the rock-bottom wages generally paid to local laborers, ex-soldiers demanded compensation two to three times higher than prevailing rates. Several veterans, for example, requested jobs as storemen, demanding $15 per week instead of the standard pay of $5 or $6. When the committee announced that there were thirty road-building jobs available for veterans, ex-servicemen lobbied for a daily wage of $2 instead of $1.25. According to committee member Percy George, one veteran requested a hundred acres of land and a $1000 advance in recognition of his military service.[104] George later testified that after hearing the veteran's request, he concluded it would be "impossible" for the committee to meet ex-soldiers' expectations. By the end of the meeting on July 21, veterans likewise questioned the utility of working with the Employment Committee. Voicing the frustrations of many, one ex-soldier ominously warned the committee, "What I want, you cannot give me."[105]

The day after the strained Employment Committee meeting, one of the largest uprisings in the history of British Honduras erupted on the streets of Belize Town. Constable David Rowland was walking along East Canal Street on the south side of the capital when he encountered BWIR veteran Thomas Graham around 7:30 p.m. As Sergeant Graham and a group of men passed the constable, Graham allegedly shouted: "We are going to give them hell tonight." Unsure how to interpret the ex-servicemen's outburst, Rowland simply walked past Graham and continued his patrol without confronting the sergeant or his companions.[106] An hour later, Colonel James Cran was resting on his veranda when he heard the sound of breaking glass. Cran ran to the street and watched in shock as eight to ten BWIR veterans, dressed in their military uniforms and marching in formation, smashed the window of Brodie's department store using large walking sticks. Hoping to end the disturbance before it escalated, Cran pleaded with the men to leave the street immediately and to discuss their grievances with him. The group of veterans quickly dismissed the colonel's offer to mediate on their behalf. Taking matters into their own hands, the men ordered Cran to "go away" and warned him to keep his distance from the contingent for the rest of the night. As Cran tried to reason with the veterans, they pushed him aside and marched to Hofius & Hildebrandt department store, where they also broke every glass window.[107]

Cran followed the veterans and watched as the former soldiers, now surrounded by a crowd of approximately seventy civilian onlookers, smashed the windows of six additional stores in rapid succession. "Working on the sound of a whistle," the men marched in front of each business, waited for the leader to give the signal, and then methodically struck the glass until the lead soldier blew the whistle a second time. Significantly, the veterans made no attempt to enter the vandalized stores or to remove any goods. "They were acting under discipline during the whole of this time and absolutely no attempt was made at looting at all," Cran later testified. "Even the articles which were exposed in the windows, which they had broken and which could be easily reached, were not touched by the Contingent." Struck by the ex-soldiers' coordinated movements, the colonel surmised that the demonstration was "part of a carefully prepared programme."[108]

BWIR veteran Frederick McDonald was sitting at the Territorial Club with Percy George when a visitor rushed in and announced that ex-soldiers were "raising hell" on the other side of town. Hoping to quell the upheaval, McDonald ran to Albert Street, where he encountered Colonel Cran and at least ten rebellious veterans. After advising Cran to go home immediately, McDonald approached one of the ringleaders, Sergeant H. H. H. Vernon, and entreated him to stop his men from vandalizing any further property. When Vernon refused, McDonald then approached the protestors directly but was rebuffed once more. As McDonald continued to negotiate with his former BWIR comrades, two or three ex-soldiers suddenly ran toward him, raising their sticks menacingly. McDonald called their bluff, asking the men "what the hell" they meant to do and reminding them that he was still "their Sergeant Major."[109]

By invoking his military rank, Regimental Sergeant Major Frederick McDonald summoned his wartime authority in an attempt to reign in his former subordinates. During the war, the decorated warrant officer had been the highest-ranking nonwhite soldier in the British Honduras Contingent, commanding the respect and obedience of black and colored enlisted men. The sergeant major's authority carried much less weight in the streets of Belize Town, however. Militant ex-soldiers might still respect their former commander enough not to physically assault him—they put down their sticks and fled when McDonald challenged them—but they disregarded his pleas to resolve their grievances through negotiation rather than mass action. When McDonald approached Sergeant Henry Ogaldez and urged him to share any grievances he had with Colonel Cran, the former non-commissioned officer replied, "Not for hell." When McDonald ordered Private Rufus Hall to leave the streets at once, the ex-soldier reminded McDonald that he was no longer in charge. "Oh, this is not Mesopotamia, this is not Egypt," Hall fumed, "this is Belize."[110]

Other alignments had changed since the war as well. During the uprising in Taranto, Italy, in December 1918, noncommissioned officers failed to join the six-day protest, electing instead to articulate their grievances through a petition to the Secretary of State for the Colonies. In British Honduras, however, former noncommissioned officers and ex-privates joined forces as protestors in the streets of Belize Town. Sergeants Thomas Graham and H. H. H. Vernon led the initial demonstration, marching at the head of the formation and giving signals with their whistles. Sergeant Ogaldez brazenly rebuffed Frederick McDonald's pleas for restraint, and Lance Corporal George Hulse threatened to assault the former sergeant major. Witnesses later testified that at least one other noncommissioned officer, Quartermaster Sergeant J. H. Grant, also participated in the protest.[111] Most significantly, ex-soldiers allegedly met in the home of Corporal Charles Sutherland to formulate plans for the uprising.[112]

The coordinated protest by ex-servicemen erupted into a full-blown popular rebellion around 8:50 p.m. when the capital's electric generator failed.[113] As Belize Town plunged into darkness, civilian women, men, and children flooded the streets and began looting the major department and grocery stores. Within minutes of the power failure, merchant Henry Melhado witnessed crowds of people hauling "sewing machines, gramophones [sic], bundles of clothing, and various other things" across the Swing Bridge.[114] Captain Herbert Stoyle, on guard at the power station, watched helplessly as "hundreds of women, men, and contingent men" passed by with "tremendous loads" of goods. The women, he noted with dismay, were "passing with their dresses full of loot and coming back again for more."[115]

"SERIOUS DISCONTENT" [195]

Armed with walking sticks, axes, hatchets, and fence palings, the mixed crowd of veterans and civilians attacked several white homes as well.[116] Many white observers believed that the uprising was a concerted attack on the colony's white elite. "Every white man in the streets," Governor Hutson recalled, "carried his life in his hands."[117] Another white resident insisted that "anybody with a white face" incurred the wrath of the crowd.[118] According to police officer Joseph Blades, the protestors boldly proclaimed, "This is our country and we want to get the white man out."[119] William Hoar, keeper of the Belize Prison, similarly testified that the protestors hurled racialized threats as they made their way across the capital. Standing on North Front Street, Hoar watched as seventy to eighty veterans and civilians crossed the Swing Bridge, reportedly shouting, "We are going to kill the white sons of bitches tonight" and "This is the black man's night." When the crowd spotted Hoar, they chased him and threatened to "smash his skull."[120] He ultimately escaped unscathed, but several other white residents were not so fortunate.

Duncan Fraser, managing director of Broadie's dry goods and hardware business, left home to check on the store and inadvertently crossed paths with a group of three hundred to four hundred protestors. After someone in the crowd spotted Fraser, several veterans beat him with fence palings, leaving him bloody and "senseless."[121] Percy George, secretary of the Returned Soldiers' Welfare Committee, endured a fifteen-minute assault at the hands of four or five ex-servicemen. As a crowd of civilians looked on, veterans repeatedly struck George on his back, shoulders, and legs and then kicked him at the base of his spine.[122] Superintendent of Police Robert Wyatt approached a group of riotous veterans and cried out, "Peace, boys, peace."[123] In response, returned soldiers beat him "black and blue" while a crowd of civilians "jeered and laughed and danced." Several minutes into the thrashing, an ex-private rescued Wyatt from his former comrades and escorted the dazed policeman to the South Street Police Station.[124] Phillip Matthews sustained severe head wounds after Privates Stephen Panting and Patrick Hamilton chased him through his house, pounding him with sticks. Unlike most victims, Matthews, an officer in the British Honduras Territorial Force, managed to fight off his attackers. Trading blows with the two ex-servicemen, Matthews knocked Hamilton to the ground and kicked Panting three times in the stomach before the men finally fled.[125]

Despite "some forebodings and intimations of trouble," the violent upheaval on the night of July 22 "came as a shock" to local authorities and totally overwhelmed the capital's understaffed police force.[126] Beating victim

Duncan Fraser, echoing the sentiments of many whites, later testified that the rebellion "was the biggest surprise of my life."[127] Robert Wyatt likewise confessed that he "had not anticipated any outbreak" among returned soldiers.[128] The massive uprising also caught Governor Eyre Hutson by surprise. Unlike other governors in the region, Hutson had elected not to request additional military or naval support during demobilization and did not increase the colony's standing security forces once BWIR veterans returned. Even after he was warned on July 18 that there was a "strong undercurrent of ill-feeling" among ex-soldiers, Hutson "still placed trust in the loyalty of the majority of the Contingent."[129]

Therefore, on the night of the rebellion, the Belize Town police force included only thirty-nine men, six of whom were new recruits.[130] At the height of the uprising, around 11:00 p.m., the meager force faced an "enormous" crowd of three to four thousand people, approximately one-fourth of the capital's total population.[131] As protestors overpowered the police, only thirty-five members of the British Honduras Territorial Force, the colony's local militia, reported for emergency duty. Terrified by the size and intensity of the mass uprising, Governor Hutson feared that the rioters would seize power and compel him to "haul down the [British] flag."[132]

As colonial authorities retreated to Drill Hall, anticipating an imminent defeat, a small group of BWIR veterans tried once again to quell the rebellion. Sometime between 11:30 p.m. and midnight, Frederick McDonald and fellow noncommissioned officer Corporal R. J. McKoy stood on the north side of the Swing Bridge and issued a call for volunteers to help restore order. McDonald blew his whistle to attract attention and shouted: "Any loyal men of the contingent fall in under me." Five or six men, including Samuel Haynes, immediately stepped forward and began detaining suspected looters. McDonald continued to solicit volunteers among the crowd until he had assembled a unit of ten to fifteen ex-soldiers. Under McDonald's direction, the veterans marched through town, clearing suspected looters from pillaged stores and businesses. "Seeing men in uniform," McDonald later testified, "the people took fright and came out in quick time offering . . . no resistance." The sergeant major posted a pair of veterans to keep guard at each store that was cleared in case the looters returned. Once his unit had successfully cleared and secured four pillaged stores, McDonald reported his progress to Colonel Cran, who remained holed up at Drill Hall along with other white residents. McDonald informed Cran that his men were unarmed and facing a hostile crowd and requested that members of the Territorial Force relieve the veterans as soon as possible.[133] Shortly after 1:00 a.m., a group of colonial officials guarded by members of the Territorial Force read the Riot Act and began clearing the remaining protestors from the street.

The rebellion finally subsided at daybreak on July 23, as the remaining civilians and ex-servicemen gradually dispersed and wandered home. In the light of day, the scope of the damage became clear. Insurance claims for the nine-hour uprising exceeded $138,000.[134] Ten of the city's largest stores had been wrecked, leaving a trail of broken glass and ruined merchandise throughout downtown. Every pane of glass in Miss Staine's boarding house was smashed, and several private homes of white businessmen suffered extensive damage as well. Significantly, no public buildings or government properties were damaged, nor did the rioters make any attempt to storm Government House, even though, as Governor Hutson openly acknowledged, it remained completely unguarded all night.[135] These findings call into question historian Peter Ashdown's widely accepted claim that the rebellion was a "clumsy attempt at a coup d'état."[136] Given veterans' pre-riot focus on economic grievances, it is likely that the upheaval on July 22 targeted the colony's white merchant elite rather than the colonial state itself.

In the days following the rebellion, tensions ran high in Belize Town as rumors swirled that civilians would return to the streets.[137] Colonial officials relied on Frederick McDonald, Samuel Haynes, and other "loyal" veterans to maintain law and order and ensure that no further unrest took place. Governor Hutson confessed privately that it was "humiliating" to realize the "influence and power" of black and colored veterans.[138] However, on July 23, the beleaguered governor authorized McDonald and Captain Greville Hulse to assemble a group of sixty to seventy veterans to patrol the streets of Belize Town and to guard white-owned businesses. The following morning, the men watched as the British naval warship HMS *Constance* arrived in English Caye, near Belize Town. Under the command of a British officer, Captain E. C. Kennedy, one hundred white British marines and a machine gun crew disembarked in the colony and established a command center at Drill Hall. The heavily armed naval party assumed command of local security operations, while Governor Hutson continued to utilize BWIR veterans to perform police duties. Following the governor's declaration of martial law, Colonel Cran swore in forty-five ex-servicemen as special constables and authorized them to begin arresting suspected rioters and looters. According to McDonald, the first men they arrested were six former BWIR comrades: Privates Blackwood, Willocks, Hall, Gaboret, Hamilton, and Domingo.[139]

[198] CHAPTER 5

In the wake of the rebellion, veterans held a series of meetings in Belize Town to discuss their grievances and determine their next steps. The first meeting took place on the afternoon of July 23 at the C. US Theatre. During the gathering, attendees established a new veterans' association, the British Honduras Contingent Committee (BHCC), to "represent them in everything in connection with their welfare."[140] Significantly, the six men elected to serve on the BHCC included veterans who had spearheaded the rebellion *and* those who had suppressed it, bringing together militant and reformist leaders. H. H. H. Vernon chaired the committee, which also included Samuel Haynes, Percival Gentle, I. E. Lewis, J. H. Grant, and A. P. Bowen.[141] Like in previous organizing efforts, noncommissioned officers monopolized the key positions in the BHCC. Five of the six elected committee members had served as NCOs during the war, while only one member, A. P. Bowen, had been a private. Furthermore, no white veterans served on the BHCC, although at least one white officer, Captain Greville Hulse, attended the July 23 meeting where the group was established. It is unclear if white servicemen refused to participate in the BHCC or if black and colored veterans excluded their former officers from the committee.

Two days after the uprising, on July 24, the BHCC met with Governor Hutson to discuss veterans' concerns. Before the committee members had an opportunity to speak, the governor opened the meeting by condemning the rebellion and announced that there would be a "full enquiry" into the "felonious acts" committed in Belize Town. Then, in a thinly veiled warning to the militant members of the committee who participated in the protest, he stated: "I hope none of you here have had any part in those acts, because I might remind you that you are still wearing His Majesty's uniform [and] are in his service under oath, and are expected to observe his laws and keep the peace."[142]

Sergeant Vernon, speaking on behalf of the BHCC, outlined several concerns to the governor, nearly all of which dealt with economic matters. He pressed Hutson to clarify the aims and responsibilities of the Employment Committee, address the high cost of clothing and other non-food items, and provide further information about the proposed land settlement program for veterans. Vernon also asked if veterans would receive a refund of the money they had contributed during the war for separation allowances. Along with these economic matters, Vernon inquired about the shooting of Private Hamilton, a BWIR veteran, during the uprising, requesting that the BHCC "be supplied with a copy of the evidence" the government had collected about the incident.[143] Striking a conciliatory tone, Vernon distanced himself from the popular upheaval on July 22 and,

"SERIOUS DISCONTENT" [199]

instead, presented the BHCC as the respectable voice of the nascent veterans' movement.

On the heels of the meeting with Governor Hutson, the leaders of the BHCC convened a second gathering with veterans on July 25, drawing a large crowd "at which nearly all ranks were present."[144] Tensions ran high as the men debated the governor's response to their grievances. The leaders of the BHCC attempted to provide an update about their meeting with Hutson, but the attendees seized the opportunity to air their grievances. Angered by ongoing rumors that local merchants were recruiting white immigrants to fill vacant positions in Belize Town, some men proposed that they send a deputation to meet with the governor to stipulate that "no further European clerks be brought to the Colony."[145] The men also demanded justice for their wounded comrade, Private Hamilton. Unsatisfied by the governor's response to their questions about the shooting, they called for the immediate arrest and court-martial of the suspected white assailant, Captain Franco. According to witnesses, one veteran yelled, "We want Captain Franco arrested by 4 o'clock this evening."[146] Others accused the BHCC of siding with Franco instead of defending Hamilton. Two of Hamilton's friends, Privates Blackwood and Willcox, were forcibly escorted out of the theater after becoming "excited" and disruptive. The meeting eventually became "disorderly": attendees hurled "sarcastic remarks" at the BHCC and "roaring and shouting" filled the theater.[147]

In response to mounting anger and demands for immediate redress, Samuel Haynes rose to address the meeting. Haynes, according to a witness, "spoke in a most forceful manner to the men."[148] He ordered veterans to "remain loyal" and "warned them to be exceedingly careful in the way they went about their grievances."[149] Invoking his position as the secretary of the BHCC, Haynes claimed that the "powers of the Committee were limited" and that they had no authority to intervene in the criminal case involving Private Hamilton and Captain Franco. Frederick McDonald later credited Haynes with squashing calls to confront Governor Hutson: "Had he not spoken in the manner in which he did . . . the meeting would have ended in possible disruption."[150] After Haynes admonished the men, McDonald recalled, the "meeting was brought to a conclusion," and the "members of the contingent went away quietly."[151] In his account of the meeting, Haynes emphasized his moderating influence on fellow veterans. "At the close of my address," he boasted, "about fifteen of the men thanked me personally for some of the points I had brought to their notice."[152]

FIGURE 5.2. Samuel Alfred Haynes. Schomburg Center for Research in Black Culture, Photographs and Prints Division, The New York Public Library.

Civilian activists, hoping to harness momentum from the rebellion, also planned a public meeting at the C. US Theatre on July 25, gathering just a few hours after the meeting held by the BHCC. On flyers announcing the event, organizers invited "men[,] women[,] and children" from the "labouring classes" to attend, a tacit acknowledgment of the important role that women and youth played in the uprising.[153] The meeting was organized by seasoned activist Claude Smith, a black man who had previously been targeted by colonial officials for defending small farmers.[154] Local authorities fretted that the public gathering could incite further unrest while conceding privately that there was "nothing in the law to render such a meeting illegal" and that "anyone who cared had a legal right to attend it."[155]

Yet, Haynes was determined to keep ex-soldiers from joining Smith's nascent campaign to organize the colony's working class. Fearful that veterans would attend the public meeting, Haynes told the men that "such a gathering was prohibited" and insisted that "no member of the contingent was to attend." Furthermore, on the evening of the event, Haynes traveled to the theater and "inspected each row of seats," searching for ex-soldiers. In subsequent testimony, he reported: "I found about 8 members of the contingent present with their lady friends, and I requested that they leave the building immediately. This they did without any hesitation."[156] According to Haynes, he only returned home after he completed his search of the theater and ensured that "no member of the contingent was present."[157]

In the weeks following the rebellion, forty men were arrested, including at least fourteen BWIR veterans.[158] Tried before a special session of the Supreme Court, thirty-one individuals were convicted of criminal offenses related to the uprising. The court handed down the longest sentences to three ex-servicemen convicted of assault: Private Rufus Hall, the veteran who boldly reminded Frederick McDonald that he was no longer in Mesopotamia, was convicted of attacking fellow veteran P. C. Francis with a brick and received a sentence of six years' imprisonment with hard labor; and the two veterans who beat and kicked Percy George—Privates W. Grant and A. Willocks—were each sentenced to five years' imprisonment with hard labor. Protestors convicted of nonviolent offenses received sentences of six months in prison.[159]

The three-member Riot Commission appointed to investigate the rebellion concluded that the "ring leaders throughout were returned soldiers of the British Honduras Contingent." The uprising in Belize Town, according to the commission, was caused by economic distress, racial animosity toward the capital's white residents, and "the presence of a considerable number of returned soldiers with extravagant claims and pretensions."[160] While members of the Riot Commission sought to invalidate ex-soldiers' grievances, other commentors argued that militant veterans had given voice to the "general dis-satisfaction" among the colony's laboring class. In his testimony to the commission, school master George Bennett asserted that veterans had been transformed by their experiences overseas during the war. BWIR volunteers had enlisted with "patriotism and loyalty akin to worship," but returned home filled with "bitter resentment." As Bennett explained, "these soldiers have been abroad and have seen the progress of other countries and knowing the colony as their home and its condition and that large sums of money have been spent [,] they naturally have a feeling that politically the colony is very backward." "I believe the rioting had a political aspect," he proclaimed, "and was a demonstration."[161]

Colonial authorities rewarded "loyal" contingent men materially and symbolically for their role in suppressing the popular uprising. Shortly after the rebellion, Frederick McDonald became the new Assistant Superintendent of Police in Belize Town and temporarily served as the Superintendent of Police after the governor removed Robert Wyatt from the post due to his poor leadership during the crisis.[162] McDonald, Hutson later testified, had performed "loyal and yeoman service" on behalf of the colonial government.[163] Samuel Haynes received a special commendation in recognition of his loyalty from the Secretary of State for the Colonies. To appease other veterans, Governor Hutson established a new Labour Bureau Office in August 1919 to assist ex-servicemen in finding employment. For men who could not secure jobs in the private sector, the state-run Labour Bureau provided temporary relief work, employing forty veterans by October 1919.[164] Hutson also petitioned imperial authorities for a £10,000 loan so that the local government could hire up to 150 unemployed veterans to work on road construction and land reclamation projects across the colony.[165]

Whereas colonial authorities celebrated McDonald and Haynes for their loyalty during the uprising, some Belize Town residents reviled the veterans' reformist politics. Four days after the rebellion, William Hoar, keeper of the Belize Prison, was standing on the steps of the North Side Police Station when Annie Flowers, a cook for a leading merchant family, approached a group of women standing nearby. Flowers, speaking in "as loud a voice as possible," reportedly declared, "The black man have no pluck. The women have to be behind them all the time or else they do nothing; but if they were all like me, I would take their [white men's] wives and daughters and bloody well live with them: that would teach them that this country belongs to the blacks." Threatening to "shove hat pins in the eyes of the bloody white men" the next time there was an uprising, Flowers reportedly vowed that she would work to clear all whites out of Belize Town. When the warship of British Marines leaves, she allegedly added, "we will know what to do with the white bastards."[166]

Conclusion

In April 1920, four months after the criminal trials of the rioters concluded, Samuel Haynes sent an unexpected appeal to Governor Hutson. Writing in his role as secretary of the BHCC, Haynes pleaded for the release of all BWIR veterans who had been incarcerated following the uprising in Belize Town. The imprisoned men, Haynes maintained, had no ability to support their families while confined in prison. As a result, their dependents were experiencing extreme financial hardship, forced to "earn their livelihood under the most hazardous and trying circumstances" and to secure food and other necessities from local merchants on credit.[167]

Although Haynes petitioned for the veterans' early release, he continued to condemn the uprising that they had spearheaded, calling the protest a "regretful occurrence" and "the deplorable riot of 22 July, 1919." Rather than affirming the veterans' grievances, Haynes lobbied the governor to pardon all incarcerated ex-servicemen in recognition of their wartime service to the empire. The veterans' "splendid record of service coupled with the physical strain borne by these men for a worthy cause," he argued, should be "taken into due consideration." Explicitly framing the potential pardon as an act of imperial gratitude, he urged the governor to release ex-soldiers from prison on May 24, 1920—Empire Day.[168]

In his appeal, Haynes maintained a studious silence regarding the fate of the civilians who were also arrested and imprisoned for their role in the uprising. Instead, he crafted his appeal solely on behalf of ex-soldiers, omitting any references to the civilian men, women, and children who protested alongside militant veterans in July 1919. In doing so, he worked to fracture the bonds of solidarity that developed on the streets of Belize Town between ex-servicemen and civilians during the uprising. His message was clear: veterans merited special consideration from the state; civilians did not.

Governor Hutson swiftly rejected Haynes's appeal despite its narrow framing on behalf of ex-soldiers. In his response to Haynes's letter, the governor argued that the incarcerated veterans had "misconducted themselves" and that he did "not feel justified in interfering with the sentence of the Court."[169] When Haynes subsequently asked if he could appeal directly to the colony's Chief Justice on behalf of incarcerated veterans, Hutson insisted that "no good object would be served" in petitioning the court.[170] And in a confidential letter to the Secretary of State for the Colonies, Hutson even questioned Haynes's loyalty, labeling the reformist veteran as a "troublesome agitator."[171]

In the aftermath of the uprising, Haynes helped to establish a new division of the UNIA in Belize Town, serving as the group's general secretary. Despite his involvement in the UNIA, Haynes continued to boast about his role in quelling the popular uprising by ex-servicemen and civilians in Belize Town. In a 1927 article published in the *Negro World*, Haynes recounted how he "saved a number of white men—British, Scot, Irish, German, and American—from probably wholesale massacre at the hands of an infuriated contingent of returned soldiers" in the summer of 1919. In recognition of his loyal service and "restraining influence," Haynes reported, he garnered "the commendation of the Secretary of State for the Colonies in a special dispatch to the Governor of the Colony."[172] Three years later, he once again highlighted his part in suppressing the July 1919 rebellion, depicting his former comrades as hotheaded drunkards. "If the truth were told, it was I whose appeal to sobriety and reason saved the handful of Europeans in Belize from a savage massacre when the returned soldiers rioted in an orgy of rum in the summer of 1919," he wrote. "I rose to the occasion and silenced the radicals."[173]

CHAPTER SIX

"Equal Reward for Equal Service"

VETERANS' POLITICS IN POSTWAR TRINIDAD

All that [the returned soldier] has is the satisfaction which arises from the consciousness that he has done his duty—that he has fought to save the world . . . [for] democracy. But it is democracy of a poor type which allows him to go unrewarded and uncared for, and, which seems to twit him for having served the Empire.

—"DISCHARGED SOLDIERS," *ARGOS*, MAY 22, 1919

The spirit of unrest, which seems to have swept over the world as one of the consequences of the great war, has visited us; and in Trinidad it appears to have taken the form of a desire on the part of some irresponsible self-appointed agitators and so-called popular leaders, to stir up strife through an exaggeration of the extent of those prejudices.

—"THREEFOLD FOLLY," *PORT OF SPAIN GAZETTE*, JULY 29, 1919

IN JULY 1919, FIFTY-THREE men gathered in Port of Spain, Trinidad, to establish the Returned Soldiers' and Sailors' Council (RSSC), an organization to "protect the interests" of newly discharged World War I veterans.[1] The founding members of the council, likely aware of swirling rumors that disaffected ex-soldiers were secretly plotting a rebellion, took great pains to assure colonial officials about their moderate aims and approach. In a letter to local authorities, the men pledged that the council would submit "their grievances in a proper constitutional manner before the Government for redress."[2] Indeed, the council's motto, "One

[205]

Aim, One Empire, One Responsibility," presented ex-soldiers' demands for fair compensation as part of a shared effort to strengthen the bonds of the empire. The RSSC's cable address likewise underscored the council's public embrace of imperial patriotism: correspondents could direct their telegrams to the RSSC using the word "LOYALTY" (see fig. 6.1).[3]

Even as the leaders of the RSSC used the language of imperial patriotism to allay colonial officials' fears about the new association, they resolutely maintained that their status as British subjects entitled them to just compensation and self-appointed representation, suturing their call for enhanced financial benefits to broader debates about democratic governance in the British Caribbean. The founding members resolved that they had a right to lobby the government directly rather than pleading for aid through the Discharged Soldiers Central Authority (DSCA), the committee established by colonial officials to oversee the welfare of ex-servicemen. They also insisted that Trinidadian veterans deserved equitable compensation—not charity or handouts—in recognition of their wartime service in the British armed forces. They endeavored to build an autonomous organization where former soldiers and sailors could elect their own officers, discuss collective grievances, and negotiate with local and imperial authorities. Ultimately, they argued for and prefigured participatory politics that challenged Crown colony rule, even as they professed their allegiance to the empire.

The RSSC established its headquarters at 49 Duncan Street, in a predominantly black, working-class neighborhood in Port of Spain. The council invited veterans to come together to share "pressing matters affecting their interests" at afternoon meetings held one to two times per week.[4] RSSC leaders highlighted the fact that the council was a representative body, unlike the DSCA, which was led by white men who had been appointed by the governor. Speaking directly to black veterans, an advertisement for the council proclaimed that the RSSC was "started for you" and "by your own people." The council's elected leaders pledged to fight "honestly, fearlessly, truthfully, and well" in their pursuit of justice for Trinidad's war veterans.[5]

In the wake of World War I, returned soldiers established new veterans' organizations across the British Caribbean. In Trinidad, veterans launched not only the RSSC but also the Soldiers and Sailors Union (SSU) within weeks of demobilization in 1919. That same year, former private Tubal Uriah "Buz" Butler established the Grenada Union of Returned Soldiers in St. George's with the support of newspaper editor and labor activist T. A. Marryshow. In Jamaica, veterans launched at least three organizations

"EQUAL REWARD FOR EQUAL SERVICE" [207]

FIGURE 6.1 Letterhead of the Returned Soldiers' and Sailors' Council. National Archives of Trinidad and Tobago.

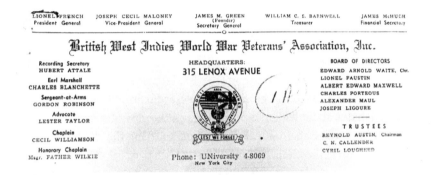

FIGURE 6.2 Letterhead of the British West Indies World War Veterans' Association, Inc. Jamaica Archives and Records Department.

during the 1920s: the St. Ann's Comrades of the War Association, the Jamaica Ex-Service Men Association, and the Ex-BWIR Association.[6] In Barbados, veterans founded the Old Comrades' Association.[7] Former soldiers even established veterans' associations while living abroad in the United States. The British West Indies World War Veterans' Association, initially led by Sergeant John W. Moses of Jamaica, was founded in New York in 1928 and remained active until at least the 1950s (see fig. 6.2).[8] In addition to welcoming ex-soldiers, the association also permitted women to join and hold office through its ladies' auxiliary.[9]

Veterans' associations mounted grassroots advocacy, mutual aid, and commemoration initiatives, providing a vehicle for ex-soldiers to agitate for financial support and civic recognition through collective action. They employed a range of tactics to advance the veterans' cause—petitioning government officials and holding protest marches as well as sponsoring rumshop reunions and participating in solemn war remembrance events. Founded and headquartered in urban locales like Port of Spain, Kingston,

St. George's, and New York, the associations were led by and centered their efforts on ex-soldiers who settled in cities following demobilization. Veterans and their civilian supporters built these new associations from the ground up, growing membership through personal ties and local outreach efforts and operating independently from the veterans' movement in Britain. The fragmentary and incomplete records left behind by these groups make it impossible to quantify precisely how many men joined their ranks, and the reported membership numbers range widely. At the inaugural meeting of the Grenada Union of Returned Soldiers, forty-two men paid the entrance fee to join the association; meanwhile, the leaders of the British West Indies World War Veterans' Association in New York boasted that their group had 1,300 members and was "planning to purchase ground and build their headquarters in Harlem at a cost of $75,000."[10]

Returned soldiers in Trinidad, outraged by the paltry benefits provided by the colonial government, rallied around the principle of "equal reward for equal service" to argue that BWIR servicemen were entitled to the same compensation given to war veterans in Britain.[11] However, intense debates about leadership, tactics, and the government's obligation to ex-soldiers roiled the nascent movement, spurring the creation of rival groups. At the same time, colonial officials, distrustful of returned soldiers, worked to undermine the RSSC, refusing to recognize or negotiate with its leaders and insisting that the DSCA was the sole body that could assess the needs of ex-servicemen. This chapter explores how veterans, civilian activists, and colonial officials in Trinidad wrestled over *who* could represent veterans and *what* compensation veterans deserved from the state. Ex-soldiers' embattled efforts to build an autonomous movement in Trinidad have been overlooked by scholars, who have instead focused their analysis on the spectacular rise of organized labor in the colony and the militant strikes that erupted in the final weeks of 1919. Yet, as historian Kelvin Singh acknowledges in his foundational political history of this period, "the issue of the returned soldiers" was "the main focus of attention" for nearly all of 1919.[12] Thus, by examining ex-servicemen's activism during this period, we can uncover the shared economic grievances that spurred the veterans' and labor movements and the debates over tactics that ultimately splintered working-class soldiers from civilian strikers.

Fraught Homecomings

In the early months of 1919, Trinidadians anxiously awaited news about the return of the BWIR and prepared to welcome home their sons, brothers, husbands, and friends who had soldiered overseas during the war. More than 1,400 men from Trinidad and Tobago had joined the BWIR, making the colony the third largest enlistment site for the regiment after Jamaica and Panama. Just weeks before demobilizing soldiers were scheduled to start arriving en masse, the editors of the *Argos* published a grim assessment of the men's economic prospects. "The outlook for the Discharged Soldier in Trinidad is far from re-assuring. If he be disabled his prospects are dismal," the newspaper pronounced in May 1919.[13] After demobilization, veterans had little hope of returning to their prewar occupations because their former positions had been "permanently filled" by replacement workers or eliminated altogether. "In Trinidad . . . the man who gave up his berth to don the King's uniform now finds that he did so for good," the *Argos* reported.[14] For disabled veterans, the economic landscape was a "hundred times worse." Colonial authorities had no special provisions in place to aid servicemen who had lost limbs, suffered from severe physical ailments, or experienced mental illness. With no hope of securing a job, Trinidad's disabled veterans "were expected by the Authorities to live on fresh air and scenery."[15]

Contrary to the *Argos*'s claim, colonial officials in Trinidad had begun formulating plans for reintegrating both able-bodied and disabled veterans into the labor market nearly two years prior to demobilization, when Governor John Chancellor established the Discharged Soldiers Central Authority in August 1917 to oversee veterans' transitions to civilian life.[16] Handpicked by the governor, the men who led the Authority hailed from Trinidad's white economic and political elite. George F. Huggins, a prominent merchant, planter, and financier, served as chair.[17] Other members included Legislative Council members William Kay and Henry Fuller, engineer Daniel Hahnk, attorney J. B. L. Todd, and police inspector J. Denis Lenagan.[18]

From the outset, the DSCA prioritized keeping colonial expenditures low rather than aiding veterans. The Authority sought to sharply curtail the state's financial obligation to veterans by shifting responsibility to private employers, local aid organizations, and even the men themselves. The Authority argued that discharged soldiers must be "encouraged to . . . get work as much as possible"; and, therefore, they should "be given as little money as possible."[19] Rather than creating new organizations to address the specific needs of veterans, the DSCA aimed to use "existing bodies and organisations in order to secure the most efficient results with the lowest expense to the Colony."[20] In a similar vein, the Authority proposed that veterans should receive disability pensions and other allowances based on rates established in 1915 rather than the more generous rates announced by the imperial government in 1917. The higher pension scale, they claimed, was "based on European requirements" and "would be an unwarrantable burden on the Colony." Furthermore, the DSCA predicted that the special provisions for "unmarried wives and illegitimate children" included in the 1917 pension guidelines would be "subject to considerable abuse" if granted to BWIR veterans.[21] Thus, DSCA members, rather than throwing their support behind BWIR soldiers' ongoing fight for equal compensation, labored to institutionalize inequality and restrict postwar financial support for the soldiers and their families.

Since it looked to private employers, rather than the state, to aid returning soldiers, the DSCA placed ads in local newspapers requesting employers to inform the Authority about available job openings. Urging employers to aid veterans out of a "sense of duty and goodwill," the Authority called on local "Estates, Stores, Factories, [and] Oilfields" to hire ex-servicemen.[22] Further, the DSCA established an employment committee to assist veterans in returning to their old civilian jobs or, if that was impossible, to obtain new positions. The committee also provided free tools for men who could demonstrate proficiency in carpentry, tailoring, or other skilled trades.[23]

Yet, like in British Honduras during this same period, conflicts quickly erupted between the employment committee, which pushed veterans to accept any available job, and ex-soldiers, who insisted that their military service qualified them for well-paying positions. Predictably, local elites mocked ex-servicemen's pursuit of upward mobility. "Cases have been known to occur when youths who before their enlistment had been garden servants have gone to the [Employment] Committee for clerical work, when their very applications disclosed the fact that they were absolutely unfitted for such employment," the editors of the *Trinidad Guardian* decried. "Some ex-soldiers have been placed twice, and even thrice, in work but . . . by their unreasonable demands disgust the employer and return to give further worry to the Authority."[24]

Ex-soldiers, in turn, argued that the DSCA's employment committee was ineffective and alleged that potential employers refused to hire black veterans.[25] One jobless veteran, writing from southern Trinidad, refuted the claim that ex-servicemen were unwilling to work. "I have made several efforts, and I am still out of employment. It is very hard after having tramped to the theatre of war to get no reward."[26] Another unemployed veteran claimed that some employers turned down job seekers who had served in the BWIR. "Just think of that and after doing what was right by answering the call of the Empire voluntarily. Now we are considered a disgrace to our country." Voicing the disappointment

"EQUAL REWARD FOR EQUAL SERVICE" [211]

of many ex-servicemen, he described the "daily regret" that he felt after seeking aid from hostile employers and indifferent colonial officials. "We have been from place to place seeking employment and can't get even the employment that we were engaged in at the time we answered the call of King and Country," he wrote. "Are we to be ruined or to continue as a disgrace in the face of it all? No assistance is the daily cry to us, and many are men of family. Is this a British Island?" Facing financial ruin, the beleaguered veteran concluded that he and his BWIR comrades had "assisted in winning the war of all wars," but had ultimately "lost our war at home."[27]

Some unemployed Trinidadian veterans sought work abroad; however, they did so independently rather than through state-sponsored initiatives, making it difficult to quantify exactly how many men left the island in the months following demobilization. Several ex-servicemen, following long-established labor migration routes, sailed across the Gulf of Paria to Venezuela, hoping to secure jobs in the port city of Güiria or on cocoa estates in the village of Yacua.[28] The DSCA's employment committee paid for a small number of veterans to return to Panama, where they had presumably worked in the Canal Zone before they enlisted.[29] Others headed north to the United States, joining thousands of fellow West Indians who settled in New York after the war.[30] Describing the labor conditions in New York in 1919, J. M. Green, a former sergeant in the BWIR, reported that the city was overrun with job seekers. "There are more unemployed men in this City than one can count, and with the numerous strikes on it is hardly safe for a stranger to go and take a job at any factories," he noted. After one week of job hunting, Green concluded that "any man who can earn six dollars per week in Trinidad can live much happier than one who is working for five dollars per day in New York."[31] Traveling abroad, as Green quickly discovered, did not provide veterans with a guaranteed path to stable employment or any employment at all.

Veterans who sought to become smallholders rather than seeking full-time employment as wage laborers could apply for financial support through the DSCA's land settlement scheme. Under the terms of the program, ex-servicemen who received a good conduct discharge sheet could apply for five acres of rural Crown land in Trinidad or on the neighboring island of Tobago to establish their own estate. Veterans who successfully cultivated their allotment with "cocoa, coconuts, limes, or other staple products" would receive the title to the land as a free grant after five years. To help veterans establish their smallholdings, the DSCA offered two short-term loans. Eligible men could receive £10 to cover the cost of tools, land clearance, and other initial expenses and a second £10 to pay for the construction of a house on the allotment.[32]

Returned soldiers who pursued free land through the DSCA's program faced daunting restrictions. Not only did they have to formally apply for the program, appearing in person at a meeting of the DSCA and proving that they were "suitable" to become smallholders, but those applicants who were approved for an allotment of Crown land had to reside on the property full time and could not sublet it during the five-year probationary period. In addition, the Authority explicitly discouraged veterans from acquiring land in adjoining plots—or "blocks"—that would have permitted groups of ex-soldiers to live and work in proximity. And its mandate that veterans grow "staple crops" on the land prevented men from pursuing other commercial uses for the property.

The DSCA's land settlement scheme elicited swift and vocal disapproval. In an editorial published in early July 1919, the *Argos* highlighted numerous shortcomings. The paper questioned the modest amount of Crown land offered to veterans as well as the Authority's recommendation that ex-soldiers establish separate estates rather than selecting neighboring land parcels to form contiguous blocks with fellow veterans. "The allotment of a mere five-acre block savours of niggardliness, especially when we consider the large areas of Crown lands held up," the *Argos* declared, "while the recommendation against the block system indicates a lack of real inside knowledge of the subject."[33] The paper reminded readers that previous land settlement programs for veterans—including the effort to resettle hundreds of black soldiers who fought with the British in the War of 1812—had utilized the block system, creating company villages in southern Trinidad where their descendants continued to live over a century later.[34] Additionally, the *Argos* criticized the DSCA loan program. It was unreasonable to expect veterans to clear the land, buy seeds and tools, build a house, and support themselves and their families with such paltry financial support. "In view of the present cost of living, of materials, etc., the niggardly advance of £10 recommended, is wholly inadequate and sounds extremely ridiculous." Without major revisions to the terms of the program, the *Argos* warned, the land settlement initiative was "likely to remain a mere *paper* scheme."[35]

Standing in solidarity with veterans, other civilian commentators offered similarly stirring rebukes of the land settlement scheme. Edwin Harper, in the poem "Lest We Forget," juxtaposed the self-sacrificing patriotism of soldiers with the appalling parsimony of the local bureaucrats charged with their care. Published in the pages of the *Argos*, the poem functioned simultaneously as an ode to Trinidadian soldiers and a public indictment of imperial ingratitude. Harper countered elite discourses that minimized, mocked, or erased Trinidadian soldiers' wartime service, instead portraying servicemen as valiant volunteers who dutifully helped "the dear motherland" to "stay a Hunnish hand."[36]

In the poem's opening stanzas, Harper returned to the early years of World War I, invoking the fevered local military recruitment campaign and Trinidadian soldiers' perilous journeys from "Iere," the Amerindian name for the island, to distant overseas conflict zones. He constructed a map of martial sacrifice, referencing soldiers' deployments to the "blood-strewn fields of France," "Afric's eastern shores," "Mesopotamia's Eden," and "Italia's ground," to mark the multiple sites where BWIR servicemen labored, fought, and died to secure the Allies' victory.

Trinidadian soldiers, in Harper's rendering, were betrayed "sons" of the empire—faithful yet forsaken. Despite their crucial contributions to the Allies' victory, they had failed to garner public recognition or fair compensation. Harper, condemning this erasure, referred to the state's obligation to veterans as an unpaid debt, a language also widely used by colonial troops in the French empire in the aftermath of the war.[37] In the poem's closing stanzas, he took aim at the land settlement scheme:

> Now they're come back to the land,
> We seem just to forget,
> To give them even a brother's hand
> Or recognise the debt.
> Just think! Five acres is the price
> As compensation fair,
> A value put on sacrifice
> On land and sea and air.[38]

Beyond its particular shortcomings, the editors of the *Argos* maintained, the land settlement scheme exposed a fundamental problem with the DSCA; namely, it was not a representative body. Drawn from the colony's white professional and merchant classes, the "gentlemen who formed the committee" lacked any "real inside knowledge of the wishes of the people." Most notably, they failed to grasp the severe financial constraints facing returned soldiers, who lacked the capital and other resources necessary to establish themselves as small farmers. If colonial authorities wanted to develop "a more comprehensive and practicable" land settlement scheme, then they would have to create "a larger and more representative committee" to consider the needs of veterans.[39] The editors called for a committee whose members were "more in touch with the people" and had "more intimate knowledge of the humbler classes," a representative body that was "in fuller sympathy" with the "needs, ambitions and aspirations" of ex-servicemen. Without an overhaul in the membership of the DSCA, the editors warned, the land settlement scheme risked "going down to posterity as a colossal failure."[40]

Other critics of the land settlement scheme echoed the point that veterans should have a voice in determining how the government rewarded their wartime service. In doing so, they challenged a central tenet of Crown colony rule by insisting that returned soldiers—not government appointees—were best equipped to formulate veterans' policy. Unwilling to leave his fate in the hands of the DSCA, one ex-serviceman proposed that colonial officials should create "a larger and more representative committee—in which discharged soldiers should be equitably represented."[41] Another correspondent, writing to the editors of the *Argos*, enjoined veterans to mobilize collectively. "The 'ex-soldier' must remember that to succeed he must help himself, and not leave everything (or anything), entirely to the Government or anybody else." Instead of accepting the "paltry 5 acres" offered in the land settlement scheme, he should "organise himself into a representative body to look after his interests."[42] By harnessing their critiques of the land settlement scheme to calls for deliberative democracy, veterans and their allies challenged the exclusion of working-class black men from local governance in Trinidad.

As frustrations mounted, veterans increasingly bypassed the DSCA and endeavored to place their concerns directly before colonial officials. On June 18, a group of ex-soldiers descended upon the Red House, the colony's seat of government, hoping to meet with the acting governor. According to newspaper reports, the men "would have nothing to do with the Discharged Soldiers organisation" and demanded to "lay their grievances" before the government instead.[43] Three weeks later, on July 3, a group of 123 ex-soldiers outlined their grievances in a petition to local authorities. Condemning the "inequitable and improper treatment" that they had endured during their military service, the men emphasized the BWIR's status as an imperial regiment and pressed the government to provide them with veterans' benefits equal to those allotted to British soldiers in the metropole. "Being troops of His Majesty's Forces, we were always under the impression that we were eligible to [receive] the same emoluments and privileges as other regiments of the British Army," the petitioners explained. However, the local government had failed to provide unemployment benefits, billeting allowances, and other forms of financial assistance to men who served in the BWIR, leaving veterans to question their regiment's "real position" in the British armed forces.[44]

By mid-July, several observers urged colonial officials to address the growing disaffection among veterans. "It is regrettable to observe that there is a strong wave of discontent, gradually yet steadily, sweeping over the spirit of our returned soldiers," the *Argos* reported. If "prompt action is not taken," the paper warned, the "serious" situation could spur unrest.[45] Likewise, Lieutenant Colonel Maxwell Smith, in a confidential assessment submitted to the acting governor on July 16, warned that a "spirit of discontent" was present among ex-soldiers. A former BWIR officer, Smith had served in the regiment's Eighth Battalion and was one of the officers who had exposed the secret meetings of the Caribbean League at Taranto, Italy. This time, he readily acknowledged veterans' economic grievances and advised colonial authorities to remedy the situation. In order to avoid accusations of racial discrimination, Smith opined that he was "strongly in favour of the men receiving the full ration allowance" and he also recommended that veterans receive bonus pay at the reduced rate of 10s. 6d. for twenty-six weeks. "On the whole I think it adviseable not to discriminate between the Native and European except in so far as local conditions as compared to with those obtaining in England warrant it," he counseled. "I more especially urge this as a very strong feeling of discontent was noticeable amongst the men . . . while on active service owning to certain discriminations made between them and the Europeans."[46] Three days after Smith drafted his report, tensions boiled over onto the streets of Port of Spain.

"A Blot on Our Fair Reputation"

On the morning of July 19, hundreds of spectators assembled at Queen's Park Savannah in Port of Spain to participate in the empire-wide Peace Day festivities.[47] The celebrations, which marked the signing of the Treaty of Versailles, featured a grand ceremonial military parade by local troops. In a symbolic recognition of their contribution to Britain's victory, former members of the BWIR were invited to march at the front of the procession. Approximately 132 BWIR veterans—one hundred men from the Eighth Battalion and thirty-two men from the First and Second Battalions— paraded around the Savannah under the command of Maxwell Smith, the white officer who had secretly warned colonial authorities about mounting ill-feeling among ex-soldiers.[48]

While scores of veterans opted to take part in the parade, "a considerable number of other returned soldiers" assembled at the Savannah but refused to fall in. Instead, they "made disparaging remarks about their comrades who were in uniform . . . especially about those who were taking part in the parade." As participating veterans marched past in formation, dissident veterans booed and heckled their former BWIR comrades. Alarmed by the dissident veterans' public acts of defiance, G. H. May, the Inspector General of the Constabulary, speculated that some ex-soldiers had refused to join the parade "because they were disappointed at not being armed." The former soldiers had "possessed themselves of ammunition whilst on active service" and had planned to "shoot down all the officers," he alleged.[49]

Two days after the disturbance at Queen's Park Savannah, the confrontations escalated dramatically when local residents attacked white British sailors from the HMS *Dartmouth*.[50] Angered by recent reports about white mobs assaulting, robbing, and killing black West Indian seamen in England, black residents in Port of Spain unleashed their ire on white sailors docked in the capital.[51] "Crowds of the *hoi polloi*, with whom were unfortunately, some of the returned soldiers," reported the *Port of Spain Gazette*, "were out on the streets with the determination to beat the whites."[52] The melee began on the evening of July 21 when two men— Vernon Davis and Arthur Harris—physically assaulted white sailors who were walking in downtown Port of Spain near the intersection of Park Street and St. Vincent Street. Soon, "a crowd of 50 persons pounced down upon" the sailors "from all directions," beating them with sticks, stones, and an iron ball tied to a string.[53] Bystanders, including women and boys, cheered on the attack, shouting, "beat him, beat him" and "run for your life or I will kill you."[54] As the victims fled, the men accosted a second group of white sailors from the *Dartmouth* who were riding on the city's tram car. When the tram car stopped at the intersection of Frederick Street and Oxford Street, the men jumped onboard and started beating sailors with fists and a large tree branch. During the tram car attack, one assailant reportedly screamed: "You white b[astard], you pay for all."[55] Crowds armed with bottles, sticks, and razors also attacked white sailors on Prince Street, hurling so many projectiles that "people who live[d] in the vicinity of the fights had to close their windows and doors in order to be secure from the rain of stones." In the aftermath of the confrontations, seven sailors from the *Dartmouth* were admitted to the local hospital due to their injuries.[56]

According to the Inspector General of the Constabulary, the assailants also taunted white sailors in a particularly charged way—by recounting their sexual encounters with white women. In a report submitted days after the disturbance, G. H. May claimed that the assailants had made "very lewd and disparaging remarks" to the sailors "about the white race and about their women folk."[57] Local authorities in Trinidad, as elsewhere in the British Caribbean, already feared that returning veterans and seamen would pursue intimate relationships with white women in the colonies, emboldened by their sexual experiences in Europe during the war. Governor Eyre Hutson, writing in the aftermath of the July 1919 uprising in British Honduras, concluded that veterans' interracial sexual liaisons had made a "dangerous and regrettable impression on them."[58] Jamaican constable Herbert Thomas likewise suggested that some ex-soldiers, having discovered a "totally different" class of white women while abroad, no longer respected "buckra [white] ladies" at home.[59] And in his memoir, Percy Fraser, Superintendent of Prisons in Trinidad, claimed without evidence that returned soldiers made good on their threats and committed "unlawful acts" against local white women. In the months following the veterans' return, he alleged, it was "unsafe for any white woman to go out in the night unescorted."[60]

Trinidad's establishment press swiftly condemned the disturbances as "disgraceful," "foolish," and "suicidal."[61] The violent upheaval on Peace Day, the *Port of Spain Gazette* fumed, was part of a subversive campaign to "galvanize . . . class and colour hatred between the various sections of our hitherto peaceful community." Arguing that the capital's racially and ethnically diverse population had lived together "in a state of remarkable and creditable amity" before the war, the paper insisted that the Peace Day disturbances signaled an unprecedented "outbreak of . . . hooliganism on the part of the lowest classes." The *Gazette* cast blame on "irresponsible self-appointed agitators and so-called popular leaders" for "stir[ring] up strife through an exaggeration of [racial and class] prejudices." The paper alleged that radicalized veterans, too, played a central role in stoking unrest. "Returned soldiers, imbued, no doubt, with the false socialistic ideals with which they have come into contact over the other side, are playing an unfortunate part in disseminating these ideals amongst their more credulous and less educated listeners." While the paper claimed to support the "legitimate aspirations of the people," it dismissed the street protests by black civilians and veterans as "absolute foolishness."[62]

In a clear warning to would-be protestors, the *Gazette* declared that imperial officials would not tolerate further unrest in the colony. The "Imperial Government is strong enough and determined enough to put down with a heavy hand any serious attempt at hooliganism on a large scale," the paper proclaimed. "The agitation of a few noisy and untruthful demagogues, therefore, seeking to stir up class and colour prejudice and hatred in our midst, is merely an act of three-fold folly." Instead of taking to the streets, counseled the *Gazette*, protestors should "refrain from . . . lawlessness" and "publicly and privately repudiate those guilty thereof."[63]

Terrified by the prospect of additional unrest, members of Trinidad's white elite responded to the disturbances by calling for "prompt and stringent measures" to protect white lives and property. In a "confidential and urgent" letter to the acting governor, six of the colony's most prominent white men, including DSCA chairman George F. Huggins, outlined a militarized counteroffensive. The rising "tide of popular inclination," as they termed it, was dangerously antiwhite. A "substantial minority of the black population openly proclaims that it has no further use for the white man, and means to eliminate him," they charged. "The palpable absurdity of such an idea in no way robs it of its danger or diminishes its attractiveness to the negro mind." Since whites could not rely on the "black constabulary" to defend their lives in a crisis, they urged the governor to mobilize the colony's resources so that "the services of every white man available may be utilized to the best advantage." The letter writers betrayed the depth of their racial paranoia as they recommended that the governor seize all available firearms and explosives from local gun dealers and arm the colony's white men. They further requested a standing body of white troops to help maintain order and pressured the government to establish fortified safety zones where white women and children could hide during an emergency if all else failed.[64]

These white elites, panicked by displays of black self-assertion, insisted that colonial rule in Trinidad was being subverted by the "mischievous and systematic exploiting of the race question." Identifying three sources of antiwhite sentiment, the men blamed the global "wave of labour unrest" in 1919, returning veterans, and the *Argos* newspaper. While condemning ex-soldiers for introducing "revolutionary ideas" from abroad, the letter writers leveled their harshest criticisms at the local antiestablishment paper. "The impunity with which this irresponsible publication has for a long time past been permitted to circulate all kind of revolutionary, seditious, and mischievous literature is regarded as a scandal by all the serious members of this community," they seethed. "Unless some speedy method can be evolved of either suppressing or muzzling this poisonous organ, a catastrophe is inevitable."[65]

Huggins and his co-petitioners closed their frantic missive by acknowledging that the war had also transformed a second aspect of race relations in Trinidad—the status of Indians. In a shockingly forthright description of colonial divide-and-rule strategies, the men stated that white plantation owners had once relied on indentured Indian laborers to act as a buffer against black uprisings. With the end of indentureship in 1917, however, the white minority could no longer depend on Indians to serve as a "safeguard against trouble with the negroes." The "'creole coolie' will either remain an interested spectator," they speculated, "or join the mob."[66]

Colonial authorities acknowledged the presence of racial friction in Trinidad but denied alarmist reports that a racial conflagration was imminent. "If the white people in the Colony would only cease cackling and spreading and enlarging on the wild rumors going around," the Inspector General of the Constabulary bristled, "the situation would soon be clear."[67] After consulting with the Legislative Council, acting governor Gordon resolved that a garrison of white troops was not needed to maintain order. Further, he declined to suppress the *Argos*, noting that the content of the paper had "recently undergone a change for the better." Assuring the Colonial Office that the "feeling of class hatred" was quickly subsiding, Gordon stressed that the "majority of the more responsible black and coloured people" did not harbor any racial animosity against whites. As long as the respectable black and colored residents in the capital remained loyal, he surmised, the popular classes were not likely to rebel.[68]

Whether or not they believed an antiwhite uprising was imminent, local authorities and business elites alike agreed that disaffected veterans had stoked the "spirit of unrest" in Trinidad, an assessment subsequently echoed by historians.[69] Yet, in a letter to the editor of the *Port of Spain Gazette*, one former sergeant explained that the disturbance at Queen's Park Savannah reflected postwar tensions among veterans from different BWIR battalions over labor and status rather than a radical antiwhite critique. Like their comrades in British Honduras, veterans in Trinidad debated the meaning of their military service and the best way to address their grievances. According to the letter writer, the veterans who marched proudly in uniform during the parade generally hailed from the battalions that had been deployed in France during the war, while the hecklers had served in the battalions that fought in the Middle East. The ex-soldiers who toiled as laborers in France, the letter writer alleged, were "subject to abuse and ridicule" from their comrades who participated in combat in Palestine, presumably because they had been relegated to noncombatant roles for the entire war. "We were enlisted under the same conditions as every other soldier but were converted into Labour Corps on arrival in France without the extra pay given to a Labour corps, so that if any of the men have a grievance or grievances, we are the ones," he insisted.

"We certainly laboured under far more colour or racial disadvantage than they did, so I fail to see why they should misbehave themselves in this disgraceful manner." The ex-sergeant argued that the hecklers ultimately "disgraced themselves and the King's uniform" by disrupting the Peace Day parade. Insisting that all soldiers had made important contributions to the war effort, he challenged notions of martial heroism that exalted only fighting troops. Signing his public letter with the pseudonym "One of the Labourers," he argued that Trinidadian soldiers who served in non-combatant roles during the war had distinguished themselves by faithfully completing their military service and refraining from any "misconduct."[70]

In the aftermath of the attacks on white sailors, the police apprehended and charged only two men for their roles in the melee, despite witness statements that as many as fifty people participated.[71] Arthur Harris and Vernon Davis were charged with "assaulting and beating" three sailors from the *Dartmouth*.[72] Harris was convicted of assaulting seaman J. C. Clews and sentenced to pay a £10 fine or three months imprisonment with hard labor. Davis was convicted of assaulting two other seamen and sentenced to three months imprisonment with hard labor.[73] Neither defendant was a BWIR veteran, and there is no direct evidence that ex-soldiers joined the crowd in beating the *Dartmouth* seamen on Peace Day, despite inflammatory claims in the local press.[74] Indeed, in the criminal trials held just days after the attacks, none of the eyewitnesses alleged that veterans participated in the melee. Neither did the police.

The acting governor, anxious to forestall any further social unrest, sought to appease ex-servicemen by offering a modest financial concession. William Gordon announced that all BWIR veterans would receive their ration allowance at the British Army rate of 2s. 1d. per day instead of the significantly lower pay rate allocated for native troops.[75] In a letter to the Secretary of State for the Colonies, Gordon conceded that the pay dispute was "causing much discontent" and noted that the members of the colony's Executive Council and Finance Committee agreed with his decision to grant ex-BWIR servicemen the same allowance as British troops. The increased pay rate, he estimated, would cost the state approximately £1800, an expense that he hoped the imperial government would fully reimburse.[76] The Army Council, however, rebuffed the idea of pay equality, ruling that BWIR veterans should be paid at the "local rate for native soldiers" rather than the higher rate for veterans in the UK.[77] The Secretary of State for the Colonies, in his reply, did not comment on Gordon's decision to equalize the ration allowance for BWIR veterans in Trinidad. Instead, he simply reported that he would not "press the Army Council to accept" the higher rate of pay.[78] The £1800, then, would have to come from local coffers.

Mobilizing Veterans

Unsatisfied with the scanty compensation offered by the colonial government, veterans began to organize collectively to pursue more robust financial support. On July 25, less than a week after the Peace Day disturbances at Queen's Park Savannah, fifty-three men established the Returned Soldiers' and Sailors' Council in Port of Spain.[79] The founding president of the RSSC was a thirty-eight-year-old writer and activist named Algernon Burkett. Born into a military family, Burkett described himself as a "very humble journalist and a Man of the African Race."[80] His father had served in the West India Regiment, fighting in West Africa during the Second Anglo-Ashanti War (1873–74). Burkett proudly invoked his father's military service, noting that he had witnessed the siege of Kumasi, the capital of the Ashanti Empire, and took part in the Volta Expedition.[81] During World War I, Burkett had recruited 138 men in Trinidad and Barbados for the BWIR, sometimes sharing the stage with Arthur Cipriani at fundraisers and recruiting events in Port of Spain.[82] In a letter to colonial officials on behalf of the RSSC, Burkett emphasized his contribution to the wartime mobilization campaign, proclaiming that he was "the first man [in Trinidad] to assist the Mother Country in the matter of the recruitment of men for service at the front."[83]

Significantly, Burkett, unlike the many others who helped establish the RSSC, was a civilian. He had not served in the BWIR or any other military unit and, instead, spent the war years at home in the West Indies. Burkett never explained why he recruited scores of men "who did their share for King and Country" but failed to enlist himself.[84] He certainly met the age and literacy requirements for the BWIR, but it is possible he had a medical condition that disqualified him from service. He may also have declined to enlist due to familial obligations or other personal reasons.

Burkett affirmed his solidarity with veterans by invoking their shared socioeconomic, gendered, and racial ties as working-class black men. Describing returned soldiers as his "kinsmen," he linked his leadership of the RSSC to his previous efforts to mobilize Trinidad's black laborers.[85] "As one who is interested in the welfare of the returned soldier ... the son of the cook; the son of the wharfman and others who belong to the same class with myself," he wrote, "I claim 'first right' to say something for him."[86] Burkett insisted that veterans' fight for equal compensation was

FIGURE 6.3 Algernon Burkett. From Algernon Burkett, *Trinidad: A Jewel of the West Or, 100 Years of British Rule* (London: Francis & Co., 1914).

an integral part of the larger struggle for decent pay and working conditions by black civilians in the colony. And he insisted that he was the ideal person to lead the veterans' fight.

Colonial officials in Trinidad immediately questioned Burkett's motives and cast doubt on his leadership of the RSSC. They suspected that Burkett had taken an interest in the nascent veterans' movement for pecuniary rather than patriotic reasons. Local police, in a report to colonial authorities, described Burkett as a "clever and cunning trickster" who lived "on his wits" and was "always ready to champion the cause of anyone able or willing to pay him for his service." Before taking up the cause of veterans, the police contended, Burkett had run afoul of the law for receiving goods as a commission agent but refusing to pay the bill. He had also posed as a solicitor and bilked unsuspecting clients out of attorney's fees.[87] Then, Burkett founded an association for cane farmers, which collapsed, according to the police, after the members discovered he was having "the time of his life at their expense."[88] The cane farmers physically attacked Burkett at one of their meetings, and he quickly moved on to champion other causes. During the war, Burkett had written "letters and petitions galore" on behalf of BWIR soldiers' unlettered dependents, plying his services at a fixed rate and garnering "a good sum" for his efforts.[89] All told, Burkett had been convicted on five criminal charges in Trinidad between 1911

"EQUAL REWARD FOR EQUAL SERVICE" [223]

and 1918, including two counts of assault and battery and one count of larceny.[90]

Under Burkett's leadership, the RSSC mobilized rapidly to stoke public support for veterans. The council held its first public meeting on the afternoon of August 15. One thousand spectators assembled on the grounds of Woodford Square in Port of Spain to participate in the inaugural gathering. Burkett was joined on the stage by over sixty guests, including BWIR officer Lieutenant Colonel H. A. de Boissiere, who chaired the event. The program featured speeches by de Boissiere, Burkett, Private Fitz Blanche, playwright Cecil Cobham, local businessmen, and one unnamed "lady."[91] In the advertisements for the meeting, the RSSC announced that the event would feature updates about the land settlement scheme, a resolution to thank "certain officers" for protecting Trinidadian soldiers during the war, and "important nonpolitical matters" (see fig. 6.4).[92] Thus, from the outset, the council explicitly positioned itself as a nonpartisan veterans' association.

Speaking to the massive crowd at Woodford Square, Burkett declared that he was determined to "get the Government to do a little more" for returned veterans. He specifically criticized the DSCA's land settlement scheme for ex-soldiers, echoing previous critiques made by the *Argos*. Denouncing the initiative as "illogical, unholy, and inequitable," Burkett countered that colonial officials should award each veteran no less than twenty acres of land as well as a cash grant of £50. He further questioned why the DSCA did not include any black or colored representatives, given that most Trinidadian veterans of the BWIR were black. If veterans wanted to "get sympathy" for their cause, Burkett argued, they needed someone of their own race to champion their interests. Heralding the RSSC as the rightful voice of the veterans' movement, he announced that over five hundred ex-servicemen had joined the council in the three weeks since it was founded. Burkett encouraged veterans to place their trust in him and urged ex-soldiers and sailors to "shout their grievances until their sacrifices of life-blood and their duty had been adequately compensated by the Government."[93]

Even though Burkett railed against the DSCA, he stressed that the RSSC would fight for veterans solely through legal forms of advocacy, debunking rumors that returned servicemen in Trinidad were covertly planning an uprising. Veterans joined the RSSC "to get their grievances righted in a constitutional manner," he insisted. Members of the council "would not employ poisonous gas, dum dum bullets, nor Jack Johnsons," a reference to the famous African American heavyweight boxing champion,

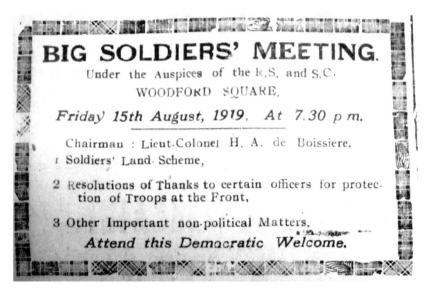

FIGURE 6.4 Advertisement for Returned Soldiers' and Sailors' Council public meeting in Port of Spain, Trinidad, 1919. *Argos*, August 5, 1919, 7.

in their fight for just compensation. Instead, the "Jack Johnsons they will employ will be the re-echoing sound of their united appeal in Downing Street," he declared to the cheering crowd. Linking the veterans' movement to celebrations of the British Empire, the RSSC meeting concluded with attendees singing two patriotic anthems: "Rule Britannia" and "God Save the King."[94]

One week after the inaugural meeting of the RSSC, Trinidad's most celebrated soldier, Captain Arthur Cipriani, returned home along with the last contingent of the colony's BWIR soldiers. Disembarking in Port of Spain on August 22, the white officer rode on horseback at the head of the homecoming parade and was heralded as the "King of Egypt" for his work on behalf of BWIR servicemen during their tour in the Middle East. Cipriani spoke to fellow soldiers at the official homecoming celebration, countering Burkett's strident demands for a robust land settlement program with a paternalistic call for law and order and respectful negotiation with government officials. In an address that would define his subsequent political style, Cipriani offered to champion the cause of veterans as long as they "played the game" with colonial authorities and deferred to his leadership. He reminded returning servicemen that they remained liable to military law during their first twenty-eight days at home and warned his comrades to avoid confrontations with local police and steer clear of unscrupulous friends. Moreover, he counseled veterans to report their grievances about outstanding gratuities to him or other former officers rather than "abusing the Paymaster" in heated confrontations. Seeking to avoid further clashes between ex-servicemen and the local government, Cipriani cautioned veterans not to take matters into their own hands. "Do not go about making fools of yourselves," he proclaimed to rousing applause. "Nobody is out to do you, everybody is out to help."[95]

Cipriani maneuvered to position himself as the rightful leader of Trinidad's nascent veterans' movement by assailing Burkett's competence and authority. Speaking to former soldiers at Greyfriars Hall on September 6, Cipriani acknowledged the leaders of the RSSC for establishing the colony's first veterans' organization but argued that veterans could most effectively address their grievances in an association comprised entirely of former soldiers rather than a "mixed council" with civilian leadership. Cipriani invoked his work with the local recruitment campaign and his spirited defense of court-martialed BWIR soldiers in Egypt as proof of his leadership acumen, reminding ex-servicemen that he had "stood by them when the days were dark." In order to settle their latest grievances, he argued, veterans needed to address the "proper authorities" and petition through the "proper channels." Instead of attacking the local government's parsimony, Cipriani maintained that local leaders were obligated to spend the colony's limited resources in a responsible and sustainable manner. "It would be almost criminal for the Government to give large sums of money to each returned soldier to lick out," he pronounced, parroting well-worn stereotypes about black profligacy. Rather, he urged veterans to ask the government for a limited "concession" that would support unemployed men for a fixed period.[96]

Refuting the claims of many ex-servicemen and their allies, Cipriani insisted that the colonial government had never promised to reward soldiers with land grants or other forms of financial support beyond the standard military pay as a condition of enlistment. "There was no contract" between the government and veterans regarding postwar compensation, he averred; therefore, ex-soldiers should refrain from "writing impertinent letters to the Colonial Secretary or making demonstrations which were not a credit to the Regiment to which they belonged." Instead, echoing the sentiments of veterans in metropolitan Britain, Cipriani argued that the "moral obligation" between veterans and the state extended to the "whole community" as well. Civilians on the home front had lived in "comfort, peace, and plenty" during the war years because of the sacrifices of BWIR soldiers. Hence, veterans should seek assistance from civilians rather than solely seeking recompense from the government. Finally, to conclude his deeply paternalistic and conciliatory speech, Cipriani assured veterans that he could "get the most out of the Government" if they allowed him to negotiate on their behalf and did not "hinder his work by abusing people" in the colonial administration.[97]

In response to Cipriani's speech, two ex-soldiers, Carlos Pollonais and Emanuel Billouin, called for the creation of a new veterans' organization. Pollonais and Billouin argued that the RSSC was "improperly constituted" and, in a clear attack on Burkett's leadership, that the "wrong men were at the head of affairs." The veterans present at Greyfriars Hall agreed. They unanimously selected Cipriani as the president of the new group, initially called the Soldiers and Sailors Union and later renamed the Soldiers' League.[98] Joining Cipriani on the association's seven-member steering committee were five veterans—including Billouin and Pollonais—along with one civilian who served as the secretary.[99]

The local press fawned over Cipriani's address at Greyfriars Hall, hailing it as "the most thrilling and sincere speech ever delivered" in the colony.[100] Some black activists, however, decried his conciliatory approach. Bruce McConney, a labor organizer and member of the Trinidad Workingmen's Association (TWA), blasted Cipriani for establishing a new veterans' group and ridiculed his deferential stance toward the colonial administration. In a letter to the *Argos*, McConney predicted that Cipriani's efforts to limit veterans' appeals for financial assistance would have "a most baneful effect on the minds of the soldiers" and "produce very inharmonious effects" on civilians as well.[101] Furthermore, he argued that Cipriani, as a white commissioned officer, could never appreciate the "sufferings" endured by rank-and-file soldiers because he had served in "comfort and luxury" during the war.[102] "Mr. Cipriani does not identify himself with the boys and therefore cannot be relied upon to do his best for them in any circumstance what[so]ever," McConney charged.[103] "This arrogant talker, from start to finish, equivocates, irritates, provokes, exasperates, and tantalizes every thinkful [*sic*] mind, freed from the blinding influence of prejudice."[104]

The nascent veterans' movement in Trinidad splintered in the wake of Cipriani's speech at Greyfriars Hall. In the absence of membership rolls and meeting minutes for both the RSSC and the SSU, it is difficult to discern the precise demographics or internal workings of either association. However, it is clear that both the establishment press and colonial officials viewed the RSSC's Burkett with suspicion. Seeking to undermine Burkett's claim that he volunteered as a recruiter for the BWIR during the war, the *Port of Spain Gazette* alleged that the RSSC president had actually "sent a formal claim" to the Commandant of the Local Forces demanding £125 for "enlisting of a certain number of recruits."[105] "What developments will follow? What next?" the paper huffed incredulously. In a confidential assessment of the RSSC, the governor of Trinidad railed that the association was "composed of a few of the men of the lower class with imaginary grievances" that Burkett had "got together for his own purpose."[106]

The leaders of the RSSC, seeking to garner legitimacy for the association, lobbied colonial authorities for official recognition. During a meeting in Port of Spain, they passed a resolution that reiterated the council's commitment to addressing veterans' grievances in a "constitutional manner" and called for the government and the DSCA to recognize the "duly elected heads" of the RSSC.[107] Unbeknownst to them, however, members of the DSCA were secretly pressuring colonial officials to deny the council recognition. In a private memo to the Colonial Secretary, the DSCA attacked Burkett's role as president of the RSSC, suggesting that he was an opportunistic agitator. "The Central Authority is of the opinion that . . . it would be a mistake to recognise any intermediary who is not himself a discharged soldier, since it is obviously to the advantage of the party who acts in this capacity to incite dissatisfaction," they wrote.[108] The DSCA had already prevented Burkett from attending their meetings to represent RSSC members; now, it claimed that it was "a matter of urgency" that the colonial government take a clear stance regarding the RSSC as well. Siding with the DSCA, colonial authorities refused to recognize the RSSC as a veterans' organization, dismissing ex-soldiers' claim that they should be able to choose their own representatives. Instead, officials maintained that the DSCA was responsible for "deal[ing] with all questions affecting discharged soldiers" and that no other group would be permitted to fulfill that role.[109] The acting governor even declined Burkett's request for a three-minute in-person meeting to discuss veterans' grievances.[110]

Burkett challenged the government's position by invoking a central plank in the Allies' wartime rhetoric—the principle of self-determination. The RSSC, he argued, reflected the genuine will of veterans, unlike the DSCA, whose white leaders had been appointed by the governor and had no connection to the BWIR. "These Returned Soldiers respectfully urge their British right to bring their grievances to the notice of the King's representative through any mouthpiece they may care to select," Burkett wrote in a letter to the Colonial Secretary.[111] Trinidad's war veterans should not be beholden to arbitrary decisions made by the DSCA when they were fully capable of forming their own association and negotiating directly with the government. Burkett further speculated that colonial officials refused to recognize the RSSC precisely because it was an autonomous, black-led veterans' association. During the war years, white elites had directed the military recruitment campaign and led the BWIR as the regiment's officers. Yet, with the creation of the RSSC, black men threatened to subvert white control over veterans' affairs. Because of "the colour of his skin," Burkett alleged, the government deemed that he was "not worthy to sit on a Body constituted for the express purpose of settling the wrongs of his own people."[112]

Meanwhile, Cipriani remained silent about the all-white leadership of the DSCA and the government's refusal to recognize the RSSC. And, despite publicly announcing his own rival veterans' association, he never sought official recognition from colonial authorities for the SSU. Instead of entering the charged debate over race and popular representation, the white ex-officer continued to argue that Trinidad's business elite, rather than the state, should help veterans get on their feet economically. "I am out to get what I can for the returned soldier," he announced during a speech at St. John's Hall. Cipriani argued that ex-servicemen should receive a "money grant" to aid in their transition to civilian life, but he failed to specify the exact amount or terns of the proposed grant. He did, however, suggest how the grants could be funded. The "money ought to come from those . . . merchants of this colony who have profiteered during the war," he declared.[113]

Cipriani increasingly railed against Trinidad's merchant class, extending the critique that he first articulated during the military recruitment campaign. The colony's affluent "millionaires," he contended, benefited economically from the war but refused to support the BWIR. Yet, the SSU president offered few details on how he planned to secure financial support from local merchants or the specific compensation that veterans should receive. Instead, the charismatic speaker traveled extensively, giving lectures about the war and regaling audiences with tales from his experiences as a BWIR officer. He devoted little time to lobbying local authorities or organizing fellow veterans. Cipriani, as Kelvin Singh argues, would ultimately "embark on a course of action that was to characterize his subsequent career as a political leader: a rhetorical display of moral indignation on behalf of those he sought to represent, followed by compromise with the colonial authorities, which deprived those he represented of the substance of their demands."[114]

Burkett continued to pressure local officials to address the plight of veterans, but he was rebuffed at every turn. Outraged by the government's refusal to negotiate with the RSSC, Burkett denounced colonial

"EQUAL REWARD FOR EQUAL SERVICE" [229]

authorities and insisted that his status as a British subject entitled him to equitable treatment. "It is an extremely painful and sad fact to state that every complaint—every grievance—brought to the notice of the Acting Governor, The Hon. William Montgomery Gordon, has been given the cold shoulder and up to now remains unanswered," he wrote. "I respectfully beg to protest on behalf of Returned Soldiers, and, as President of this Humble Council as well as in the capacity of a citizen of the Empire." Colonial authorities, Burkett continued, had a responsibility to investigate "the grievances of over 1000 Black Sons of the Empire who have fought and died for British Honour." In his critique of colonial authorities, Burkett appealed to imperial patriotism, race pride, and democratic citizenship, weaving together postwar discourses that are often imagined as discrete and conflicting. Instead, he claimed the right to speak on behalf of the "Black Sons of the Empire" as a fellow black "citizen," offering a "vernacular theorization of imperial citizenship" similar to other British colonials of color in the postwar period.[115] Pushing against the strictures of Crown colony rule, Burkett demanded that local authorities not only address veterans' grievances but honor their repeated call to participate in democratic governance. Burkett concluded his letter dramatically, writing: "If the Governor investigates and the charges I make turn out unfounded, I am willing to give my life for the mistake."[116]

Stonewalled at home, Burkett appealed directly to high-ranking officials in England, including Members of Parliament, Cabinet ministers, and Field Marshall Douglass Haig. In doing so, he pursued a long-standing strategy of soliciting imperial authorities to rectify unjust decisions by officials in the colonies.[117] Since the local government had "bluntly refused" to address the concerns of ex-soldiers, Burkett dispatched a telegram to the Secretary of State for the Colonies on behalf of the RSSC, calling for an official investigation into the treatment of veterans in Trinidad. The telegram highlighted veterans' economic grievances, decrying the nonpayment of war gratuities and other promised military allowances.[118] The RSSC also wrote a letter to the Secretary of State for War, pleading for increased pensions for ex-servicemen and their dependents. Insisting that there was a "most grave dissatisfaction" among veterans in Trinidad, the council offered to partner with the War Office to ensure that ex-soldiers and their families received proper compensation. "This is a serious matter . . . and this humble body pledges itself to give every assistance it possibly can so as to set at rest grievances which might carry unpleasant results," the RSSC warned.[119]

[230]   CHAPTER 6

The council also tried to use the circum-Caribbean press to draw attention to the dire conditions facing ex-soldiers in Trinidad. Traditionally, the colony's two major dailies, the *Port of Spain Gazette* and the *Trinidad Guardian*, devoted extensive coverage to the colonial administration.[120] Yet, as Burkett noted angrily, the establishment press "refuses to publish anything" critical of the government's treatment of veterans. Only the *Argos*, which Burkett touted as a "splendid little journal and the only sincere friend of the masses," publicly condemned the government's inaction.[121] Frustrated by the "miserable lack of Journalistic Backbone" in Trinidad, the RSSC president dispatched a letter to the editor of the Jamaica *Daily Gleaner*, the most influential and widely circulated newspaper in the British Caribbean. Hoping to "place before the world at large the gross dissatisfaction now rampant in Trinidad among the Returned Soldiers of His Majesty's B. W. I. Regt.," Burkett explained that many ex-soldiers were still awaiting their military backpay and other promised financial compensation months after demobilization. When veterans sought answers from local officials, Burkett claimed, the Military Paymaster responded dismissively by shrugging his shoulders, or, worse, hurling "some insulting epitheth [*sic*]." Thus, Burkett implored the editor of the *Daily Gleaner* to publish his exposé to shed light on the desperate "condition now existing in Trinidad in connection with those poor men who have helped to save the Empire."[122]

The manager of the *Daily Gleaner*, after reading Burkett's explosive allegations, declined to publish the letter. Instead, unbeknownst to Burkett, the *Daily Gleaner* staff passed the letter along to Jamaica's colonial secretary, who, in turn, immediately sent a copy to colonial authorities in Trinidad.[123] In response to Burkett's exposé, Trinidad's governor insisted that the RSSC and its leaders lacked credibility, and his administration was "doing everything possible" to address veterans' grievances. "This Government . . . has declined to recognize the Council, and the refusal of the local press to publish his letter is an indication of the public feeling with respect to Mr. Burkett, and of the unreliability of his assertions," he explained in a reply to Governor Probyn of Jamaica.[124] The publication of the letter by the Jamaican press, he continued, would "serve no useful purpose."[125] Burkett's damning missive never saw the light of day.

Even as Burkett wrestled with colonial authorities, he affirmed the RSSC's steadfast support of the British Empire and stressed the council's "unswerving loyalty to the Throne."[126] He also reiterated that veterans should seek redress strictly within the bounds of the law, doing so "decently, orderly, quietly and insistently."[127] In a public letter to returned

"EQUAL REWARD FOR EQUAL SERVICE" [231]

soldiers in early October 1919, the RSSC president acknowledged that veterans had "real solid grievances," but he counseled them to be patient and demonstrate "some more of Job's splendid virtue." "What I wish you to do is to act very orderly," he stressed. "Do not abuse anybody. Do not in any way offend anybody. I do not say if you are struck to strike back. Rather run away. Play coward." Burkett, in his persistent disavowal of violent protest, encouraged veterans to place their faith in imperial officials in London who could intervene on their behalf against local authorities in Trinidad. Connecting the history of British abolitionism to the fight for veterans' compensation, Burkett maintained that imperial officials would ensure that black ex-servicemen received proper compensation for their wartime service. "The great minds across the Seas will give you everything that belongs to you," he promised. "If Britain can pay £30,000,000 for your liberation when you did nothing for her then she will not pay you for your services when you helped to save the Empire? Oh yes, she will."[128]

The establishment press in Trinidad, however, insisted that the colonial government had already fulfilled its obligation to veterans and accused ex-servicemen of conniving to bilk the state. In a fictionalized portrayal of a DSCA meeting, an anonymous writer for the *Port of Spain Gazette* described the committee as "a goose which lays golden eggs for the benefit of ex-soldiers of the British West Indies Regiment." Determined to take full advantage of the committee's largesse, veterans eagerly "set forth claims and petitions." In this dramatic account, an ex-soldier who worked as a butler before the war—but "aspires now to office life"—demands a typewriter so that he can "qualify for a clerkship"; others ask for sewing machines, money for new civilian clothes, or acres of free land, all based on dubious claims. Instead of carefully investigating veterans' requests, the writer alleges, the DSCA dispensed financial support to veterans based on their ability to craft a "pitiful tale." Like Shakespeare's King Lear, who "gave his kingdom in exchange for eloquent speeches," the committee fell prey to men who possessed "the gifts of the Blarney." Calling for the DSCA to develop more stringent and uniform policies for assessing veterans' appeals, the writer declared: "Every man who went to serve King and Country offered . . . the supreme sacrifice. . . . Let us not go into heroics over them; but let us not forget either what is our duty to them."[129]

The *Trinidad Guardian* used far more acerbic language, lambasting ex-soldiers who demanded financial assistance from the state as "unemployable" and habitually indolent. In an editorial entitled "The Discharged Soldiers Problem," the *Guardian* alleged that "a number of" veterans "had never done any serious or consistent work before they enlisted, and have no intentions, if they can avoid it, of ever doing any work again now released from army discipline."[130] Insisting that some able-bodied veterans chose to survive by "persistent mendicancy" rather than honest labor, the paper argued that colonial authorities should leave the men to fend for themselves. The "sooner this class of grumbler is made to realise that he will not be permitted to consider himself a perpetual charge upon the community, the better it will be for him and the colony in general," the *Guardian* concluded.[131]

Local police and magistrates likewise viewed black veterans with hostility and used the courts to compel ex-soldiers to "behave themselves."[132] Veterans who challenged the police received swift punishment. Ex-private Norman Niblett was sentenced to pay thirty shillings or undergo fourteen days imprisonment for shaking a stick in the face of a constable.[133] Another former private, Hypolite Londea, was fined £2 or ordered to serve fourteen days imprisonment with hard labor for supposedly blocking a footpath.[134] Even Burkett faced harassment by the police. On the evening of October 28, a police detective accosted the RSSC president, claiming that there was an outstanding warrant for his arrest. When Burkett arrived at the police station, however, he was informed that the warrant was actually for a different man, who was accused of "raising money under false pretenses."[135] Angered by the wrongful arrest, Burkett threatened to pursue legal action against the detective and two other senior constables unless he was granted "adequate compensation."[136] Ultimately, in an important victory for Burkett, the detective who falsely detained him was fined £2 and punished with "28 days' confinement to the barracks."[137] Perhaps buoyed by this win, Burkett redoubled his efforts to garner official recognition for the RSSC.

"Whenever Society is in Travail Liberty is Born"

In November 1919, after months of failing to secure a meeting with colonial authorities through official channels, Burkett and the members of the RSSC tried a new tactic—direct action.[138] On the evening of November 12, over one hundred veterans marched through the streets of Port of Spain to Government House, the Victorian Italianate mansion that served as the governor's official residence.[139] Determined to register their plight with the governor, the men waited outside the mansion's gates for John Chancellor to appear. When the governor finally emerged from Government House for his nightly drive, the assembled ex-soldiers stood at attention and saluted. Then, Burkett, speaking on behalf of the council, briefly addressed Chancellor. "Your Excellency, these gallant men are returned soldiers of the King," he declared. "They come to welcome you back to Trinidad and to show you by their presence that they have grievances." Following his remarks, Burkett presented the governor with a homemade emblem featuring a picture of Lady Justice with the phrase "British Justice" printed below. The inscription on the emblem stoically invoked veterans' wartime sacrifices and the empire's obligation to its colonial troops. "We have done our duty nobly," it read. "We bring back wounds and a greater Britain." Rattled by the large crowd of veterans outside of Government House, Chancellor scrambled to assuage the men's discontent, promising RSSC members that the local government, under his leadership, would remedy their concerns. "Soldiers, I have heard of all your grievances. They are now before me and I am investigating them myself," he asserted, "and very soon the fullest satisfaction will be given to you."[140]

The following day, Chancellor convened the colony's Executive Council to discuss ex-soldiers' grievances.[141] During the closed-door meeting, Chancellor refuted claims that the colonial government had a legal obligation to veterans; however, he conceded that "it was desirable" to "allay" the "general dissatisfaction" among ex-servicemen to ensure public order. By providing additional financial support, he argued, colonial officials could "make the men realise that the Government was grateful to them, for the sacrifices they made on behalf of their country."[142] He proposed that any gratuity or land grant to local war veterans be dispensed equally to all ex-soldiers, regardless of rank or service regiment, ensuring that members of the all-white Merchants' and Planters' Contingent, as well as BWIR veterans, would receive a payout. After securing the approval of the Executive Council, Chancellor also pledged to discuss the proposed compensation scheme with members of the DSCA "before taking action."[143] Yet, in keeping with the fundamentally autocratic nature of Crown colony government, the governor failed to consult the leaders of the RSSC and SSU, let alone solicit feedback on his proposal from the one hundred RSSC members who had bravely marched to Government House to confront him the day before.

On the heels of the Executive Council meeting, Chancellor fielded more questions about veterans' grievances, this time during a session of the Legislative Council. Stephen Laurence, a colored physician and unofficial member of the Council, pressed Chancellor to acknowledge the "large amount of dissatisfaction among returned soldiers" and to outline a plan to address their concerns. It is unclear if Laurence's request was in direct response to the RSSC's protest at Government House or his personal interactions with BWIR veterans; however, it marked the first time that a Legislative Council member publicly addressed Trinidadian veterans' mounting discontent. Under fire from the RSSC and the Legislative Council, Chancellor sought to present himself as a skilled and tactful administrator. He reported that colonial authorities were giving "earnest attention" to "the treatment of the returned soldiers" and promised to make an announcement "within a fortnight" about the government's plans to stem the discontent.[144]

As Chancellor scrambled to craft a proposal that could allay veterans' grievances, dockworkers in Port of Spain went on strike to secure higher wages and overtime pay. The strike began on November 15, after the major shipping companies refused to negotiate with activists from the Trinidad Workingmen's Association who were representing the dockworkers. The TWA, under the leadership of David Headley and Barbadian stevedore James Braithwaite, boasted over one thousand members with branches in Port of Spain and San Fernando. The association had supported workers in previous industrial disputes and embraced strikes "as an instrument of social progress."[145] Within days, other workers in and around the capital began protesting for higher wages, too. City council workers in Port of Spain went on strike on November 21. Estate laborers employed by the Trinidad Land and Finance Company and coal carriers at the Archer Coaling Company followed suit three days later.[146]

Meanwhile, the shipping companies continued to rebuff the TWA's efforts to negotiate on behalf of striking dockworkers. Instead, determined to crush the strike, they employed strikebreakers on the wharves starting on November 24.[147] As the standoff between workers and managers intensified, the dockworkers' strike became "a racial and class confrontation," radicalizing poor and working-class black residents across the capital.[148] As one historian notes, "The dockworkers were winning widespread sympathy from large sections of the Black population in Port of Spain and were beginning to attract Black slum dwellers and unemployed to their cause."[149] Hoping to build a working-class coalition, TWA activists lectured daily in Port of Spain's Woodford Square to galvanize public support for the strikers and bring new workers into the labor movement.

Algernon Burkett, although not a member of the TWA, published an open letter to the strikers in the *Argos*. However, instead of celebrating the industrial action, he attempted to de-escalate the strikes. Burkett expressed solidarity with the aims of the strike, affirming that workers were "entitled to higher wages" and "had every right to live in comfort and ease," but questioned the TWA's militant tactics. Instead, he admonished

"EQUAL REWARD FOR EQUAL SERVICE" [235]

workers to return to the bargaining table and negotiate with employers in "cool headed" fashion rather than issuing "harsh and unreasonable" ultimatums. "I think you have struck prematurely and clumsily," he chided, advising that "strikes are not intended as instruments of revenge" and that the TWA should "not precipitate strikes for strike-sake."[150] Seeking to extend his influence beyond the RSSC, Burkett convened a meeting with the strikers one day after his letter was published in the *Argos*. As a crowd assembled at the corner of Marine Square and St. Vincent Street in Port of Spain, he began to address the strikers but was immediately shouted down. "After a few vain attempts," one newspaper reported, Burkett "gave up the idea and took his departure."[151] Burkett would remain on the sidelines as "strikitis" spread across the colony.[152]

Facing widespread unrest, colonial officials convened a private gathering with returned soldiers at the Red House in Port of Spain on the morning of November 25.[153] In a concerted move to sideline the RSSC, however, Governor Chancellor tapped Burkett's rival Arthur Cipriani to provide a list of BWIR veterans to invite to the meeting. Obliging the governor's request, Cipriani supplied a list of forty-seven ex-servicemen for the event, including three members of his SSU steering committee.[154] Neither Burkett nor the RSSC's secretary L. Milner-Jones were invited to attend.

Chancellor unveiled the government's new compensation plan for veterans to the handpicked group of former officers and enlisted men during the closed-door meeting.[155] Rejecting the principle of equal compensation, the governor refused to grant BWIR veterans the same demobilization allowances and unemployment benefits issued to British soldiers in the metropole. Instead, Chancellor deftly reworked the language of wartime sacrifice and mutual obligation to justify the state's parsimony. In England, he argued, one-third of military-aged men had served in the armed forces during the war, and all available material resources had been diverted to the war effort. In Trinidad, only one in thirty eligible men had served in the BWIR, and the economic dislocations of the war were minimal compared to those in the metropole. In light of these differences, declared Chancellor, the colonial state could not justify compensating BWIR veterans on par with English soldiers.[156] Simply put, Trinidadians had not sacrificed enough to reap the same postwar rewards as Englishmen.

As an act of "gratitude," the government agreed to pay each ex-soldier a $72 final settlement in local currency, which was equal to approximately £15.[157] Veterans could receive the full payment in cash through six monthly installments of $12, or they could request tools or other items of equivalent value to start a small business. As a third option, ex-soldiers could receive five acres of land and $24 in cash to be paid in monthly installments. Men who chose the land grant had to cultivate at least one acre of the property within the first year to retain their grant.[158]

The gratuity offered under Chancellor's plan provided short-term financial relief to BWIR veterans, albeit significantly less than their metropolitan counterparts. Given that the average unskilled worker in Port of Spain earned $24–$30 per month, the government's $72 gratuity provided soldiers with the equivalent of three months' salary. After receiving the gratuity, as one historian suggests, veterans who had already secured civilian employment would have been better off than most laboring people. And the $12 per month payment would have kept a single unemployed veteran from destitution for six months—though it was not enough to support a family. Veterans who hoped to establish themselves as small farmers were on even shakier ground: the substantial $48 deduction to cover the cost of land left them with little money to buy tools, seed, or other essential supplies, and given that much of the Crown land granted to ex-servicemen was located in remote areas, the cost of relocating, clearing the land, and cultivating it in one year would prove too much for many would-be smallholders.[159] But for BWIR veterans in urban areas and small towns, the gratuity offered a temporary buffer from the worst effects of the postwar economic downturn.

Burkett immediately criticized the new compensation scheme for veterans, noting that it fell far short of what was provided to veterans in Britain. Speaking out on behalf of "the coloured (negro) soldiers of the B. W. I. R.," the RSSC president insisted that "black heroes" were "entitled to the same army benefits as Imperial troops." He promised to continue the fight for just compensation for ex-servicemen and pledged to alert "Big Authorities across the seas" about veterans' unresolved financial grievances in Trinidad. Burkett also publicly chastised Arthur Cipriani for joining forces with colonial authorities to discredit Burkett's work as RSSC president. "To you, Capt. Cipriani, I am very sorry to see that you forgot yourself by telling the Governor that I was misleading the soldiers. But, of course, you are out to save somebody's skin—You know fully well that I am right."[160]

Veterans and their allies in the press joined Burkett in panning the compensation scheme, characterizing it as "absurd" and "a burning shame."[161] Critics pointed out three major shortcomings of the government's plan. First, the £15 gratuity was substantially less than the £25 that ex-servicemen had requested and did not provide enough aid for unemployed men to support their households. Given the wartime surge in the costs of clothing, food, and other consumer goods, the gratuity did not allow veterans to achieve even a semblance of financial security. "I am quite sure that every soldier, when he received his final balance, had to spend seven-eighths of it in clothing alone—to say nothing of the other necessaries of life—added to that unemployment in six out of ten cases," one veteran noted with exasperation. "With the foregoing facts staring us in the face, can any reasonable man admit that a gratuity of £15 is sufficient compensation for services rendered? I submit not."[162] Second, under the government's plan, all veterans received the same gratuity irrespective of their length of military service. Thus, a soldier who enlisted in 1917 received the same £15 gratuity as a soldier who joined in 1915 despite serving far less time. The third and most pervasive criticism of the government's compensation scheme was that it dispersed the gratuity to veterans in monthly installments rather than one lump-sum payment. Under the "paltry instalment system," ex-soldiers had to wait six months before receiving their full gratuity. Given "the present high cost of living," veterans could "do nothing with any single instalment of twelve dollars" from the government.[163] The meager monthly payments, the editors of the *Argos* calculated, would be "easily swallowed up in the purchase of an ordinary suit of khaki . . . a few pieces of underclothing or a pair of boots and a hat."[164]

Veterans received their first installment of the gratuity, which some men referred to derisively as the "$12 dole," in early December. The *Argos* mocked colonial officials for the meager financial support provided to ex-servicemen and claimed that many veterans, "after securing their windfall," quickly used the money "to have a good time." The "smallness of the amount prevented the majority of the men from investing it in anything of consequence," the paper reported, "with the result that the spirit shops came in for a roaring trade. By nightfall, it is safe to assume, that so little was left of the first instalment that it could have been carried in a thimble!"[165] More seriously, the *Argos* alleged that cash-strapped veterans were "falling into the hands of the moneylenders" who charged exorbitant interest rates ranging from 120 to 240 percent. Destitute ex-servicemen who were unable to secure loans were forced to buy goods on credit and at inflated prices from unscrupulous local merchants. Thus, the *Argos* warned, the "installment system operates harshly against the men whom it is intended to benefit," pushing veterans into further misery and debt rather than helping them to budget the gratuity.[166]

The colonial government's belated act of "gratitude" did little to remedy the financial hardship and discrimination that veterans faced in Trinidad. Walter Eversley, a former corporal in the BWIR, knew these problems all too well. In December 1919, just as the first gratuity payment was being issued, Eversley documented his job search in a letter to the *Trinidad Guardian*. Seeking employment as a mechanic, Eversley interviewed at the Trinidad Electric Company and was promised a position. But when he returned the next day to finalize his employment, he was directed to seek work elsewhere. The manager, Eversley alleged, had been advised "not [to] give employment to any returned soldiers." Denouncing the "narrow-minded individuals" who discriminated against veterans, Eversley questioned why his sacrifices on behalf of the empire went unrewarded. "Three years ago, I left Central America and proceeded to Jamaica and there enlisted and served with the B. W. I. Regiment. My discharge sheet shows that my character was exemplary," he wrote. "Is this the treatment to be meted out to a man who has thrown up lucrative employment to serve King and Country?"[167] Eversley's desperate query went unanswered.

Conclusion

Three days before Christmas 1919, John Chancellor wrote to the Secretary of State for the Colonies summarizing his efforts to resolve veterans' grievances in Trinidad. Sounding a triumphant note, the governor reported that veterans had readily accepted the government's compensation plan, ending months of intense uncertainty and unrest. The dispersal of gratuity payments, he claimed, had "abated much of the bitterness of the returned soldiers toward the Government" and "had a good effect."[168] Explaining the specific terms of the plan, Chancellor stated that it was designed to provide a final round of financial support to ex-servicemen without requiring protracted government oversight. "As the majority of the returned soldiers were uneducated men," he wrote, "it was desirable that the arrangements for dealing with them should be simple and that any concession granted should be free from restrictions and conditions which would be irksome to the men and difficult for the Government to enforce."[169] State parsimony and administrative convenience, in the end, trumped veterans' pleas for equal compensation.

The governor vaunted that the compensation plan had another salubrious effect—undercutting the power of Burkett and the RSSC. In the aftermath of demobilization, he recalled, "the discontent among the soldiers at their treatment was acute, and agitators were taking advan-

"EQUAL REWARD FOR EQUAL SERVICE" [239]

tage of that feeling to increase the general unrest in the Colony." Burkett and the RSSC, the governor alleged, had recklessly "fomented" a "feeling of dissatisfaction" among veterans. However, after the local government announced the new compensation plan, "organized agitation . . . ceased, and the Returned Soldiers and Sailors Council . . . lost much of its influence."[170] The government's swift action, boasted Chancellor, had prevented "ill disposed persons" from stoking discontent and engaging in "agitation of an objectionable character."[171]

One day after dispatching his triumphant letter to the Secretary of State for the Colonies, Chancellor did make one minor concession to local veterans. In response to persistent criticism, the governor agreed to issue the remainder of the gratuity payment as a lump sum rather than six monthly installments. Veterans who elected to receive the cash payout, the *Argos* reported, could pick up their money on Christmas Eve.[172] After veterans' months-long battle for equitable financial compensation from the state, the final cash payment on Christmas Eve was likely greeted with a mix of relief and resignation, viewed as an early Christmas present by some men and as a lump of coal by others who compared it to the more generous payment given to ex-soldiers in the metropole.

Algernon Burkett continued to lead the RSSC, though the organization faded from public view after the final gratuity payment was dispersed. Given the absence of local press coverage, it is unclear if the veterans' association met regularly after December 1919. However, Burkett was still wrestling privately with officials about the terms of the gratuity as late as 1929, protesting the government's "unjust refusal" to remit payments to Trinidadian veterans who enlisted outside of the colony during World War I.[173] Fragmentary archival records also reveal that colonial authorities kept a close eye on Burkett's activities, monitoring his efforts to organize cane farmers in southern Trinidad and a planned speaking tour of England in 1923. In their surveillance reports, local police continued to disparage Burkett, insisting that he was anathema to the colony's respectable class. "No person with any sense of decency be they black or white," a detective noted with disdain, "would have anything to do with him."[174] Writing to the Colonial Office nearly two decades after the RSSC's founding, Trinidad's acting governor portrayed Burkett as an unrepentant charlatan. "Mr. Burkett," he alleged dismissively, "preys on the credulity of ignorant people."[175]

Burkett's rival Arthur Cipriani would also continue to advocate for BWIR veterans in the interwar years, occasionally writing letters to colonial officials on behalf of disabled and destitute former comrades. However, in the wake of the final gratuity payment in 1919, he swiftly abandoned his efforts to build an autonomous veterans' organization and, instead, joined the colony's burgeoning labor movement. During the 1920s, Cipriani would invoke his wartime advocacy on behalf of BWIR soldiers to position himself as a champion of the "barefoot man," Trinidad's black and Indian laboring poor. Yet, Cipriani would remain committed to a reformist model of politics that emphasized negotiation with colonial authorities and fidelity to the British Empire. As one scholar notes, Cipriani "believed strongly in the British Empire and British justice and was adamant in his view that all reforms must be sought through the constitutional process and within the imperial framework and not through violence. His was essentially the politics of moderation."[176] This reformist approach—modeled by Cipriani, Samuel Haynes, and other former soldiers—would shape movements for democratic governance, racial equality, and economic opportunity across the British Caribbean in the postwar period.

Epilogue

ON THE MORNING of November 11, 1922, ten thousand people gathered in Kingston, Jamaica, to witness the unveiling and dedication of the island's official World War I memorial. Unveiled on the fourth anniversary of the Armistice, the towering twenty-nine-foot monument commemorated the lives of over 1,130 Jamaican servicemen who perished during the war. Designed by two Jamaican architects and constructed using locally quarried stone and marble, the monument consisted of a massive white cross placed atop an octagonal base. The gleaming white structure, surrounded by beds of richly hued plumbago and hibiscus flowers and draped in Union Jacks, stood as the centerpiece in the newly commissioned Memorial Square, constructed at the cost of £3000. The two inscriptions on the monument, rendered in simple block lettering, highlighted the memorial's dual function as a commemoration of local loss and as a symbol of imperial belonging. The first inscription, chiseled on a marble slab on the stone base, dedicated the monument "In Memory of the Men of Jamaica who fell in the Great War." The second inscription, borrowing the consolatory words etched on cenotaphs in the British Isles, proclaimed: "Their name liveth for evermore."[1]

Shortly before 11:00 a.m., as relatives of the deceased assembled in a specially designated seating area and thousands of "uninvited" spectators crowded on nearby streets and rooftops, acting governor Herbert Bryan ascended the dais to officially dedicate the new memorial.[2] In a brief address, Bryan lauded the "sons of Jamaica," who sacrificed their lives to guarantee the security of the British Empire. Along with other fallen "sons of the Empire," Jamaica's war dead joined a valiant fraternity of men who fell in the service of the king. Declaring that their sacrifices were not in vain, the governor charged the people of Jamaica to retain the "indomitable spirit" that led thousands of their countrymen to face the threat of death so that the "Empire might stand." "O People of Jamaica," he proclaimed, "Let us remember, and charge our children to remember, that these who saved our mortal heritage cast away their own."[3]

The political significance of the new memorial and the ritualized acts of mourning that accompanied its unveiling did not escape the editors of the *Daily Gleaner*. In an editorial published two days after the ceremony, the paper argued that the cenotaph was more than a "local manifestation of feeling" for the island's deceased soldiers. It was also a "symbolic representation" of Jamaicans' "feeling for the Empire" and "continued solidarity" with Britain. Despite moments of imperial "backslidings" in the postwar years, the *Gleaner* maintained, metropolitan officials remained committed to advancing the "personal liberty" of colonial subjects throughout the realm. And Jamaicans of all classes, recognizing the sovereign's commitment to "justice and freedom," remained loyal to the king and to the "spirit" of his empire. "Let no one be mistaken: in spite of all that may be said in moments of peace, when men are prone to be critical and discontented: if the Empire were threatened again . . . [w]hat Jamaica did in 1915 and after, she would do again and more, much more."[4]

The language of imperial patriotism pervaded some popular commemorations of the Armistice in the British Caribbean as well. On the same day that thousands of Kingstonians dedicated the cenotaph in memory of their deceased "sons," the editors of the *Labour Leader*, the organ of the Trinidad Workingmen's Association, reflected on the meaning of the war for colonials of color. Armistice Day, the editors surmised, held "far greater" significance for black West Indians than it did for "any of the Caucasian races" that fought in World War I. For the descendants of enslaved Africans, the war had provided the first opportunity to repay Britons for the "ransom of twenty million sterling" that "Victoria the Good paid to set their forefathers free." By offering their lives as soldiers, black servicemen had repaid "in blood" their ancestors' "long outstanding debt to the British Empire," the *Labour Leader* insisted. Thus, on Armistice Day, black subjects in the British Caribbean not only celebrated the empire's wartime victory but also the paying off of a historic obligation for the abolition of slavery. "The love, the devotion, and the loyalty of the West Indian for the Throne" led black troops to lay down their lives for the preservation of His Majesty's empire, the paper proclaimed. Having saved the British Empire and repaid the debt for emancipation, West Indians now solely possessed a "debt of gratitude" for the Mother Country's beneficence.[5]

FIGURE 7.1 Dedication of the Jamaica War Memorial, 1922. Courtesy of National Library of Jamaica.

By the 1920s, public commemorations of World War I in the British Caribbean often portrayed BWIR soldiers as paragons of imperial loyalty and dutiful black subjects. Even militant organizations like the Trinidad Workingmen's Association suggested that the war had given the "dusky sons of Africa" an opportunity to be "obedient to the call of Empire." "The path of glory which has been trod by the sons of Trinidad and Tobago" who served in the war, the *Labour Leader* mused, reflected "an attachment to their King and to the Country of their adoption akin to that which the Jews manifested for beloved Zion."[6] Yet, these narratives elided the intense battles over race, imperial belonging, and equal rights that soldiers fought during and after the war and glossed over the racist hardships that black soldiers endured within the British Army. Instead, commentators portrayed the war as a bloody catalyst for heightened imperial unity. By voluntarily enlisting for military service, black and colored West Indians had supposedly repaid their ancestors' debts to Britain and earned recognition for the "ancient and loyal" Caribbean colonies.[7]

Some BWIR veterans countered this whitewashed narrative, insisting that Britain had betrayed black soldiers and failed to uphold the promise of martial interracialism. In the poem "Hypocrisy," published in the *Negro World* in 1923, Ernest Mair boldly denounces Britain's treatment of West Indian servicemen.[8] The Jamaican ex-corporal disputes official narratives of the British Army as a multiracial martial brotherhood, instead portraying white English soldiers as hypocritical, racist, and cowardly. In the poem, Mair credits colonial soldiers from Britain's vast empire with winning the war for the Allied powers and condemns imperial officials for refusing to acknowledge nonwhite troops' military contributions.

> Forth from the East and from the West,
> From North and South they came,
> The captives' sons arose to save
> Their captor's race from shame!
> Dupes of autocracy,
> They shed their rich red Afric blood
> To save democracy.
>
> And now the fearful strife is o'er
> Now that the battle is won,
> Oppression is the base reward
> Of every Afric son.

Castigating England as the "queen of hypocrites," Mair portends that black people across the British Empire will soon overcome the "cruel rod" of oppression that they endure under colonial rule: "Sure as the rising of the sun / Dispels the gloom of night / Your paths of wrong to darkness lead/ While Negroes from your bondage freed / Shall rise to greet the light!" [9]

Through articles in local newspapers, other veterans charged that the soaring rhetoric of the war years rang hollow for former members of the BWIR. Clennell Wickham, in an article published in the *Barbados Weekly Herald*, described the lessons he learned as a young sergeant in the regiment. "Patriotism," he noted, "is a purely civilian asset to be resumed after the duration [of the war] . . . one does not think much of any body except himself when toiling in full marching order up a hill with a gradient of one in two." A soldier is "not regarded as having done the King a good turn by enlisting," he added wryly. Reflecting on the treatment of BWIR veterans, Arthur Cipriani echoed Ernest Mair's claim that West Indian soldiers had failed to garner the respect and compensation they deserved. But instead of blaming imperial bureaucrats in London, Cipriani directed his anger at local civilians and colonial administrators in Trinidad. "It is quite true that very few promises made [to BWIR soldiers] have been fulfilled. It is quite true that a great deal of hardship and injustice has been heaped on the Returned Soldiers. It is quite true that the ingratitude of our people has been galling, bitter and disappointing," Cipriani fumed. The BWIR "has all too often been ridiculed, the services of those men all too often discounted," he continued, by "the large majority of the Colony's sons who stayed at home and grew fat, sleek, and wealthy off the sacrifices of their sons and brothers."[10]

Contestations over the meaning of the war and the politics of imperial patriotism profoundly shaped the development and trajectory of veterans' organizations in the interwar era. In the months following demobilization, BWIR veterans seemed poised to emerge as a powerful new interest group. As this book has shown, between 1919 and 1920, ex-servicemen across the region formed autonomous veterans' associations and pressured local authorities to provide cash gratuities, land grants, and temporary employment. Between 1920 and 1921, ex-servicemen garnered a further concession from colonial authorities: pardons for the Taranto mutineers. Shortly after Arthur Cipriani launched his campaign to expose Brigadier General Cary-Barnard's abuses at Taranto, Jamaican legislator H. A. L. Simpson began pressuring imperial authorities to pardon the forty-nine former BWIR soldiers held in Jamaica for military offenses. Simpson's effort garnered the support of the *Daily Gleaner*, which called on the governor to intercede on behalf of the imprisoned veterans. Challenging official narratives about the mutineers, the *Gleaner* suggested that the ex-soldiers were "young men of intelligence" who bore "the stamp of respectability." The paper, moreover, questioned why veterans who volunteered "as freemen to assist in wiping out autocracy" were "brought back to the West Indies as prisoners."[11] Bowing to mounting pressure from veterans and their civilian allies, Secretary of State for the Colonies Alfred Milner pardoned forty-seven of the forty-nine ex-soldiers imprisoned in Jamaica in October 1920 and ordered that the men should be permitted to return to their home colonies.[12] That same month, Governor Charles O'Brien pardoned two Taranto mutineers in Barbados, and Governor John Chancellor of Trinidad followed suit in 1921.[13]

However, in the wake of these significant victories, the nascent veterans' movement sputtered. As ex-servicemen dedicated to negotiation and constitutional forms of agitation took the helm of veterans' organizations in Trinidad, British Honduras, Jamaica, and elsewhere in the region, these nascent groups offered few opportunities for rank-and-file members to participate in the process of lobbying the state. Cipriani's injunction that ex-servicemen should report their grievances to their former officers instead of "making fools" of themselves by confronting authorities directly underscored the top-down model of leadership that stymied mass mobilization among veterans.[14] Despite veterans' strong sense of collective identity and public venerations of martial sacrifice, veterans' organizations during the 1920s suffered from low membership and ill-defined agendas. Significantly, only one of the three veterans' organizations founded in Jamaica in the 1920s survived more than one year. The most enduring organization, the Jamaica Old Comrades' Association, declared that it was "strictly non-political" and listed the governor as its honorable president.[15] Even the British West Indies World War Veterans' Association in Harlem, which existed for at least two decades, focused its efforts on mutual aid initiatives and commemorative projects rather than political advocacy. Indeed, the association welcomed "high officials of the State . . . to become honorary members."[16]

Thus, when men and women in the British Caribbean spoke of the First World War in the 1920s, they increasingly invoked heroic narratives about the dead instead of acknowledging the urgent needs of surviving BWIR veterans in their own communities. Tellingly, during the war memorial dedication ceremony in Kingston in November 1922, most ex-servicemen were relegated to a viewing area across the street from the memorial and were not invited to take part in the military review. Only a small number of disabled veterans in wheelchairs were allowed on the memorial grounds during the ceremony (see fig. 7.2). While colonial governments continued

FIGURE 7.2 Disabled veterans at the dedication of the Jamaica War Memorial, 1922. Courtesy of National Library of Jamaica.

to provide some economic programs for veterans—especially in Jamaica, where the government launched a land-settlement initiative, provided short-term loans, and allotted £20,000 for public works jobs—public officials increasingly concentrated their efforts on commemorating the war through memorials and annual celebrations rather than tending to the material needs of the living.[17] By the early 1930s, ex-soldiers reported that they were living "in a most deplorable condition," facing unemployment and "permanent sickness" due to their military service.[18] In Jamaica, hundreds of impoverished veterans—adorned in their military ribbons—held hunger marches in the streets of downtown Kingston to call attention to their desperate plight.[19] According to former sergeant D. S. Wynter, the BWIR's disabled veterans endured especially dire circumstances. "You should see the survivors of the Halifax Blizzard," he reported in a 1934 letter to the West India Committee in London. "Some are in the Mad House or Asylum [,] others on the pauper roll [,] others naked all from want of employment, some destitute in Cuba and prefer to remain owing to the existing conditions here" in Jamaica, Wynter alleged.[20]

By examining popular claims-making and imperial policy in the wartime British Caribbean, *Democracy's Foot Soldiers* sheds new light on the racialized and gendered nature of military mobilization, the multiple uses of the language of imperial patriotism, and the impact of military service on BWIR veterans' political consciousness. This book also helps to explain why Arthur Cipriani, Samuel Haynes, and other

FIGURE 7.3 Political cartoon celebrating Arthur Cipriani's election to Trinidad's Legislative Council in 1925. *Labour Leader*, February 11, 1925, 7.

well-known ex-soldiers ultimately rose to prominence as leaders of civilian organizations rather than veterans' groups. After receiving the support of black and colored laborers due to his work on behalf of the BWIR, Cipriani won the presidency of the Trinidad Workingmen's Association in 1923 and led the group until his death in 1945. He also enjoyed an unprecedented string of electoral victories, serving in Trinidad's reformed Legislative Council from 1925 to 1945 and as mayor of Port of Spain from 1929 to 1940.[21] During Cipriani's campaign for the Legislative Council, former BWIR comrades appealed to voters on his behalf, recalling how he had "stood firm" in support of the regiment's black soldiers.[22] Championing the rights of the "unwashed and unsoaped," Cipriani lobbied for an eight-hour working day, minimum wage, compulsory education, workers' compensation, and universal suffrage during the interwar years.[23] He also pushed for more West Indian men to be appointed to high-ranking civil service positions and campaigned tirelessly against racial discrimination.[24] Yet, Cipriani never questioned the "ultimate moral rightness of the British Empire" or demanded an end to colonial rule.[25]

Although colonial officials devoted declining attention to veterans' affairs in the interwar period, former BWIR soldiers continued to gather periodically for reunions, patriotic celebrations, protests, and funerals in the British Caribbean and the United States until at least the onset of

FIGURE 7.4 Twenty-five-year reunion of Jamaica's 1st BWIR contingent, 1940. Jamaica Archives and Records Department, Orrett Photographs Collection, 7-130-1.

World War II.[26] These gatherings provided space for ex-soldiers to foster their own narratives about their military service and renew the friendships they formed with comrades during the war years. A surviving photograph captures a reunion of the first contingent of Jamaican soldiers during an event commemorating the twenty-fifth anniversary of their departure on the *Verdala* (see fig. 7.4). Taken in November 1940, the photograph shows the men—now all middle-aged—dressed formally in their Sunday best, including jackets and ties for most. One man even wears a striped, three-piece suit complete with a matching hat and cane. Along with their civilian attire, some of the assembled men also don military insignia and medals—visual reminders of their former rank and status in the BWIR. As this photograph demonstrates, former soldiers commemorated their military service and affirmed their identity as BWIR veterans long after they returned home from the war.

Recent commemorations of the centennial of World War I ignited new debates about the experiences of BWIR soldiers and the war's political legacy. In England, a growing cadre of community activists, scholars, filmmakers, and writers have sought long overdue recognition for black British servicemen, including those who served in the BWIR. Yet, on both sides of the Atlantic, there remains a dearth of popular knowledge about West Indians' myriad contributions to the war effort and their fight for equality. While conducting research in Jamaica, Trinidad, Barbados, and elsewhere in the Caribbean, I discovered this firsthand as community members expressed surprise when I explained the focus of my work. Many people I encountered insisted that West Indian men had not served in World War I or assumed that I was actually interested in researching World War II. Even the military personnel charged with preserving the history of West Indian military service stated that they had been taught very little about the thousands of men who soldiered in the BWIR. During an informal tour of the Jamaica Military Museum and Library at Up Park Camp, my guide stated that the museum focused on the history of the West India Regiment and the current Jamaica Defence Force (JDF) and contained few artifacts from the BWIR. During a visit to the World War I memorial in Kingston, now dedicated to fallen soldiers from both World Wars, I spoke with one of the JDF soldiers assigned to guard the monument (see fig. 7.5). After explaining my interest in the historic cenotaph, the soldier suggested that only a few Englishmen from the island had served in World War I and that no black men had volunteered. Like many other people I encountered, he erroneously believed that black and colored West Indians had first served en masse in Europe and the Middle East during World War II rather than World War I.

Interviewed in the early years of the twenty-first century, the last surviving BWIR veterans offered a mixed assessment of their military experience.[27] George Blackman, a colored volunteer from Barbados, enlisted as a teenager and served with the Fourth Battalion in France and Italy. Interviewed in 2002, the 105-year-old ex-soldier recounted several examples of racist slights from German prisoners of war as well as British comrades. He leveled his harshest criticism, however, at colonial officials for not providing sufficient support for returning veterans. "When the war finish, there was nothing," Blackman lamented. "The only thing that we had is the clothes and the uniform that we got on. The pants, the jacket and the shirt and the boots. You can't come home naked." Calling attention to the ambiguous position of former colonial soldiers in postcolonial societies, Blackman complained that he was not eligible for a military pension from Britain or Barbados. "England don't have anything to do with me now. England turned me over," he reported. "Barbadians rule Barbados now."[28] Eugent Clarke, a former private who lived to be 108 years old, echoed

FIGURE 7.5 Jamaica War Memorial in National Heroes' Park. Photo by author.

Blackman's distaste for war, vividly recalling the harrowing working and living conditions in wartime France. While Clarke was able to collect a small pension from the Jamaica Legion, he shared Blackman's critique of postwar social and economic conditions in the Caribbean. Advising the next generation of activists on the unfinished struggle for rights and recognition, Clarke declared: "You must demand justice. It's the hardest thing to get in Jamaica. There's no love can come in without justice. Give every man equal rights—pay him a good day's pay for a good day's work—that's justice."[29]

ACKNOWLEDGMENTS

I LOVE THE ACKNOWLEDGEMENTS section of books. Ever since I began reading scholarly books as a college student, I have always taken time to read the acknowledgments. I often read every single line. For me, the acknowledgments offer a rare, behind-the-scenes peak into the author's life: their scholarly trajectory, career milestones, friendships, and family. For years, I have imagined what I would write in the acknowledgments when I completed this book. It is a surreal moment to finally reach this stage.

I am pleased to acknowledge the financial support that I received to research and write this book. I received fellowships from the Alpha Kappa Alpha Educational Advancement Foundation, American Historical Association, Coordinating Council for Women in History, Duke University, Ford Foundation, Fulbright Program, Institute for Citizens & Scholars, Mellon Foundation, Mustard Seed Foundation, and Social Science Research Council. While at Dartmouth College, I received the Walter and Constance Burke Research Initiation Award, a Junior Faculty Fellowship, and a research grant from the Nelson A. Rockefeller Center for Public Policy and the Social Sciences. At Princeton University, I have received financial support from the Department of African American Studies and the University Committee on Research in the Humanities and Social Sciences. Along with these fellowships, I received crucial support from several diversity pipeline programs, including the Mellon Mays Undergraduate Fellowship (MMUF), Moore Undergraduate Research Apprentice Program (MURAP), and Institute for Recruitment of Teachers (IRT) Associate Program. I am incredibly proud to be a product of these trailblazing programs to diversify the professoriate.

During my undergraduate years, several professors at Columbia University encouraged me to pursue graduate studies and prepared me for the long road ahead. Barbara Fields and Eric Foner introduced me to the historian's craft, setting an example of scholarly excellence that continues to inspire me. Karen Barkey, Mignon Moore, and Nancy Woloch connected me to valuable research opportunities both on and off campus. Reginald Hildebrand at the University of North Carolina at Chapel Hill supervised my first independent research project as a MURAP fellow and offered brilliant insights on the research and writing process.

[253]

I started the research for this book as a graduate student at Duke University, where I learned from a distinguished group of scholars in the History and African and African American Studies departments. My dissertation advisor, John D. French, introduced me to the field of Latin American history, helped me to secure numerous rounds of international research funding, and provided rigorous feedback on my initial drafts. John also organized several Latin American Studies workshops at Duke where I was able to present my work. David Barry Gaspar spent countless hours discussing Caribbean history and historiography with me and encouraged me to imagine my own research agenda as a Caribbeanist. Jolie Olcott has been a steadfast source of inspiration, support, and advice as I have worked to complete this book. Conversations with Gunther Peck and Vincent Brown pushed me to clarify the stakes of my work and wrestle with the complex subjectivities of soldiers. I am also grateful to Michaeline Crichlow, Raymond Gavins, Lawrence Goodwin, Nathalie Hartman, and Charles Payne for their mentorship during my time at Duke. My classmates in History, African and African American Studies, and the Center for Latin American and Caribbean Studies provided camaraderie and friendship during my time in Durham. While in graduate school, I also spent a transformative year as a Fulbright fellow at the Institute for Gender and Development Studies at The University of the West Indies, St. Augustine in Trinidad. I would like to thank Bridget Brereton, Gabrielle Hosein, Patricia Mohammed, and Rhoda Reddock for their generosity and mentorship.

Like all historians, I am profoundly indebted to the archivists and librarians who work tirelessly to safeguard, preserve, and catalog historical materials. I would like to acknowledge the staff at all the archives, museums, and libraries listed in this book's bibliography. I am especially grateful to Mary Alpuche at the Belize Archives and Records Department for locating several previously unpublished photographs of the British West Indies Regiment. I also received valuable assistance from Karen Proverbs at the Barbados Department of Archives; Kasiya Halstad, Marcella Phillips, Claude Stewart, and Marsha Vassal at the Jamaica Archives; Nicole Bryan and Bernadette Worrell at the National Library of Jamaica; and Marcella Thompson, Avalon Dougan, and Malachi Alexis at the National Archives of Trinidad and Tobago. I would also like to thank the librarians at Duke University, Dartmouth College, and Princeton University who secured materials for me through Borrow Direct and Interlibrary Loan.

I was fortunate to begin my faculty career at Dartmouth College in the African and African American Studies (AAAS) program. As chair of

ACKNOWLEDGMENTS [255]

AAAS, Antonio Tillis offered sage advice and expert mentorship. Celia Naylor guided my transition to campus during my first year with extraordinary kindness and good humor. I wrote the earliest drafts of this book alongside Aimee Bahng and Rashauna Johnson at coffee shops across the Upper Valley. I will always treasure the time that we spent thinking, writing, and laughing together. Colleagues Robert Baum, Robert Bonner, Michael Chaney, Adrienne Clay, Soyica Colbert, Ayo Coly, Judy Danna, Margaret Darrow, Laura Edmondson, Alysia Garrison, Gretchen Gerzina, Lourdes Gutiérrez Najera, Trica Keaton, Deborah King, Chelsey Kivland, Vincent Mack, Abigail Neely, Tanalís Padilla, Elizabeth Pérez, Julia Rabig, Russell Rickford, Naaborko Sackeyfio-Lenoch, Silvia Spitta, Roberta Stewart, Michelle Warren, Derrick White, and Barbara Will offered astute commentary on my work and helped me to navigate the tenure track. Lynn Higgins, in her role as associate dean for interdisciplinary and international studies, allocated funding to help me complete additional archival research in the Caribbean. With support from Dartmouth's James O. Freedman Presidential Scholars Program, I had the pleasure of working with a wonderful group of undergraduate research assistants. Many thanks to Tailour Garbutt, Jennifer Gargano, Chloe Jones, Bennie Niles IV, Lauryn Overton, Erick Ramirez, Rachel Sands, Meredith Shaw, and Eirik Voll.

When I moved to Princeton University in 2017, I was blessed to join the phenomenal crew in the Department of African American Studies. I cannot imagine a better environment to write my first book. Anna Arabindan-Kesson, Wendy Belcher, Ruha Benjamin, Wallace Best, Lorgia García Peña, Eddie Glaude, Joshua Guild, Tera Hunter, Marcus Lee, Kinohi Nishikawa, Naomi Murakawa, Chika Okeke-Agulu, Imani Perry, Keeanga-Yamahtta Taylor, and Autumn Womack are remarkably thoughtful and generous colleagues. I am especially grateful to Eddie and Tera for their visionary leadership of the department and steadfast support for junior faculty. Staff members Shanda Carmichael, Anthony Gibbons Jr., Sonia Hollis, Jana Johnson, Elio Lleo, April Peters, and Dionne Worthy have provided pivotal support for my research and teaching. I would also like to thank Rashidah Andrews, Catherine Clune-Taylor, Ada Ferrer, Hanna Garth, Tod Hamilton, Rosina Lozano, Angela Maxam, Shawn Maxam, Mitch McEwen, Dan-el Padilla Peralta, LaFleur Stephens-Dougan, Nicole Myers Turner, Momo Wolapoye, Vanilla Wolapoye, and Corrina Zeltsman for their encouragement. Rachel Price has been an unwavering source of support as we both navigated the challenges of research and teaching while raising toddlers during the pandemic. A talented group of Princeton undergraduates helped me to catalog my unwieldly collection of paper copies and digital photographs from numerous archives. I am pleased to acknowledge Kimberly Cross, Emily Dickinson, Amanda Eisenhour, Ozichi Okorom, Avanequé Pennant, Katherine Powell, and Ariel Sylvain for their assistance.

My research has been greatly enriched by conversations with students, scholars, and community members over the years. I appreciate everyone who took the time to attend one of my presentations, read draft chapters, or share relevant materials. I want to acknowledge the helpful feedback and advice that I have received from Leslie Alexander, Emma Amador, Yesenia Barragan, Nathalie Batraville, Peter Beattie, Takkara Brunson, Deidre Hill Butler, Ginetta Candelario, Matthew Childs, Kaysha Corinealdi, Christina Davidson, Eric Duke, Alexander Eastman, Aisha Finch, Christianna Fryar, Julia Gaffield, Guadalupe García, Ernest Gibson, Jorge Giovanetti, Jaira Harrington, Randal Jelks, Grace Sanders Johnson, Jessica Marie Johnson, Rhonda Jones, Natasha Lightfoot, Treva Lindsay, Minkah Makalani, John Morrow Jr., Michelle Moyd, Kennetta Hammond Perry, Andrea Queenley, Melina Pappademos, Leah Wright Rigueur, Neil Roberts, Fannie Rushing, Jeffrey Sammons, Paula Marie Seniors, Elizabeth Shesko, Michelle Scott, Matthew Smith, Frances Peace Sullivan, Sasha Turner, Chantelle Verna, and Chad Williams. I also received valuable feedback on my research during invited lectures at Buffalo State University, Columbia University, Duke University, University of Sussex, Villanova University, and the Philosophical Society of Trinidad and Tobago. I am especially indebted to Dalea Bean, Devyn Spence Benson, Natanya Duncan, Anne Eller, Julie Greene, and Lara Putnam for sharing relevant sources with me and offering detailed suggestions that strengthened my work. Lara also served as my mentor during my year as a Woodrow Wilson Career Enhancement Fellow and has continued to be a treasured interlocutor.

Over the many years that it took to complete this book, I worked closely with an amazing group of academic coaches and editors. Michelle Boyd provided expert coaching as I worked to build a productive and sustainable writing practice. Susan Whitlock read the entire manuscript and improved every page with her meticulous editing. Rachel Hynson helped me to sharpen my arguments and hone my voice as a writer. Nicole DiMella secured permissions for the photographs republished in this book. Ruth Bloom retrieved several files for me from the National Archives in England. I would also like to acknowledge Ron Draddy for creating the book's maps, and Max Burns for designing the chart.

The incredible staff at Princeton University Press shepherded my manuscript through the publication process with extraordinary skill and care. Priya Nelson embraced this project from the beginning and worked tirelessly to ensure that it would be published in a timely manner. Emma Wagh provided expert feedback and crucial guidance as I navigated each stage of the publication process. I am also indebted to production editor Angela Piliouras and copyeditor Sherry Howard Salois for their excellent work. It was truly a joy to work with the talented staff at Princeton University Press. Three anonymous readers provided incisive comments on the manuscript. I appreciate the time and effort they put into reading my work and composing such detailed reports. I would also like to thank Debbie Gershenowitz at the University of North Carolina Press for several generative conversations about the project.

My close friends have celebrated with me in good times and encouraged me in moments of self-doubt. I am grateful to Jamila Webb, Keesha Ball, Michelle Burton, Emily Robinson, Jasmine Collins, Katherine Williams, Kwamena Aidoo, Lindsay Dunn, and Becky Robinson for our lifelong friendships. Thank you for always reminding me that my work is only one part of who I am. Aimee Bahng, Devyn Spence Benson, Natanya Duncan, Rashauna Johnson, Crystal Sanders, Shatema Threadcraft, and Danielle Terrazas Williams are brilliant scholars and even better human beings. One of the best things about becoming a historian is the friendships that I have built with these phenomenal women. I am so grateful that we are all walking this path together.

My family is the greatest blessing in my life. My loved ones have supported me in every way imaginable as I worked to complete this book. I am thankful for my aunts, uncles, and cousins in the Conley and Goldthree/Goldthreate families for lifting me up with their prayers, visits, and calls. My aunt Janis Perry has purchased dozens of books for me since I was a little girl and fostered my love for reading. My late grandparents—Ellie Banks Conley, James Monroe Conley, and Gertrude Goldthreate Sowell—taught me about the rich history of our family, our communities, and our people. Their stories about life in the Jim Crow South made me want to become a historian. My stepmother Vernisia Goldthree has kept me covered in prayer and always reminds me that "all is well." My brother Clarence Goldthree has cheered me on every step of the way. My niece Tyanna Sillas and nephew Dallas Haymore amaze me with their kindness, intelligence, and resilience. My daughter Nuri is the light of my life. She is the most loving person I have ever met—and the most inquisitive, too! Now that this book is done, I hope that I will be able to answer a few more of her questions. There are no words that can adequately express how much my mother, Judy Conley Goldthree, has done to support me on this journey. For my entire life, she has moved mountains to ensure that I could pursue my dreams. Her fierce and unwavering love is the driving force behind this book and everything else that I have accomplished in my life.

I completed this book while navigating profound loss and grief. My dad, Clarence Michael Lee Goldthree, passed away in 2021. He was an extraordinary father and my biggest champion. In 2023, my great aunt Mary Lucille Brown Cotten and my beloved sister Angelica Haymore left us as well. These three sudden and unexpected deaths have been a painful reminder of the uncertainties of life. I wish we could all be together again to celebrate the book's arrival and so many other special moments.

Last, but most importantly, I praise God, who makes all things possible. Thank you, Jesus, for guiding my steps. In all seasons, I hold fast to this truth: "Surely goodness and mercy shall follow me all the days of my life, and I will dwell in the house of the Lord forever." Amen.

NOTES

Introduction

Epigraph 1: "Report of UNIA Meeting," *Negro World*, July 17, 1920, reprinted in Robert A. Hill, ed., *The Marcus Garvey and Universal Negro Improvement Association Papers*, vol. II (Berkeley: University of California Press, 1983), 411.

Epigraph 2: C. L. R. James, *The Life of Captain Cipriani: An Account of British Government in the West Indies* (Durham, NC: Duke University Press, 2014), 69.

1. On Butler's return to the Grenada following the war, see "Arrival of Grenada Contingent from Egypt," *West Indian* Mail Edition, June 20, 1919, 1.

2. "Grenada Union of Returned Soldiers," *West Indian* Mail Edition, September 26, 1919, 2.

3. "Grenada Union of Returned Soldiers," *West Indian* Mail Edition, September 26, 1919, 2.

4. "Grenada Union of Returned Soldiers," *West Indian* Mail Edition, September 12, 1919, 1.

5. W. Richard Jacobs, ed., *Butler Versus the King: Riots and Sedition in 1937* (Port of Spain, Trinidad: Key Caribbean Publications, 1976), 56–57. See also W. Richard Jacobs, "Butler: A Life of Struggle," in *In the Spirit of Butler: Trade Unionism in Free Grenada* (St. George's Grenada: Fedon Publishers, 1982), 34–35; Nyahuma Obika, *An Introduction to the Life and Times of T.U.B. Butler, the Father of the Nation* (Port of Spain, Trinidad: Caribbean Historical Society, 1983), 8–11.

6. On the Trinidad Workingmen's Association, see Brinsley Samaroo and Cherita Girvan, "The Trinidad Workingmen's Association and the Origins of Popular Protest in a Crown Colony," *Social and Economic Studies* 21, no. 2 (1972): 205–22; Kelvin Singh, *Race and Class Struggles in a Colonial State: Trinidad 1917-1945* (Calgary: University of Calgary Press, 1994); José Andrés Fernández Montes de Oca, "'No Race Question': Garveyism and Trinidad's Labor Movement in the Age of Black Internationalism, 1919-1925," in *Global Garveyism*, eds. Ronald J. Stephens and Adam Ewing (Gainesville: University Press of Florida, 2019), 242–64.

7. Jacobs, *Butler Versus the King*.

8. On Butler's political activism in Grenada and Trinidad, see Obika, *Introduction to the Life*; Jerome Teelucksingh, *Ideology, Politics, and Radicalism of the Afro-Caribbean* (New York: Palgrave Macmillan, 2016), 91–130; Singh, *Race and Class Struggles*, 161–85; Jerome Teelucksingh, *Caribbean Liberators: Bold, Brilliant and Black Personalities and Organizations* (Palo Alto, CA: Academica Press, 2013), 41–84.

9. Military recruitment in Australia and India was also carried out on a voluntary basis during World War I. In contrast, conscription was formally instituted in Britain, Canada, and New Zealand, and scholars have noted that recruitment practices in Britain's African colonies were often highly coercive. Other Allied Powers also used conscription to increase the size of their armed forces. The French Army mobilized soldiers through conscription in France and the French Empire throughout the war

[259]

[260] NOTES TO INTRODUCTION

years, while the United States instituted conscription shortly after entering the war in 1917. See Ashley Jackson and James E. Kitchen, "The British Empire and the First World War: Paradoxes and New Questions," in *The British Empire and the First World War*, ed. Ashley Jackson (New York: Routledge, 2016), 6–8.

10. "Just a Little Bunch of Islands in the Sea," *West Indian*, September 19, 1915, 4.

11. On "martial interracialism," see also Reena N. Goldthree, "Writing War and Empire: Poetry, Patriotism, and Public Claims-Making in the British Caribbean," in *Caribbean Military Encounters*, eds. Shalini Puri and Lara Putnam (New York: Palgrave MacMillan, 2017), 53–55.

12. "The Jamaica Contingent," *Port of Spain Gazette*, June 30, 1915, 11.

13. "Enthusiastic Recruiting Meeting," *Port of Spain Gazette*, August 31, 1915, 8.

14. There is a substantial literature on the ideology of racial democracy in Latin America and the Caribbean. For an insightful overview of the scholarship, see Paulina L. Alberto and Jesse Hoffnung-Garskof, "'Racial Democracy' and Racial Inclusion: Hemispheric Histories," in *Afro-Latin American Studies: An Introduction*, eds. Alejandro de la Fuente and George Reid Andrews (Cambridge: Cambridge University Press, 2018), 264–316. For an analysis of the origins and development of this discourse in the British Caribbean, see Henrice Altink, *Public Secrets: Race and Colour in Colonial and Independent Jamaica* (Liverpool: Liverpool University Press, 2019); Maziki Thame, "Racial Hierarchy and the Elevation of Brownness in Creole Nationalism," *Small Axe* 21, no. 3 (2017): 111–23. For discussions of the politics of race and military service, see Nicola Foote and René Harder Horst, *Military Struggle and Identity Formation in Latin America: Race, Nation, and Community During the Liberal Period* (Gainesville: University Press of Florida, 2010); Ada Ferrer, *Insurgent Cuba: Race, Nation, and Revolution, 1868–1898* (Chapel Hill: University of North Carolina Press, 2005).

15. Cedric L. Joseph, "The British West Indies Regiment, 1914–1918," *Journal of Caribbean History* 2 (1971): 94–124; W. F. Elkins, "A Source of Black Nationalism in the Caribbean: The Revolt of the British West Indies Regiment at Taranto, Italy," *Science and Society* 34, no. 1 (1970): 99–103; Glenford Howe, "In the Crucible of Race: Race, Power, and Military Socialization of West Indian Recruits during the First World War," *Journal of Caribbean Studies* 10 (1995): 163–81; Glenford Howe, *Race, War and Nationalism: A Social History of West Indians in the First World War* (Kingston, Jamaica: Ian Randle Publishers, 2002); Richard Smith, *Jamaican Volunteers in the First World War: Race, Masculinity, and the Development of National Consciousness* (Manchester, England: Manchester University Press, 2004); Winston James, *Holding Aloft the Banner of Ethiopia: Caribbean Radicalism in Early Twentieth-Century America* (New York: Verso, 1998), 52–66; Anne Spry Rush, *Bonds of Empire: West Indians and Britishness from Victoria to Decolonization* (New York: Oxford University Press, 2011), 119–28; Stephen Bourne, *Black Poppies: Britain's Black Community and the Great War* (Cheltenham, England: The History Press, 2014), 62–76; Barry Renfrew, *Britain's Black Regiments: Fighting for Empire and Equality* (Cheltenham, England: History Press, 2020), 141–239; Anna Maguire, *Contact Zones of the First World War Cultural Encounters across the British Empire* (Cambridge: Cambridge University Press, 2021); Dominiek Dendooven, *The British West Indies Regiment: Race and Colour on the Western Front* (Yorkshire, England: Pen and Sword, 2023).

NOTES TO INTRODUCTION [261]

16. "Our Boys God Bless Them," *West Indian*, February 28, 1919, 1.

17. Claude McKay, "Letter to the *Negro World*," January 14, 1920, cited in Winston James, "Letters from London in Black and Red: Claude McKay, Marcus Garvey and the Negro World," *History Workshop Journal* 85 (2018): 290.

18. Eduardo V. Morales, "An Address to the Returned Soldiers of the B. W. I. Regiment," *Workman*, July 26, 1919, 5.

19. George Padmore, "Hitler Makes British Drop Color Bar," *The Crisis* 48 (March 1941): 74.

20. Ray Costello, *Black Tommies: British Soldiers of African Descent in the First World War* (Liverpool: Liverpool University Press, 2015), 160; Bourne, *Black Poppies*, 71. For other studies that adopt similar lines of argument, see Elkins, "A Source of Black Nationalism," 101; Tony Martin, "Revolutionary Upheaval in Trinidad, 1919: Views from British and American Sources," *Journal of Negro History* 58, no. 3 (1973): 313–26; O. Nigel Bolland, *On the March: Labour Rebellions in the British Caribbean, 1934–39* (Kingston, Jamaica: Ian Randle Publishers, 1995), 27–34; Howe, *Race, War and Nationalism*, 155–71; Smith, *Jamaican Volunteers*, 122–51; James, *Holding Aloft the Banner*, 52–66. For important exceptions, see Rush, *Bonds of Empire*, 125–28; Renfrew, *Britain's Black Regiments*, 234.

21. Karin Barber, ed., *Africa's Hidden Histories: Everyday Literacy and Making the Self* (Bloomington: Indiana University Press, 2006), 6.

22. All BWIR volunteers who enlisted before November 1916 were required to pass a literacy test.

23. On literacy in the BWIR compared to white British regiments, see "The West Indian Abroad," *Port of Spain Gazette*, September 16, 1919, 9; "Our Boys God Bless Them," *West Indian*, February 28, 1919, 1. See also, Rush, *Bonds of Empire*, 125–26. Scholars have previously noted that British Caribbean migrants also had very high literacy rates during this period. James, *Holding Aloft the Banner*, 78–80; Lara Putnam, *Radical Moves: Caribbean Migrants and the Politics of Race in the Jazz Age* (Chapel Hill: University of North Carolina Press, 2013), 128–29.

24. Thavolia Glymph, *The Women's Fight: The Civil War's Battles for Home, Freedom, and Nation* (Chapel Hill: University of North Carolina Press, 2020), 4.

25. Gordon K. Lewis, *Main Currents in Caribbean Thought: The Historical Evolution of Caribbean Society in Its Ideological Aspects, 1492–1900* (Lincoln: University of Nebraska Press, 2004), 239–40.

26. David Killingray, "'A Good West Indian, a Good African, and, in Short, a Good Britisher': Black and British in a Colour-Conscious Empire, 1760–1950," *The Journal of Imperial and Commonwealth History* 36, no. 3 (2008): 363–81; Michelle Ann Stephens, *Black Empire: The Masculine Global Imaginary of Caribbean Intellectuals in the United States, 1914–1962* (Durham, NC: Duke University Press, 2005); Faith Smith, *Strolling in the Ruins: The Caribbean's Non-sovereign Modern in the Early Twentieth Century* (Durham, NC: Duke University Press, 2023); Rush, *Bonds of Empire*; Marc Matera, *Black London: The Imperial Metropolis and Decolonization in the Twentieth Century* (Berkeley: University of California Press, 2015).

27. Smith, *Strolling in the Ruins*, 6.

28. Gregory Mann, *Native Sons: West African Veterans and France in the Twentieth Century* (Durham, NC: Duke University Press, 2006), 4.

[262] NOTES TO INTRODUCTION

29. Laurence Cole and Daniel L. Unowsky, *The Limits of Loyalty: Imperial Symbolism, Popular Allegiances, and State Patriotism in the late Habsburg Monarchy* (New York: Berghahn Books, 2007), 2.

30. Unlike traditional definitions of ideology, the notion of a political language does not assume that the ideas being expressed are internalized or held by those who articulate them. On the four competing definitions of ideology, see Michael J. Cormack, *Ideology* (Ann Arbor: University of Michigan Press, 1992), 9–13.

31. James C. Scott, *Domination and the Arts of Resistance: Hidden Transcripts* (New Haven: Yale University Press, 1990), 136.

32. By the early twentieth century, most British Caribbean colonies were governed through Crown colony rule. Only two colonies—Barbados and the Bahamas—maintained the Old Representative System of government. On Crown colony rule, see Derek O'Brien, "The Commonwealth Caribbean and the Westminster Model," in *The Oxford Handbook of Caribbean Constitutions*, ed. Derek O'Brien, Richard Albert, and Se-shauna Wheatle (Oxford, England: Oxford University Press, 2020), 134–37.

33. An elected borough council was reestablished in stages between 1914 and 1917. By 1917, all members of the council were elected. O. Nigel Bolland, *The Politics of Labour in the British Caribbean: The Social Origins of Authoritarianism and Democracy in the Labour Movement* (Kingston, Jamaica: Ian Randle, 2001), 140; Singh, *Race and Class Struggles*, 14; Selwyn D. Ryan, *Race and Nationalism in Trinidad and Tobago: A Study of Decolonization in a Multiracial Society* (Toronto, Canada: University of Toronto Press, 1972), 24–27.

34. Patrick E. Bryan, *The Jamaican People, 1880–1902* (Kingston, Jamaica: University of the West Indies Press, 2000), 11–21.

35. Hilary McD. Beckles, *Great House Rules: Landless Emancipation and Workers' Protest in Barbados, 1838–1938* (Kingston, Jamaica: Ian Randle, 2004), 187.

36. For an overview of the causes of migration, see Elizabeth M. Thomas-Hope, "The Establishment of a Migration Tradition: British West Indian Movements to the Hispanic Caribbean in the Century after Emancipation," in *Caribbean Social Relations*, ed. Colin G. Clarke (Liverpool: University of Liverpool, 1978), 66–81; Bonham C. Richardson, "Caribbean Migrations, 1838–1985," in *The Modern Caribbean*, ed. Franklin W. Knight and Colin A. Palmer (Chapel Hill: University of North Carolina Press, 2014), 203–28; James, *Holding Aloft the Banner*, 9–49.

37. Michaeline A. Crichlow, *Negotiating Caribbean Freedom: Peasants and the State in Development* (Lanham, MD: Lexington Books, 2005), 53; James, *Holding Aloft the Banner of Ethiopia*, 22; Elizabeth McLean Petras. *Jamaican Labor Migration: White Capital and Black Labor, 1850–1930* (Boulder, CO: Westview Press, 1988).

38. Bonham Richardson, *Panama Money in Barbados, 1900–1920* (Knoxville: University of Tennessee Press, 1986), 3; Julie Greene, "Entangled in Empires: British Antillean Migrations in the World of the Panama Canal," in *Crossing Empires: Taking U.S. History into Transimperial Terrain*, ed. Kristin L. Hoganson and Jay Sexton (Durham, NC: Duke University Press, 2020), 227.

39. Richardson, *Panama Money in Barbados*, 100–11; Dawn Marshall, "The History of West Indian Migrations: The Case of the West Indies," *Caribbean Review* 11, no. 1 (1982): 15–31; Putnam, *Radical Moves*.

NOTES TO INTRODUCTION [263]

40. On British Caribbean migration to the United States, see James, *Holding Aloft the Banner*; Irma Watkins-Owens, *Blood Relations: Caribbean Immigrants and the Harlem Community, 1900–1930* (Bloomington: Indiana University Press, 1996); Glenn A. Chambers, *From the Banana Zones to the Big Easy: West Indian and Central American Immigration to New Orleans, 1910–1940* (Baton Rouge: Louisiana State University Press, 2019); Tyesha Maddox, *A Home Away from Home: Mutual Aid, Political Activism, and Caribbean American Identity* (Philadelphia: University of Pennsylvania Press, 2024). On British Caribbean migration to South America, see Sidney M. Greenfield, "Barbadians in the Brazilian Amazon," *Luso-Brazilian Review* 20, no. 1 (1983): 44–64; Howard Johnson, "Barbadian Migrants in the Putumayo District of the Amazon, 1904–11," in *Caribbean Migration: Globalized Identities*, ed. Mary Chamberlain (New York: Routledge, 2002), 182–93; Elaine P. Rocha and Frederick Alleyne, "'*Millie Gone to Brazil*': Barbadian Migration to Brazil in the Early 20th Century," *Journal of the Barbados Museum and Historical Society* 58 (2012): 1–42; Nicola Foote, "British Caribbean Women Migrants and Domestic Service in Latin America, 1850–1950s: Race, Gender and Colonial Legacies," in *Colonization and Domestic Service: Historical and Contemporary Perspectives*, ed. Victoria K. Haskins and Claire Lowrie (New York: Routledge, 2015), 289–308; Putnam, *Radical Moves*; Winthrop Wright, *Café con Leche: Race, Class, and National Image in Venezuela* (Austin: University of Texas Press, 1990), 64, 77–78, 92.

41. Smith, *Strolling in the Ruins*, 3. There is substantial scholarship on Caribbean migration in the Americas during this period. For an overview of the historiography, see Lara Putnam, "Borderlands and Border Crossers: Migrants and the Greater Caribbean, 1840–1940," *Small Axe* 18, no. 1 (2014): 7–21.

42. Peter Way, "Black Service . . . White Money: The Peculiar Institution of Military Labor in the British Army during the Seven Years' War," in *Workers Across the Americas: The Transnational Turn in Labor History*, ed. Leon Fink, (New York: Oxford University Press, 2011, 62. See also Erik-Jan Zürcher, *Fighting for a Living: A Comparative Study of Military Labour 1500–2000* (Amsterdam: Amsterdam University Press, 2013); Michelle Moyd, "Soldiering On: A Research Agenda" (unpublished paper, copy in possession of the author, 2014); Simeon Man, *Soldiering through Empire: Race and the Making of the Decolonizing Pacific* (Oakland: University of California Press, 2018); Khary Oronde Polk, *Contagions of Empire: Scientific Racism, Sexuality, and Black Military Workers Abroad, 1898–1948* (Chapel Hill: University of North Carolina Press, 2020); Radhika Singha, *The Coolie's Great War: Indian Labour in a Global Conflict, 1914–1921* (New York: Oxford University Press, 2020); Samuel Fury Childs Daly, "War as Work: Labor and Soldiering in History—Review Essay," *International Labor and Working-Class History* 103 (2023): 375–80.

43. Lara Putnam, *Radical Moves*, 21–48.

44. On BWIR volunteers from Brazil, see George B. Mitchell to Earl Curzon of Kedleston (Foreign Office), March 25, 1919, CO 318/350, file 26492, TNA. On the response to the war among British Caribbean migrants in Costa Rica, see Ronald Harpelle, *West Indians of Costa Rica: Race, Class, and the Integration of an Ethnic Minority* (Montreal: McGill-Queen's University Press, 2001), 44. On BWIR volunteers from Nicaragua, see "A Pathetic Consul," *Jamaica Times*, February 5, 1916, 31. On BWIR recruitment in Panama, see Reena N. Goldthree, "'A Greater Enterprise

[264] NOTES TO INTRODUCTION

than the Panama Canal': Migrant Labor and Military Recruitment in the World War I–Era Circum-Caribbean," *Labor: Studies in Working-Class History of the Americas* 13, no. 3–4 (2016): 57–82.

45. Melvin E. Page, ed., *Africa and the First World War* (Basingstoke: Palgrave Macmillan, 1987); Arthur E. Barbeau and Florette Henri, *The Unknown Soldiers: African-American Troops in World War I* (New York: Da Capo Press, 1996); Mann, *Native Sons*; Dirk van Galen Last with Ralf Futselaar, *Black Shame: African Soldiers in Europe, 1914-1922*, trans. Marjolijn de Jager (New York: Bloomsbury Academic, 2015); Adriane Lentz-Smith, *Freedom Struggles: African Americans and World War I* (Cambridge: Harvard University Press, 2009); Michelle R. Moyd, *Violent Intermediaries: African Soldiers, Conquest, and Everyday Colonialism in German East Africa* (Athens: Ohio University Press, 2014); Jeffrey T. Sammons and John H. Morrow, *Harlem's Rattlers and the Great War: The Undaunted 369th Regiment and the African American Quest for Equality* (Lawrence: University Press of Kansas, 2014); Chad Williams, *Torchbearers of Democracy: African American Soldiers in the World War I Era* (Chapel Hill: University of North Carolina Press, 2010); Polk, *Contagions of Empire*; Michael Joseph, "First World War Veterans and the State in the French and British Caribbean, 1919–1939." *First World War Studies 10, no. 1 (2019):* 31–48.

46. Chad Williams, "A Mobilized Diaspora: The First World War and Black Soldiers as New Negroes," in *Escape from New York: The New Negro Renaissance beyond Harlem*, ed. Davarian L. Baldwin and Minkah Makalani (Minneapolis: University of Minnesota Press, 2013), 248.

47. "All in Favour Say 'Aye,'" *Workman*, July 5, 1919, 4.

48. Jane Nardal, "Black Internationalism," *La Dépêche africaine*, February 15, 1928, cited in T. Denean Sharpley-Whiting, *Negritude Women* (Minneapolis: University of Minnesota Press, 2002), 105.

49. On constructions of masculinity in the nineteenth- and early-twentieth century British Caribbean, see Aviston D. Downes, "Boys of the Empire: Elite Education and the Construction of Hegemonic Masculinity in Barbados, 1875–1920," in *Interrogating Caribbean Masculinities: Theoretical and Empirical Analyses*, ed. Rhoda Reddock (Kingston, Jamaica: University of the West Indies Press, 2004), 105–36; Mimi Sheller, *Citizenship from Below: Erotic Agency and Caribbean Freedom* (Durham, NC: Duke University Press, 2012), 89–113; Brian L. Moore and Michele A. Johnson, *Neither Led Nor Driven: Contesting British Cultural Imperialism in Jamaica, 1865–1920* (Kingston, Jamaica: University of the West Indies Press, 2004), chaps. 4–5.

50. Dalea Bean, *Jamaican Women and the World Wars: On the Front Lines of Change* (Basingstoke, U.K.: Palgrave Macmillan, 2018), 87–114.

51. Bean, *Jamaican Women and the World Wars*, 88.

52. Lentz-Smith, *Freedom Struggles*, 6.

53. On the central role of violence in making and sustaining the British Empire, see Caroline Elkins, *Legacy of Violence: A History of the British Empire* (New York: Alfred A. Knopf, 2022).

54. *Census of Jamaica and its Dependencies: Taken on the 3rd April, 1911* (Kingston, Jamaica: Government Printing Office, 1912), 7.

NOTES TO CHAPTER 1 [265]

55. Henry W. Lofty, *Report on the Census of Barbados, 1911–1921* (Bridgetown, Barbados: Advocate, 1921), 21.

56. University of the West Indies Census Research Programme and the Trinidad and Tobago Central Statistical Office, comp., *Leeward Islands Census 1891 with Tabular Statements and Report*, in *Census Reports from the British West Indies, 1891–1921* (Port of Spain, Trinidad: Central Statistical Office, 1964), 1.

Chapter One: The "Color Question"

Epigraph: Lord Dundonald to the Colonial Office, November 23, 1914, CO 318/333, file 46453, The National Archives (hereafter TNA), Kew, England.

1. For a description of the meeting, see "A New Society," *Daily Gleaner*, September 17, 1914, 14.

2. For a copy of the resolution to Raymond Poincaré, see *Daily Chronicle*, September 17, 1914, n.p., reprinted in Robert A. Hill, ed., *The Marcus Garvey and Universal Negro Improvement Association Papers*, vol. 1 (Berkeley: University of California Press, 1983), 70–71.

3. For the text of the resolution to Lewis Harcourt, see Marcus Garvey, Universal Negro Improvement and Conservation Association and African Communities League to Rt. Hon. Lewis Harcourt, September 16, 1914, CO 137/705, file 41210, TNA. A summary of the resolution was announced in the press a day before the meeting; see "A New Society," *Daily Gleaner*, September 14, 1914, 4.

4. Marcus Garvey, Universal Negro Improvement and Conservation Association and African Communities League to Rt. Hon. Lewis Harcourt, September 16, 1914, CO 137/705, file 41210, TNA.

5. Travers Buxton to Marcus Garvey, October 21, 1914, reprinted in Hill, *Marcus Garvey*, 1:81; William Manning to Marcus Garvey, September 19, 1914, reprinted in Hill, *Marcus Garvey*, 1:72.

6. "UNIA Memorial Meeting," December 4, 1914, *Daily Chronicle*, reprinted in Hill, *Marcus Garvey*, 1:95.

7. Handwritten File Note [signature illegible], October 28, 1914, CO 137/705, file 41210, TNA.

8. Captain A. A. Cipriani, *Twenty-Five Years After: The British West Indies Regiment in The Great War* (Port of Spain: Trinidad Publishing, 1940), 7.

9. Cipriani, *Twenty-Five Years After*, 7–8.

10. Marcus Garvey, "A Talk with Afro-West Indians: The Negro Race and its Problems" (1914), in Hill, *Marcus Garvey*, 1:55. On Garvey's family background and early activism, see Tony Martin, *Race First: The Ideological and Organizational Struggles of Marcus Garvey and the Universal Negro Improvement Association* (Dover, MA: Majority Press, 1976), 3–7; Rupert Lewis, *Marcus Garvey: Anti-Colonial Champion* (Trenton, NJ: Africa World Press, 1988); Robert A. Hill, "'Comradeship of the More Advanced Races': Marcus Garvey and the Brotherhood Movement in Britain, 1913–14," *Small Axe* 17, no. 1 (2013): 50–70; Adam Ewing, *The Age of Garvey: How a Jamaican Activist Created a Mass Movement and Changed Global Black Politics* (Princeton, NJ: Princeton University Press, 2014), 15–44. On Cipriani, see Gérard Besson, "A Tale of Two Families: The De Boissiers & the Ciprianis of Trinidad," paper

[266] NOTES TO CHAPTER 1

presented to the 22nd Annual Conference of Caribbean Historians, St. Augustine, Trinidad, April 1990; C. L. R. James, *The Life of Captain Cipriani: An Account of British Government in the West Indies* (Nelson, Lancashire: Coulton, 1932).

11. For a detailed discussion of the development and consolidation of white Creole identity in nineteenth-century Barbados, see David Lambert, *White Creole Culture, Politics and Identity During the Age of Abolition* (Cambridge: Cambridge University Press, 2005). On the cosmopolitan white elite in Trinidad, see Bridget Brereton, "The White Elite of Trinidad, 1838–1950," in Johnson and Watson, *The White Minority in the Caribbean*, 32–70.

12. For a discussion of the early West India Regiments, see Roger Norman Buckley, *Slaves in Red Coats: The British West India Regiments, 1795–1815* (New Haven, CT: Yale University Press, 1979); Tim Lockley, *Military Medicine and the Making of Race: Life and Death in the West India Regiments, 1795–1874* (New York: Cambridge University Press, 2020); David Lambert, *Soldiers of Uncertain Rank: The West India Regiments in British Imperial Culture* (New York: Cambridge University Press, 2024).

13. Kristin L. Hoganson, *Fighting for American Manhood: How Gender Politics Provoked the Spanish-American and Philippine-American Wars* (New Haven: Yale University Press, 1998), 9.

14. David Lloyd George infamously referred to Britain's Caribbean colonies as "the slums of the empire." Eric Williams, *From Columbus to Castro: The History of the Caribbean, 1492–1969* (New York: Vintage, 1984), 443.

15. "Enthusiastic Recruiting Meeting," *Port of Spain Gazette*, August 31, 1915, 8.

16. B. B. Cubitt (War Office) to the Under Secretary of State for the Colonies (Colonial Office), September 2, 1914, CO 318/333, file 33355, TNA.

17. The title for this section is from a handwritten note by R. A. Wiseman, September 1, 1914, CO 152/342, file 33037, TNA. For a chronological account of Governor Manning's response to the outbreak of war, see William Manning to Lewis Harcourt, October 20, 1914, CO 137/705, file 43763, TNA.

18. Herbert G. De Lisser, *Jamaica and the Great War* (Kingston, Jamaica: Gleaner, 1917), 9.

19. De Lisser, *Jamaica and the Great War*, 10.

20. "The Censorship," *Daily Gleaner*, August 4, 1914, 6.

21. "The City Churches and the War," *The Mirror*, August 4, 1914, 7.

22. *West India Committee Circular*, August 25, 1914, 404.

23. "Barbados-The gift of 2,240,000 lbs. of sugar," *West Indian Committee Circular*, September 22, 1914, 431; Officer Administering the Government of the Leeward Islands to Secretary of State for the Colonies, September 4, 1914, CO 152/342, file 33764, TNA; T. A. V. Best to Secretary of State for the Colonies, September 18, 1914, CO 152/342, file 39480, TNA; Governor of Jamaica to Secretary of State for the Colonies, September 19, 1914, CO 137/704, file 35916, TNA. For the total financial contribution of the British Caribbean colonies to the war effort, see Table B.1 in Glenford D. Howe, *Race, War and Nationalism: A Social History of West Indians in the First World War* (Kingston, Jamaica: Ian Randle Publishers, 2002), 203–4. Colonial officials, military recruiters, and local elites frequently used the phrase "ancient and loyal colonies" to highlight the longstanding ties between Britain and her colonies in

NOTES TO CHAPTER 1   [267]

the Caribbean. For examples, see "Fine Function," *Daily Gleaner*, May 31, 1915, 14; "The Bahamas Contingent," *Daily Gleaner*, September 30, 1915, 6; "Enrolling Men for War Contingent from Jamaica," *Daily Gleaner*, October 8, 1915, 13; Charles Prestwood Lucas, ed., *The Empire at War*, vol. 2 (Humphrey Milford: Oxford University Press, 1923), 359, 370.

24. Haddon-Smith to Harcourt, December 16, 1914, CO 23/274/394, cited in Gail Saunders, *Race and Class in the Colonial Bahamas, 1880–1960* (Gainesville: University Press of Florida, 2016), 100.

25. "War and Bananas," *Daily Gleaner*, August 10, 1914, 10.

26. File 7/12/154, "Jamaica Memories" Collection, Jamaica Archives (hereafter JA), Spanish Town, Jamaica.

27. *Clarion*, December 9, 1915, quoted in Peter Ashdown, "Marcus Garvey, the UNIA and the Black Cause in British Honduras, 1914–1949," *Journal of Caribbean History* 15 (1981): 43.

28. I have not been able to locate this letter. However, Lewis Harcourt, Secretary of State for the Colonies, mentions this initial correspondence in a letter to the War Office in April 1915. Lewis Harcourt to Kitchener, April 22, 1915, CO 318/333, file 50043, TNA.

29. Officer Administering the Government of the Leeward Islands to the Secretary of State for the Colonies, August 31, 1914, CO 152/342, file 33037, TNA.

30. War Office, *Manual of Military Law: War Office, 1914* (London: His Majesty's Stationary Office, 1914), 471, 843.

31. Handwritten note by R. A. Wiseman, September 1, 1914, CO 152/342, file 33037, TNA.

32. Handwritten note by Gilbert Grindle, CO 152/342, file 33037, TNA.

33. The War Cabinet voted to deploy cavalry and infantry divisions from the Indian Army in France on August 28, 1914. David Omissi, ed., *Indian Voices of the Great War: Soldiers' Letter, 1914–18* (New York: St. Martin's Press, 1999), xiii, 2; "British Reinforcements," *Jamaica Times*, September 5, 1914, 6.

34. Heather Streets, *Martial Races: The Military, Race and Masculinity in British Imperial Culture, 1857–1914* (New York: Manchester University Press, 2004), 1–13, 93–101.

35. Kaushik Roy, "Race and Recruitment in the Indian Army, 1880–1918," *Modern Asian Studies* 47, no. 4 (2013): 1312; S. D. Pradhan, "Indian Army and the First World War," in *India and World War I*, ed. Dewitt C. Ellinwood and S. D. Pradhan (New Delhi: Manohar, 1978), 56.

36. Streets, *Martial Races*, 100.

37. "British Reinforcements," *Jamaica Times*, September 5, 1914, 6.

38. A. B. Ellis, *The History of the First West India Regiment* (London: Chapman and Hall, 1885), 166–68; 170–77; 286–97.

39. Cedric L. Joseph, "The British West Indies Regiment," *Journal of Caribbean History* 2 (1971): 94; Ellis, *History of the First*, 317–32.

40. Ellis, *History of the First*, 24.

41. Ellis, *History of the First*, 19.

42. Handwritten note by R. A. Wiseman, September 1, 1914, CO 152/342, file 33037, TNA.

[268] NOTES TO CHAPTER 1

43. Handwritten note by R. A. Wiseman, September 1, 1914, CO 152/342, file 33037, TNA.

44. Handwritten note by E. R. Darnley, September 1, 1914, CO 152/342, file 33037, TNA.

45. Handwritten note by E. R. Darnley, September 1, 1914, CO 152/342, file 33037, TNA.

46. Handwritten note by R. A. Wiseman, September 1, 1914, CO 152/342, file 33037, TNA; Handwritten note by Gilbert Grindle, CO 152/342, file 33037, TNA.

47. Handwritten note by R. A. Wiseman, September 1, 1914, CO 152/342, file 33037, TNA.

48. Handwritten note by Gilbert Grindle, CO 152/342, file 33037, TNA.

49. Handwritten note by R. A. Wiseman, September 1, 1914, CO 152/342, file 33037, TNA.

50. A commerce destroyer is a navy vessel used to intercept or destroy an enemy's merchant vessel. B. B. Cubitt to the Under Secretary of State for the Colonies, September 2, 1914, CO 318/333, file 33355, TNA.

51. Lewis Harcourt to Governor William Manning, September 8, 1914, 1B/5/29/21, JA.

52. The title for this section is from Dr. A. A. Myers to the Editors of the West India Committee Circular, November 7, 1914, reprinted "Letters to the Editor-The Proposed West Indies Contingent," *West India Committee Circular*, December 15, 1914, 598. Governor William Manning reviewed a copy of the Colonial Office's letter on October 9, 1914. The first two members of his staff reviewed the letter on October 6, 1914. For date received notations on the cover page of the letter, see Lewis Harcourt to William Manning, September 8, 1914, 1B/5/29/21, JA.

53. Lara Putnam, "Nothing Matters but Color Transnational Circuits, the Interwar Caribbean, and the Black International," in *From Toussaint to Tupac: The Black International Since the Age of Revolution*, ed. Michael O. West, William G. Martin, and Fanon Che Wilkins (Chapel Hill: University of North Carolina Press, 2009), 114.

54. For early proposals for a Jamaican military contingent, see "Another Suggestion," *Daily Gleaner*, August 31, 1914, 4; "Military Men on the Canal Zone," *Daily Gleaner*, September 5, 1914, 14; "Why Not Use Our W. I. R.," *Jamaica Times*, September 5, 1914, 15; "Contingent for Europe," *Daily Gleaner*, September 5, 1914, 14; "Volunteer Force," *Daily Gleaner*, September 17, 1914, 10; "The Forum of Gleaner Readers," *Daily Gleaner*, September 29, 1914, 4; "Opinions of Gleaner Readers," *Daily Gleaner*, October 13, 1914, 10.

55. "Backwoodsman" proposed that the Jamaican government cover for the contingent's basic expenses, which he estimated at £350 per year, while private donations from patriotic residents could support the widows and orphans of fallen soldiers. Once Jamaica recruited its contingent, he confidently predicted that Trinidad, Barbados, British Guiana, and the smaller islands would promptly raise their own regiments as well. To demonstrate his commitment to the war effort, "Backwoodsman" pledged to contribute £1 1s. "every month as long as the war lasts" to a family of a disabled or slain soldier. To make good on his offer, he enclosed £2 2s. for the months of August and September along with his letter. "Another Suggestion," *Daily Gleaner*, August 31, 1914, 4.

NOTES TO CHAPTER 1 [269]

56. "Contingent for Europe," *Daily Gleaner,* September 5, 1914, 14.

57. Ellis, *History of the First,* 3.

58. Joseph, "British West Indies Regiment," 94.

59. Private Samuel Hodge, a member of the Fourth Battalion of the WIR, received the Victoria Cross in 1867 for "his bravery at the storming and capture of the stockaded town of Tubabecolong, in the kingdom of Barra, River Gambia" during a battle in the First Gambia Campaign in West Africa. For the complete citation, see *The London Gazette,* January 4, 1867, Issue 23205, Page 84. Lance-Corporal William James Gordon, a member of the First Battalion of the WIR, received the Victoria Cross in 1892 for his "his bravery and self-devotion" during the Second Gambia Campaign in West Africa. For the complete citation, see *The London Gazette,* December 9, 1892, Issue 26532, Page 7217.

60. Historian Julie Greene estimates that "150,000 to 200,000 people had traveled to the Canal Zone from the islands of the Caribbean" by the time the canal was completed in 1914. Approximately eighty thousand of the Caribbean migrants hailed from Jamaica. These figures include migrants who signed a labor contract with the Isthmian Canal Commission as well as those who traveled on their own. Julie Greene, "Entangled in Empires: British Antillean Migrations in the World of the Panama Canal," in *Crossing Empires: Taking U.S. History into Transimperial Terrain,* ed. Kristin L. Hoganson and Jay Sexton (Durham, NC: Duke University Press, 2020), 228. For estimates of the total number of contract workers who immigrated to Panama during the construction of the US-led canal project, see Olive Senior, *Dying to Better Themselves: West Indians and the Building of the Panama Canal* (Kingston, Jamaica: University of the West Indies Press, 2014), 184. See also Michael L. Conniff, *Black Labor on a White Canal: Panama, 1904-1981* (Pittsburgh, PA: University of Pittsburgh Press, 1985); George W. Westerman, *Los inmigrantes antillanos en Panamá* (Panamá: Impresora de la Nacion, 1980); Velma Newton, *The Silver Men: West Indian Labour Migration to Panama, 1850-1914* (Kingston, Jamaica: Ian Randle Publishers, 2004); Joan Flores-Villalobos, *The Silver Women: How Black Women's Labor Made the Panama Canal* (Philadelphia: University of Pennsylvania Press, 2023).]

61. Kim Johnson, "How 'Badjohn' Became A Word," *Trinidad and Tobago Express,* June 22, 2008.

62. William H. Gale, "Annual Report for Commerce and Industry for 1914 (First Section)," March 8, 1915, RG 84, Vol. 082, Foreign Service Posts of the Department of State, Panama, Colon Consulate, National Archives and Records Administration, College Park, MD.

63. "Military Men on the Canal Zone," *Daily Gleaner,* September 5, 1914, 14; For a detailed discussion of West Indians' role in the construction of the Panama Canal and West Indian life in the Canal Zone, see Julie Greene, *The Canal Builders: Making America's Empire at the Panama Canal* (New York: The Penguin Press, 2009), chapter three. On the response to the outbreak of World War I among West Indians in Panama, see Reena N. Goldthree, "'A Greater Enterprise Than the Panama Canal': Migrant Labor and Military Recruitment in the World War I-Era Circum-Caribbean," *Labor: Studies in Working-Class History of the Americas* 13, no. 3–4 (2016): 57–82.

[270] NOTES TO CHAPTER 1

64. Stephen A. Hill, *Who's Who in Jamaica, 1916* (Kingston, Jamaica: The Gleaner Company, 1916), 39; Stephen A. Hill, *Who's Who in Jamaica, 1919-1920* (Kingston, Jamaica: The Gleaner Company, 1919), 52.

65. De Lisser, *Jamaica and the Great War*, 31-33; "Why Not Use Our W.I.R.," *Jamaica Times*, September 5, 1914, 15; "Volunteer Force," *Daily Gleaner*, September 17, 1914, 10.

66. William Manning to Lewis Harcourt, October 20, 1914, CO 137/705, file 43763, TNA.

67. Joseph, "British West Indies Regiment," 94.

68. As historian Richard Smith points out, the arms-bearing tradition in the British Caribbean was historically linked to white colonists' anxieties about property rights and racial domination. Smith, *Jamaican Volunteers in the First World War*, 48-51; James Burk, *Handbook of the Sociology of the Military*, ed. Giuseppe Caforio, (New York: Springer, 2003), 111-30.

69. "A Suggestion," *Daily Gleaner*, September 4, 1914, 4; De Lisser, *Jamaica and the Great War*, 31.

70. "W. I. Regiment and the War," *Daily Gleaner*, October 27, 1914, 6.

71. "Opinion of Gleaner Readers," *Daily Gleaner*, October 13, 1914, 10.

72. "The West Indian Offer of Service," *West Indian Committee Circular*, October 20, 1914, 481.

73. William Manning to Lewis Harcourt, October 20, 1914, CO 137/705, file 43763, TNA.

74. Cipriani, *Twenty-Five Years After*, 7.

75. "Notes of Interest," *West India Committee Circular*, November 3, 1914, 520.

76. Thomas C. Holt, *The Problem of Freedom: Race, Labor, and Politics in Jamaica and Britain, 1832-1938* (Baltimore, MD: Johns Hopkins University Press, 1991); Catherine Hall, *Civilising Subjects: Metropole and Colony in the English Imagination, 1830-1867* (Chicago: University of Chicago Press, 2002); Christopher Taylor, *Empire of Neglect: The West Indies in the Wake of British Liberalism* (Durham, NC: Duke University Press, 2018).

77. Louis S. Meikle, *Confederation of the British West Indies versus Annexation to the United States: A Political Discourse on the West Indies* (New York: Negro Universities Press, 1969, 1912c); "British West Indies To Be Sold to the United States," *Northern News*, April 8, 1916, Vol. 9-10, 1; "The Talk About the Sale of the West Indies To America," *Northern News*, April 15, 1916, Vol. 9-11, 1. These rumors resurfaced in the aftermath of World War I; see Jamaica Imperial Association to Colonial Secretary (Jamaica), October 23, 1919, in H. Bryan, Acting Governor to Viscount Milner, October 31, 1919, CO 137/733, file 65916, TNA; "Editorialettes," *The Workman*, August 30, 1919, p.4; "Lord Rothmere Suggest Sale of West Indian Islands," *The Workman*, September 20, 1919, p.1; "Editorialettes," *The Workman*, October 4, 1919, 4; "Interesting News from the West Indian Islands," *The Workman*, October 18, 1919, 2.

78. Arch Dale, "Shoulder to Shoulder," *The Grain Growers' Guide*, August 1914, n.p. *The Grain Growers' Guide* was published in Winnipeg, Canada by farmers' organizations in the "prairie" provinces of Manitoba, Saskatchewan, and Alberta. Professor John Herd Thompson kindly brought this image to my attention and provided background about the publication.

NOTES TO CHAPTER 1 [271]

79. W.H. Steele Mitchell, *Daily Express*, reprinted in "Letters to the Editor," *West India Committee Circular*, November 17, 1914, 550.

80. Lieut.-General Douglas Mackinnon Baillie Hamilton Cochrane (The Earl of Dundonald), *My Army Life* (London: Edward Arnold & Co, 1926), 1–19, 302–3.

81. Lord Dundonald to the Colonial Office, November 23, 1914, CO 318/333, file 46453, TNA.

82. "Proposed West Indian Contingent," Lord Dundonald to the Colonial Office, November 23, 1914, CO 318/333, file 46453, TNA.

83. Handwritten note by R. A. Wiseman, November 26, 1914, CO 318/333, file 46453, TNA.

84. Handwritten note by R. A. Wiseman, November 26, 1914, CO 318/333, file 46453, TNA.

85. Handwritten note by Gilbert Grindle, November 26, 1914, CO 318/333, file 46453, TNA.

86. Handwritten note by G. V. Fiddes, December 1, 1914, CO 318/333, file 46453, TNA.

87. Handwritten note by Gilbert Grindle, November 26, 1914, CO 318/333, file 46453, TNA; Handwritten note by G. V. Fiddes, December 1, 1914, CO 318/333, file 46453, TNA.

88. H. J. Read (on behalf of Lewis Harcourt) to War Office, December 8, 1914, CO 318/333, file 46453, TNA.

89. H. J. Read (on behalf of Lewis Harcourt) to War Office, December 8, 1914, CO 318/333, file 46453, TNA.

90. B. B. Cubitt to the Under-Secretary of State, Colonial Office, December 14, 1914, CO 318/333, file 50043, TNA.

91. Harcourt outlined in concerns with the War Office's December 1914 proposal in a letter to Lord Stamforham in April 1915. See Lewis Harcourt to Lord Stamforham, April 20, 1915, CO 318/333, file 50043, TNA.

92. Dundonald, *My Army Life*, 306; Lord Dundonald to the Under-Secretary of State, Colonial Office, December 30, 1914, CO 318/333, file 50043, TNA.

93. Under-Secretary of State to Lord Dundonald, December 28, 1914, quoted in Dundonald, *My Army Life*, 306.

94. The title for this section is from "The West Indies and the War," *Federalist and Grenada People*, June 19, 1915, 2.

95. Governor Leslie Probyn to Lewis Harcourt, October 27, 1914, CO 28/284, file 44093, TNA.

96. Dr. A.A. Myers to the Editors of the West India Committee Circular, November 7, 1914, reprinted "Letters to the Editor-The Proposed West Indies Contingent," *West India Committee Circular*, December 15, 1914, 598.

97. Dr. A. A. Myers to the Editors of the West India Committee Circular, November 7, 1914, reprinted "Letters to the Editor-The Proposed West Indies Contingent," *West India Committee Circular*, December 15, 1914, 598.

98. "The West Indies and the War," *Federalist and Grenada People*, June 19, 1915, 2.

99. De Lisser, *Jamaica and the Great War*, 33; Howe, *Race, War and Nationalism*, 34; "The Mixed British Army," Barbados *Globe and Colonial Advocate*, February 12, 1915, n.p.

[272] NOTES TO CHAPTER 1

100. *The Clarion*, August 12, 1915, 177, quoted in Howe, *Race, War and Nationalism*, 34.

101. *The Clarion*, August 12, 1915, 177, quoted in Howe, *Race, War and Nationalism*, 34.

102. "Now in Training for Service at the Front," *Daily Gleaner*, October 5, 1915, 6.

103. Frank Cundall, *Jamaica's Part in the Great War, 1914–1918* (London: IOJ, by the West India Commission, 1925), 109.

104. C. L. R. James, *Life of Captain Cipriani*, 23.

105. Anthony De V. Phillips, "Go Ahead England, Barbados is Behind You: Barbadian Responses to the Outbreak of the Great War," in *Before and After 1865: Education, Politics and Regionalism in the Caribbean*, ed. Brian Moore and Swithin Wilmot (Kingston, Jamaica: Ian Randle, 1998), 346.

106. Lewis Harcourt to William Manning, February 10, 1915, 1B/5/29/22, JA.

107. Governor Hadden-Smith to Bonar Law, August 7, 1915, CO 321/282, file 40055, TNA; Director General, Army Medical Services to W.S. Mitchell, July 8, 1915, CO 321/282, file 40055, TNA.

108. Governor Hadden-Smith to Bonar Law, August 7, 1915, CO 321/282, file 40055, TNA.

109. Governor Manning to Bonar Law, April 15, 1916, CO 137/715, TNA. Rushie-Gray's service with the West India Regiment is discussed in Smith, *Jamaican Volunteers in the First World War*, 65.

110. Minute, May 3, 1916, CO 137/715, file 20904, TNA; Minute, May 15, 1916, CO 137/715, file 20904, TNA.

111. William Manning to Bonar Law, June 23, 1916, 1B/5/23/5, JA.

112. Pension Claims for Egbert Watson, WO 364/4505, TNA.

113. George I. Brizan, *Brave Young Grenadians-Loyal British Subjects: Our People in The First and Second World War* (San Juan, Trinidad: Paria Publishing Company, 2002), 33.

114. Pension Claims for Alonzo Nathan, WO 364/2665, TNA.

115. Norman Manley, "The Autobiography of Norman Washington Manley," *Jamaica Journal* 7, no.1, (March–June 1973), 6.

116. Manley, "Autobiography," 5.

117. Manley, "Autobiography," 7.

118. Manley, "Autobiography," 5–6.

119. "Coloured Men as Recruits," *The Port of Spain Gazette*, June 16, 1915, 5.

120. "Coloured Men as Recruits," *The Port of Spain Gazette*, June 16, 1915, 5.

121. Joseph, "British West Indies Regiment," 98.

122. Lord Stamfordham to Lewis Harcourt, April 17, 1915, CO 318/333, file 50043, TNA.

123. Lewis Harcourt to Lord Stamforham, April 20, 1915, CO 318/333, file 50043, TNA.

124. Lord Stamforham to Lewis Harcourt, April 22, 1915, CO 318/333, file 50043, TNA; War Office to Secretary of State, Colonial Office, May 19, 1915, CO 137/712, TNA.

125. Lewis Harcourt to Kitchener, April 22, 1915, CO 318/333, file 50043, TNA; War Office to Secretary of State, Colonial Office, May 19, 1915, CO 137/712, TNA.

NOTES TO CHAPTER 1 [273]

126. "The Jamaica War Contingent Fund," *Daily Gleaner*, May 14, 1915, 13; "The Jamaica War Contingent Fund," *Daily Gleaner*, May 26, 1915, 13.

127. "The Jamaica War Contingent Fund," *Daily Gleaner*, May 28, 1915, 13.

128. "Men of Trinidad!," *Port of Spain Gazette*, June 5, 1915, 9.

129. "For King and Empire," *Port of Spain Gazette*, June 29, 1915, 5.

130. The (London) *Times*, October 25, 1915, 7.

131. See, for example, "Message from the King," *Federalist and Grenada People*, October 27, 1915, n.p.

132. *The London Gazette*, October 26, 1915, quoted in Cundall, *Jamaica's Part*, 27.

133. "Britain's Myriad Voices Call," *The West Indian*, July 24, 1915, 4.

134. "From the Negro Improvement Society," *Jamaica Times*, November 13, 1915, reprinted in Hill, *Marcus Garvey*, I:163–64.

135. Brian L. Moore and Michele A. Johnson, *Neither Led nor Driven: Contesting British Cultural Imperialism in Jamaica, 1865-1920* (Kingston, Jamaica: University of the West Indies Press, 2004), 308.

136. For examples, see "Jamaica Patriotic League," *Daily Gleaner*, September 27, 1915, 14; "Jamaica Patriotic League," *Jamaica Times*, October 2, 1915, 7; "Jamaica Patriotic League," *Daily Gleaner*, October 18, 1915, 14; "Jamaica Patriotic League," *Daily Gleaner*, October 25, 1915, 14.

137. The annual commemoration of the end of slavery in the British Caribbean is celebrated on August 1. On the establishment and early activism of the UNIA in Jamaica, see Tony Martin, *Race First: The Ideological and Organizational Struggles of Marcus Garvey and the Universal Negro Improvement Association* (Westport, CT: Greenwood Press, 1976), 6–7; Natanya Duncan, *An Efficient Womanhood: Women and the Making of the Universal Negro Improvement Association* (Chapel Hill: University of North Carolina Press, 2025), 30–31.

138. Marcus Garvey, Jnr., "A Talk with Afro-West Indians. The Negro Race and its Problems," in Hill, *Marcus Garvey*, 1:62.

139. Meikle, *Confederation of the British*, 38.

140. Meikle, 6. For a history of the idea of a West Indian federation, see Eric D. Duke, *Building a Nation: Caribbean Federation in the Black Diaspora* (Gainesville: University Press of Florida, 2016).

141. Meikle, *Confederation of the British*, 6.

142. "West Indian Confederation," *Daily Argosy*, August 5, 1914, 8; "Great Scheme," *Daily Gleaner*, August 22, 1914, 10; Marcus Garvey strongly endorsed Meikle's proposal for a West Indian federation in a lengthy letter to the *Daily Gleaner*, see "The Forum of Gleaner Readers," *Daily Gleaner*, August 26, 1914, 4.

143. For more information about Hubert Hill Cain's involvement in the UNIA in British Honduras, see Peter Ashdown, "Marcus Garvey, the UNIA and the Black Cause in British Honduras, 1914–1949," *Journal of Caribbean History* 15 (1981), 41–55.

144. The requirements for enlistment in the BWIR are discussed extensively in Chapter Two. For a brief overview of the requirements for enlistment, see "The Conditions of Enlistment," *Jamaica Times*, October 9, 1915, 15.

145. "The West Indies and the War," *Federalist and Grenada People*, June 19, 1915, 2.

[274] NOTES TO CHAPTER 2

Chapter Two: "Every True Son of the Empire"

Epigraph 1: "From the Negro Improvement Society," *Jamaica Times*, November 13, 1915, n.p. reprinted in Robert A. Hill, ed., *The Marcus Garvey and Universal Negro Improvement Association Papers*, vol. 1 (Berkeley: University of California Press, 1983), 163.

Epigraph 2: George Padmore, "Hitler Makes British Drop Color Bar," *The Crisis* 48, no. 3 (1941): 74.

1. C. L. R. James, *Beyond a Boundary* (Durham, NC: Duke University Press, 1993), 30.

2. James, *Beyond a Boundary*, 31.

3. James, *Beyond a Boundary*, 31.

4. "Just a Little Bunch of Islands in the Sea," *West Indian*, September 19, 1915, 4.

5. Vincent Brown, *Tacky's Revolt: The Story of an Atlantic Slave War* (Cambridge, MA: Harvard University Press, 2020), 6.

6. War Office to Secretary of State, Colonial Office, May 19, 1915, CO 137/712, The National Archives (hereafter TNA), Kew, England.

7. B. B. Cubitt, War Office to Under Secretary of State, Colonial Office, June 25, 1915, CO 318/336, file 29508, TNA.

8. Separation allowances were designed to "provide for the maintenance of the family of the soldier when he is unavoidably separated from them by the exigencies of the public service, or to assist in maintaining the dependants of the soldier, other than wives and children, in the same degree of comfort as they enjoyed" prior to his enlistment. Until December 1917, soldiers who applied for separation allowances for their dependents were required to make a weekly allotment from their pay to contribute toward the separation allowance, with the government contributing the balance. Separation allowance payments were determined by the soldier's rank, number of dependents, and place of residence. War Office, *Regulations for the Issue of Separation Allowance and Allotments of Pay During the Present War* (London: HMSO, 1915), 5.

9. B. B. Cubitt, War Office to Under Secretary of State, Colonial Office, June 25, 1915, CO 318/336, file 29508, TNA.

10. H. J. Read (for Bonar Law) to Secretary of State for War, War Office, July 7, 1915, CO 318/336, file 29508, TNA.

11. For the various separation allowance scales for the British Army, see War Office, *Regulations for the Issue*, 46; For the various separation allowance scales for the West India Regiment, see B.B. Cubitt, War Office to Under Secretary of State, Colonial Office, July 17, 1915, CO 318/336, file 29508, TNA.

12. The final terms regarding the colonies' contribution to separation allowances would not be fixed until September 1915. See E. R. Darnley (Colonial Office) to J. B. Crosland (War Office), September 14, 1915, CO 318/336, file 43957, TNA; A. Pickard (War Office) to E.R. Darnley (Colonial Office), September 22, 1915, CO 318/336, file 43957, TNA.

13. B. B. Cubitt, War Office to Under Secretary of State, Colonial Office, July 17, 1915, CO 318/336, file 29508, TNA.

14. Handwritten note by Gilbert Grindle, July 20, 1915, CO 318/336, file 33039, TNA.

NOTES TO CHAPTER 2 [275]

15. Handwritten note by Gilbert Grindle, July 20, 1915, CO 318/336, file 33039, TNA.

16. "The Jamaica Contingent," *Jamaica Times*, August 7, 1915, 14.

17. "The Proposed Trinidad Contingent," *Port of Spain Gazette*, June 25, 1915, 3.

18. "The Government and the People," *Port of Spain Gazette*, June 25, 1915, 2.

19. "The Proposed Trinidad Contingent," *Port of Spain Gazette*, June 25, 1915, 3.

20. George Basil Haddon-Smith to Lewis Harcourt, June 7, 1915, CO 321/281, file 26449, TNA; William Manning to Gilbert Grindle, August 5, 1915, CO 137/710, file 36649, TNA.

21. The title for this section is from "Recruiting in Trinidad," *Port of Spain Gazette*, September 1, 1915, 11. For a draft of the telegram, see Bonar Law to the West Indian Colonies, July 20, 1915, CO 318/336, file 33039, TNA. The Governor of the Windward Islands stated that he received the official telegram on July 21, 1915. "The West Indian Contingent," *Daily Argosy*, August 1, 1915, 5.

22. "West Indians Volunteer," *The New York Times*, June 4, 1915, 4; In a speech to the Legislative Council, Governor George Le Hunte of Trinidad stated that Governor Manning approached him about raising a battalion of 1,200 soldiers for the BWIR, which is lower than the figure quoted by the *The New York Times*. "The Legislature," *Port of Spain Gazette*, June 26, 1915, 5.

23. "The Legislature," *Port of Spain Gazette*, June 26, 1915, 5; Charles Prestwood Lucas, ed., *The Empire at War*, vol. 2 (London: Oxford University Press), 417.

24. H. J. Read to Secretary of State for War, War Office, July 7, 1915, CO 318/336, file 33039, TNA.

25. For population estimates for the British Caribbean by colony, see Joseph C. Ford and Frank Cundall, *The Handbook of Jamaica for 1916* (Kingston, Jamaica: Government Printing Office, 1916), 22–23.

26. These figures are taken from the 1911 official census, cited in Ford and Cundall, *Handbook of Jamaica for 1916*, 37.

27. "The Men and the War," *Daily Gleaner*, June 5, 1915, 8.

28. "Recruiting in Trinidad," *Port of Spain Gazette*, September 1, 1915, 11.

29. A.A. Cipriani, *Twenty-Five Years After: The British West Indies Regiment in the Great War 1914–1918* (Port of Spain: Trinidad Publishing, 1940), 9.

30. "Britain's Myriad Voices Call," *West Indian*, July 24, 1915, 4.

31. "Recruiting in Trinidad," *Port of Spain Gazette*, September 1, 1915, 11.

32. For coverage of Indian soldiers in the Great War, see "Our Fine Indian Troops," *Jamaica Times*, September 5, 1914, 6.

33. "The Men and the War," *Daily Gleaner*, June 5, 1915, 8.

34. B. B. Cubitt to Under Secretary of State for the Colonies (Colonial Office), August 16, 1915, CO 318/336, file 37888, TNA.

35. Handwritten note by R. A. Wiseman, August 17, 1915, CO 318/336, file 37888, TNA.

36. B. B. Cubitt to Under Secretary of State for the Colonies, October 25, 1915, CO 318/336, file 49130, TNA.

37. "The Jamaica Contingent," *Port of Spain Gazette*, June 30, 1915, 11. The remaining members of the inaugural War Contingent Committee were Frank Jackson, John Barclay, S. Couper, and J. Tapley. John Barclay was the Secretary of the

[276] NOTES TO CHAPTER 2

Jamaica Agricultural Society and S. Couper served as the Director of the Government Railway. Joseph C. Ford and Frank Cundall, *The Handbook of Jamaica for 1919* (Kingston: Government Printing Office, 1919), 592.

38. For a list of the members appointed to the inaugural Barbados Recruiting Committee in August 1915, see "Report of the Recruiting Committee," August 11, 1917, CO 28/292, TNA.

39. "A Sweepstake," *Daily Gleaner*, January 14, 1915, 13.

40. Arthur Cipriani, "The Carnival," *Port of Spain Gazette*, February 7, 1915, 6. See also Errol G. Hill, "Calypso and War," *Black American Literature Forum* 23, no.1 (1989): 69–71.

41. "Help for the Motherland," *Port of Spain Gazette*, June 2, 1915, 11.

42. "Mr A. A. Cipriani and Red Cross Nurses," *Port of Spain Gazette*, September 5, 1915, 6.

43. Cipriani, *Twenty-Five Years After*, 9.

44. The title for this section is from "Just a Little Bunch of Islands in the Sea," *West Indian*, September 19, 1915, 4.

45. "Enthusiastic Recruiting Meeting," *Port of Spain Gazette*, August 31, 1915, 8; C. L. R. James, *The Life of Captain Cipriani: An Account of British Government in the West Indies* (Nelson, Lancashire: Coulton, 1932), 25.

46. "Enthusiastic Recruiting Meeting," *Port of Spain Gazette*, August 31, 1915, 8.

47. Cipriani, *Twenty-Five Years After*, 9.

48. Commenting on the central role that ministers played in circulating information, a Jamaican BWIR recalled: "Ministers on Sunday tell them [the news]. Ministers on the pulpit Sunday tell them. And when the Minister tell them they believe what [the] Minister say. So if you even get a paper and read it and tell them, they say: 'But the Minister never tell we so Sunday!'" "Life in Jamaica in the Early Twentieth Century: A Presentation of Ninety Oral Accounts" (unpublished transcripts housed at Institute of Social and Economic Research, University of the West Indies, Mona, Kingston, Jamaica), Volume: Parish of Trelawny, Respondent: 81TMa, "Mr. G.—Ex-Serviceman," 21.

49. "Life in Jamaica in the Early Twentieth Century: A Presentation of Ninety Oral Accounts," Volume: Parish of St. Catherine, Respondent: 51StcMa, "World War I Volunteer," 19.

50. Herbert G. de Lisser, *Jamaica and the Great War* (Kingston, Jamaica: Gleaner), 70.

51. For an analysis of middle-class and elite women's contributions to the war effort in Jamaica, see Dalea Bean, *Jamaican Women and the World Wars: On the Front Lines of Change* (Cham, Switzerland: Palgrave Macmillan, 2018). On women's activism in British Honduras during the war years, see Anne S. Macpherson, *From Colony to Nation: Women Activists and the Gendering of Politics in Belize, 1912–1982* (Lincoln: University of Nebraska Press, 2007), 58–59.

52. de Lisser, *Jamaica and the Great War*, 69.

53. Nicoletta F. Gullace, "White Feathers and Wounded Men: Female Patriotism and the Memory of the Great War," *Journal of British Studies* 36, no. 2 (1997): 183.

54. *The Antigua Sun*, August 25, 1915, 3, quoted in Glenford D. Howe, *Race, War and Nationalism: A Social History of West Indians in the First World War* (Kingston, Jamaica: Ian Randle Publishers, 2002), 53.

NOTES TO CHAPTER 2 [277]

55. "Women for the Cause!," *Daily Gleaner*, May 17, 1917, 8.

56. Macpherson, *From Colony to Nation*, 50–58.

57. *Clarion*, December 30, 1915, n.p, quoted in Macpherson, *From Colony to Nation*, 58.

58. "A Notable Day at Montego Bay," *Daily Gleaner*, November 17, 1915, 13.

59. "The Great Recruiting Demonstration at Montego Bay," *Daily Gleaner*, November 18, 1915, 14.

60. "Great Recruiting Movement in the Parishes of Jamaica," *Daily Gleaner*, December 3, 1915, 13.

61. "Information Regarding Rates of Pay, Separation Allowances, and Pensions for the Men Joining the Jamaica War Contingents," 1B/5/77/108-1926, Jamaica Archives (hereafter JA), Spanish Town, Jamaica. [See "Recruiting in the City," *Port of Spain Gazette*, August 15, 1915, 3—slightly different rate quoted].

62. "Inside the Recruiting Office," *Port of Spain Gazette*, September 30, 1915, 3.

63. Moore and Johnson, *Neither Led Nor Driven: Contesting British Cultural Imperialism in Jamaica, 1865-1920* (Kingston, Jamaica: University of the West Indies Press, 2004), see chapter 9.

64. "Ocho Rios Recruiting Meeting," *Daily Gleaner*, December 15, 1915, 13.

65. "The King Needs You!," *The Dominica Chronicle*, January 13, 1917, quoted in Irving W. André and Gabriel J. Christian, *For King and Country: The Service and Sacrifice of the Dominican Soldier* (Brampton, Ontario: Pont Casse Press, 2008), 45.

66. Simon Rogers, "There were no parades for us," *The Guardian*, November 6, 2002, http://www.guardian.co.uk/uk/2002/nov/06/britishidentity.military.

67. "Ocho Rios Recruiting Meeting," *Daily Gleaner*, December 15, 1915, 13.

68. "Meeting Held," *Daily Gleaner*, October 25, 1915, 14.

69. "Message from the King," *Federalist and Grenada People*, October 27, 1915, 2.

70. "The Call of the Empire for More Recruits," *Daily Gleaner*, December 17, 1915, 11.

71. "The Call of the Empire for More Recruits," *Daily Gleaner*, December 17, 1915, 11.

72. "The Motherland's Call," *Daily Gleaner*, November 29, 1915, 14.

73. "A Notable Day at Montego Bay," *Daily Gleaner*, November 17, 1915, 13.

74. For a fascinating history of war-related calypsos in Trinidad, see Hill, "Calypso and War," 61–88.

75. John Cowley, *Carnival, Canboulay and Calypso: Traditions in the Making* (Cambridge: Cambridge University Press, 1996), 207.

76. "Demerarian Goes with the Barbados Contingent," *Daily Argosy*, June 22, 1915, 6.

77. Aviston D. Downes, "Boys of the Empire: Elite Education and the Construction of Hegemonic Masculinity in Barbados, 1875-1920," in *Interrogating Caribbean Masculinities: Theoretical and Empirical Analyses*, ed. Rhoda Reddock (Kingston, Jamaica: University Press of the West Indies, 2004), 129.

78. "Message from the King," *Federalist and Grenada People*, October 27, 1915, 2.

79. Timothy Stapleton, "Visual Symbols and Military Culture in Britain's West African Colonial Army (c.1900–60)," *International Journal of Military History and Historiography* 41, no. 1 (2020): 42–73; Heather Streets, *Martial Races: The Military,*

Race, and Masculinity in British Imperial Culture, 1857–1914 (Manchester: Manchester University Press, 2004), 201–2, 207–10; Christopher Leach, "Uniforms and Commercial Culture: Constructing a Vision of Warfare in Pre-Great War Britain," *Cultural History* 10, no. 1 (2021): 31–60; Jane Tynan, *British Army Uniform and the First World War: Men in Khaki* (New York: Palgrave Macmillan, 2014).

80. Streets, *Martial Races*, 201.

81. Adriane Lentz-Smith, *Freedom Struggles: African Americans and World War I* (Cambridge: Harvard University Press, 2009), 81.

82. Gregory Mann, *Native Sons: West African Veterans and France in the Twentieth Century* (Durham: Duke University Press, 2006), 93–95.

83. Michelle Moyd, *Violent Intermediaries: African Soldiers, Conquest, and Everyday Colonialism in German East Africa* (Athens: Ohio University Press, 2014), 13–14.

84. Marc Goodman and V. Rushton, "A Jamaica Past, Being a Glimpse into History's Bloodiest Battlefield: A Visit with Jamaica's Last Surviving World War I Veteran," *Jamaican Historical Society Bulletin* 11, no.3 (1999/2000): 54.

85. For an analysis of the communication networks that connected the British West Indies to Central America, see Lara Putnam, "'Nothing Matters But Color': Transnational Circuits, the Interwar Caribbean, and the Black International," in *From Toussaint to Tupac: The Black International since the Age of Revolution*, ed. Michael O. West, William G. Martin, and Fanon Che Wilkins (Chapel Hill: University of North Carolina Press, 2009), 107–9. See also Lara Putnam, *Radical Moves: Caribbean Migrants and the Politics of Race in the Jazz Age* (Chapel Hill: University of North Carolina Press, 2013).

86. De Lisser, *Jamaica and the Great War*, 97.

87. "Bocas-Del-Toro Volunteers," *Daily Gleaner*, November 22, 1915, 11; "Jamaica's Loyal Sons Coming Home to Enlist for the War," *Daily Gleaner*, December 28, 1915, 6; "They Remembered England," *Daily Gleaner*, December 29, 1915, 8; "Recruits from Colón," *Daily Gleaner*, February 7, 1916, 14.

88. "Recruits from Colón," *Daily Gleaner*, February 7, 1916, 14.

89. "West Indians in Panama," *Port of Spain Gazette*, November 17, 1915, 9.

90. W.A. Hume, "Wait to Fight for Empire," *Daily Gleaner*, November 23, 1915, 13.

91. For a detailed treatment of the BWIR recruitment campaigns in Panama, see Reena N. Goldthree, "'A Greater Enterprise Than the Panama Canal': Migrant Labor and Military Recruitment in the World War I-Era Circum-Caribbean," *Labor: Studies in Working-Class History of the Americas* 13, no. 3–4 (2016): 57–82.

92. "A Pathetic Consul," *Jamaica Times*, February 5, 1916, 31.

93. "West Indians in Panama," *Port of Spain Gazette*, November 17, 1915, 9.

94. Stephen A. Hill, *Who's Who in Jamaica, 1919–1920* (Kingston, Jamaica: Gleaner, 1920), 242.

95. "West Indians in Panama Rallying Round the Flag," *Panama Morning Journal*, May 14, 1917, 1.

96. Hill, *Who's Who in Jamaica, 1919–1920*, 242.

97. "Volunteers for the British Army," *Panama Star & Herald*, May 11, 1917, enclosed in Claude Mallet to Arthur Balfour, June 6, 1917, CO 318/343/8, file 34370, TNA; "Volunteers for the British Army," *Panama Morning Journal*, July 7,

NOTES TO CHAPTER 2 [279]

1917, enclosed in Claude Mallet, Recruitment of British West Indians at Panama, CO 318/343/28, file 45461, TNA.

98. Cited in Putnam, "Nothing Matters but Color," 114.

99. *Panama Morning Journal*, May 22, 1917, 7.

100. "What Do They Know of England," *Panama Morning Journal*, May 18, 1917, 4. For another example of this rhetoric see, "West Indians Leave for War," *Panama Morning Journal*, May 18, 1917, 1.

101. Claude Mallet to Arthur Balfour, June 6, 1917, CO 318/343, file 34370, TNA.

102. "Recruiting Starts in Colon Today," *Panama Morning Journal*, May 29, 1917, 7.

103. The BWIR included 441 soldiers from the Bahamas, 533 from British Honduras, 229 from the Leeward Islands, 359 from St. Lucia, and 305 from St. Vincent.

104. The BWIR recruitment campaign in Panama in 1917 garnered 2,091 volunteers. This figure does not include the previous groups of BWIR volunteers who departed from Panama in 1915 and 1916. Hill, *Who's Who in Jamaica, 1919–1920*, 242; Goldthree, "A Greater Enterprise," 66–67.

105. "Fathers and Sons," *Daily Gleaner*, October 6, 1921, 6.

106. The BWIR included 397 officers and 15,204 soldiers of other ranks. For the official enlistment figures, see West Indian Contingent Committee, *Reports and Accounts for the Nine Months ended 30th September, 1919* (London: West India Committee Rooms, 1920); Lucas, *Empire at War*, 335.

107. When calculating Jamaica's BWIR enlistment figures, military authorities on the island counted men who volunteered locally as well as men who volunteered in Panama and traveled to Jamaica to complete the final steps in the enlistment process. However, as newspaper reports and personnel records make clear, the men who volunteered in Panama for the BWIR hailed from across the British Caribbean and were not solely Jamaican. Therefore, when assessing BWIR enlistment patterns, I focus on where soldiers resided when they volunteered for the regiment rather than their colony of origin. Hill, *Who's Who in Jamaica, 1919–1920*, 244–45; Goldthree, "A Greater Enterprise."

108. O. Nigel Bolland, *On the March: Labour Rebellions in the British Caribbean, 1934–39* (Kingston, Jamaica: Ian Randle Publishers, 1995), 27.

109. According to the surviving nominal rolls, at least 73 men who were already living in England joined the BWIR in 1916. This figure does not include white officers who resided in England and were later assigned to the regiment. "Nominal Roll of Men Who Have Enlisted in England Since 3rd June, 1916," enclosed in War Office to Under Secretary of State for the Colonies, July 8, 1916, CO 318/340, TNA; "Enlistments in England Since 23rd July, 1916," enclosed in War Office to Under Secretary of State for the Colonies, August 31, 1916, CO 318/340, TNA; "Further Recruits Who Have Enlisted in England for the British West Indies Regiment," enclosed in War Office to Under Secretary of State for the Colonies, September 29, 1916, CO 318/340, TNA; "Further Roll of Recruits," enclosed in War Office to Under Secretary of State for the Colonies, November 28, 1916, CO 318/340, TNA. For geographic information about some of the men's place of enlistment in England, see "Further Roll of Recruits Who Have Enlisted in England Since 30th August, 1916," enclosed in War Office to Under Secretary of State for the Colonies, October 1916, CO 318/340, TNA; "Further

Roll of Recruits Who Enlisted in England During October, 1916," enclosed in War Office to Under Secretary of State for the Colonies, November 4, 1916, CO 318/340, TNA.

110. In general, volunteers had to between the ages of 19 and 38 to enlist unless they had previously served in the military. Veterans who desired to enlist in the BWIR could sign up until age forty-five. For the complete enlistment requirements, see "Notice: Barbadians for Service with the British Army," *Barbados Globe and Colonial Advocate*, June 23, 1915, n.p; "Information Regarding Rates of Pay, Separation Allowances, and Pensions for Men Joining the Jamaica War Contingents," 1B/5/77/108-1926, JA.

111. "Notice: Barbadians for Service with the British Army," *Barbados Globe and Colonial Advocate*, June 11, 1915, n.p.

112. Lucas, *Empire at War*, 2: 336.

113. De Lisser, *Jamaica and the Great War*, 71.

114. David Killingray, "Race and Rank in the British Army in the Twentieth Century," *Ethnic and Racial Studies* 10, no. 3 (1987): 276–90.

115. Bonar Law to the Governors of Jamaica, Leeward Islands, Barbados, Trinidad, and British Guiana, December 18, 1915, CO 318/336, TNA.

116. *Census of Jamaica and its Dependencies: Taken on the 3rd April, 1911* (Kingston, Jamaica: Government Printing Office, 1912), 7.

117. B. B. Cubitt to Under Secretary of State, Colonial Office, December 14, 1915, CO 318/336, file 57697, TNA.

118. The military attestation forms for the BWIR were destroyed sometime in the 1920s after the Military Paymaster and colonial officials deemed that the final deadline for filing new claims for veteran's compensation had passed.

119. "Recruiting in Colony for BWI Regiment," November 23, 1917, CO 28/292, TNA.

120. "Report on Island's Recruiting," *Daily Gleaner*, August 23, 1916, 14; *Census of Jamaica*, 28.

121. Frank Holmes, *The Bahamas During the Great War* (Nassau: The Tribune, 1924), 28–29; "Our Men for the Front," *West Indian*, September 5, 1915, 3.

122. "Items of News," *Port of Spain Gazette*, September 8, 1915, 4.

123. "Recruiting in Colony for BWI Regiment," November 23, 1917, CO 28/292, TNA; Lucas, *Empire at War*, 364.

124. "Ocho Rios Recruiting Meeting," *Daily Gleaner*, December 15, 1915, 13.

125. Downes, "Boys of the Empire," 128.

126. Lucas, *Empire at War*, 364.

127. C. L. R. James, *The Black Jacobins: Toussaint L'Ouverture and the San Domingo Revolution* (New York: Vintage, 1989 [1963c]), 403.

128. Hill, *Who's Who in Jamaica*, 246; "Report on Island's Recruiting," *Daily Gleaner*, August 23, 1916, 14.

129. Lucas, *Empire at War*, 348.

130. G. B. Haddon-Smith to A. Bonar Law, September 15, 1915, CO 321/282, TNA.

131. Holmes, *Bahamas During the Great War*, 25; Howe, *Race, War and Nationalism*, 59.

132. "Our Recruits," *Daily Gleaner*, March 8, 1917, 16.

NOTES TO CHAPTER 2 [281]

133. "Cycling Salvador at the Front," *Port of Spain Gazette*, September 2, 1915, 9.

134. "Items of News," *Port of Spain Gazette*, September 8, 1915, 4.

135. "Mr. A. Cipriani's Application for Commission in West India Contingent," November 15, 1915, File Folder 29/1916, Box 3–96 (1916), Colonial Secretary's Office Papers, National Archives of Trinidad and Tobago (hereafter NATT).

136. "Items of News," *Port of Spain Gazette*, January 4, 1916, 4; "The Trinidad Breeders Association and Mr. A.A. Cipriani," *Port of Spain Gazette*, January 8, 1916, 3.

137. "Jamaica Memories" Collection, File 7/12/129, JA.

138. "Life in Jamaica in the Early Twentieth Century: A Presentation of Ninety Oral Accounts," Volume: Parish of St. Ann, Respondent: 45STaFc, "Mrs. E. and her Husband," 4, Erna Brodber Oral History Project, Sir Arthur Lewis Institute for Social and Economic Studies Documentation and Data Centre, The University of the West Indies, Mona, Jamaica.

139. "Life in Jamaica in the Early Twentieth Century: A Presentation of Ninety Oral Accounts," Volume: Parish of St. Andrew, Respondent: 41StaMb, "The Fisherman," 2, Erna Brodber Oral History Project, Sir Arthur Lewis Institute for Social and Economic Studies Documentation and Data Centre, The University of the West Indies, Mona, Jamaica.

140. Hill, *Who's Who in Jamaica*, 247.

141. Lucas, *Empire at War*, 418.

142. "Disappointed Candidates for the Front," *Daily Argosy*, September 5, 1915, 7.

143. "Disappointed Candidates for the Front," *Daily Argosy*, September 5, 1915, 7.

144. "Recruiting in Demerara," *Port of Spain Gazette*, September 5, 1915, 11.

145. "Late Happenings in the Rural Districts," *Daily Gleaner*, November 19, 1915, 10.

146. "Late Barbados News," *Port of Spain Gazette*, September 11, 1915, 7.

147. "Boy Scout Concert," *Port of Spain Gazette*, September 12, 1915, 9.

148. Howe, *Race, War and Nationalism*, 66.

149. Hill, *Who's Who in Jamaica*, 247.

150. Howe, *Race, War, and Nationalism*, 64.

151. "Report of the Recruiting Committee," August 11, 1917, CO 28/292, TNA.

152. "Report of the Recruiting Committee," August 11, 1917, CO 28/292, TNA.

153. Hadden-Smith to Walter Long, September 5, 1917, CO 321/295, file 48584, TNA; "Report of Colonial Surgeon Working on the V.D. Ordinance," enclosed in Hadden-Smith to Walter Long, December 9, 1918, CO 321/300, file 1170, TNA.

154. Howe, *Race, War and Nationalism*, 70.

155. Howe, *Race, War and Nationalism*, 70.

156. *Census of the Colony of Trinidad and Tobago, 1911*, 22–23.

157. Moore and Johnson, *Neither Led nor Driven*, 212; *Census of Jamaica*, 10.

158. "Securing Volunteers in St. Ann," *Daily Gleaner*, November 15, 1915, 13.

159. "Jamaica's Loyal Sons Coming Home to Enlist for the War," *Daily Gleaner*, 6.

160. Lucas, *Empire at War*, 348.

161. "Securing Volunteers in St. Ann," *Daily Gleaner*, November 15, 1915, 13.

162. Hill, *Who's Who in Jamaica*, 247.

163. "To Those Who Have Not Enlisted," *Port of Spain Gazette*, September 9, 1915, 4.

[282] NOTES TO CHAPTER 2

164. "Imposter in Khaki Uniform," *Daily Gleaner*, December 16, 1915, 6.

165. "Imposter in Khaki Uniform," *Daily Gleaner*, December 16, 1915, 6.

166. "Cowardly Slackers," *Port of Spain Gazette*, September 4, 1915, 9.

167. "Stoning Recruits," *Port of Spain Gazette*, September 11, 1915, 9.

168. "Soldiers of the King," *Port of Spain Gazette*, September 10, 1915, 11.

169. Life in Jamaica in the Early Twentieth Century: A Presentation of Ninety Oral Accounts," Volume: St. Andrew Parish, Respondent: 39StaFc, ". . . the world let go now," 49, Erna Brodber Oral History Project, Sir Arthur Lewis Institute for Social and Economic Studies Documentation and Data Centre, The University of the West Indies, Mona, Jamaica.

170. "Life in Jamaica in the Early Twentieth Century: A Presentation of Ninety Oral Accounts," Volume: St. Andrew Parish, Respondent: 39StaFc, ". . . the world let go now," 50, Erna Brodber Oral History Project, Sir Arthur Lewis Institute for Social and Economic Studies Documentation and Data Centre, The University of the West Indies, Mona, Jamaica.

171. Winston James, *Holding Aloft the Banner of Ethiopia* (London: Verso, 1998), 54.

172. "The Man Who Is the Island's Backbone," *Jamaica Times*, July 13, 1918, 8.

173. 7/12/43, "Jamaica Memories" collection, JA.

174. Howe, *Race, War and Nationalism*, 223.

175. "Big Recruiting Meeting at Gayle Yesterday," *Daily Gleaner*, October 28, 1915, 13.

176. "Life in Jamaica in the Early Twentieth Century: A Presentation of Ninety Oral Accounts," Volume: St. Andrew Parish, Respondent: 39StaFc, ". . . the world let go now," 49.

177. "Life in Jamaica in the Early Twentieth Century: A Presentation of Ninety Oral Accounts," Volume: St. Andrew Parish, Respondent: 39StaFc, ". . . the world let go now," 49.

178. Hill, *Who's Who in Jamaica*, 247.

179. "News and Topics in Brief," *West Indian*, September 5, 1915, 4.

180. "Recruiting in the City," *Port of Spain Gazette*, August 15, 1915, 3.

181. "Report of the Recruiting Committee," August 11, 1917, CO 28/292, TNA.

182. "Letter to the Editor from A Creole," *Clarion*, November 4, 1915, 520.

183. "Native Troops," *Daily Gleaner*, August 11, 1915, 8.

184. "The Mixed British Army," *Barbados Globe and Colonial Advocate*, February 12, 1915, n.p.

185. "Message from the King," *Federalist and Grenada People*, October 27, 1915, 2.

186. "Mischievous Utterings," *Port of Spain Gazette*, September 12, 1915, 6.

187. "The Man Who Is the Island's Backbone," *Jamaica Times*, July 13, 1918, 8.

188. *Newhaven Chronicle*, November 18, 1915, quoted in Richard Smith, *Jamaican Volunteers in the First World War: Race, Masculinity, and the Development of National Consciousness* (Manchester: Manchester University Press, 2004), 70.

189. Smith, *Jamaican Volunteers*, 70.

190. De Lisser, *Jamaica and the Great War*, 117.

191. "Compulsion in Jamaica," *Daily Gleaner*, March 12, 1917, 8.

192. "The Call for Men," *Daily Gleaner*, March 12, 1917, 8.

NOTES TO CHAPTER 2   [283]

193. "Opinions on Compulsion Bill," *Daily Gleaner*, March 24, 1917, 1.

194. "The Question of Compulsion in this Colony," *Daily Gleaner*, March 19, 1917, 4.

195. William Manning to Walter Long, June 15, 1917, CO 137/723, file 34825, TNA; "Conscription," *Daily Gleaner*, April 3, 1917, 11.

196. "Military Service Law, 1917," in *The Laws of Jamaica Passed in the Year 1917* (Kingston: Government Printing Office, 1918).

197. For population data on the Chinese community in Jamaica, see *Census of Jamaica*, 7, 28.

198. Acting Governor of Jamaica to Walter Long, September 29, 1917, CO 137/722, file 52680, TNA.

199. "The Jamaica Contingent," *Port of Spain Gazette*, June 30, 1915, 11; For additional examples of this rhetoric, see "The Call of the Empire," *Daily Argosy*, June 24, 1915, 4; "For England," *Daily Argosy*, June 29, 1915, 4; "The Song of Our Boys," *West Indian*, September 19, 1915, 4; Rev. J. W. Graham and Tom Redcam, *Round the Blue Light* (Kingston: Jamaica Times Printery, 1918), 5.

200. Cipriani, *Twenty-Five Years After*, 9.

201. West India Committee to Bonar Law, June 29, 1915, CO 318/336, file 30143, TNA.

202. H. J. Read (for Bonar Law) to the Governors of Trinidad and British Guiana, July 6, 1915, CO 318/336, file 30143, TNA; Handwritten note by Gilbert Grindle, July 2, 1915, file 30143, TNA.

203. Wilfred Collet to Secretary of State for the Colonies, July 15, 1915, quoted in Macpherson, *From Colony to Nation*, 57.

204. Wilfred Collet to Secretary of State for the Colonies, August 27, 1915, quoted in Macpherson, *From Colony to Nation*, 57.

205. Captain H. Dow, *Record of Service of Members: The Trinidad Merchants' and Planters' Contingent 1915 to 1918* (Trinidad: Printed by the Government Printer, 1925), ix.

206. Cipriani, *Twenty-Five Years After*, 9.

207. "Letter By A. A. Cipriani," *Mirror*, August 16, 1915, quoted in Brinsley Samaroo and Cherita Girvan, "The Trinidad Workingmen's Association and the Origins of Popular Protest in a Crown Colony," *Social and Economic Studies* 21, no. 2 (1972): 211–12.

208. "Mr. A. A. Cipriani and His 'Boycotting' Charge," *Port of Spain Gazette*, September 3, 1915, 9.

209. "Mr. A. A. Cipriani and His 'Boycotting' Charge," *Port of Spain Gazette*, September 3, 1915, 9.

210. Howe, *Race, War and Nationalism*, 48; James, *Holding Aloft the Banner*, 55.

211. Cipriani, *Twenty-Five Years After*, 9.

212. George Huggins to A. Bonar Law, November 4, 1915, CO 295/503, file 51237, TNA.

213. A. S. Bowen to Captain Warner, December 6, 1915, CO 295/503, file 57711, TNA.

214. Handwritten note by F. G. A. Butler, November 5, 1915, CO 295/503, file 51237, TNA.

[284] NOTES TO CHAPTER 3

215. Handwritten note by R. A. Wiseman, November 6, 1915, CO 295/503, file 51237, TNA.

216. Handwritten note by C. A. Darley, November 6, 1915, CO 295/503, file 51237, TNA; Handwritten note by Gilbert Grindle, November 6, 1915, CO 295/503, file 51237, TNA.

217. "Another Serious Complaint Against the Police," *Port of Spain Gazette*, October 22, 1915, 9.

218. Handwritten note by Gilbert Grindle, November 15, 1915, CO 295/503, file 51237, TNA.

219. F. G. A. Butler to George Huggins, November 16, 1915, CO 295/503, file 51237, TNA.

220. Dow, *Record of Service of Members*, xiii, 34.

221. Michèle Levy, introduction to *The Man Who Ran Away and Other Stories of Trinidad in the 1920s and 1930s*, by Alfred Mendes (Kingston, Jamaica: University of the West Indies Press, 2006).

222. Levy, introduction, xxiv.

223. Alfred H. Mendes, *The Autobiography of Alfred Mendes, 1871–1991* (Kingston, Jamaica: University of the West Indies Press, 2002), 43.

224. Mendes, *Autobiography*, 48.

225. Mendes, *Autobiography*, 60–61.

226. *Beacon*, May 1933, 21, quoted in Levy, introduction, xv.

227. James, *Beyond a Boundary*, 30–31.

228. For the rank of men who joined the Merchants' and Planters' Contingent, see The West Indian Contingent Committee, *Report and Accounts for the Six Months ended 31st December, 1918* (London: The West India Committee Rooms, 1919), n.p.

229. Samaroo and Girvan, "Trinidad Workingmen's Association," 211.

230. "Barbados Citizens Contingent," *Port of Spain Gazette*, November 7, 1915, 7.

231. "Barbados Citizens Contingent," *Port of Spain Gazette*, November 7, 1915, 7; "Barbados Citizens Contingent Fund," *Port of Spain Gazette*, November 19, 1915, 2.

232. *West Indian*, November 25, 1915, 2.

233. Henry W. Lofty, *Report of the Census of Barbados, 1911–1921* (Bridgetown: Advocate, 1921), 14.

234. "Jamaica Slackers," *Daily Gleaner*, October 25, 1915, 13.

235. "Answering Homeland's Call," *Daily Gleaner*, November 6, 1915, 14.

236. "Topics of the Day: The Other Young Men," *Daily Gleaner*, November 27, 1915, 8.

237. "Linstead Recruiting Meeting," *Daily Gleaner*, January 27, 1917, 22.

238. Lucas, *Empire at War*, 377–78.

239. Lucas, *Empire at War*, 377.

240. Leslie Probyn to Walter Long, July 31, 1918, CO 137/726, file 42533, TNA.

Chapter Three: "Humiliations and Disillusion"

Epigraph: Lt. Col. Charles Wood-Hill, *A Few Notes on the History of the British West Indies Regiment*, 6.

NOTES TO CHAPTER 3 [285]

1. On James O. Sands's work as a photographer, see Krista Thompson, *An Eye for the Tropics: Tourism, Photography, and Framing the Caribbean Picturesque* (Durham, NC: Duke University Press, 2007), 95, 317.

2. Tina Campt, *Image Matters: Archive, Photography, and the African Diaspora in Europe* (Durham, NC: Duke University Press, 2012), 46.

3. On the family photograph as a tool to project family lineage and racial, gender, and class respectability, see Campt, *Image Matters*, 46–50. On respectability and the colored middle class in the colonial Bahamas, see Gail Saunders, *Race and Class in the Colonial Bahamas, 1880–1960* (Gainesville: University Press of Florida, 2016), 42–46.

4 Etienne Dupuch, *A Salute to Friend and Foe: My Battles, Sieges and Fortunes* (Nassau, Bahamas: The Tribune, 1982), 31, 33.

5. Dupuch, *Salute to Friend and Foe*, 31–32; Etienne Dupuch, *Tribune Story* (London: Ernest Benn, 1967), 26.

6. Dupuch, *Salute to Friend and Foe*, 31.

7. C. A. Wickham, "Work in the Army," *Barbados Weekly Herald*, July 12, 1919, 4.

8. Ashley Jackson and James E. Kitchen, "The British Empire and the First World War: Paradoxes and New Questions," in *The British Empire and the First World War*, ed. Ashley Jackson (New York: Routledge, 2016)," 6.

9. A. E. Horner, *From the Islands of the Sea: Glimpses of a West Indian Battalion in France* (Nassau, Bahamas: Guardian Office, 1919), 36.

10. Unsigned letter to Roland Green, July 27, 1918, CO 318/347, The National Archives, Kew, England (hereafter TNA); Roland Green to Secretary of State for the Colonies, October 25, 1918, CO 318/347, TNA.

11. Dupuch, *Tribune Story*, 27.

12. For an overview of British Army regulations during World War I, see War Office, *Manual of Military Law* (London: HMSO, 1914); War Office, *The King's Regulations and Orders for the Army 1912. Reprinted with Amendments published in Army Orders up to 1st August, 1914* (London: HMSO, 1914).

13. C. A. Wickham, "First Impressions of the Army," *Barbados Weekly Herald*, June 28, 1919, 5.

14. War Office, *Manual of Military Law*, 370–455.

15. Dupuch, *Salute to Friend and Foe*, 44.

16. Dupuch, *Salute to Friend and Foe*, 31–85.

17. Cedric L. Joseph, "The British West Indies Regiment, 1914–1918," *Journal of Caribbean History* 2 (1971): 94–124; Glenford D. Howe, *Race, War and Nationalism: A Social History of West Indians in the First World War* (Kingston, Jamaica: Ian Randle Publishers, 2002); Richard Smith, *Jamaican Volunteers in the First World War: Race, Masculinity, and the Development of National Consciousness* (Manchester, England: Manchester University Press, 2004); Winston James, *Holding Aloft the Banner of Ethiopia: Caribbean Radicalism in Early Twentieth-Century America* (New York: Verso, 1998), 52–66; Dominiek Dendooven, *The British West Indies Regiment: Race and Colour on the Western Front* (Yorkshire, England: Pen and Sword, 2023); Barry Renfrew, *Britain's Black Regiments: Fighting for Empire and Equality* (Cheltenham, England: History Press, 2020), 141–239.

[286] NOTES TO CHAPTER 3

18. The title for this section is from "The Trinidad Contingent in England," *Port of Spain Gazette*, November 9, 1915, 2. As discussed in chapter 2, some West Indian men were already residing in England when the BWIR was established and subsequently joined the regiment. On the enlistment process for the BWIR in England, see Frank Cundall, *Jamaica's Part in the Great War, 1915–1918* (London: IOJ, by the West India Commission, 1925), 29.

19. Trinidad's first contingent of BWIR volunteers departed on September 18, 1915. There were 443 soldiers in the contingent. See "Departure of Trinidad's Contingent," *Port of Spain Gazette*, October 6, 1915, 9; C. B. Franklin, *Trinidad and Tobago Year Book* (Port-of-Spain: Franklin's Electric Printery, 1919), xxxvii.

20. "The Trinidad Contingent in England," *Port of Spain Gazette*, November 9, 1915, 2.

21. Adriane Lentz-Smith, *Freedom Struggles: African Americans and World War I* (Cambridge, MA: Harvard University Press, 2011), 118.

22. Vere E. Johns, "Tommy Atkins and the War," *New York Age*, July 8, 1933, 5.

23. "The Trinidad Contingent in England," *Port of Spain Gazette*, November 9, 1915, 2.

24. A. A. Cipriani, *Twenty-Five Years After: The British West Indies Regiment in The Great War, 1914–1918* (Port of Spain: Trinidad Publishing, 1940), 16.

25. Dupuch, *Salute to Friend and Foe*, 36.

26. Dupuch, *Salute to Friend and Foe*, 35.

27. For accounts of illness on the troopships, see Cipriani, *Twenty-Five Years After*, 16; Wood-Hill, *Few Notes*, 2; John Hutson to W. L. C. Phillips (Acting Colonial Secretary), January 12, 1917, CO 28/291/4, TNA.

28. Dupuch, *Salute to Friend and Foe*, 35.

29. Dupuch, *Salute to Friend and Foe*, 35.

30. Cipriani, *Twenty-Five Years After*, 16; C. B. Franklin, *Trinidad and Tobago Year Book* (Port of Spain: Franklin's Electric Printery, 1919), viii.

31. Dupuch, *Salute to Friend and Foe*, 35.

32. John Hutson to W. L. C. Phillips (Acting Colonial Secretary), January 12, 1917, CO 28/291/4, TNA.

33. Wood-Hill, *Few Notes*, 2.

34. Wood-Hill, *Few Notes*, 9; James, *Holding Aloft the Banner*, 59.

35. Ross Wilson, "The Burial of the Dead: The British Army on the Western Front, 1914–18," *War & Society* 31, no. 1 (2012): 22–41. On mortuary practices in the British Caribbean, see Yanique Hume, "Death and the Construction of Social Space: Land, Kinship, and Identity in the Jamaican Mortuary Cycle," in *Passages and Afterworlds: Anthropological Perspectives on Death in the Caribbean*, ed. Maarit Forde and Yanique Hume (Durham, NC: Duke University Press, 2018), 109–38; Vincent Brown, *The Reaper's Garden: Death and Power in the World of Atlantic Slavery* (Cambridge, MA: Harvard University Press, 2008).

36. Johns, "Tommy Atkins and the War," 5.

37. Cipriani, *Twenty-Five Years After*, 16.

38. Johns, "Tommy Atkins and the War," 5.

39. Johns, "Tommy Atkins and the War," 5.

40. For a detailed account of BWIR soldiers' tragic voyage on the *Verdala* in March 1916, see Major G. V. Hart to the Governor of Bermuda, March 29, 1916,

NOTES TO CHAPTER 3 [287]

enclosed in G. M. Bullock to War Office, March 30, 1916, CO 318/339, TNA. For the number of soldiers in Jamaica's Third Contingent, see Cundall, *Jamaica's Part in the Great War*, 26.

41. *Minutes of the Legislative Council of Jamaica for the Year 1917* (Kingston, Jamaica: Government Printing Office, 1918), Appendix No. XXI. War Office staff members claimed that the Admiralty made the decision to divert the *Verdala* to Halifax without consulting them. Army Council to the Secretary of the Admiralty, April 21, 1916, CO 318/339, TNA.

42. Major G. V. Hart to the Governor of Bermuda, March 29, 1916, enclosed in G. M. Bullock to War Office, March 30, 1916, CO 318/339, TNA.

43. Stephen Bourne, *Black Poppies: Britain's Black Community and the Great War* (Stroud, Gloucestershire: The History Press, 2014), 66.

44. Major G. V. Hart to the Governor of Bermuda, March 29, 1916, enclosed in G. M. Bullock to War Office, March 30, 1916, CO 318/339, TNA. On the conditions on the *Verdala*, see also Fred Cole, file 7/12/11, "Jamaica Memories Collection," Jamaica Archives and Records Department, Archives Unit (hereafter JA), Spanish Town; "Voyage of the Third Contingent," *Daily Gleaner*, May 17, 1916, 4.

45. G. M. Bullock to War Office, March 30, 1916, CO 318/339, TNA.

46. "Voyage of the Third Contingent," *Daily Gleaner*, May 17, 1916, 4.

47. "The Warrior Sons of Jamaica—Sufferer in Blizzard," *Daily Gleaner*, May 6, 1916, 13.

48. "Voyage of the Third Contingent," *Daily Gleaner*, May 17, 1916, 4.

49. Howe, *Race, War, and Nationalism*, 80.

50. "Voyage of the Third Contingent," *Daily Gleaner*, May 17, 1916, 4.

51. G. M. Bullock to War Office, March 30, 1916, CO 318/339, TNA.

52. "Voyage of the Third Contingent," *Daily Gleaner*, May 17, 1916, 4.

53. "The Warrior Sons of Jamaica—Sufferer in Blizzard," *Daily Gleaner*, May 6, 1916, 13.

54. "Voyage of the Third Contingent," *Daily Gleaner*, May 17, 1916, 4.

55. "The Warrior Sons of Jamaica—Sufferer in Blizzard," *Daily Gleaner*, May 6, 1916, 13.

56. Herbert G. de Lisser, *Jamaica and the Great War* (Kingston, Jamaica: Gleaner, 1917), 111.

57. De Lisser, *Jamaica and the Great War*, 111.

58. "Sufferers in Third Contingent," *Daily Gleaner*, May 4, 1916, 10.

59. At least 391 soldiers from Jamaica's Third Contingent were discharged from the BWIR as medically unfit. Stephen A. Hill, *Who's Who in Jamaica, 1919–1920* (Kingston: Gleaner, 1920), 240.

60. Fred Cole, file 7/12/11, "Jamaica Memories Collection," JA; "Nominal Roll of N.C.O.'s and Men, British West Indies Regiment Returned to Colonies in Hospital Ship 'Dover Castle' 26th August, 1916," CO 318/340, TNA.

61. Victor Grueber to Colonial Secretary (Jamaica), May 10, 1926, 1B/5/77/705-1926, JA.

62. Typewritten File Note by Arthur Herbert Pinnock, May 25, 1926, 1B/5/77/705-1926, JA.

63. "The Trinidad Contingent in England," *Port of Spain Gazette*, November 9, 1915, 2.

64. David Killingray, "'A Good West Indian, a Good African, and, in Short, a Good Britisher': Black and British in a Colour-Conscious Empire, 1760–1950," *The Journal of Imperial and Commonwealth History* 36, no. 3 (2008): 363–81, quotation on page 372. See also, Brian L. Moore and Michele A. Johnson, *Neither Led Nor Driven: Contesting British Cultural Imperialism in Jamaica, 1865–1920* (Kingston, Jamaica: University of the West Indies Press, 2004), ch. 9; Anne Spry Rush, *Bonds of Empire: West Indians and Britishness from Victoria to Decolonization* (New York: Oxford University Press, 2011).

65. "The West Indian Contingent," *West India Committee Circular*, October 5, 1915, 431.

66. On racist ideology in Britain, see Peter Fryer, *Aspects of British Black History* (London: Index Books, 1993), 29–33.

67. As historian Kennetta Hammond Perry has argued, since the nineteenth century "people of African descent [have] employed British subjecthood and adapted discourses of Britishness by leveraging claims to imperial belonging and citizenship in a challenge to metropolitan elites' ideas about their place within the Empire and colonial society." Kennetta Hammond Perry, *London is the Place for Me: Black Britons, Citizenship, and the Politics of Race* (New York: Oxford University Press, 2015), 27.

68. Kevin Gordon, *Seaford and Eastbourne in the Great War* (Barnsley, England: Pen & Sword Military, 2014), 96.

69. Winston James, "The Black Experience in Twentieth-Century Britain," in *Black Experience and the Empire*, ed. Phillip D. Morgan and Sean Hawkins (New York: Oxford University Press, 2006), 349.

70. Caroline Bressey, "Looking for Work: The Black Presence in Britain, 1860–1920," *Immigrants and Minorities* 28, nos. 2–3 (2010): 164–82; Jeffrey Green, *Black Edwardians: Black People in Britain, 1901–1914* (New York: Frank Cass Publishing, 1998); Marc Matera, *Black London: The Imperial Metropolis and Decolonization in the Twentieth Century* (Oakland: University of California Press, 2015), 22–23.

71. Robert A. Hill, "'Comradeship of the More Advanced Races': Marcus Garvey and the Brotherhood Movement in Britain, 1913–14," *Small Axe* 17, no. 1 (2013): 50–70; W. F. Elkins, "Hercules and the Society of Peoples of African Origin," *Caribbean Studies* 11, no. 4 (1972): 47–59; James, "Black Experience," 349–54; Ron Ramdin, *The Making of the Black Working Class in Britain* (Brookfield, VT: Gower, 1987), 47–57.

72. Gordon, *Seaford and Eastbourne in the Great War*, 24.

73. Cundall, *Jamaica's Part in the Great War*, 28.

74. "News from Our Soldier Boys," *Nassau Guardian*, January 1, 1916, 2. On the initial reception of the BWIR in England, see also Anna Maguire, *Contact Zones of the First World War: Cultural Encounters Across the British Empire* (Cambridge: Cambridge University Press, 2021), 57–61.

75. "News from Our Soldier Boys," *Nassau Guardian*, January 1, 1916, 2.

76. "Letters from our Soldiers," *Jamaica Times*, March 25, 1916, 11.

77. "Gunner Billouin Writes from Seaford," *Port of Spain Gazette*, December 30, 1915, 9.

78. Horner, *From the Islands of the Sea*, 13.

79. "The Trinidad Contingent in England," *Port of Spain Gazette*, November 9, 1915, 2.

NOTES TO CHAPTER 3 [289]

80. "And Still They Come," *Port of Spain Gazette*, November 11, 1915, 8.

81. "Letters From Our Soldiers," *Jamaica Times*, January 1, 1916, 17.

82. "The West Indian Contingent," *West India Committee Circular*, October 19, 1915, 452.

83. "Seaford Where the West Indian Contingent Camp is Situated," *Daily Gleaner*, October 27, 1915, 13.

84. "The West Indian Contingent," *West India Committee Circular*, October 19, 1915, 452.

85. "The West Indian Contingent," *West India Committee Circular*, October 19, 1915, 452.

86. British Caribbean newspapers selectively republished letters from soldiers and only printed those that would aid in local recruitment efforts. For example, the editors of the Grenada *West Indian* acknowledged that they "did not want to inflame public opinion during the war," so they "suppressed many of the letters of complaint and protest" that they received from BWIR soldiers. Also, British military censors reviewed soldiers' letters and often intercepted those that contained information about troop movement or accounts that could undermine morale. "Our Boys, God Bless Them," *West Indian* (Mail Edition), February 28, 1919, 1. See also, Howe, *Race, War, and Nationalism*, 46; Maguire, *Contact Zones*, 60.

87. "The First Seven Hundred," *Jamaica Times*, February 8, 1919, 5.

88. "The Fortnight at Seaford Camp," *West India Committee Circular*, November 2, 1915, 474–75.

89. For descriptions of the daily routine for BWIR soldiers at North Camp, see "The Fortnight at Seaford Camp," *West India Committee Circular*, November 2, 1915, 474–75; "Our Boys at the Front," *Port of Spain Gazette*, December 31, 1915, 3; "Letters from Our Soldiers," *Jamaica Times*, March 25, 1916, 11; Cundall, *Jamaica's Part in the Great War*, 28.

90. "From Seaford Camp, and the Firing Lines," *Daily Gleaner*, January 29, 1916, 11.

91. "Gunner Billouin Writes from Seaford," *Port of Spain Gazette*, December 30, 1915, 9.

92. "Letter from a Trinidadian at Seaford," *Port of Spain Gazette*, January 11, 1916, 10; Howe, *Race, War, and Nationalism*, 92–93.

93. Howe, *Race, War, and Nationalism*, 92–94.

94. "From Seaford Camp, and the Firing Lines," *Daily Gleaner*, January 29, 1916, 11.

95. "Our Boys at the Front," *Port of Spain Gazette*, December 31, 1915, 3.

96. "Letters from Members of the Trinidad Contingent," *Port of Spain Gazette*, November 6, 1915, 3.

97. Gordon, *Seaford and Eastbourne in the Great War*, 130.

98. Gordon, *Seaford and Eastbourne in the Great War*, 130.

99. Cipriani, *Twenty-Five Years After*, 10. See also, Glenford Howe, "Military-Civilian Intercourse, Prostitution and Venereal Disease among Black West Indian Soldiers during World War I," *Journal of Caribbean History* 31, no. 1–2 (1997): 89–90.

100. "Letters from Members of the Trinidad Contingent," *Port of Spain Gazette*, November 6, 1915, 3s

101. "And Still They Come," *Port of Spain Gazette*, November 11, 1915, 8; "Letters from Our Soldiers," *Jamaica Times*, January 1, 1916, 17; "Our Boys at Seaford," *Port of Spain Gazette*, January 7, 1916, 3. BWIR soldiers also reported that some white British soldiers called them "darkies." See, for example, "A Darkie and a Tommy," *Port of Spain Gazette*, February 16, 1919, 11.

102. On English ideas about race, empire, and colonial difference, see Catherine Hall, *Civilising Subjects: Metropole and Colony in the English Imagination 1830–1867* (Chicago: University of Chicago Press, 2002).

103. Wood-Hill, *Few Notes*, 2.

104. "From Seaford Camp, and the Firing Lines," *Daily Gleaner*, January 29, 1916, 11.

105. "Our Boys at Seaford Camp," *Port of Spain Gazette*, December 4, 1915, 3.

106. "Letters from our Soldiers," *Jamaica Times*, January 1, 1916, 17.

107. "British West Indies Regiment," *West India Committee Circular*, February 24, 1916, 71.

108. "Our Boys," *Dominica Chronicle*, February 9, 1916, 8.

109. "From Seaford Camp, and the Firing Lines," *Daily Gleaner*, January 29, 1916, 11.

110. Cundall, *Jamaica's Part in the Great War*, 28; Wood-Hill, *Few Notes*, 2; Gordon, *Seaford and Eastbourne in the Great War*, 132.

111. According to the online database of the Commonwealth War Graves Commission, nineteen BWIR soldiers are buried at Seaford Cemetery in England. In addition, thirty BWIR soldiers are buried at Plymouth (Efford) Cemetery in England. On the deaths of BWIR soldiers at North Camp in Seaford, see "British West Indies Regiment: Some Notes from Seaford," *West India Committee Circular*, January 27, 1916, 30; "The West Indian Contingent," *West Indian Committee Circular*, February 10, 1916, 48; "British West Indies Regiment," *West Indian Committee Circular*, February 24, 1916, 70.

112. The poems were written in the autograph book of Miss E. Burton, a nurse at Surrey Convalescent Home (also known as Seaford War Hospital) in Seaford, England. There are 23 poems written by BWIR soldiers in the autograph book. Autograph Book by Miss E. Burton, IWM Misc. 200/292, Imperial War Museum, London, England.

113. Hilary R. Buxton, "'Crutches as Weapons': Reading Blackness and the Disabled Soldier Body in the First World War," in *Men and Masculinities in Modern Britain: A History for the Present*, ed. Matt Houlbrook, Katie Jones, and Ben Mechen (Manchester: Manchester University Press, 2024), 88–110; Howe, *Race, War, and Nationalism*, 167–68; Peter Fryer, *Staying Power: The History of Black People in Britain* (London: Pluto Press, 1984), 297.

114. Private Lionel W. French, untitled handwritten poem, October 27, 1915, IWM Misc. 200/2928, Imperial War Museum.

115. Private Jacob Stanislaus Cunningham, untitled handwritten poem, 1915, in Autograph Book by Miss E. Burton, IWM Misc. 200/2928, Imperial War Museum.

116. Cunningham, untitled handwritten poem, in Autograph Book by Miss E. Burton, IWM Misc. 200/2928, Imperial War Museum.

117. Wood-Hill, *Few Notes*, 2.

NOTES TO CHAPTER 3 [291]

118. On the relocation of the BWIR from England to Egypt, see War Office to Colonial Office, February 10, 1916, CO 318/339, TNA; War Office to Colonial Office, February 22, 1916, CO 318/339, TNA; War Office to Colonial Office, June 10, 1916, CO 318/339, TNA; Cundall, *Jamaica's Part in the Great War*, 30.

119. Ralph A. Campbell to General Officer, Commanding-in-Chief, Southern Command, Salisbury, June 20, 1916, enclosed in War Office to Colonial Office, June 10, 1916, CO 318/339, TNA. On the experiences of disabled BWIR soldiers in England during World War I, see Buxton, "Crutches as Weapons."

120. Dupuch initially served in the BWIR's Fifth Battalion in Egypt before transferring to the Fourth Battalion in France in 1917.

121. Dupuch, *Salute to Friend and Foe*, 54.

122. Dupuch, *Salute to Friend and Foe*, 55.

123. Brett A. Berliner, *Ambivalent Desire: The Exotic Black Other in Jazz-age France*. (Amherst: University of Massachusetts Press, 2002), 9. For the estimated population of black residents in France before 1914, see Mark Hewitson, conclusion to *What Is a Nation?: Europe 1789–1914*, ed. Timothy Baycroft and Mark Hewitson (New York: Oxford University Press, 2006), 326.

124. John Horne, "Immigrant Workers in France during World War I," *French Historical Studies* 14, no. 1 (1985): 59.

125. On African American soldiers in France, see Adriane Lentz-Smith, *Freedom Struggles*, ch.4; Chad Williams, *Torchbearers of Democracy: African American Soldiers in the World War I Era* (Chapel Hill: University of North Carolina Press, 2010), ch.3. On the Fijian Labour Corps in France, see John Starling and Ivor Lee, *No Labour, No Battle: Military Labour during the First World War* (Stroud: Spellmount, 2009), 264–66.

126. Horner, *From the Islands of the Sea*, 18. On Alfred Horner's background, see Richard Smith, "Loss and Longing: Emotional Responses to West Indian Soldiers during the First World War," *Roundtable: The Commonwealth Journal of International Affairs* 103, no.2, (2014): 249.

127. Mary Louise Pratt, *Imperial Eyes: Travel Writing and Transculturation* (New York: Routledge, 1992), 7.

128. Cundall, *Jamaica's Part in the Great War*, 58–70. See also the regimental war diaries for the BWIR in France, TNA, WO 95/338/1; WO 95/338/2; WO 95/409/3; WO 95/409/4; and WO 95/495/3.

129. Until November 1916, all volunteers for the BWIR had to pass a literacy test demonstrating their ability to read and write in English in order to enlist in the regiment.

130. Paul J. Bailey, "'An army of workers': Chinese Indentured Labour in First World War France," in *Race, Empire, and First World War Writing*, 35–52; Xu Guoqi, *Strangers on the Western Front: Chinese Workers in the Great War* (Cambridge: Harvard University Press, 2011); Tyler Stovall, "Colour-Blind France? Colonial Workers during the First World War," *Race & Class* 35, no. 2 (1993): 35–55.

131. Lieutenant H. R. Wakefield, "Chinese Labour in France," WO 106/33, TNA.

132. Horner, *From the Islands*, 51.

133. Dupuch, *Salute to Friend and Foe*, 66.

134. Dupuch, *Salute to Friend and Foe*, 66.

[292] NOTES TO CHAPTER 3

135. The scholarship on the relationship between World War I and the emergence of anti-imperialism in the colonized world is vast. For examples of studies that highlight the role of World War I veterans from Africa and the African Diaspora, see Howe, *Race, War, and Nationalism*; James K. Matthews, "World War I and the Rise of African Nationalism: Nigerian Veterans as Catalysts of Change," *The Journal of Modern African Studies* 20, no. 3 (1982): 493–502; Smith, *Jamaican Volunteers*; Chad Williams, "A Mobilized Diaspora: The First World War and Black Soldiers as New Negroes," in *Escape from New York: The New Negro Renaissance Beyond Harlem*, ed. Davarian L. Baldwin and Minkah Makalani (Minneapolis: University of Minnesota Press, 2013), 247–69.

136. Dupuch, *Salute to Friend and Foe*, 55.

137. On "stranger intimacy," see Nayan Shah, *Stranger Intimacy: Contesting Race, Sexuality and the Law in the North American West* (Berkeley: University of California Press, 2011).

138. Horner, *From the Islands*, 55.

139. Horner, *From the Islands*, 56.

140. For examples of this rhetoric, see "Vive La France!," *West Indian* (Mail Edition), July 4, 1919, 1; "Sergeant Willie Jeffers of Montserrat in Transit for His Home," *Workman*, July 26, 1919, 8; "The Returned Soldiers Friendly Column," *Jamaica Times*, August 16, 1919, 14.

141. "Sergeant Willie Jeffers of Montserrat in Transit for His Home," *Workman*, July 26, 1919, 8.

142. "The Returned Soldiers Friendly Column," *Jamaica Times*, August 16, 1919, 14.

143. On African Americans' depictions of race relations in wartime France, see Lentz-Smith, *Freedom Struggles*, 99, 121, 129; Williams, *Torchbearers of Democracy*, ch.4.

144. Horner, *From the Islands*, 54.

145. Horner, *From the Islands*, 53.

146. Horner, *From the Islands*, 53.

147. Horner, *From the Islands*, 50.

148. Horner, *From the Islands*, 51.

149. Smith, "Loss and Longing," 250.

150. See, for example, Lucy Bland, "White Women and Men of Colour: Miscegenation Fears in Britain after the Great War," *Gender & History* 17, no. 1 (2005): 29–61; Tyler Stovall, "Love, Labor, and Race: Colonial Men and White Women in France during the Great War," in *French Civilization and its Discontents: Nationalism, Colonialism, Race*, ed. Tyler Stovall and Georges Van den Abbeele (Lanham, MD: Lexington Books, 2003), 297–323.

151. Richard S. Fogarty, "Race and Sex, Fear and Loathing in France during the Great War," *Historical Reflections/Réflexions Historiques* 34, no. 1 (2008): 52.

152. Richard S. Fogarty, *Race and War in France: Colonial Subjects in the French Army, 1914–1918* (Baltimore, MD: Johns Hopkins University Press, 2012), ch. 6; Tyler Stovall, "The Color Line behind the Lines: Racial Violence in France during the Great War," *American Historical Review* 103, no.3 (1998): 761–62.

153. Margaret Darrow, *French Women and the First World War: War Stories of the Home Front* (New York: Berg, 2000), 53–97.

NOTES TO CHAPTER 4 [293]

154. Marie de La Hire, *La femme française: son activité pendant la guerre* (Paris: Librarie Jules Tallandier, 1917), quoted in Darrow, *French Women*, 58.

155. Stovall, "Love, Labor, and Race," 302.

156. Darrow, *French Women*, ch. 3.

157. Dupuch, *Salute to Friend and Foe*, 33–34.

158. Howe, "Military-Civilian Intercourse," 92.

159. *The Clarion*, June 1, 1916, 599, cited in Howe, "Military-Civilian Intercourse," 91.

160. Dupuch, *Salute to Friend and Foe*, 69.

161. Dupuch, *Salute to Friend and Foe*, 69.

162. Mark Whalan, "'The Only Real White Democracy' and the Language of Liberation: The Great War, France, and African American Culture in the 1920s," in *Paris, Capital of the Black Atlantic: Literature, Modernity, and Diaspora*, ed. Jeremy Braddock and Jonathan P. Eburne (Baltimore, MD: Johns Hopkins University Press, 2013), 52–77.

163. Stovall, "Love, Labor, and Race," 297.

164. Fogarty, *Race and War in France*, 61–62.

165. Fogarty, *Race and War in France*, 65; Joe Lunn, "'Les Races Guerrieres': Racial Preconceptions in the French Military about West African Soldiers during the First World War." *Journal of Contemporary History* 34, no. 4 (1999): 517–36.

166. Kimloan Hill, "Sacrifices, Sex, Race: Vietnamese Experiences in the First World War," in *Race, Empire, and First World War Writing*, ed. Santanu Das (New York: Cambridge University Press), 61.

167. Lucie Cousturier, *Des Inconnus chez moi* (Paris: Editions de la Sirene, 1920), quoted in Stovall, "Love, Labor, and Race," 306.

Chapter Four: An "Insubordinate Spirit Prevailed"

1. Unsigned Letter to Mr. Prince Alfred, July 18, 1918, Colonial Secretary's Office Papers (hereafter CSO Papers), File Folder 4/1919, Box 1–193 (1919), National Archive of Trinidad and Tobago (hereafter NATT), Port of Spain.

2. Unsigned Letter to Mr. Prince Alfred, July 18, 1918, CSO Papers, File Folder 4/1919, Box 1–193 (1919), NATT.

3. Lt. Col. P.J. Fearen to Headquarters, XXI Corps, July 22, 1918, CSO Papers, File Folder 4/1919, Box 1–193 (1919), NATT.

4. Lt. Col. P.J. Fearen to Headquarters, XXI Corps, July 22, 1918, CSO Papers, File Folder 4/1919, Box 1–193 (1919), NATT; Commander-in-Chief of the Egyptian Expeditionary Force to Governor of Trinidad and Tobago, November 5, 1918, CSO Papers, File Folder 4/1919, Box 1–193 (1919), NATT.

5. Lt. Col. C. Wood-Hill to Headquarters, Anzac Mounted Division, September 14, 1918, CSO Papers, File Folder 4/1919, Box 1–193 (1919), NATT.

6. Lt. Col. C. Wood-Hill to Headquarters, Anzac Mounted Division, September 14, 1918, CSO Papers, File Folder 4/1919, Box 1–193 (1919), NATT; Commander-in-Chief of the Egyptian Expeditionary Force to Governor of Trinidad and Tobago, November 5, 1918, CSO Papers, File Folder 4/1919, Box 1–193 (1919), NATT; J. R. Chancellor to the Commander-in-Chief of the Egyptian Expeditionary Force, January 1919, CSO Papers, File Folder 4/1919, Box 1–193 (1919), NATT.

[294]   NOTES TO CHAPTER 4

7. Officials in Trinidad finally identified Private Roberts as the anonymous letter writer in late March 1919, eight months after his letter was confiscated and four months after the Armistice. The surviving records do not explicitly state Roberts' race. However, nearly all privates in the BWIR were black or colored, while the regiment's officers were white. Governor J.R. Chancellor to the Commander-in-Chief of the Egyptian Expeditionary Force, March 22, 1919, CSO Papers, File Folder 4/1919, Box 1–193 (1919), NATT.

8. The forty-two signatories included sixteen soldiers from Jamaica, five from Barbados, five from Grenada, four from British Guiana, three from the Bahamas, three from British Honduras, two from Trinidad, two from St. Vincent, one from Montserrat, and one from St. Lucia. The petition was not dated, but several references in the text suggest that it was written during the second half of 1918. See Petition from Charles Callender, W. E. Julien, A. Johnson, et. al to Governor Charles O'Brien (Barbados), n.d., CO 318/348, file 16801, TNA. In an account published shortly after the war, Sergeant P. E. Vasquez recalled that a group of sergeants in the First and Second Battalions of the BWIR met while stationed in the Middle East to "appeal for the long due raise of pay," likely a reference to Army Order No. 1. See P. E. Vasquez, "The B. W.I. on the Dead Sea," *Clarion*, December 18, 1919, 672–3.

9. The petition was not dated, but several references in the text suggest that it was written during the second half of 1918. Petition from Charles Callender, W.E. Julien, A. Johnson, et. al to Governor Charles O'Brien (Barbados), n.d., CO 318/348, file 16801, The National Archives (hereafter TNA), Kew, England.

10. Petition from Charles Callender, W.E. Julien, A. Johnson, et. al to Governor Charles O'Brien (Barbados), n.d., CO 318/348, file 16801, TNA.

11. Petition from Charles Callender, W.E. Julien, A. Johnson, et. al to Governor Charles O'Brien (Barbados), n.d., CO 318/348, file 16801, TNA.

12. By 1918, petitioning was a well-established aspect of black and colored West Indians' protest politics. Beginning in the late eighteenth century, free people of color, and less frequently enslaved men and women, regularly petitioned the Crown and local legislative bodies to protest mistreatment and discrimination. After emancipation in 1834 and "full freedom" in 1838, black and colored West Indians used petitions as a vehicle to solicit support from Queen Victoria and to register demands for improved material, social, and political standing with local colonial officials. Significantly, I have not found any examples of BWIR soldiers petitioning King George V, which perhaps reflects a more nuanced understanding of the division of authority and responsibility in the imperial bureaucracy.

13. Petition from Charles Callender, W.E. Julien, A. Johnson, et. al to Governor Charles O'Brien (Barbados), n.d., CO 318/348, file 16801, TNA.

14. Until November 1916, all volunteers for the BWIR had to pass a literacy test demonstrating their ability to read and write in English to enlist in the regiment. While scholars have documented that British Caribbean immigrants in the United States and Central America had high literacy rates, they have not considered how nearly universal literacy in the BWIR shaped soldiers' protest strategies. On literacy rates among British West Indian immigrants, see Lara Putnam, *Radical Moves: Caribbean Migrants and the Politics of Race in the Jazz Age* (Chapel Hill: University of North Carolina Press, 2013), 128–29; Winston James, "Explaining Afro-Caribbean

NOTES TO CHAPTER 4 [295]

Social Mobility in the United States: Beyond the Sowell Thesis," *Comparative Studies in Society and History* 44, no. 2 (2002): 232–34.

15. A. E. Horner, *From the Islands of the Sea: Glimpses of a West Indian Battalion in France* (Nassau, Bahamas: Guardian, 1919), 50.

16. See, for example, O. Nigel Bolland, *On the March: Labour Rebellions in the British Caribbean, 1934–39* (Kingston, Jamaica: Ian Randle Publishers, 1995), 27–34; Glenford D. Howe, *Race, War and Nationalism: A Social History of West Indians in the First World War* (Kingston, Jamaica: Ian Randle Publishers, 2002), chapter Ten; Winston James, *Holding Aloft the Banner of Ethiopia: Caribbean Radicalism in Early Twentieth-Century America* (New York: Verso, 1998); Tony Martin, "Revolutionary Upheaval in Trinidad, 1919: Views from British and American Sources," *Journal of Negro History* 58, no. 3 (1973): 313–26; Richard Smith, *Jamaican Volunteers in the First World War: Race, Masculinity, and the Development of National Consciousness* (Manchester: Manchester University Press, 2004), chapter Six.

17. Ray Costello, *Black Tommies: British Soldiers of African Descent in the First World War* (Liverpool: Liverpool University Press, 2015), 160.

18. W. F. Elkins, "A Source of Black Nationalism in the Caribbean: The Revolt of the British West Indies Regiment at Taranto, Italy." *Science and Society* 34, no. 1 (1970): 103.

19. *Hansard* HC Deb., 20 November 1917, vol. 99 cc 991–2; *Hansard* HC Deb., 26 November 1917, vol. 99 cc 1631–5; War Office, "Army Order 1, Royal Warrant—Increase in Pay for Soldiers," *Army Orders, January, 1918* (London: His Majesty's Stationary Office, 1918), in CO 318/347, The National Archives (hereafter TNA), Kew, England.

20. The provisions of Army Order were applied retroactively to September 29, 1917. War Office, "Army Order 1, Royal Warrant—Increase in Pay for Soldiers," *Army Orders, January, 1918* (London: His Majesty's Stationary Office, 1918), 3–6, in CO 318/347, TNA.

21. The original rate of pay for imperial troops was established by Royal Warrant on December 1, 1914. Under Army Order 1 of 1918, the minimum daily wage for privates rose by 6d. while the basic pay for other ranks increased by 3d. War Office, "Army Order 1, Royal Warrant—Increase in Pay for Soldiers," *Army Orders, January, 1918* (London: His Majesty's Stationary Office, 1918), 4–5 in CO 318/347, TNA.

22. War Office, "Army Order 1, Royal Warrant—Increase in Pay for Soldiers," *Army Orders, January, 1918* (London: His Majesty's Stationary Office, 1918), 4, in CO 318/347, TNA.

23. The qualifying period for proficiency pay was reduced from two years to six months. See War Office, "Army Order 1, Royal Warrant—Increase in Pay for Soldiers," *Army Orders, January, 1918,* 3. For the new regulations concerning hospitalized soldiers' pay, see page, 6.

24. War Office, "Army Order 1, Royal Warrant—Increase in Pay for Soldiers," *Army Orders, January, 1918,* 3–4.

25. HC Debates, 26 November 1917, vol. 99, cc1631–3.

26. For enlistment figures for the Dominions, see War Office, *Statistics of the Military Effort of the British Empire During the Great War, 1914–1920,* (London: His Majesty's Stationary Office, 1922), 756, 773. While soldiers from the Dominions

were excluded from Army Order No. 1, soldiers in the all-white South African Overseas Expeditionary Force were awarded the benefits of the order through a special provision.

27. David Killingray and James Matthews, "Beasts of Burden: British West African Carriers in the First World War," *Canadian Journal of African Studies / Revue Canadienne des Études Africaines* 13, no. 1/2 (1979): 10; War Office, *Statistics of the Military*, 754, 772, 777.

28. According to historian Michael Francis Snape, the Non-Combatant Corps "was never very large and at no point mustered more than 3,000 conscientious observers during the First World War." Michael Francis Snape, *God and the British Soldier: Religion and the British Army in the First and Second World Wars* (New York: Routledge, 2005), 193.

29. For the total number of British, Dominion, Indian, and Colonial Troops mobilized for the First World War, see War Office, *Statistics of the Military*, 756.

30. War Office, "Army Order 1, Royal Warrant—Increase in Pay for Soldiers," *Army Orders, January, 1918*, 3–7.

31. General Edmund Allenby first wrote to the War Office on February 6, 1918, to inquire about Army Order No.1. The letter is referenced in G.F. Watterson, War Office to General Edmund Allenby, March 27, 1918, CSO Papers, File Folder 2/1919, Box 1–193 (1919), NATT.

32. Under Allenby's command, British forces captured Beersheba on October 31, 1917, Gaza on November 7, 1917, and Jerusalem on December 10, 1917. For an overview of these campaigns from official dispatches, see *A Brief Record of the Advance of the Egyptian Expeditionary Force Under the Command of General Sir Edmund H. H. Allenby, July 1917 to October 1918*, Second Edition (London: His Majesty's Stationary Office, 1919), 1–9; for a scholarly treatment of Allenby's role in these key victories, see Matthew Hughes, *Allenby and British Strategy in the Middle East, 1917–1919* (London: Frank Cass, 1999).

33. Matthew Hughes, "Allenby, Edmund Henry Hynman, first Viscount Allenby of Megiddo (1861–1936)," in *Oxford Dictionary of National Biography*, Oxford University Press, 2004; online ed., May 2008, http://www.oxforddnb.com/view/article /30392; David R. Woodward, *Hell in the Holy Land: World War I in the Middle East* (Lexington: University of Kentucky Press, 2006), 82.

34. Woodward, *Hell in the Holy Land*, 82–83.

35. Colonel Reginald Edmund Maghlin Russell to Wavell, August 6, 1937, Liddell Hart Centre for Military Archives, Allenby MSS 6/8/74, quoted in Woodward, *Hell in the Holy Land*, 85.

36. G.F. Watterson, War Office to General Edmund Allenby, March 27, 1918, CSO Papers, File Folder 2/1919, Box 1–193 (1919), NATT.

37. The BWIR established a depot at Withnoe Camp near Plymouth, England in January 1916. For mentions of the location of the depot, see "The West Indian Contingent," *West India Committee Circular*, February 10, 1916, 48; "British West Indies Regiment," *West India Committee Circular*, March 9, 1916, 93; Frank Cundall, *Jamaica's Part in the Great War, 1914–1918* (London: Pub. for the Institute of Jamaica by the West India Committee, 1925), 28. For Allenby's letter, see General Edmund Allenby to War Office, May 9, 1918, CSO Papers, File Folder 2/1919, Box 1–193 (1919), NATT.

NOTES TO CHAPTER 4 [297]

38. For examples of this rhetorical strategy, see J. Challenor Lynch to T. E. Fell, Colonial Secretary (Barbados), October 9, 1918, CO 28/294, file 56561, TNA; Colonel C. Wood-Hill to Sir John Chancellor, Governor of Trinidad and Tobago, November 26, 1918, CSO Papers, File Folder 2/1919, Box 1–193 (1919), NATT; West Indian Contingent Committee to Walter Long, December 30, 1918, CO 318/347, file 63228, TNA; West Indian Contingent Committee to Alfred Milner, January 15, 1919, CO 318/347, file 3414, TNA.

39. On the development of the ideology of respectability in the British Caribbean during the nineteenth and early twentieth centuries, see Brian L. Moore and Michele A. Johnson, *Neither Led Nor Driven: Contesting British Cultural Imperialism in Jamaica, 1865–1920* (Mona, Jamaica: University of the West Indies Press, 2004); Catherine Hall, *Civilising Subjects: Metropole and Colony in the English Imagination, 1830–1867* (Chicago: University of Chicago Press, 2002), 115–39; Brian L. Moore, *Cultural Power, Resistance, and Pluralism: Colonial Guyana, 1838–1900* (Barbados: University of the West Indies Press, 1995); Bridget Brereton, *Race Relations in Colonial Trinidad, 1870–1900* (New York: Cambridge University Press, 1979), chapters 4 and 5; Anne Spry Rush, *Bonds of Empire: West Indians and British-ness from Victoria to Decolonization* (Oxford: Oxford University Press, 2011), 2–4.

40. General Edmund Allenby to War Office, May 9, 1918, File Folder 2/1919, Box 1–193 (1919), Colonial Secretary's Office Papers, NATT; G.F. Watterson, War Office to General Edmund Allenby, June 18, 1918, CSO Papers, File Folder 2/1919, Box 1–193 (1919), NATT.

41. G.F. Watterson, War Office to General Edmund Allenby, June 18, 1918, CSO Papers, File Folder 2/1919, Box 1–193 (1919), NATT.

42. B. B. Cubitt to Colonial Office, August 2, 1918, CO 318/347, TNA.

43. James, *Holding Aloft the Banner*, 62.

44. Sergeant J. E. Lewis to Lieutenant Colonel Cran, February 22, 1918, CO 123/296, file 65699, TNA.

45. In regard to pay, the 1915 telegram which outlined the final terms for the creation of the BWIR stated: "Pay at British rates would commence from date of embarkation at Colony of concentration and would be borne by Imperial funds as well as all other expenses connected with the contingent from that date until date of return to respective colonies of recruitment." See Secretary of State for the Colonies to Governors and Administrators of the West Indian Colonies, July 28, 1915, copy enclosed in CO 318/348, TNA.

46. Petition from Charles Callender, W. E. Julien, A. Johnson, et. al to Governor Charles O'Brien (Barbados), n.d., CO 318/348, file 16801, TNA.

47. The West Indian Contingent Committee was "established at a meeting held at the Colonial Office on August 30th, 1915, at the instance of the Right Hon. A. Bonar Law, M.P., Secretary of State for the Colonies." Throughout its existence (1915–1920), the Contingent Committee used the offices and staff of the powerful West India Committee to carry out its work. See West Indian Contingent Committee, *Report of the Committee for the Ten Months ended June 30th, 1916* (London: The West India Committee Rooms, 1916), 2.

48. For the committee's membership list, see West Indian Contingent Committee, *Report of the Committee*, 1.

[298]   NOTES TO CHAPTER 4

49. "Minutes a Meeting of the General Purposes Committee," June 25, 1918, West Indian Contingent Committee Minute Book, ICS 97 1/6/1, Institute for Commonwealth Studies, London, England; "Minutes a Meeting of the General Purposes Committee," November 1, 1918, West Indian Contingent Minute Book, ICS 97 1/6/1, Institute for Commonwealth Studies.

50. "Minutes a Meeting of the General Purposes Committee," June 25, 1918, West Indian Contingent Committee Minute Book, ICS 97 1/6/1, Institute for Commonwealth Studies.

51. J. C. Hope, V. C. Thomas, E. F. Packer, et. al. to J. Challenor Lynch, August 2, 1918, CO 28/294, file 56561, TNA.

52. For a description of the educational background and socioeconomic status of the petitioners, see J. Challenor Lynch to T. E. Fell, Colonial Secretary (Barbados), October 9, 1918, CO 28/294, file 56561, TNA.

53. Private J.C. Hope was awarded the Distinguished Conduct Medal in October 1918. Hope, while "wounded in four places, including a broken arm," assisted a fellow soldier to travel over a mile back to camp. For the complete citation, see *Supplement to the London Gazette*, October 21, 1918, Issue 30961, Page 12349.

54. J.C. Hope, V.C. Thomas, E.F. Packer, et. al. to J. Challenor Lynch, August 2, 1918, CO 28/294, file 56561, TNA.

55. J.C. Hope, V.C. Thomas, E.F. Packer, et. al. to J. Challenor Lynch, August 2, 1918, CO 28/294, file 56561, TNA.

56. I have not been able to locate the original petitions of the soldiers from Dominica, St. Kitts and Nevis, and Montserrat. However, T.A.V. Best, Acting Governor of the Leeward Islands, offered a summary of the documents in a letter to Governor John Chancellor of Trinidad. Unfortunately, Governor Best did not state if the petitions were mailed from BWIR soldiers in the Middle East or Western Europe. T. A. V. Best to John Chancellor, Governor of Trinidad and Tobago, December 28, 1918, CSO Papers, File Folder 2/1919, Box 1–193 (1919), NATT.

57. Howe, *Race, War and Nationalism*, 161.

58. On Lynch's tenure in the Legislative Council and his antipathy towards the laboring classes, see Bonham C. Richardson, *Panama Money in Barbados 1900–1920* (Knoxville: University of Tennessee Press, 1985), 106, 131, 133.

59. Brian Stoddart, "Cricket and Colonialism in the English-speaking Caribbean to 1914: Towards a Cultural Analysis," in *Pleasure, Profit, Proselytism: British Culture and Sport at Home and Abroad*, ed. J. A. Mangan (Totowa, NJ: Frank Cass, 1988), 243; Richardson, *Panama Money in Barbados*, 106.

60. J. Challenor Lynch to T.E. Fell, Colonial Secretary (Barbados), October 9, 1918, CO 28/294, file 56561, TNA.

61. J. Challenor Lynch to T.E. Fell, Colonial Secretary (Barbados), October 9, 1918, CO 28/294, file 56561, TNA.

62. J. Challenor Lynch to T.E. Fell, Colonial Secretary (Barbados), October 9, 1918, CO 28/294, file 56561, TNA.

63. Charles O'Brien to Walter H. Long, October 14, 1918, CO 28/294, file 56561, TNA.

64. The War Office initially decided that "slightly coloured gentlemen" could be nominated for temporary commissions in October 1917. However, the War Office's

NOTES TO CHAPTER 4 [299]

decision was not widely communicated until April 1918, leading most BWIR soldiers to believe that black and colored men were still barred from commissions. See Secretary of State for the Colonies to Governor of Barbados, October 20, 1917, CO 28/292/37, TNA; B. B. Cubitt to Under Secretary of State, Colonial Office, April 26, 1918, CO 318/347, TNA; Handwritten File Note by E. R. Darnley, December 18, 1918, CO 28/294, file 56561, TNA.

65. *Hansard* HC Deb., November 14, 1918, vol 110, cc2884-5, https://api.parliament.uk/historic-hansard/commons/1918/nov/14/british-west-india-regiment#column_2884.

66. Deborah Cohen, *The War Come Home: Disabled Veterans in Britain and Germany, 1914–1939* (Berkeley: University of California Press, 2001), 1.

67. Lt.-Col. Charles Wood-Hill, *A Few Notes on the History of the British West Indies Regiment* (n.p., n.d.), 9.

68. Two BWIR battalions served in combat during the war. Soldiers in the First and Second Battalions fought against Turkish forces in the Middle Eastern theater in Palestine from August to September 1918. For a description of their combat activities, see Commander-in-Chief, Egyptian Expeditionary Force to War Office, December 17, 1918, CSO Papers, File Folder 2020/1919, Box 2020–2980 (1919), NATT.

69. Colonel C. Wood-Hill to Sir John Chancellor, Governor of Trinidad and Tobago, November 26, 1918, CSO Papers, File Folder 2/1919, Box 1–193 (1919), NATT.

70. Colonel C. Wood-Hill to Sir John Chancellor, Governor of Trinidad and Tobago, November 26, 1918, CSO Papers, File Folder 2/1919, Box 1–193 (1919), NATT.

71. C.P. Coote to Lady Matilde Mallet, December 10, 1918, reprinted in *Letters from the Trenches During the Great War* (Shipston-on-Stour: King's Stone Press, n.d.), 28.

72. On the BWIR recruitment drives in Panama, see Reena Goldthree, "'A Greater Enterprise than the Panama Canal': Migrant Labor and Military Recruitment in the World War I–Era Circum-Caribbean," *Labor: Studies in Working-Class History of the Americas* 13, no. 3–4 (2016): 57–82; Richardson, *Panama Money in Barbados*, 217.

73. On BWIR soldiers' experiences in wartime France, see Reena N. Goldthree, "'Vive La France!': Afro-Caribbean Soldiers and Interracial Intimacies on the Western Front, 1915–19," *Journal of Colonialism and Colonial History* 7, no. 3 (2016), doi:10.1353/cch.2016.0040.

74. Sir Etienne Dupuch, *Salute to Friend and Foe: My Battles, Sieges and Fortunes* (Nassau: The Tribune, 1982), 78.

75. Dupuch, *Salute to Friend and Foe*, 78. Reginald Elgar Willis enlisted in the Fifth Jamaica War Contingent on January 1, 1917, and departed Jamaica with the contingent on March 31, 1917. Stephen A. Hill, *Who's Who in Jamaica, 1919–1920* (Kingston, Jamaica: Gleaner, 1920), 255.

76. C.P. Coote to Lady Matilde Mallet, December 10, 1918, reprinted in *Letters from the Trenches*, 28.

77. The First, Second, and Fifth Battalions remained in the Middle East until 1919. For the numbers of BWIR officers and men at Taranto, see General Headquarters (GH), Italy to War Office, December 19, 1918, CO 318/347, TNA; War Diary, Ordinance Depot, Taranto, Italy, November 1918, WO 95/4256, TNA.

[300]   NOTES TO CHAPTER 4

78. On November 19, 1918, Captain W. I. Hamlin noted that Base Headquarters had granted permission for military officials to use soldiers from the Third, Fourth, Sixth, Seventh, and Ninth Battalions "for the purposes of Labour." However, it was unusual for soldiers to perform sanitation duties for other military units, particularly for civilian corps that were themselves hired to perform such menial duties. War Diary, Ordinance Depot, Taranto, Italy, November 1918, WO 95/4256, TNA.

79. While the general outline of the mutiny is well known, the exact chronology and causes of the uprising are less understood. Some scholars, for example, have argued that BWIR soldiers at Taranto rose in protest against the racist policies of the base commandant, Brigadier-General Cyril Darcy Vivien Cary-Barnard. During his tenure at Taranto, Cary-Barnard enforced strict racial segregation on the base, relegating BWIR soldiers to segregated canteens and the Native Labour Hospital. However, he did not assume command at Taranto until February 4, 1919, nearly two months after the mutiny. Therefore, his policies could not have played a role in sparking the protest. For the quotation, see Dupuch, *Salute to Friend and Foe*, 78.

80. Base Commandant, Taranto to War Office, December 9, 1918 (B.C. 119), CO 318/347, TNA; Richard Smith, *Jamaican Volunteers*, 130. In addition to the events outlined above, the official history of British military operations in Italy during the Great War states that "stones were thrown at two officers and a bomb was thrown into the tent of a regimental quartermaster-sergeant" during the Taranto mutiny. Brigadier-General Sir James E. Edmonds, *Military Operations, Italy, 1915–1919* (London: H.M. Stationery Office, 1949), 386–87.

81. Secret Telegram, Base Commandant, Taranto to War Office, December 9, 1918, CO 318/347, TNA.

82. Secret Telegram, Base Commandant, Taranto to War Office, December 10, 1918, CO 318/347, TNA.

83. The War Office confirmed the decision to disband the Ninth Battalion on January 4, 1919, and military authorities at Taranto permanently disbanded the unit on January 19, 1919. See Base Routine Orders, Taranto Base, January 20, 1919, WO 95/4255, TNA; War Diary, Ordinance Depot, Taranto, Italy, January 1919, WO 95/4256, TNA.

84. Secret Telegram, Base Commandant, Taranto to War Office, December 10, 1918, CO 318/347, TNA.

85. Telegram, General Headquarters (GH), Italy to War Office, December 12, 1918, CO 318/347; War Diary, Ordinance Depot, Taranto, Italy, December 1918, WO 95/4256, TNA.

86. Telegram, Inspector-General of Communications (IGC), Italy to War Office, December 11, 1918, CO 318/347, TNA.

87. Telegram, Base Commandant, Taranto to War Office, December 12, 1918, CO 318/347, TNA.

88. Telegram, General Officer Commanding, Italy to War Office, December 13, 1918, CO 318/347, TNA.

89. Petition from M. Murphy and 179 signatures to Secretary of State for the Colonies, December 6, 1918, CO 28/294, TNA.

90. Petition from M. Murphy and 179 signatures to Secretary of State for the Colonies, December 6, 1918, CO 28/294, TNA.

NOTES TO CHAPTER 4 [301]

91. Rudyard Kipling, "The Heathen," http://battlepoetry.com/kip/heathen/heathen.htm.

92. Acting Sergeant Robert Richards was initially charged with manslaughter for fatally wounding Private Pinnock. However, he was convicted on the lesser charge of "conduct prejudicial to good order and military discipline" and sentenced to six months in prison with hard labor. His sentence was ultimately reduced to only two months' imprisonment. War Diary of the Seventh Battalion, British West Indies Regiment, January 16, 1919, WO 95/4262, TNA; Julian Putkowski and Julian Sykes, *Shot at Dawn: Executions in World War One by Authority of the British Army Act*, (London: Leo Cooper, 1999), 264.

93. Handwritten File Note by G. E. A. Grindle, December 13, 1918, CO 318/347, file 60323, TNA.

94. The following number of soldiers were arrested from each battalion: Fourth Battalion (12 soldiers), Sixth Battalion (12 soldiers), Seventh Battalion (5 soldiers), Eighth Battalion (2 soldiers), Ninth Battalion (37 soldiers), Tenth Battalion (3 soldiers), and Eleventh Battalion (1 soldier). Register of Field General Courts Martial, WO 213/27, TNA.

95. War Office, *Manual of Military Law* (London: HMSO, 1914), 50.

96. Register of Field General Courts Martial, WO 213/27, TNA.

97. After the Armistice, all outstanding death sentences for military offenses were commuted to penal servitude, and no further death sentences for military infractions were carried out. Soldiers found guilty of murder and other serious civil crimes, however, still faced the death penalty. Cathryn Corns and John Hughes-Wilson, *Blindfold and Alone: British Military Executions in the Great War* (London: Cassell, 2001), 401.

98. Howe, *Race, War and Nationalism*, 189–90.

99. Corns and Hughes-Wilson, *Blindfold and Alone*, 401.

100. Gunner William E. Lewis (Royal Field Artillery), Private Jack Braithwaite (Otago New Zealand), and Acting Corporal Jesse Robert Short (Northumberland Fusiliers, Tyneside Irish) were executed for mutiny during the Great War. Mahmoud Mohamed Ahmed, a laborer in the Egypt Labour Corps, was also executed for mutiny. For a complete listing of all British and colonial soldiers and laborers executed during the war, see Corns and Hughes-Wilson, *Blindfold and Alone*, Appendix 2.

101. The British Army executed 306 soldiers and laborers during the Great War. The vast majority of executed men were convicted of desertion (266 out of 306). Corns and Hughes-Wilson, *Blindfold and Alone*, 51, 447.

102. Privates James A. Mitchell (First Battalion) and Albert Denny (Eighth Battalion) were executed for murder, while Private Hubert A. Clarke (Second Battalion) was executed for striking a superior officer. Private Herbert Morris (Sixth Battalion) was executed for desertion. For a detailed account of the circumstances that led these soldiers to be condemned to death, see Julian Putkowski and Julian Sykes, *Shot at Dawn: Executions in World War One by Authority of the British Army Act*, 195–96, 230–32, 264.

103. Elkins, "Source of Black Nationalism," 101.

104. Wood-Hill, *A Few Notes on the History*, 10.

105. Corns and Hughes-Wilson, *Blindfold and Alone*, 380.

106. Wood-Hill, *A Few Notes on the History*, 10.

[302] NOTES TO CHAPTER 4

107. H. Fitz M. Stacke, *The Worcestershire Regiment in the Great War* (Kidderminster, 1928), quoted in Elkins, "Source of Black Nationalism," 101; Smith, *Jamaican Volunteers*, 131.

108. General Henry Thullier to War Office, Secret Dispatch, December 29, 1918, CO 318/350, TNA.

109. Smith, *Jamaican Volunteers*, 133.

110. Major Maxwell Smith to General Henry Thullier, December 27, 1918, CO 318/350, TNA.

111. On the central role that fraternal and civic associations played in promoting black internationalism and regional unity in the West Indian migratory sphere, see Lara Putnam, "Nothing Matters but Color Transnational Circuits, the Interwar Caribbean, and the Black International," in *From Toussaint to Tupac: the Black International Since the Age of Revolution*, ed. Michael O. West, William G. Martin, and Fanon Che Wilkins (Chapel Hill: University of North Carolina Press, 2009), 107–30. On the emergence of friendly societies as a response to crown colony government in the British Caribbean colonies, see Glen Richards, "Friendly Societies and Labour Organisation in the Leeward Islands, 1912–19," in *Before and After 1865: Education, Politics and Regionalism in the Caribbean*, ed. Brian Moore and Swithin Wilmot (Kingston, Jamaica: Ian Randle, 1998), 136–49.

112. "The Order of the Foresters Here," *Daily Gleaner*, June 8, 1915, 4.

113. "Brilliant Masonic Function Held on Wednesday Night," *Daily Gleaner*, December 12, 1919, 10.

114. Sergeant Pouchet's first name and home colony are not included in any of the reports on the Caribbean League. However, there is a soldier named Sergeant Leon Charles Pouchet, Regimental Number 11533, listed among the rolls of BWIR volunteers from Trinidad. Leon Charles Pouchet enlisted in the Fourth Trinidad Contingent and departed for the war on July 7, 1917. Before joining the BWIR, he resided in Port of Spain and listed his wife as his next of kin. See "Nominal Roll of all the Contingents that have left Trinidad and Joined the B. W. I. Regiment," CSO Papers, File Folder 1792/1918, Box 1009–1936 (1918), NATT; C. B. Franklin, *Trinidad and Tobago Year Book* (Port-of-Spain: Franklin's Electric Printery, 1919), xlvii.

115. Major Maxwell Smith to General Henry Thullier, December 27, 1918, CO 318/350, TNA.

116. Major Maxwell Smith to General Henry Thullier, December 27, 1918, CO 318/350, TNA.

117. Major Maxwell Smith to General Henry Thullier, January 3, 1919, CO 318/350, TNA.

118. War Diary, Ordinance Depot, Taranto, Italy, December 23, 1918, WO 95/4256, TNA.

119. The third meeting of the Caribbean League was held at the sergeants' mess of the Eighth Battalion of the BWIR. See Major Maxwell Smith to General Henry Thullier, January 3, 1919, CO 318/350, TNA.

120. Major Maxwell Smith to General Henry Thullier, January 3, 1919, CO 318/350, TNA.

121. Major Maxwell Smith to General Henry Thullier, January 3, 1919, CO 318/350, TNA.

NOTES TO CHAPTER 4 [303]

122. General Henry Thullier to War Office, Secret Dispatch, December 29, 1918, CO 318/350, TNA.

123. Handwritten File Note by E. R. Darnley, January 16, 1919, CO 318/350, file 2590, TNA.

124. Handwritten File Note by G. E. A. Grindle, January 17, 1919, CO 318/350, file 2590, TNA.

125. Colonial Office to Leslie Probyn, January 24, 1919, CO 318/350, TNA.

126. Colonial Office to The Officer Administering the Government of British Honduras, January 24, 1919, CO 318/350, TNA; Colonial Office to Wilfred Collet (British Guiana), January 24, 1919, CO 318/350, TNA; Colonial Office to W.L. Allardyce (Bahamas), January 24, 1919, CO 318/350, TNA; Colonial Office to J.R. Chancellor (Trinidad and Tobago), January 24, 1919, CO 318/350, TNA; Colonial Office to G.B. Haddon-Smith (Windward Islands), January 24, 1919, CO 318/350, TNA; Colonial Office to C.R.M. O'Brien (Barbados), January 24, 1919, CO 318/350, TNA; Colonial Office to The Officer Administering the Government of the Leeward Islands, January 24, 1919, CO 318/350, TNA.

127. For a complete account of Alfred Milner's career in the colonial service, see Colin Newbury, "Milner, Alfred, Viscount Milner (1854–1925)," in *Oxford Dictionary of National Biography*, Oxford University Press, 2004; online ed., Oct 2008, http://www.oxforddnb.com/view/article/35037. For the debate over the authorship of the Balfour Declaration, see W. T. Mallison, "The Balfour Declaration: An Appraisal," in *The Transformation of Palestine*: *Essays on the Origin and Development of the Arab-Israeli Conflict*, ed. Ibrahim Abu-Lughod (Evanston, IL: Northwestern University Press, 1987), 66–95; William D. Rubinstein, "The Secret of Leopold Amery," *Historical Research* 73, no. 181 (2000): 176, 184–85.

128. West Indian Contingent Committee to Walter Long, December 30, 1918, CO 318/347, file 63228, TNA.

129. West Indian Contingent Committee to Alfred Milner, January 15, 1919, CO 318/347, file 3414, TNA.

130. West Indian Contingent Committee to Walter Long, December 30, 1918, CO 318/347, file 63228, TNA.

131. West Indian Contingent Committee to Alfred Milner, January 15, 1919, CO 318/347, file 3414, TNA.

132. West Indian Contingent Committee to Alfred Milner, January 15, 1919, CO 318/347, file 3414, TNA.

133. West Indian Contingent Committee to Walter Long, December 30, 1918, CO 318/347, file 63228, TNA.

134. West Indian Contingent Committee to Alfred Milner, January 15, 1919, CO 318/347, file 3414, TNA.

135. Francis Fleming was the former governor of the Leeward Islands. James Hayes-Saddler was the former governor of the Windward Islands. Frederic M. Hodgeon was the former governor of Barbados and of British Guiana. George Le Hunte was the former governor of Trinidad and Tobago. R. B. Llewelyn was the former governor of the Leeward Islands. Sydney Olivier was the former governor of Jamaica. William Grey Wilson of the former governor of the Bahamas.

136. Governor Charles O'Brien to Secretary of State for the Colonies, January 28, 1919, CO 318/347, file 3414, TNA.

[304] NOTES TO CHAPTER 4

137. Handwritten File Note by G. E. A. Grindle, January 31, 1919, CO 318/347, file 7242, TNA.

138. H. T. Allen, "Pay of the British West Indies Regiment," January 30, 1919, CO 318/348, file 5991, TNA.

139. These other "coloured units" were the Fiji Labour Company, Bermuda Royal Garrison Artillery, Cape Coloured Labour Battalion, Cape Corps Infantry, Cape Auxiliary Horse Transport Corps, and Cape Coloured Labour Section. E.R. Darnley estimated the total enlistment for these six units to be approximately eight thousand men. Colonial Office, "Draft Memorandum for the War Cabinet: Question of extending to various coloured Colonial Contingents the full benefits of Army Order No.1 of 1918," February 1919, CO 318/347, file 7242, TNA.

140. H. T. Allen, "Pay of the British West Indies Regiment," January 30, 1919, CO 318/348, file 5991, TNA.

141. Handwritten File Note by G. E. A. Grindle, January 31, 1919, CO 318/347, file 7242, TNA.

142. Handwritten File Note by Alfred Milner, February 4, 1919, CO 318/347, file 7242, TNA.

143. Colonial Office, "Draft Memorandum for the War Cabinet: Question of extending to various coloured Colonial Contingents the full benefits of Army Order No.1 of 1918," February 1919, CO 318/347, file 7242, TNA.

144. Colonial Office, "Draft Memorandum for the War Cabinet."

145. Colonial Office, "Draft Memorandum for the War Cabinet."

146. B. B. Cubitt to the Under Secretary of State, Colonial Office, February 18, 1919, CO 318/350, file 10950, TNA.

147. Under Army Order No. 17 of 1919, soldiers received a gratuity of £5 for the first year of military service and an additional 10s. per month for every month of service after the first year for a maximum of forty-eight months. See United Kingdom, Hansard, HC Deb (13 February 1919), vol. 112 cc 294–5W.

148. Handwritten File Note by E. R. Darnley, February 20, 1919, CO 318/350, file 10950, TNA.

149. Telegram from the Secretary of State for the Colonies to February 21, 1919, CO 318/350, file 10950, TNA; Handwritten File Note by E. R. Darnley, February 20, 1919, CO 318/350, file 10950, TNA.

150. In his letter, Cubitt did not specify what other "coloured units" might also retroactively receive the benefits of Army Order No.1, but the likely units included the Fiji Labour Company, Bermuda Royal Garrison Artillery, Cape Coloured Labour Battalion, Cape Corps Infantry, Cape Auxiliary Horse Transport Corps, and Cape Coloured Labour Section. B. B. Cubitt to the Under Secretary of State, Colonial Office, February 18, 1919, CO 318/350, file 10950, TNA.

151. The West Indian Contingent Committee also boasted about its role in securing the benefits of Army Order No. 1 for BWIR soldiers in its closing report for 1918. The West Indian Contingent Committee, *Report and Accounts for the Six Months ended 31st December, 1918* (London: The West India Committee Rooms, 1919), n.p.

152. Gregory Mann, *Native Sons: West African Veterans and France in the Twentieth Century* (Durham: Duke University Press, 2006), 83.

153. Testimony of Greville William Charles Hulse, September 8, 1919, *Report of the Riot Commission*, CO 123/296, file 65699, TNA.

NOTES TO CHAPTER 5 [305]

154. Arthur A. Cipriani to the Colonial Secretary (Trinidad and Tobago), November 29, 1919, reprinted in Cipriani, *Twenty-Five Years After: The British West Indies Regiment in The Great War* (Port of Spain: Trinidad Publishing, 1940), 60.

155. Major J. B. Thursfield to Arthur Cipriani, September 30, 1919, reprinted in Cipriani, *Twenty-Five Years After*, 65.

156. Report by Major J. B. Thursfield, September 30, 1919, reprinted in Cipriani, *Twenty-Five Years After*, 62.

Chapter Five: "Serious Discontent"

Epigraph 1: Handwritten note by Gilbert Grindle, October 22, 1919, CO 318/352, file 64434, TNA.

Epigraph 2: Claude McKay, "Letter to the Negro World," January 14, 1920, cited in Winston James, "Letters from London in Black and Red: Claude McKay, Marcus Garvey and the *Negro World*," *History Workshop Journal* 85 (2018): 290.

1. On Lord Hankey's work with the War Council, see Lord Hankey, *The Supreme Command, 1914–1918*, vol. 1 (London: George Allen and Unwin, 1961), 3–10, 237–332.

2. J. R. H. Homfray to Lord Hankley, January 14, 1919, CO 318/350, file 10550, The National Archives (hereafter TNA), Kew, England.

3. Typewritten note by Lord Hankey, February 12, 1919, on J. R. H. Homfray to Lord Hankey, January 14, 1919, CO 318/350, file 10550, TNA.

4. Piers W. North to Colonial Office, January 6, 1919, CO 318/352, file 7723, TNA.

5. Leslie Probyn to Viscount [Alfred] Milner, May 22, 1919, CO 137/731, file 34400, TNA.

6. Address by Charles O'Brien to Barbadian Planters, July 30, 1919, reprinted in Robert A. Hill, ed., *The Marcus Garvey and Universal Negro Improvement Association Papers*, vol. 11 (Durham: Duke University Press, 2011), 241.

7. Herbert T. Thomas, *The Story of a West Indian Policeman or Forty-seven Years in the Jamaica Constabulary* (Kingston, Jamaica: Gleaner, 1927), 214.

8. Captain Percy L. Fraser, *Looking over my Shoulder: Forty-Seven Years a Public Servant, 1885–1932* (San Juan, Trinidad: Lexicon Trinidad, 2007), 8.

9. Fraser, *Looking Over My Shoulder*, 8.

10. On the central role of voluntary and philanthropic organizations in postwar Britain, see Deborah Cohen, *The War Come Home: Disabled Veterans in Britain and Germany, 1914–1939* (Berkeley: University of California Press, 2001), 15–61.

11. The title for this section is from J. R. H. Homfray to Lord Hankley, January 14, 1919, CO 318/350, file 10550, TNA.

12. Homfray's January 1919 letter reached the Colonial Office on February 17, 1919.

13. B. B. Cubitt to Under Secretary of State, Colonial Office, February 7, 1919, CO 318/350, file 8424, TNA.

14. Handwritten note by E. R. Darnley, February 18, 1919, CO 318/350, file 10550, TNA. The Colonial Office had initiated plans to station a warship near Jamaica during demobilization before receiving Homfray's letter. Secretary of the Admiralty to Under Secretary of State, Colonial Office, February 7, 1919; Viscount [Alfred] Milner to Governor of Jamaica, February 15, 1919; and G. V. Fiddes to Secretary of the Admiralty, February 20, 1919, all in CO 318/350, file 8424, TNA.

[306] NOTES TO CHAPTER 5

15. Secretary of State for the Colonies to Officer Administering the Government (British Honduras) and to Governor of the Bahamas, February 20, 1919, CO 318/350, file 10550, TNA.

16. Secretary of State for the Colonies to Governors of Trinidad, Barbados, British Guiana, and the Windward and Leeward Islands, February 20, 1919, CO 318/350, file 10550, TNA.

17. Charles O'Brien, February 21, 1919, "Unrest in the West Indies," GH 3/5/1, LT/S/1, Barbados Department of Archives (hereafter BDA), Black Rock, Barbados; William L. Allardyce to Admiral Morgan Singer, February 23, 1919, reprinted in Hill, *Marcus Garvey*, 11:171.

18. Charles O'Brien to Viscount [Alfred] Milner, March 5, 1919, "Scheme of Organization Against Civil Disturbances," GH 3/4/4, BDA.

19. William L. Allardyce to Admiral Morgan Singer, February 23, 1919, reprinted in Hill, *Marcus Garvey*, 11:171.

20. After the withdrawal of the last garrison of white British troops from the British Caribbean in 1905, colonial authorities and local white elites repeatedly insisted that black and colored volunteers and constables could not be trusted to suppress popular uprisings. Bonham C. Richardson, *Igniting the Caribbean's Past: Fire in British West Indian History* (Chapel Hill: University of North Carolina Press, 2004), 189–91.

21. Marika Sherwood, *Origins of Pan-Africanism: Henry Sylvester Williams, Africa, and the African Diaspora* (New York: Routledge, 2011), 35–36.

22. Sherwood, *Origins of Pan-Africanism*, 109–16, 119–23; Brinsley Samaroo, "Cyrus Prudhomme David: A Case Study in the Emergence of the Black Man in Trinidad Politics," *Journal of Caribbean History* 3 (1971): 77–78.

23. E. M'Zumbo Lazare, "An Important Reminder," *Argos*, January 2, 1919, 7.

24. E. M'Zumbo Lazare, "An Important Reminder," *Argos*, January 2, 1919, 7.

25. For a biographical portrait of U. Theo McKay, see Winston James, *A Fierce Hatred of Injustice: Claude McKay's Jamaica and His Poetry of Rebellion* (Kingston, Jamaica: Ian Randle, 2001), 26–33.

26. U. Theo McKay, Letter to the Editor, January 14, 1919, in "Some Questions Which Merit Consideration of Public," *Daily Gleaner*, January 20, 1919, 5.

27. For local studies that document the rapid expansion of the UNIA in the circum-Caribbean after World War I, see Carla Burnett, "'Unity Is Strength': Labor, Race, Garveyism, and the 1920 Panama Canal Strike," *The Global South* 6, no. 2 (2012): 39–64; Adam Ewing, "Caribbean Labour Politics in the Age of Garvey, 1918–1938," *Race and Class* 55, no. 1 (2013): 23–45; Humberto García Muñiz and Jorge L. Giovannetti, "Garveyismo y racismo en el Caribe: El caso de la población cocola en la República Dominicana," *Caribbean Studies* 31, no. 1 (2003): 139–211; Frank Guridy, "'Enemies of the White Race': The Machadista State and the UNIA in Cuba," *Caribbean Studies* 31, no. 1 (2003): 107–37; Ronald Harpelle, "Cross Currents in the Western Caribbean: Marcus Garvey and the UNIA in Central America," *Caribbean Studies* 31, no. 1 (2003): 35–73; Rupert Lewis and Patrick Bryan, eds., *Garvey, His Work and Impact* (Trenton, NJ: Africa World Press, 1991); Marc C. McLeod, "'Sin dejar de ser cubanos': Cuban Blacks and the Challenges of Garveyism in Cuba," *Caribbean Studies* 31, no. 1 (2003): 75–105; Asia Leeds, "Toward the 'Higher Type of

NOTES TO CHAPTER 5 [307]

Womanhood': The Gendered Contours of Garveyism and the Making of Redemptive Geographies in Costa Rica, 1922–1941," *Palimpsest: A Journal on Women, Gender, and the Black International* 2, no. 1 (2013): 1–27; Ronald J. Stephens and Adam Ewing, eds., *Global Garveyism* (Gainesville: University Press of Florida, 2019); Frances Peace Sullivan, "'Forging Ahead' in Banes, Cuba: Garveyism in a United Fruit Company Town," *New West Indian Guide* 88 (2014): 231–61.

28. "Advice of the Negro to Peace Conference," *Negro World*, November 30, 1918, reprinted in Hill, *Marcus Garvey*, 1:302–3.

29. U.S. Postal Censorship Report, November 7, 1919, RG 165, 10218-261/2, National Archives and Records Administration, Washington, DC, reprinted in Hill, *Marcus Garvey*, 11:109.

30. Tony Martin, "Marcus Garvey and Trinidad, 1912–1947," in *The Pan-African Connection: From Slavery to Garvey and Beyond* (Dover, MA: Majority Press, 1983), 64.

31. W. M. Gordon (Acting Governor) to Viscount [Alfred] Milner, June 18, 1919, CO 295/521, file 41273, TNA.

32. Cecil Clementi (Officer Administering the Government, British Guiana) to Viscount [Alfred] Milner, May 10, 1919, CO 111/623/7345, National Archives of the United Kingdom, reprinted in Hill, *Marcus Garvey*, 11:205–6; Charles O'Brien to Viscount [Alfred] Milner, July 14, 1919, "Unrest in the West Indies," GH 3/5/1, LT/S/1, BDA.

33. Martin, "Marcus Garvey and Trinidad," 66–67.

34. For an analysis of W. A. Domingo's political trajectory, see Winston James, *Holding Aloft the Banner of Ethiopia: Caribbean Radicalism in Early Twentieth-Century America* (New York: Verso, 1998), 41, 50–51, 94, 269–70.

35. "Reconstruction in the West Indies," *West Indian*, March 23, 1919, reprinted in Hill, *Marcus Garvey*, 11:187.

36. "Reconstruction in the West Indies," *West Indian*, March 23, 1919, reprinted in Hill, *Marcus Garvey*, 11:187.

37. W. F. Elkins, "Suppression of the *Negro World* in the British West Indies," *Science & Society* 35, no. 3 (1971): 345.

38. W. M. Gordon to Viscount [Alfred] Milner, June 18, 1919, CO 295/521, file 41273, TNA; W. M. Gordon to Wilfred Collet, June 10, 1919, CO 295/521, file 41273, TNA.

39. For the exchange between colonial administrators in British Guiana and U.S. consular officials regarding the circulation of the *Negro World* and other black publications from the United States, see George Chamberlin to Robert Lansing, May 9, 1919, RG 59, 811.918/129, National Archives and Records Administration; Cecil Clementi to Viscount [Alfred] Milner, May 10, 1919, CO 111/623/7345, National Archives of the United Kingdom; B. H. Bayley to George E. Chamberlin, May 31, 1919, RG 59, 811.918/130, National Archives and Records Administration; George E. Chamberlin to Robert Lansing, June 2, 1919, RG 59, 811.918/130, National Archives and Records Administration, all reprinted in Hill, *Marcus Garvey*, 11:199–204, 205–6, 209–10.

40. For an overview of black veterans' activism following World War I, see Chad Williams, "A Mobilized African Diaspora: The First World War, Military Service, and Black Soldiers as New Negroes," in *Escape from New York: The New Negro Renaissance*

[308] NOTES TO CHAPTER 5

Beyond Harlem, ed. Davarian L. Baldwin and Minkah Makalani (University of Minnesota Press, 2013), 247–69.

41. Thomas, *Story of a West Indian,* 216.

42. *Jamaica Times,* May 17, 1919, 10.

43. Minutes of the Meeting of the Privy Council, July 18, 1919, 1B/5/3/32, Jamaica Archives (hereafter JA), Spanish Town.

44. Secretary of State for the Colonies Alfred Milner recommended this strategy in a telegram to all West Indian governors in February 1919. For a copy of Milner's telegram, see Secretary of State for the Colonies to Governor of Trinidad, February 8, 1919, Colonial Secretary's Office Papers (hereafter CSO Papers), File Folder 926/1919, Box 231-1266 (1919), National Archive of Trinidad and Tobago (hereafter NATT), Port of Spain, Trinidad.

45. On the plan to send veterans to their home parishes for welcome-home festivities, see "Return of the Contingents," *Northern News,* April 19, 1919, 1; "Montego Bay Will Give Contingent Men Warm Welcome," *Northern News,* April 26, 1919, 1; Thomas, *Story of a West Indian,* 214–20.

46. BWIR veterans were officially demobilized after a twenty-eight-day transitional furlough period at home. During this period, they still received daily wages and had the right to wear their uniform. "Army Demobilization Regulations, Part III, Chapter XXXIII: British West Indies Regiment," CO 318/355, file 7060, TNA. For the average final payment allotted to BWIR veterans, see Secretary of State of the Colonies to Governor of Trinidad, March 18, 1919, CSO Papers, File Folder 926/1919, Box 231-1266 (1919), NATT.

47. "Sober Thought About Our Returning Soldiers," *Jamaica Times,* April 12, 1919, 6.

48. "Information Regarding Rates of Pay, Separation Allowances, and Pensions for the Men Joining the Jamaica War Contingents," 1B/5/77/108-1926, JA.

49. On rates of legal marriage in the British Caribbean, see Rhoda E. Reddock, *Women, Labour and Politics in Trinidad and Tobago* (London: Zed Books, 1994), 60; Anne S. Macpherson, *From Colony to Nation: Women Activists and the Gendering of Politics in Belize, 1912–1982* (Lincoln: University of Nebraska Press, 2007), 128–29; Brian L. Moore and Michele A. Johnson, *Neither Led Nor Driven: Contesting British Cultural Imperialism in Jamaica, 1865–1920* (Kingston, Jamaica: University of the West Indies Press, 2004), 329–30.

50. Reddock, *Women, Labour and Politics,* 61; Janet Henshall Momsen, ed., introduction to *Women and Change in the Caribbean: A Pan-Caribbean Perspective* (Bloomington, IN: Indiana University Press, 1993), 1.

51. Reddock, *Women, Labour and Politics,* 70.

52. Henry W. Lofty, *Report on the Census of Barbados, 1911–1921* (Bridgetown: Advocate, 1921), Appendix B.

53. Charles O'Brien to Viscount [Alfred] Milner, July 14, 1919, "Unrest in the West Indies," GH 3/5/1, LT/S/1, BDA.

54. Thomas, *Story of a West Indian,* 217.

55. "Peace Day Observed with Enthusiasm in Jamaica," *Daily Gleaner,* July 21, 1919, 1, 13.

56. Glen Richards, "Race, Class and Labour Politics in Colonial Jamaica, 1900–1934," in *Jamaica in Slavery and Freedom: History, Heritage and Culture,* ed.

NOTES TO CHAPTER 5 [309]

Kathleen E. A. Monteith and Glen Richards (Kingston, Jamaica: University of the West Indies Press, 2002), 350.

57. Jamaica Federation of Labour to Viscount [Alfred] Milner, CO 137/732, file 463878, TNA.

58. Draft reply, September 3, 1919, CO 137/732, file 463878, TNA.

59. Law No. 17 of 1919, "Temporary Registration of Voters Law," in Robert Johnston to Viscount [Alfred] Milner, July 9, 1919, CO 137/732, file 44170, TNA.

60. Propertied adult women in British Honduras gained the right to vote in 1912. Macpherson, *From Colony to Nation*, 37, 47. On the women's suffrage campaign in Jamaica, see Linnette Vassell, "The Movement for the Vote for Women 1918–1919," *Jamaican Historical Review* 15, no. 11 (1993): 40–54; Dalea Bean, *Jamaican Women and the World Wars: On the Front Lines of Change* (Basingstoke, England: Palgrave Macmillan, 2018),115–49.

61. Joseph C. Ford and Frank Cundall, *The Handbook of Jamaica for 1920* (Kingston, Jamaica: Government Printing Office, 1920), 658.

62. Ford and Cundall, *The Handbook of Jamaica for 1920*, 658; Bean, *Jamaican Women*, 115–49.

63. Frank Cundall, *The Handbook of Jamaica for 1921* (Kingston, Jamaica: Government Printing Office, 1921), 600.

64. Cundall, *Handbook of Jamaica for 1921*, 600–1.

65. "The Returned Soldiers Friendly Column," *Jamaica Times*, June 28, 1919, 14.

66. Cundall, *Handbook of Jamaica for 1921*, 600.

67. Leslie Probyn to Secretary of State for the Colonies, June 22, 1919, CO 137/732, file 37053, TNA.

68. Claude Mallet to Earl Curzon of Kedleston, Foreign Office, February 24, 1919, CO 318/350, file 19715, TNA.

69. For estimates of the number of British Caribbean immigrants to Cuba during this period, see Marc C. McLeod, "Undesirable Aliens: Race, Ethnicity, and Nationalism in the Comparison of Haitian and British West Indian Immigrant Workers in Cuba, 1912–1939," *Journal of Social History* 31, no. 3 (1998): 599; Philip A. Howard, *Black Labor, White Sugar: Caribbean Braceros and Their Struggle for Power in the Cuban Sugar Industry* (Baton Rouge: Louisiana State University Press, 2015), 65. On the history of British Caribbean migration to Cuba, see Robert Whitney and Graciela Chailloux Laffita, *Subjects or Citizens: British Caribbean Workers in Cuba, 1900–1960* (Gainesville: University Press of Florida, 2013.); Jorge L. Giovannetti-Torres, *Black British Migrants in Cuba: Race, Labor, and Empire in the Twentieth-century Caribbean, 1898–1948* (New York, NY: Cambridge University Press, 2020).

70. "News of the Week," *Barbados Weekly Herald*, January 17, 1920, 6. On ex-soldiers' emigration from Barbados to Cuba, see "Late Barbados News," *Port of Spain Gazette*, September 19, 1919, 5; "Late Barbados News," *Port of Spain Gazette*, November 7, 1919, 4; "Telegrams-The Returned Soldiers," *St. Croix Avis*, September 12, 1919, 3; "Telegrams-Emigration to Cuba," *St. Croix Avis*, September 12, 1919, 3.

71. "Items of News," *Port of Spain Gazette*, May 12, 1920, 4.

72. "Local News-Habour Notes," *Dominica Chronicle*, September 20, 1919, 7; Glenford D. Howe, *Race, War and Nationalism: A Social History of West Indians in the First World War* (Kingston, Jamaica: Ian Randle Publishers, 2002), 191, 199.

[310] NOTES TO CHAPTER 5

73. Robert Johnstone to Viscount [Alfred] Milner, August 14, 1919, CO 137/733, file 50990, TNA.

74. "Last Monday's Disorderly Scenes," *Port of Spain Gazette* July 23, 1919, 3; "Riotous End to Peace Rejoicings," *Trinidad Guardian*, July 23, 1919, 8.

75. The title for this section is from Testimony of David Samuel Rowland, September 24, 1919, *Report of the Riot Commission*, CO 123/296, file 65699, TNA.

76. Testimony of James Cran, September 26, 1919, *Report of the Riot Commission*, CO 123/296, file 65699, TNA; "Welcome to the Men of our Contingents," *The Belize Independent*, July 16, 1919, vol. 6, no. 279, 3.

77. Testimony of Samuel Alfred Haynes, September 17, 1919, *Report of the Riot Commission*, CO 123/296, file 65699, TNA.

78. "Address by His Excellency the Governor to the British Honduras Contingents," July 8, 1919, *Report of the Riot Commission*, CO 123/296, file 65699, TNA.

79. "Address by His Excellency the Governor to the British Honduras Contingents," July 8, 1919, *Report of the Riot Commission*, CO 123/296, file 65699, TNA.

80. Testimony of James Cran, September 26, 1919, *Report of the Riot Commission*, CO 123/296, file 65699, TNA. The local currency in British Honduras during this period was the British Honduras dollar.

81. Testimony of Eyre Hutson, August 27, 1919, *Report of the Riot Commission*, CO 123/296, file 65699, TNA.

82. Testimony of Robert Wyatt, September 8, 1919, *Report of the Riot Commission*, CO 123/296, file 65699, TNA.

83. Testimony of Samuel Alfred Haynes, September 17, 1919, *Report of the Riot Commission*, CO 123/296, file 65699, TNA.

84. Testimony of James Cran, September 26, 1919, *Report of the Riot Commission*, CO 123/296, file 65699, TNA.

85. Testimony of Cyril Fuller, September 22, 1919, *Report of the Riot Commission*, CO 123/296, file 65699, TNA.

86. Testimony of James Cran, September 26, 1919, *Report of the Riot Commission*, CO 123/296, file 65699, TNA.

87. Testimony of Lindsay Arthur Jeffery, September 8, 1919, *Report of the Riot Commission*, CO 123/296, file 65699, TNA; Testimony of Coralie Jane Brown, September 16, 1919, *Report of the Riot Commission*, CO 123/296, file 65699, TNA.

88. Testimony of Eyre Hutson, August 27, 1919, *Report of the Riot Commission*, CO 123/296, file 65699, TNA.

89. Macpherson, *From Colony to Nation*, 39.

90. Testimony of Frans Robert Dragten, n.d., *Report of the Riot Commission*, CO 123/296, file 65699, TNA.

91. Testimony of Frans Robert Dragten, n.d., *Report of the Riot Commission*, CO 123/296, file 65699, TNA.

92. Macpherson, *From Colony to Nation*, 39.

93. *Clarion*, July 18, 1918, quoted in Howe, *Race, War and Nationalism*, 176.

94. Kelvin Singh, *Race and Class Struggles in a Colonial State: Trinidad 1917–1945* (Kingston, Jamaica: University of the West Indies Press, 1994), 15; Jerome Teelucksingh, *Labour and the Decolonization Struggle in Trinidad and Tobago* (New York: Palgrave Macmillan, 2015), 34.

NOTES TO CHAPTER 5 [311]

95. Leslie Probyn to Viscount [Alfred] Milner, July 8, 1920, CO 318/355, file 37284, TNA.

96. G. B. Haddon-Smith to Viscount [Alfred] Milner, August 13, 1920, CO 318/355, file 45125, TNA.

97. G. B. Haddon-Smith to Viscount [Alfred] Milner, July 31, 1920, CO 318/355, file 43390, TNA; Wilfred Collet to Viscount [Alfred] Milner, August 21, 1920, CO 318/355, file 46334, TNA.

98. "The Decadence of True Patriotism," *Barbados Weekly Herald*, October 18, 1919, 4.

99. On H. H. Cain and the *Belize Independent*, see Peter Ashdown, "The Growth of Black Consciousness in Belize, 1914–1919: The Background to the Ex-Servicemen's Riot of 1919," *Belcast Journal of Belizean Affairs* 2, no. 2 (1985): 4.

100. "Welcome to the Men of our Contingents," *The Belize Independent*, July 16, 1919, vol. 6, no. 279, 3, enclosed in CO 123/296, file 65699, TNA.

101. Patriot, "Our Heroes' Arrival," *The Belize Independent*, July 16, 1919, vol. 6, no. 279, 12, enclosed in CO 123/296, file 65699, TNA.

102. Testimony of Phillip Woods, September 22, 1919, *Report of the Riot Commission*, CO 123/296, file 65699, TNA.

103. Testimony of Phillip Woods, September 22, 1919, *Report of the Riot Commission*, CO 123/296, file 65699, TNA.

104. Testimony of Percy George, September 20, 1919, *Report of the Riot Commission*, CO 123/296, file 65699, TNA.

105. Testimony of Percy George, September 20, 1919, *Report of the Riot Commission*, CO 123/296, file 65699, TNA.

106. Testimony of David Samuel Rowland, September 24, 1919, *Report of the Riot Commission*, CO 123/296, file 65699, TNA.

107. Testimony of James Cran, September 26, 1919, *Report of the Riot Commission*, CO 123/296, file 65699, TNA.

108. Testimony of James Cran, September 26, 1919, *Report of the Riot Commission*, CO 123/296, file 65699, TNA.

109. Testimony of Frederick Hubert Erskine McDonald, September 9, 1919, *Report of the Riot Commission*, CO 123/296, file 65699, TNA.

110. Testimony of Frederick Hubert Erskine McDonald, September 9, 1919, *Report of the Riot Commission*, CO 123/296, file 65699, TNA.

111. "Appendix P: List of Persons Alleged to Have Committed Offenses," *Report of the Riot Commission*, CO 123/296, file 65699, TNA.

112. Testimony of Susan Sutherland, February 5, 1921, Minute Paper 3093–20, Minute Paper Collection, Belize Archives and Records Service, Belomopan (hereafter BA). See also Macpherson, *From Colony to Nation*, 68–69.

113. Historian Peter Ashdown maintains that riotous veterans sabotaged the generator, but witnesses at the Power Station testified that the generator failed due to "a shortage of steam." The official Riot Commission likewise concluded that the power failure was not intentional. Testimony of Herbert Blin Stoyle, September 22, 1919, *Report of the Riot Commission*, CO 123/296, file 65699, TNA; *Summary Report of the Riot Commission*, CO 123/296, file 65699, TNA. BWIR veterans did target one aspect of the colony's infrastructure, however. At 9:15 p.m., veterans urged R. A. Gill,

[312] NOTES TO CHAPTER 5

an operator at the colony's Wireless Station, to "smash the instruments" to prevent outgoing telegrams. Gill, however, refused to comply. Later that evening, another veteran asked Gill to delay any telegrams, but Gill refused once more. *Report of the Riot Commission*, "Appendix E: Attempt to Delay the Sending of a Wireless Message," CO 123/296, file 65699, TNA.

114. Testimony of Henry Melhado, September 22, 1919, *Report of the Riot Commission*, CO 123/296, file 65699, TNA.

115. Testimony of Herbert Blin Stoyle, September 22, 1919, *Report of the Riot Commission*, CO 123/296, file 65699, TNA.

116. Testimony of Henry Melhado, September 22, 1919, *Report of the Riot Commission*, CO 123/296, file 65699, TNA.

117. Testimony of Eyre Hutson, August 27, 1919, *Report of the Riot Commission*, CO 123/296, file 65699, TNA.

118. Testimony of Percy George, September 20, 1919, *Report of the Riot Commission*, CO 123/296, file 65699, TNA.

119. Testimony of Joseph Blades, September 8, 1919, *Report of the Riot Commission*, CO 123/296, file 65699, TNA.

120. Testimony of William Hoar, September 22, 1919, *Report of the Riot Commission*, CO 123/296, file 65699, TNA.

121. Testimony of Duncan Fraser, September 15, 1919, *Report of the Riot Commission*, CO 123/296, file 65699, TNA.

122. Testimony of Percy George, September 20, 1919, *Report of the Riot Commission*, CO 123/296, file 65699, TNA.

123. Testimony of Joseph Clark, September 23, 1919, *Report of the Riot Commission*, CO 123/296, file 65699, TNA.

124. Testimony of Robert Wyatt, September 8, 1919, *Report of the Riot Commission*, CO 123/296, file 65699, TNA.

125. Testimony of Phillip Edwin Matthews, September 8, 1919, *Report of the Riot Commission*, CO 123/296, file 65699, TNA.

126. *Summary Report of the Riot Commission*, CO 123/296, file 65699, TNA.

127. Testimony of Duncan Fraser, September 15, 1919, *Report of the Riot Commission*, CO 123/296, file 65699, TNA.

128. Testimony of Robert Wyatt, September 8, 1919, *Report of the Riot Commission*, CO 123/296, file 65699, TNA.

129. Testimony of Eyre Hutson, August 27, 1919, *Report of the Riot Commission*, CO 123/296, file 65699, TNA.

130. *Summary Report of the Riot Commission*, CO 123/296, file 65699, TNA.

131. *Summary Report of the Riot Commission*, CO 123/296, file 65699, TNA. For additional estimates of the crowd size during the rebellion, see Testimony of Henry Melhado, September 22, 1919, *Report of the Riot Commission*, CO 123/296, file 65699, TNA; Testimony of Lindsay Arthur Jeffery, September 8, 1919, *Report of the Riot Commission*, CO 123/296, file 65699, TNA; Testimony of James Cran, September 26, 1919, *Report of the Riot Commission*, CO 123/296, file 65699, TNA.

132. Eyre Hutson to Gilbert Grindle, July 31, 1919, CO 123/295, TNA.

133. Testimony of Frederick Hubert Erskine McDonald, September 9, 1919, *Report of the Riot Commission*, CO 123/296, file 65699, TNA.

NOTES TO CHAPTER 5   [313]

134. "Exhibit 25: Riot Claims," *Report of the Riot Commission*, CO 123/296, file 65699, TNA; Testimony of Coralie Jane Brown, September 16, 1919, *Report of the Riot Commission*, CO 123/296, file 65699, TNA.

135. Testimony of Eyre Hutson, August 27, 1919, *Report of the Riot Commission*, CO 123/296, file 65699, TNA.

136. Peter Ashdown, "Race Riot, Class Warfare and 'Coup d'état: The Ex-Servicemen's Riot of July 1919," *Belcast Journal of Belizean Affairs* 3, nos. 1 & 2 (1986): 12.

137. Testimony of James Cran, September 26, 1919, *Report of the Riot Commission*, CO 123/296, file 65699, TNA.

138. Eyre Hutson to Viscount [Alfred] Milner, July 30, 1919, CO 123/295, file 108634, quoted in Ashdown, "Race Riot, Class Warfare," 10.

139. Testimony of Frederick Hubert Erskine McDonald, September 9, 1919, *Report of the Riot Commission*, CO 123/296, file 65699, TNA.

140. Appendix B: Letter from G. W. C. Hulse to J. Cran, July 23, 1919, *Report of the Riot Commission*, CO 123/296, TNA.

141. Appendix B: Letter from G. W. C. Hulse to J. Cran, July 23, 1919, *Report of the Riot Commission*, CO 123/296, TNA.

142. Appendix B to Exhibit 3 (Evidence of the Governor): Statement to the Committee of Contingent at Government House, July 24, 1919, *Report of the Riot Commission*, CO 123/296, TNA.

143. Appendix B to Exhibit 3 (Evidence of the Governor): Statement to the Committee of Contingent at Government House, July 24, 1919, *Report of the Riot Commission*, CO 123/296, TNA.

144. Testimony of Samuel Alfred Haynes, September 17, 1919, Report of the Riot Commission, CO 123/296, file 65699, TNA.

145. Testimony of Frederick Hubert Erskine McDonald, September 9, 1919, *Report of the Riot Commission*, CO 123/296, file 65699, TNA.

146. Testimony of Samuel Alfred Haynes, September 17, 1919, Report of the Riot Commission, CO 123/296, file 65699, TNA.

147. Testimony of Samuel Alfred Haynes, September 17, 1919, Report of the Riot Commission, CO 123/296, file 65699, TNA.

148. Testimony of Frederick Hubert Erskine McDonald, September 9, 1919, *Report of the Riot Commission*, CO 123/296, file 65699, TNA.

149. Testimony of Samuel Alfred Haynes, September 17, 1919, Report of the Riot Commission, CO 123/296, file 65699, TNA.

150. Testimony of Frederick Hubert Erskine McDonald, September 9, 1919, *Report of the Riot Commission*, CO 123/296, file 65699, TNA.

151. Testimony of Frederick Hubert Erskine McDonald, September 9, 1919, *Report of the Riot Commission*, CO 123/296, file 65699, TNA.

152. Testimony of Samuel Alfred Haynes, September 17, 1919, Report of the Riot Commission, CO 123/296, file 65699, TNA.

153. "Report of the Commissioners Appointed by the Governor to Inquire into the Cause and Origin of a Disturbance Which Took Place at the C. US Theatre. . . . ," Minute Paper 3547–1919, Minute Paper Collection, Belize Archive (hereafter BA).

154. Macpherson, *From Colony to Nation*, 61–62.

[314] NOTES TO CHAPTER 5

155. "Report of the Commissioners Appointed by the Governor to Inquire into the Cause and Origin of a Disturbance Which Took Place at the C. US Theatre. . . .," Minute Paper 3547–1919, Minute Paper Collection, BA.

156. Testimony of Samuel Alfred Haynes, September 17, 1919, *Report of the Riot Commission*, CO 123/296, file 65699, TNA.

157. Testimony of Samuel Alfred Haynes, September 17, 1919, *Report of the Riot Commission*, CO 123/296, file 65699, TNA.

158. The following BWIR veterans were arrested for their roles in the riot: Private H. Blackwood, Private E. Brooks, Private J. Carillo, Private B. Dalrymple, Private M. Domingo, Private S. Domingo, Private Gaboret, Private W. Grant, Private P. Hamilton, Private T. Hamilton, Private R. W. Hall, Private S. Panting, Corporal C. Sutherland, and Private A. Willocks. For the names of arrested veterans, see Testimony of William Hoar, *Report of the Riot Commission*, September 22, 1919, CO 123/296, file 65699, National Archives of the United Kingdom; Testimony of Frederick Hubert Erskine McDonald, September 9, 1919, *Report of the Riot Commission*, CO 123/296, file 65699, TNA; Macpherson, *From Colony to Nation*, 68–71.

159. Ashdown, "Race Riot, Class Warfare," 11.

160. *Summary Report of the Riot Commission*, CO 123/296, file 65699, TNA.

161. Testimony of George F. Bennett, September 16, 1919, *Report of the Riot Commission*, CO 123/296, file 65699, TNA.

162. Justifying his decision to place Robert Wyatt on a mandatory leave of absence and to relieve him of his post, Hutson wrote: "Mr. Wyatt is slovenly in appearance, is on too intimate terms with the men of the force and he has, in my opinion, neither the education nor standing to command that respect, which is in my opinion, essential, from members of the force and from the general public in Belize. He is slow to act, in fact, he has become 'stale at his job.'" Eyre Hutson to Secretary of State for the Colonies, October 22, 1919, CO 123/296, file 65768, TNA.

163. Testimony of Eyre Hutson, August 27, 1919, *Report of the Riot Commission*, CO 123/296, file 65699, TNA.

164. Eyre Hutson to Secretary of State for the Colonies, October 22, 1919, CO 123/296, file 65768, TNA.

165. Eyre Hutson to Secretary of State for the Colonies, October 30, 1919, CO 123/296, file 66222, TNA.

166. Testimony of William Hoar, September 22, 1919, *Report of the Riot Commission*, CO 123/296, file 65699, TNA. For additional information about Annie Flowers, see Macpherson, *From Colony to Nation*, 29–35, 69–70.

167. British Honduras Contingent Committee to Governor Eyre Hutson, April 22, 1920, Minute Paper Collection 1292–1920, BA.

168. British Honduras Contingent Committee to Governor Eyre Hutson, April 22, 1920, Minute Paper Collection 1292–1920, BA.

169. H. E. Phillips (Acting Colonial Secretary) to S. A. Haynes and the British Honduras Contingent Committee, April 27, 1920, Minute Paper Collection 1292–1920, BA.

170. S. A. Haynes to H. E. Phillips (Acting Colonial Secretary), April 29, 1920, Minute Paper Collection 1292–1920, BA; H. E. Phillips (Acting Colonial Secretary) to S. A. Haynes, May 3, 1920, Minute Paper Collection, BA.

NOTES TO CHAPTER 6 [315]

171. Governor Eyre Hutson to Secretary of State for the Colonies, May 10, 1920, FO 115/2619, TNA.

172. S. A. Haynes, "Through Black Spectacles," *Negro World*, August 13, 1927, 4, 10 (quotations on p. 10).

173. *Belize Independent*, June 18, 1930, quoted in Macpherson, *From Colony to Nation*, 33.

Chapter Six: "Equal Reward for Equal Service"

Epigraph 1: "Discharged Soldiers," *Argos*, May 22, 1919, 2.

Epigraph 2: "Threefold Folly," *Port of Spain Gazette*, July 29, 1919, 13.

1. Returned Soldiers' and Sailors' Council to Colonial Secretary, July 25, 1919, CSO Papers, File Folder 4623/1919, Box 4026–4967 (1919), National Archives of Trinidad and Tobago (hereafter NATT); Returned Soldiers' and Sailors' Council to Colonial Secretary, August 1, 1919, CSO Papers, File Folder 4623/1919, Box 4026–4967 (1919), NATT.

2. Returned Soldiers' and Sailors' Council to Colonial Secretary, July 25, 1919, CSO Papers, File Folder 4623/1919, Box 4026–4967 (1919), NATT.

3. The motto and cable address of the RSSC were printed on the council's official letterhead. See, for example, Returned Soldiers' and Sailors' Council to Colonial Secretary, August 1, 1919, CSO Papers, File Folder 4623/1919, Box 4026–4967 (1919), NATT.

4. "Returned Soldiers and Sailors Council," *Argos*, July 30, 1919, 8; "Returned Soldiers," *Argos*, August 19, 1919, 7.

5. "Returned Soldiers and Sailors Council," *Argos*, July 30, 1919, 8.

6. The Jamaica Ex-Service Men Association, founded in December 1922, was subsequently renamed as the Jamaica Old Comrades Association.

7. Michael Joseph, "First World War Veterans and the State in the French and British Caribbean, 1919–1939," *First World War Studies* 10, no. 1 (2019): 14, note 4.

8. "West Indian War Veterans Organize," *New York Amsterdam News*, February 1, 1928, 4. Sometime in the 1940s, the group changed its name to The British West Indies War Veterans, Incorporated. For accounts of the group's activities in the 1950s, see "Sir Francis Evans is Patron of Veterans' Ball," *New York Amsterdam News*, October 14, 1950, 20; "BWI War Veterans Association to Hold Memorial Services, Church of Crucifixion," *New York Amsterdam News*, May 19, 1951, 29.

9. For a list of officers in the ladies' auxiliary, see British West Indies War Veterans to Antigua Barbuda Progressive Society, undated letter (c.1955), Antigua Barbuda Progressive Society Records, Box 2, Folder 3, Manuscripts, Archives and Rare Books Division, Schomburg Center for Research in Black Culture, New York, NY. See also, "Conversation with a Queen," *New York Amsterdam News, November 9, 1957*, 8.

10. "West Indian War Veterans Organize," *New York Amsterdam News*, February 1, 1928, 4.

11. "In Defence of the Soldiers," *Argos*, September 29, 1919, 5.

12. Kelvin Singh, *Race and Class Struggles in a Colonial State: Trinidad 1917–1945* (Calgary: University of Calgary Press, 1994), 23.

13. "Discharged Soldiers," *Argos*, May 22, 1919, 2.

[316] NOTES TO CHAPTER 6

14. "Our Returned Soldiers," *Argos*, May 14, 1919, 11.

15. "Discharged Soldiers," *Argos*, May 22, 1919, 2.

16. The Discharged Soldiers Central Authority was established on August 16, 1917. "Discharged Soldiers," *Trinidad and Tobago Council Paper No. 3 of 1918* (Port of Spain: Government Printing Office, 1918), 2.

17. Michael Anthony, "Huggins, [Sir] George F. (1870–1941," in *Historical Dictionary of Trinidad and Tobago*, (Lanham, MD: Scarecrow Press, 1997), 292–93.

18. For the membership of the Discharged Soldiers Central Authority, see "Discharged Soldiers"; C. B. Franklin, *The Trinidad and Tobago Year Book* (Port of Spain: Franklin's Electric Printery, 1920), 196.

19. "Discharged Soldiers," 8.

20. "Discharged Soldiers," 5.

21. "Discharged Soldiers," 3.

22. "Discharged Soldier Central Authority: To Employers," *Port of Spain Gazette*, February 19, 1919, 6. See also, "Discharged Soldier Central Authority: To Employers," *Port of Spain Gazette*, February 20, 1919, 11; "Discharged Soldier Central Authority: To Employers," *Port of Spain Gazette*, February 22, 1919, 11; "Discharged Soldier Central Authority: To Employers," *Port of Spain Gazette*, March 1, 1919, 6.

23. "Discharged Soldiers Central Authority, Employment Committee Report," August 19, 1919, CSO Papers, File Folder 4623/1919, Box 4026–4967 (1919), NATT.

24. "The Discharged Soldier in Trinidad," *Trinidad Guardian*, reprinted in *Jamaica Times*, June 14, 1919, 7.

25. On the DSCA, see "The Case of Mr. T. B. Jackson," *Argos*, June 24, 1919, 5.

26. "A Soldier's Pathetic Plea," *Argos*, June 14, 1919, 2.

27. "The Returned Soldiers," *Argos*, July 8, 1919, 5.

28. "Returned Soldiers Seeking Employment in Venezuela," *Argos*, September 27, 1919, 5. On British Caribbean migration from Trinidad to Venezuela, see Lara Putnam, *Radical Moves*, 23–32.

29. "Discharged Soldiers Central Authority, Employment Committee Report," August 19, 1919, CSO Papers, File Folder 4623/1919, Box 4026–4967 (1919), NATT.

30. Irma Watkins-Owens, *Blood Relations: Caribbean Immigrants and the Harlem Community, 1900–1930* (Bloomington: Indiana University Press, 1996); Lara Putnam, "Provincializing Harlem: The 'Negro Metropolis' as Northern Frontier of a Connected Caribbean," *Modernism/Modernity* 20, no. 3 (2013): 469–84.

31. "Unemployed Men in New York," *Port of Spain Gazette*, December 14, 1919, 11.

32. "Land Settlement Scheme," June 14, 1917, CSO Papers, File Folder 4623/1919, Box 4026–4967 (1919), NATT; "Important to Returned Soldiers," *Port of Spain Gazette*, July 2, 1919, 10.

33. "The Land Settlement Scheme," *Argos*, July 9, 1919, 2.

34. John McNish Weiss, *The Merikens: Free Black American Settlers in Trinidad 1815–16* (London: McNish & Weiss, 2002); Gerald Horne, *Negro Comrades of the Crown: African Americans and the British Empire Fight the U.S. Before Emancipation* (New York, NY: NYU Press, 2013), 197–216; Rashauna Johnson, *Slavery's Metropolis: Unfree Labor in New Orleans During the Age of Revolutions* (New York: Cambridge University Press, 2016), 162–202.

NOTES TO CHAPTER 6 [317]

35. "The Land Settlement Scheme," *Argos*, July 9, 1919, 2.

36. Edwin Harper, "Lest We Forget," *Argos*, September 1, 1919, 4.

37. On World War I colonial veterans' claims of a "blood debt," see Jennifer Anne Boittin, *Colonial Metropolis: The Urban Grounds of Anti-Imperialism and Feminism in Interwar Paris* (Lincoln: University of Nebraska Press, 2010), 78–79; Gregory Mann, *Native Sons: West African Veterans and France in the Twentieth Century* (Durham, NC: Duke University Press, 2006), 183–209; David Murphy, "Race and the Legacy of the First World War in French Anti-Colonial Politics of the 1920s," in *Minorities and the First World War: From War to Peace*, ed. Hannah Ewence and Tim Grady (London: Palgrave Macmillan, 2017), 201–26.

38. Edwin Harper, "Lest We Forget," *Argos*, September 1, 1919, 4.

39. "The Land Settlement Scheme," *Argos*, July 9, 1919, 2.

40. "The Land Settlement Scheme," *Argos*, July 9, 1919, 2.

41. A. L., "The Land Settlement Scheme," *Argos*, July 12, 1919, 11.

42. "The Land Settlement Scheme," *Argos*, July 16, 1919, 11.

43. "Discharged Soldiers Visit Colonial Secretary," *Argos*, June 18, 1919, 9.

44. B. W. I. Deputation to Colonial Secretary of Trinidad and Tobago, July 3, 1919, CSO Papers, File Folder 4278/1919, Box 4026–4967 (1919), NATT; "Returned Soldiers Petition the Government," *Argos*, July 24, 1919, 3.

45. "Grave Discontent," *Argos*, July 12, 1919, 2.

46. Confidential Memo by Maxwell Smith, July 16, 1919, CSO Papers, File Folder 4623/1919, Box 4026–4967 (1919), NATT.

47. The title for this section is from "Last Monday's Disorderly Scene," *Port of Spain Gazette*, July 23, 1919, 3.

48. "Military Parade for the 'Peace Celebrations,'" *Port of Spain Gazette*, July 15, 1919, 8;[1] G. H. May, "Report by the Inspector General of the Constabulary," in W. M. Gordon (Acting Governor) to Viscount Milner, July 29, 1919, CO 295/521, file 50053, TNA.

49. G. H. May, "Report by the Inspector General of the Constabulary," in W. M. Gordon (Acting Governor) to Viscount Milner, July 29, 1919, CO 295/521, file 50053, TNA.

50. "Last Monday's Disorderly Scenes," *Port of Spain Gazette* July 23, 1919, 3; "Fate of 'Peace Day' Rioters," *Port of Spain Gazette*, July 26, 1919, 7; G. H. May, "Report by the Inspector General of the Constabulary," in W. M. Gordon (Acting Governor) to Viscount Milner, July 29, 1919, CO 295/521, file 50053, TNA.

51. G. H. May, "Report by the Inspector General of the Constabulary," in W. M. Gordon (Acting Governor) to Viscount Milner, July 29, 1919, CO 295/521, file 50053, TNA. On the anti-black race riots in England in 1919, see David Featherstone, "Politicizing In/Security, Transnational Resistance, and the 1919 Riots in Cardiff and Liverpool," *Small Axe* 22, no.3 (2018): 56–67; Jacqueline Jenkinson, *Black 1919: Riots, Racism and Resistance in Imperial Britain* (Liverpool: Liverpool University Press, 2009); Stephen Bourne, *Black Poppies: Britain's Black Community and the Great War* (History Press, 2014), 121–62. For coverage of the race riots in England in the Trinidadian press, see "Race Riots in Liverpool," *Argos*, July 9, 1919, 7; "Race Riots in England," *Argos*, July 17, 1919, 5.

52. "Last Monday's Disorderly Scenes," *Port of Spain Gazette* July 23, 1919, 3.

[318] NOTES TO CHAPTER 6

53. "'Peace Day' Rioters in Court," *Port of Spain Gazette*, July 25, 1919, 7. See also, "Fate of 'Peace Day' Rioters," *Port of Spain Gazette*, July 26, 1919, 7–8.

54. "'Peace Day' Rioters in Court," *Port of Spain Gazette*, July 25, 1919, 7; "Fate of 'Peace Day' Rioters," *Port of Spain Gazette*, July 26, 1919, 7–8. On the role of boys and women in the melee, see "Last Monday's Disorderly Scenes," *Port of Spain Gazette*, July 23, 1919, 3.

55. "Fate of 'Peace Day' Rioters," *Port of Spain Gazette*, July 26, 1919, 8.

56. "Riotous End to Peace Rejoicings," *Trinidad Guardian*, July 23, 1919, 8.

57. G. H. May, "Report by the Inspector General of the Constabulary," in W. M. Gordon (Acting Governor) to Viscount Milner, July 29, 1919, CO 295/521, file 50053, TNA.

58. Eyre Hutson to Secretary of State for the Colonies, October 22, 1919, CO 123/296, file 65768, TNA.

59. Herbert T. Thomas, *The Story of a West Indian Policeman or Forty-seven Years in the Jamaica Constabulary* (Kingston, Jamaica: Gleaner, 1927), 26.

60. Capt. Percey L. Fraser, *Looking Over My Shoulder: Forty-Seven Years a Public Servant, 1885–1932* (San Juan: Lexicon Trinidad, 2007), 8.

61. "Riotous End to Peace Rejoicings," *Trinidad Guardian*, July 23, 1919, 8; "Threefold Folly," *Port of Spain Gazette*, July 29, 1919, 13.

62. "Threefold Folly," *Port of Spain Gazette*, July 29, 1919, 13.

63. "Threefold Folly," *Port of Spain Gazette*, July 29, 1919, 13.

64. G. F. Huggins, C. de Verteuil, J. A. Bell Smythe, A. S. Bowen, A. H. McClean, and H. H. Pasea to the Colony Secretary, July 30, 1919, in W. M. Gordon (Acting Governor) to Viscount Milner, July 29, 1919, CO 295/522, file 50053, TNA.

65. G. F. Huggins, C. de Verteuil, J. A. Bell Smythe, A. S. Bowen, A. H. McClean, and H. H. Pasea to the Colony Secretary, July 30, 1919, in W.M. Gordon (Acting Governor) to Viscount Milner, July 29, 1919, CO 295/522, file 50053, TNA.

66. G. F. Huggins, C. de Verteuil, J. A. Bell Smythe, A. S. Bowen, A. H. McClean, and H. H. Pasea to the Colony Secretary, July 30, 1919, in W. M. Gordon (Acting Governor) to Viscount Milner, July 29, 1919, CO 295/522, file 50053, TNA.

67. G. H. May to Colonial Secretary, August 5, 1919, in W. M. Gordon to Viscount Milner, August 7, 1919, CO 295/522, file 50042, TNA.

68. W. M. Gordon to Viscount Milner, August 7, 1919, CO 295/522, file 50042, TNA.

69. "Threefold Folly," *Port of Spain Gazette*, July 29, 1919, 13. See, for example, Tony Martin, "Revolutionary Upheaval in Trinidad, 1919: Views from British and American Sources," *Journal of Negro History* 58, no. 3 (1973): 313–26.

70. "A Returned Soldier's View," *Port of Spain Gazette*, July 24, 1919, 7.

71. For witness statements about the number of participants, see "Fate of 'Peace Day' Rioters," *Port of Spain Gazette*, July 26, 1919, 7.

72. During the criminal trial, Inspector Matthew Costellos noted that there were "four other cases for similar offenses against the defendants," but he ultimately withdrew them. See "Fate of 'Peace Day' Rioters," *Port of Spain Gazette*, July 26, 1919, 8.

73. "Fate of 'Peace Day' Rioters," *Port of Spain Gazette*, July 26, 1919, 7–8; "Ruffians Convicted," *Trinidad Guardian*, July 26, 1919, 12.

NOTES TO CHAPTER 6 [319]

74. "Last Monday's Disorderly Scenes," *Port of Spain Gazette* July 23, 1919, 3; "Riotous End to Peace Rejoicings," *Trinidad Guardian*, July 23, 1919, 8.

75. Acting Colonial Secretary to the British West Indies Deputation, July 22, 1919, CSO Papers, File Folder 4623/1919, Box 4026–4967 (1919), NATT; Acting Colonial Secretary to Acting Receiver General, July 29, 1919, CSO Papers, File Folder 4623/1919, Box 4026–4967 (1919), NATT.

76. W. M. Gordon to Viscount Milner, August 12, 1919, CSO Papers, File Folder 4623/1919, Box 4026–4967 (1919), NATT.

77. B. B. Cubitt to Under Secretary of State, Colonial Office, October 14, 1919, File Folder 4278/1919, Box 4026–4967 (1919), NATT.

78. Milner to J. R. Chancellor, November 21, 1919, CSO Papers, File Folder 4278/1919, Box 4026–4967 (1919), NATT.

79. Returned Soldiers' and Sailors' Council to Colonial Secretary, July 25, 1919, CSO Papers, File Folder 4623/1919, Box 4026–4967 (1919), NATT; Returned Soldiers' and Sailors' Council to Colonial Secretary, August 1, 1919, CSO Papers, File Folder 4623/1919, Box 4026–4967 (1919), NATT.

80. Algernon Burkett to T. A. V. Best, October 20, 1919, CSO Papers, File Folder 4623/1919, Box 4026–4967 (1919), NATT.

81. Algernon Burkett, *Trinidad: A Jewel of the West, Or, 100 Years of British Rule* (London: Francis, 1914), n. p.

82. Algernon Burkett to Acting Governor, August 28, 1919, CSO Papers, File Folder 4623/1919, Box 4026–4967 (1919), NATT. For coverage of Burkett's military recruiting activities, see "Mr. Burkett in Barbados," *Port of Spain Gazette*, September 22, 1915, 9; "Mr. Algernon Burkett at Barbados," *Port of Spain Gazette*, February 12, 1916, 5; C. L. R. James, *The Life of Captain Cipriani: An Account of the British Government in the West Indies* (Nelson, Lancashire: Coulton, 1932), 22.

83. Algernon Burkett to T. A. V. Best, October 20, 1919, CSO Papers, File Folder 4623/1919, Box 4026–4967 (1919), NATT.

84. Algernon Burkett to T. A. V. Best, October 20, 1919, CSO Papers, File Folder 4623/1919, Box 4026–4967 (1919), NATT.

85. Algernon Burkett to Acting Governor, August 28, 1919, CSO Papers, File Folder 4623/1919, Box 4026–4967 (1919), NATT.

86. "The Land Settlement Scheme," *Argos*, September 24, 1919, 6.

87. "Algernon Burkett Before City Magistrate," *Port of Spain Gazette*, September 8, 1917, 9.

88. "Algernon A. Burkett as Known by the Police," July 4, 1921, CSO Papers, File Folder 14/1921, Box 3–988 (1921), NATT.

89. "Algernon A. Burkett as Known by the Police," July 4, 1921, CSO Papers, File Folder 14/1921, Box 3–988 (1921), NATT.

90. "Algernon A. Burkett as Known by the Police," CSO Papers, File Folder 14/1921, Box 3–988 (1921), NATT. See also, "Algernon Burkett Before City Magistrate," *Port of Spain Gazette*, September 8, 1917, 9; "Mr. Burkett Petitions Governor," *Argos*, September 24, 1917, 2; "Burkett before the Beak," *Port of Spain Gazette*, March 27, 1919, 7; "Burkett Made to Pay," *Port of Spain Gazette*, March 28, 1919, 5.

91. "Returned Soldiers and Sailors," *Trinidad Guardian*, August 16, 1919, 11; "Returned Soldiers Meeting," *Port of Spain Gazette*, August 16, 1919, 8.

[320] NOTES TO CHAPTER 6

92. "Big Soldiers' Meeting," *Argos*, August 5, 1919, 7.

93. "Returned Soldiers and Sailors," *Trinidad Guardian*, August 16, 1919, 11.

94. "Returned Soldiers and Sailors," *Trinidad Guardian*, August 16, 1919, 11.

95. "Captain Cipriani's Stirring Reply," *Trinidad Guardian*, August 23, 1919, 7.

96. "Meeting of Returned Soldiers," *Trinidad Guardian*, September 7, 1919, 9.

97. "Meeting of Returned Soldiers," *Trinidad Guardian*, September 7, 1919, 9.

98. "Meeting of Returned Soldiers," *Trinidad Guardian*, September 7, 1919, 9.

99. "Meeting of Returned Soldiers," *Trinidad Guardian*, September 7, 1919, 9.

100. "A Clarion Call," *Argos*, September 8, 1919, 5.

101. "Mr. Bruce McConney on Captain Cipriani," *Argos*, September 13, 1919, 5.

102. "Mr. Bruce McConney on Captain Cipriani," *Argos*, September 17, 1919, 6.

103. "Mr. Bruce McConney on Captain Cipriani," *Argos*, September 17, 1919, 6.

104. "Mr. Bruce McConney on Captain Cipriani," *Argos*, September 13, 1919, 5.

105. "Items of News," *Port of Spain Gazette*, September 13, 1919, 4.

106. J. R. Chancellor to the Governor of Jamaica, November 25, 1919, CSO Papers, File Folder 4623/1919, Box 4026–4967 (1919), NATT.

107. L. Milner-Jones to Colonial Secretary, August 22, 1919, CSO Papers, File Folder 4623/1919, Box 4026–4967 (1919), NATT.

108. Typed file folio memo (#15), DSCA Secretary to Acting Colonial Secretary, August 20, 1919, CSO Papers, File Folder 4623/1919, Box 4026–4967 (1919) NATT.

109. Acting Colonial Secretary to Algernon A. Burkett, August 29, 1919, CSO Papers, File Folder 4623/1919, Box 4026–4967 (1919) NATT.

110. Algernon Burkett to T. A. V. Best, October 20, 1919, CSO Papers, File Folder 4623/1919, Box 4026–4967 (1919), NATT; Acting Colonial Secretary to A. Burkett, October 25, 1919, CSO Papers, File Folder 4623/1919, Box 4026–4967 (1919), NATT.

111. Algernon Burkett to Colonial Secretary, September 1, 1919, CSO Papers, File Folder 4623/1919, Box 4026–4967 (1919) NATT.

112. Algernon Burkett to Acting Governor, August 28, 1919, CSO Papers, File Folder 4623/1919 Box 4026–4967 (1919), NATT.

113. "The West Indian Abroad," *Argos*, September 16, 1919, 6.

114. Singh, *Race and Class Struggles*, 18.

115. Lara Putnam, "Citizenship from the Margins: Vernacular Theories of Rights and the State from the Interwar Caribbean," *Journal of British Studies* 53, no.1 (2014): 164.

116. Algernon Burkett to T. A. V. Best (Acting Governor), October 20, 1919, CSO Papers, File Folder 4623/1919, Box 4026–4967 (1919), NATT.

117. For discussions of Afro-Caribbeans' use of petitions as a form of advocacy and protest, see Daniel Carpenter, *Democracy by Petition: Popular Politics in Transformation, 1790–1870* (Cambridge, MA: Harvard University Press, 2021), 164–200; Thomas Holt, *The Problem of Freedom: Race, Labor, and Politics in Jamaica and Britain, 1832–1938* (Baltimore: Johns Hopkins University Press, 1992); Jorge L. Giovannetti-Torres, *Black British Migrants in Cuba: Race, Labor, and Empire in the Twentieth-Century Caribbean, 1898–1948* (New York: Cambridge University Press, 2018).

118. "The Soldiers' Council," *Argos*, September 4, 1919, 6.

119. Returned Soldiers' and Sailors' Council to the War Office, September 1, 1919, CO 318/350, TNA.

NOTES TO CHAPTER 6 [321]

120. Bridget Brereton, introduction to James, *The Life of Captain Cipriani*.

121. Algernon Burkett to the Editor of the Jamaica *Gleaner*, September 20, 1919, CSO Papers, File Folder 4623/1919, Box 4026–4967 (1919), NATT.

122. Algernon Burkett to the Editor of the Jamaica *Gleaner*, September 20, 1919, CSO Papers, File Folder 4623/1919, Box 4026–4967 (1919), NATT.

123. M. de Cordova to Acting Colonial Secretary, October 16, 1919, CSO Papers, File Folder 4623/1919, Box 4026–4967 (1919), NATT; Acting Governor (Jamaica) to John R. Chancellor, October 21, 1919, CSO Papers, File Folder 4623/1919, Box 4026–4967 (1919), NATT.

124. J. R. Chancellor to the Governor of Jamaica, November 25, 1919, CSO Papers, File Folder 4278/1919, Box 4026–4967 (1919), NATT.

125. J. R. Chancellor to the Governor of Jamaica, November 25, 1919, CSO Papers, File Folder 4278/1919, Box 4026–4967 (1919), NATT.

126. Returned Soldiers' and Sailors' Council to the War Office, September 1, 1919, CO 318/350, TNA.

127. Algernon A. Burkett, "Advice to Returned Soldiers," *Argos*, October 1, 1919, 7.

128. Algernon A. Burkett, "Advice to Returned Soldiers," *Argos*, October 1, 1919, 7.

129. "The Aftermath," *Port of Spain Gazette*, October 12, 1919, 8.

130. "The Discharged Soldiers Problem," *Trinidad Guardian*, September 21, 1919, 6.

131. "The Discharged Soldiers Problem," *Trinidad Guardian*, September 21, 1919, 6.

132. "City Magistrate's Court," *Port of Spain Gazette*, July 3, 1919, 2.

133. "City Magistrate's Court," *Port of Spain Gazette*, July 3, 1919, 2.

134. "Causing an Obstruction," *Port of Spain Gazette*, July 26, 1919, 7.

135. "Items of News," *Port of Spain Gazette*, October 30, 1919, 4.

136. "Items of News," *Port of Spain Gazette*, October 31, 1919, 4.

137. "Items of News," *Port of Spain Gazette*, November 1, 1919, 4. See also, "Action for Assault and False Imprisonment," *Port of Spain Gazette*, November 15, 1919, 10.

138. The title for this section is from David Headley, *Monographic Labour Review*, no. 1 (1921), cited in Singh, *Race and Class Struggles*, 23.

139. "Governor Chancellor Receives Deputation of Returned Soldiers," *Argos*, November 13, 1919; "Returned Soldiers," *Trinidad Guardian*, November 13, 1919, 14.

140. "Governor Chancellor Receives Deputation of Returned Soldiers," *Argos*, November 13, 1919.

141. Under Crown colony rule, Trinidad's Executive Council was comprised of five to six official members of the Legislative Council, all of whom held key positions in the colonial administration, and one unofficial member of the Legislative Council, who was not employed in the colonial administration. Every member of the Executive Council was nominated. See William H. Mercer and A. E. Collins, eds., *The Colonial Office List for 1919: Comprising Historical and Statistical Information Respecting the Colonial Dependencies of Great Britain* (London: Waterlow & Sons, 1919), 399.

142. J. R. Chancellor to Viscount Milner, December 3, 1920, CSO Papers, File Folder 3309/1920, Box 3130–3987 (1920), NATT.

143. "Before the Executive Council," November 13, 1919, CSO Papers, File Folder 4623/1919 Box 4026–4967 (1919), NATT.

[322] NOTES TO CHAPTER 6

144. "Legislative Council," *Port of Spain Gazette*, November 15, 1919, 9.

145. Singh, *Race and Class Struggles*, 23; Brinsley Samaroo and Cherita Girvan, "The Trinidad Workingmen's Association and the Origins of Popular Protest in a Crown Colony," *Social and Economic Studies* 21, no. 2 (1972): 213–15. On the 1919 strikes in Trinidad, see also Adam Ewing, "Caribbean Labour Politics in the Age of Garvey, 1918–1938," *Race & Class* 55, no.1 (2013): 23–45; Christian Høgsbjerg, "'Whenever Society Is in Travail Liberty is Born': The Mass Strike of 1919 in Colonial Trinidad," in *The Internationalisation of the Labour Question: Ideological Antagonism, Workers' Movements and the ILO Since 1919*, ed. Holger Weiss and Stefano Bellucci (Springer International Publishing, 2019), 215–34; Jerome Teelucksingh, *Labour and the Decolonization Struggle in Trinidad and Tobago* (New York: Palgrave Macmillan, 2015), 32–37.

146. Singh, *Race and Class Struggles*, 27.

147. Singh, *Race and Class Struggles*, 25.

148. Singh, *Race and Class Struggles*, 26–7.

149. Singh, *Race and Class Struggles*, 27.

150. "Mr. Burkett's Advice to Strikers," *Argos*, November 18, 1919, 7.

151. "Items of News," *Port of Spain Gazette*, November 20, 1919, 4.

152. "Strikitis in the City," *Argos*, November 21, 1919, 5.

153. "The Government & Returned Soldiers," *Argos*, November 26, 1919, 7; "Deputations to the Governor," *Port of Spain Gazette*, November 27, 1919, 3.

154. The three members of the steering committee invited to the meeting were Emanuel Billouin, Victor Dyall, and Joseph Wood. CSO Papers, File Folder 4623/1919, Box 4026–4967 (1919), NATT.

155. "The Government & Returned Soldiers," *Argos*, November 26, 1919, 7; "Statement by Governor to the Returned Soldiers," November 25, 1919, CSO Papers, File Folder 4623/1919, Box 4026–4967 (1919), NATT.

156. "The Government and Returned Soldiers," *Argos*, November 26, 1919, 7; "Trinidad and Tobago Discharged Soldier Central Authority," Council Paper 59 of 1920, CO 298/115, TNA.

157. For the conversion rate of Trinidadian dollars to British pounds sterling, see Franklin, *The Trinidad and Tobago Year Book*, 155.

158. "The Government and Returned Soldiers," *Argos*, November 26, 1919, 7; "Trinidad and Tobago Discharged Soldier Central Authority," Council Paper 59 of 1920, CO 298/115, TNA.

159. Singh, *Race and Class Struggles*, 20.

160. Algernon Burkett, "A Matter of Public Interest," *Argos*, November 28, 1919, 7.

161. "Reward for Soldiers," *Argos,* December 2, 1919, 7.

162. "Reward for Soldiers," *Argos*, December 2, 1919, 7.

163. "Redeeming a Promise," *Argos*, December 16, 1919, 5.

164. "Redeeming a Promise," *Argos*, December 16, 1919, 5.

165. "Returned Soldiers Draw Their First $12," *Argos,* December 5, 1919, 7.

166. "The Principle of Giving," *Argos*, December 22, 1919.

167. "A Returned Soldier's Complaint," *Trinidad Guardian*, December 7, 1919, 9.

168. J. R. Chancellor to Viscount Milner, December 22, 1919, CSO Papers, File Folder 4623/1919, Box 4026–4967 (1919), NATT.

NOTES TO EPILOGUE [323]

169. J. R. Chancellor to Viscount Milner, December 22, 1919, CSO Papers, File Folder 4623/1919, Box 4026–4967 (1919), NATT.

170. J. R. Chancellor to Viscount Milner, December 22, 1919, CSO Papers, File Folder 4623/1919, Box 4026–4967 (1919), NATT.

171. J. R. Chancellor to Viscount Milner, December 22, 1919, CSO Papers, File Folder 4623/1919, Box 4026–4967 (1919), NATT.

172. "Sir John Chancellor and Returned Soldiers," *Argos*, December 24, 1919.

173. Returned Soldiers' and Sailors' Council to Secretary of State for the Colonies, May 21, 1929, CO 295/566/14, TNA.

174. "Algernon A. Burkett as Known by the Police," July 4, 1921, CSO Papers, File Folder 14/1921, Box 3–988 (1921), NATT.

175. Acting Governor (Trinidad and Tobago) to W. G. A. Ormsby-Gore, July 10, 1936, CO 295/591/5, TNA.

176. Sahadeo Basdeo, *Labour Organisation and Labour Reform in Trinidad, 1919–1939* (St. Augustine, Trinidad: Institute for Social and Economic Research, 1983), 46.

Epilogue

1. "Unveiling and Dedication of Jamaica's War Memorial, 11th November 1922," Manuscripts and Special Collections, National Library of Jamaica, Kingston.

2. According to the *Daily Gleaner*, "thousands of people who had no invitations" to the unveiling ceremony had "seized every available vantage point" near the memorial by the time the ceremony commenced. Police and military guards were dispatched to keep "the uninvited" at a "prescribed distance" from monument. "Island's War Memorial Unveiled & Dedicated: Imposing Ceremony," *Daily Gleaner*, November 13, 1922, 3.

3. "Unveiling and Dedication of Jamaica's War Memorial, 11th November 1922," Manuscripts and Special Collections, National Library of Jamaica.

4. "Lest We Forget," *Daily Gleaner*, November 13, 1922, 8.

5. "Lest We Forget," *The Labour Leader*, November 11, 1922, n.p. The editors of the *Labour Leader* reiterated this argument two years later when the Trinidad War Memorial was unveiled. "The Paths of Glory," *Labour Leader*, June 28, 1924, 4.

6. "The Paths of Glory," *Labour Leader*, June 28, 1924, 4.

7. "The Paths of Glory," *Labour Leader*, June 28, 1924, 4.

8. Ernest E. Mair, "Hypocrisy," *Negro World*, July 29, 1922, 6.

9. Mair, "Hypocrisy," 6.

10. Arthur A. Cipriani, "Why We Fought," *Labour Leader*, June 28, 1924, 5.

11. "The Quality of Mercy," *Daily Gleaner*, August 28, 1920, 8.

12. "All But Two of the British West Indies Regiment Men Who Were in the Penitentiary Have Been Pardoned," *Daily Gleaner*, October 23, 1920, 1.

13. "All But Two of the British West Indies Regiment Men Who Were in the Penitentiary Have Been Pardoned," *Daily Gleaner*, October 23, 1920, 1.

14. "Captain Cipriani's Stirring Reply," *Trinidad Guardian*, August 23, 1919, 7.

15. Frank Cundall, *Handbook of Jamaica for 1926* (Kingston, Jamaica: Government Printing Office, 1926), 617.

[324] NOTES TO EPILOGUE

16. "West Indian War Veterans Organize," *New York Amsterdam News*, February 1, 1928, 4.

17. For an overview of the economic support provided to BWIR veterans in Jamaica, see Cundall, *Handbook of Jamaica for 1926, 616*; A. S. Jelf to C. H. Eastwood, William Bennett, et. al., February 15, 1933, enclosed in C. A. L. Cliffe to I. Powell, PIN 15/1772, The National Archives (hereafter TNA), Kew, England. On the local effort to provide aid to veterans in Jamaica in the interwar years, see also Richard Smith, "'Heaven Grant You Strength to Fight the Battle for Your Race': Nationalism, Pan-Africanism and Jamaican Memory," in *Race, Empire and First World War Writing*, ed. Santanu Das (New York: Cambridge University Press, 2011), 272; Michael Joseph, "First World War Veterans and the State in the French and British Caribbean, 1919–1939," *First World War Studies* 10, no. 1 (2019): 38–43.

18. William Bennett, C. H. Eastwood, et. al. to R. E. Stubbs, October 19, 1932, PIN 15/1772, TNA.

19. "Detective Corporal's report to the Detective Inspector on Ex-British West Indies Regiment Association's March of 17 May 1933," May 18, 1933, 1B/5/79/672, Jamaica Archives (hereafter JA), Spanish Town; "Case of the Ex-Soldiers of the BWI Regiment Debated in Council," *Daily Gleaner*, May 19, 1933, 6; "Ex-Service B.W.I.R. Men," *Daily Gleaner*, May 19, 1933, 12.

20. D. S. Wynter to the Secretary of the West India Committee, May 16, 1934, PIN 15/1772, TNA.

21. Before 1925, all members of the Legislative Council in Trinidad were nominated rather than elected. Following the elections in February 1925, the Legislative Council added seven elected members based on a restricted franchise. The other eighteen members of the Legislative Council were nominated by the governor or held senior positions in the colonial administration. Jerome Teelucksingh, *Labour and the Decolonization Struggle in Trinidad and Tobago* (New York: Palgrave Macmillan, 2015), 83.

22. D. Wells, "An Ex-Soldier's Appeal," *Labour Leader*, December 20, 1924, 14; "Representative Government: A Voice from the U.S.A," *Labour Leader*, November 12, 1924, 6–7.

23. Selwyn D. Ryan, *Race and Nationalism in Trinidad and Tobago: A Study of Decolonization in a Multiracial Society* (Toronto: University of Toronto Press, 1972), 34.

24. On Cipriani's political activism during the interwar years, see Gordon K. Lewis, *The Growth of the Modern West Indies* (New York: Monthly Review Press, 1968), 203–7; Ryan, *Race and Nationalism*, 35–43; Teelucksingh, *Labour and the Decolonization Struggle*.

25. Lewis, *Growth of the Modern West Indies*, 206.

26. For descriptions of some of these gatherings, see "War Veterans to Hold Flag Ceremony Sunday," *New York Amsterdam News*, April 11, 1928, 10; "Treat to Men who Served in World War," *Daily Gleaner*, December 29, 1932, 17; "Ex-Service Men Hold Meeting on Race Course," *Daily Gleaner*, January 10, 1933, 15; "News from Abroad: War Vets Organize to Win Preferences," *New York Amsterdam News*, February 20, 1937, 11; "Dead Veterans Given Homage at Abyssinian," *New York Amsterdam News*, November 13, 1937, 23; "Ex-B.W.I.R. Assn.," *Daily Gleaner*, May 2, 1941, 5.

NOTES TO EPILOGUE [325]

27. Peter Lennon, "Dishonoured legion," *Guardian, October 6, 1999,* https://www
.theguardian.com/theguardian/1999/oct/07/features11.g23; Marc Goodman and V.
Rushton, "A Jamaica Past, Being a Glimpse into History's Bloodiest Battlefield: A
Visit with Jamaica's Last Surviving World War I Veteran," *Jamaican Historical Society Bulletin* 11, no. 3 (1999/2000): 52–57; Simon Rogers, "There were no parades for
us," Special Report: The Military: Soldiers of the Empire, *Guardian,* November 6,
2002, http://www.guardian.co.uk/military/story/0,,834475,00.html.

28. Rogers, "There were no parades for us."

29. In some interviews and news articles, Eugent Clarke's name is listed as "Ugent
Clark." Goodman and Rushton, "A Jamaica Past," 52–57; "Requiem for Ugent Clark,"
Daily Gleaner, June 15, 2002, A4. However, his name is recorded as "Eugent Clarke"
in military records. "Medal Card of Clarke, Eugent," WO 372/4/140499, TNA.

BIBLIOGRAPHY

Primary Sources

Archives and Museums Consulted

BARBADOS

Barbados Department of Archives, Black Rock
National Library Service Main Library (Bridgetown Public Library), Bridgetown

BELIZE

Belize Archives and Records Service, Belomopan

JAMAICA

Jamaica Archives, Jamaica Archives and Records Unit, Spanish Town
Jamaica Military Museum and Library, Kingston
National Library of Jamaica, Kingston
Sir Arthur Lewis Institute for Social and Economic Studies Documentation
    and Data Centre, The University of the West Indies, Mona
West Indies and Special Collections, Mona Library, The University of the West
    Indies, Mona

TRINIDAD AND TOBAGO

Chaguaramas Military History and Aerospace Museum, Chaguaramas
National Archives of Trinidad and Tobago, Port of Spain
West Indiana and Special Collections Division, The Alma Jordan Library, The
    University of the West Indies, St. Augustine

UNITED KINGDOM

British Library, Colindale and St. Pancras
Imperial War Museum, London
Institute for Commonwealth Studies Library and Archives, London
National Archives of the United Kingdom, Kew

UNITED STATES

Library of Congress, Washington, DC
National Archives and Records Administration, College Park, MD

[327]

[328] BIBLIOGRAPHY

National Archives and Records Administration, St. Louis, MO
Schomburg Center for Research in Black Culture, New York Public Library,
New York, NY

PUBLISHED PRIMARY SOURCES

Burkett, Algernon Albert. *Trinidad: A Jewel of the West, Or, 100 Years of British Rule*. London: Francis, 1914.

Census of the Colony of Trinidad and Tobago, 1911. Port of Spain, Trinidad: Government Printing Office, 1913.

Census of Jamaica and its Dependencies: Taken on the 3rd April, 1911. Kingston, Jamaica: Government Printing Office, 1912.

Census Reports from the British West Indies, 1891–1921. Port of Spain, Trinidad: Central Statistical Office, 1964.

Cipriani, A. A. *Twenty-Five Years After: The British West Indies Regiment in The Great War, 1914–1918*. Port of Spain: Trinidad Publishing, 1940.

Cundall, Frank. *The Handbook of Jamaica for 1921*. Kingston, Jamaica: Government Printing Office, 1921.

———. *The Handbook of Jamaica for 1926*. Kingston, Jamaica: Government Printing Office, 1926.

———. *Jamaica's Part in the Great War, 1915–1918*. London: IOJ, by the West India Commission, 1925.

Debates in the Legislative Council of Trinidad and Tobago, January–December 1915. Port of Spain: Government Printing Office, 1916.

De Lisser, Herbert G. *Jamaica and the Great War*. Kingston, Jamaica: Gleaner, 1917.

Dow, Captain H. *Record Service of Members of the Trinidad Merchants' and Planters' Contingent, 1915–1918*. Trinidad: Government Printery, 1925.

Dundonald, Douglas Mackinnon Baillie Hamilton Cochrane. *My Army Life*. London: Edward Arnold, 1926.

Dupuch, Sir Etienne. *A Salute to Friend and Foe: My Battles, Sieges and Fortunes*. Nassau: The Tribune, 1982.

———. *Tribune Story*. London: Benn, 1967.

Edmonds, Brigadier-General Sir James E. *Military Operations, Italy, 1915–1919*. London: H.M. Stationery Office, 1949.

Ford, Joseph C., and Frank Cundall. *The Handbook of Jamaica for 1916*. Kingston, Jamaica: Government Printing Office, 1916.

———. *The Handbook of Jamaica for 1919*. Kingston, Jamaica: Government Printing Office, 1919.

———. *The Handbook of Jamaica for 1920*. Kingston, Jamaica: Government Printing Office, 1920.

Franck, Harry A. *Roaming through the West Indies*. New York, The Century Co., 1920.

Franklin, C. B. *Trinidad and Tobago Year Book*. Port-of-Spain: Franklin's Electric Printery, 1919.

———. *Trinidad and Tobago Year Book*. Port-of-Spain: Franklin's Electric Printery, 1920.

BIBLIOGRAPHY [329]

Fraser, Capt. Percy L. *Looking Over My Shoulder: Forty-Seven Years a Public Servant, 1885–1932*. San Juan: Lexicon Trinidad, 2007.

Great Britain, Egyptian Expeditionary Force. *A Brief Record of the Advance of the Egyptian Expeditionary Force Under the Command of General Sir Edmund H. H. Allenby, July 1917 to October 1918*. 2nd ed. London: His Majesty's Stationary Office, 1919.

Hall, Lieut.-Col. L. J. *The Inland Water Transport in Mesopotamia*. London: Constable, 1921.

Hansard HC Deb., November 20, 1917, vol. 99 cc 991–2, https://api.parliament.uk /historic-hansard/commons/1917/nov/20/army-pay-increase#column_992.

Hansard HC Deb., November 26, 1917, vol. 99 cc 1631–5, https://api.parliament.uk /historic-hansard/commons/1917/nov/26/scales-of-increased-pay#column_1633.

Hansard HC Deb., November 14, 1918, vol 110, cc2884-5, https://api.parliament.uk /historic-hansard/commons/1918/nov/14/british-west-india-regiment#column _2884.

Hewitt, J. M., ed. *Silver Jubilee Magazine*. Bridgetown: Barbados Herald Press, 1935.

Hill, Robert A., ed., *The Marcus Garvey and Universal Negro Improvement Association Papers*, vol. 1. Berkeley: University of California Press, 1983.

———. *The Marcus Garvey and Universal Negro Improvement Association Papers*, vol. 11, *The Caribbean Diaspora, 1910–1920*. Durham, NC: Duke University Press, 2011.

Hill, Robert A., John Dixon, Mariela Haro Rodriguez, and Anthony Yuen, eds. *The Marcus Garvey and Universal Negro Improvement Association Papers*, vol. 13, *The Caribbean Diaspora, 1921–1922*. Durham, NC: Duke University Press, 2016.

Hill, Stephen A. *Who's Who in Jamaica, 1916*. Kingston, Jamaica: Gleaner, 1916.

———. *Who's Who in Jamaica, 1919–1920*. Kingston, Jamaica: Gleaner, 1920.

Holmes, Frank. *The Bahamas During the Great War*. Nassau: The Tribune, 1924.

Horner, A. E. *From the Islands of the Sea: Glimpses of a West Indian Battalion in France*. Nassau, Bahamas: Guardian, 1919.

James, C. L. R. *Beyond a Boundary*. Kingston, Jamaica: Sangster's Books and Hutchinson, 1963.

———. *The Case for West Indian Self-Government*. London: Hogarth Press, 1933.

———. *The Life of Captain Cipriani: An Account of the British Government in the West Indies*. Nelson, Lancashire: Coulton, 1932.

The Laws of Jamaica Passed in the Year 1917. Kingston: Government Printing Office, 1918.

Letters from the Trenches During the Great War. Shipston-on-Stour: King's Stone Press, n.d.

Lofty, Henry W. *Report on the Census of Barbados, 1911–1921*. Bridgetown, Barbados: Advocate, 1921.

Lucas, Charles Prestwood, ed. *The Empire at War*, vol. 2. London: Oxford University Press, 1923.

McDonald, Donald. *Songs of an Islander*. London: E. Stock, 1918.

Meikle, Louis S. *Confederation of the British West Indies versus Annexation to the United States: A Political Discourse on the West Indies*. New York: Negro Universities Press, 1969 [1912c].

[330] BIBLIOGRAPHY

Mendes, Alfred H. *The Autobiography of Alfred H. Mendes, 1897–1991*. Kingston, Jamaica: University of the West Indies Press, 2002.

Minutes of the Legislative Council of Jamaica for the Year 1917. Kingston, Jamaica: Government Printing Office, 1918.

Mitchell, Randolph, ed. *His Best Orations: A Summary of the Activities of Captain A. A. Cipriani*. Port of Spain: Surprise Print Shop, 1949.

Olivier, Lord Sydney. *Jamaica: The Blessed Island*. London: Faber and Faber, 1936.

Omissi, David, ed. *Indian Voices of the Great War: Solders' Letters, 1914–18*. New York: St. Martin's Press, 1999.

Owen, Stanley G. *Jamaica Marches On: A Marching and Recruiting Song for the Jamaica War Contingents*. Words by Tom Redcam. Kingston, Jamaica: Published by Astley Clerk, n. d.

Padmore, George. "Hitler Makes British Drop Color Bar." *The Crisis* 48, no. 3 (1941): 72–75.

Ramson, J. L. *"Carry On!" or Pages from the life of a West Indian padre in the field*. Kingston, Jamaica: Educational Supply, 1918.

Roberts, Walter Adolphe. *Pierrot Wounded and Other Poems*. New York: Britton Publishing, [c1919].

Smith, L. "Memoirs of a World War One Veteran." *Belizean Studies* 5, no. 2 (1977): 33–35.

Supplement to the London Gazette. October 21, 1918, Issue 30961.

Thomas, Herbert T. *The Story of a West Indian Policeman or Forty-seven Years in the Jamaica Constabulary*. Kingston, Jamaica: Gleaner, 1927.

Trinidad and Tobago Council Paper No. 3 of 1918. Port of Spain: Government Printing Office, 1918.

War Office. *Manual of Military Law*. London: HMSO, 1914.

———. *Regulations for the Issue of Separation Allowance and Allotments of Pay During the Present War*. London: HMSO, 1915.

———. *Statistics of the Military Effort of the British Empire During the Great War, 1914–1920*. London: His Majesty's Stationary Office, 1922.

West Indian Contingent Committee. *Reports and Accounts for the Nine Months ended 30th September, 1919*. London: West India Committee Rooms, 1920.

———. *Report and Accounts for the Six Months ended 31st December, 1918*. London: The West India Committee Rooms, 1919.

———. *Report of the Committee for the Ten Months ended June 30th, 1916*. London: The West India Committee Rooms, 1916.

Wheeler, L. Richard. *Desert Musings. Verse*. London, [1920].

———. "Empire Troops in Sussex During the Great War." *The Sussex County Magazine* 14 (1940): 202, 205–9.

Wickham, John, ed. *A Man with a Fountain Pen: Clennell Wilsden Wickham, 1895–1938*. Bridgetown: Nation Publishing, 1995.

Wood-Hill, Lt. Col. Charles. *A Few Notes on the History of the British West Indies Regiment*.

The Year Book of the Bermudas, the Bahamas, British Guiana, British Honduras, and the West Indies. London: Canadian Gazette, 1929.

BIBLIOGRAPHY [331]

NEWSPAPERS AND OTHER PERIODICALS

Argos (Trinidad)
Barbados Globe and Colonial Advocate
The Barbados Weekly Herald
The Clarion (British Honduras)
The Crisis (United States)
The Daily Argosy (British Guiana)
Daily Gleaner (Jamaica)
Dominica Chronicle
Federalist and Grenada People
Globe and Colonial Advocate (Barbados)
Jamaica Times
The Jamaica Churchman
Labour Leader (Trinidad)
The Mirror (Trinidad)
Nassau Guardian (Bahamas)
The Negro World (United States)
The New Belize
New York Age (United States)
New York Amsterdam News (United States)
New York Times (United States)
Northern News (Jamaica)
Panama Morning Journal
Port of Spain Gazette (Trinidad)
St. Croix Avis
The Trinidad Guardian
Voice of St. Lucia
The West Indian (Grenada)
The Workman (Panama)
West India Committee Circular (United Kingdom)

Secondary Sources

Adas, Michael. "Contested Hegemony: The Great War and the Afro-Asian Assault on the Civilizing Mission Ideology." *Journal of World History* 15, no.1 (2004): 31–64.

Alberto, Paulina L., and Jesse Hoffnung-Garskof. "'Racial Democracy' and Racial Inclusion: Hemispheric Histories." In *Afro-Latin American Studies: An Introduction,* edited by Alejandro de la Fuente and George Reid Andrews, 264–316. Cambridge: Cambridge University Press, 2018.

Alt, William E., and Betty L. Alt. *Black Soldiers, White Wars: Black Warriors from Antiquity to the Present.* Westport, CT: Praeger, 2002.

Altink, Henrice. *Destined for a Life of Service: Defining African-Jamaican Womanhood, 1865–1938.* Manchester: Manchester University Press, 2011.

———. *Public Secrets: Race and Colour in Colonial and Independent Jamaica.* Liverpool: Liverpool University Press, 2019.

André, Irving W., and Gabriel J. Christian. *For King & Country: The Service and Sacrifice of the Dominican Soldier*. Brampton, Ontario: Pont Casse Press, 2008.

Andrivon-Milton, Sabine. *La Martinique et la grande guerre*. Paris: L'Harmattan, 2005.

Anthony, Michael. "Huggins, [Sir] George F. (1870–1941)." In *Historical Dictionary of Trinidad and Tobago*. Lanham, MD: Scarecrow Press, 1997.

———. *The Making of Port of Spain: The History of Port of Spain, 1757–1939*, vol. 1. Cascade, Trinidad: Paria Publishing, 2007.

Ashdown, Peter. "The Growth of Black Consciousness in Belize 1914–1919. The Background to the Ex-Servicemen's Riot of 1919." *Belcast Journal of Belizean Affairs* 2, no. 2 (1985): 1–5.

———. "Marcus Garvey, the UNIA and the Black Cause in British Honduras, 1914–1949." *Journal of Caribbean History* 15 (1981): 41–55.

———. "Race Riot, Class Warfare and Coup d'Etat: The Ex-Servicemen's Riot of July 1919." *Belcast Journal of Belizean Affairs* 3, no. 1 (1986): 8–14.

Bailey, Paul J. "'An army of workers': Chinese Indentured Labour in First World War France." In *Race, Empire and First World War Writing*, edited by Santanu Das, 35–52. New York: Cambridge University Press, 2011.

Bakan, Abigail B. *Ideology and Class Conflict in Jamaica: The Politics of Rebellion*. Montréal: McGill-Queen's University Press, 1990.

Barbeau, Arthur E., and Florette Henri. *The Unknown Soldiers: African-American Troops in World War I*. New York: Da Capo Press, 1996.

Barber, Karin. *Africa's Hidden Histories: Everyday Literacy and Making the Self*. Bloomington: Indiana University Press, 2006.

Barriteau, Eudine. "Theorizing Gender Systems and the Project of Modernity in the Twentieth-Century Caribbean." *Feminist Review* 59 (1998): 186–210.

Bartley, Marleen A. "Land Settlement in Jamaica, 1923–1949." In *Jamaica in Slavery and Freedom: History, Heritage and Culture*, edited by Kathleen E.A. Monteith and Glen Richards, 324–39. Kingston, Jamaica: University of the West Indies Press, 2002.

Basdeo, Sahadeo. "Indian Participation in Labour Politics in Trinidad, 1919–1939." *Caribbean Quarterly* 32, no. 3/4 (1986): 50–65.

———. *Labour Organisation and Labour Reform in Trinidad, 1919–1939*. St. Augustine, Trinidad: Institute for Social and Economic Research, 1983.

Bean, Dalea. "'A Dangerous Class of Woman?': Prostitution and the Perceived Threat to Military Efficiency in Jamaica During the World Wars." *Jamaica Historical Review* 24 (2009): 42–50.

———. *Jamaican Women and the World Wars: On the Front Lines of Change*. Cham, Switzerland: Palgrave Macmillan, 2018.

———. "'This is an Empire War!": Contextualizing Issues of Britishness, Gender, and Jamaican Loyalty during World Wars I and II." In *Islands and Britishness: A Global Perspective*, edited by Jodie Matthews and Daniel Travers, 120–33. Newcastle Upon Tyne: Cambridge Scholars Publishing, 2012.

Beckles, Hilary McD. *Chattel House Blues: Making of a Democratic Society in Barbados, from Clement Payne to Owen Arthur*. Kingston, Jamaica: Ian Randle, 2004.

BIBLIOGRAPHY [333]

———. *Great House Rules: Landless Emancipation and Workers' Protest in Barbados, 1838–1938*. Kingston, Jamaica: Ian Randle, 2003.

Bender, Daniel E., and Jana K. Lipman, ed., *Making the Empire Work: Labor and United States Imperialism*. New York: New York University Press, 2015.

Benoit, Oliver. "T. Albert Marryshow and the Problems of National Identity Formation in Grenada." In *Islands and Britishness: A Global Perspective*, edited by. Jodie Matthews and Daniel Travers, 78–90. Newcastle upon Tyne: Cambridge Scholars Publishing, 2012.

Berliner, Brett A. *Ambivalent Desire: The Exotic Black Other in Jazz-age France*. Amherst: University of Massachusetts Press, 2002.

Besson, Gerard. "A Tale of Two Families: The De Boissiers & and the Ciprianis of Trinidad" (paper presented at the 22nd Annual Conference of Caribbean Historians, St. Augustine, Trinidad, April 1990).

Bland, Lucy. "White Women and Men of Colour: Miscegenation Fears in Britain after the Great War." *Gender & History* 17, no. 1 (2005): 29–61.

Bogues, Anthony. "Nationalism and Jamaican Political Thought." In *Jamaica in Slavery and Freedom: History, Heritage and Culture*, edited by Kathleen E.A. Monteith and Glen Richards, 363–87. Kingston, Jamaica: University of the West Indies Press, 2002.

———. "Politics, Nation, and PostColony: Caribbean Inflections." *Small Axe* 11 (2002): 1–30.

Boittin, Jennifer Anne. *Colonial Metropolis: The Urban Grounds of Anti-Imperialism and Feminism in Interwar Paris*. Lincoln: University of Nebraska Press, 2010.

Bolland, O. Nigel. *On the March: Labour Rebellions in the British Caribbean, 1934–39*. Kingston, Jamaica: Ian Randle Publishers, 1995.

———. *The Politics of Labour in the British Caribbean: The Social Origins of Authoritarianism and Democracy in the Labour Movement*. Princeton, NJ: Markus Wiener Publishers, 2001.

Bollettino, Maria Alessandra. "'Of equal or of more service': Black Soldiers and the British Empire in the Mid-Eighteenth-Century Caribbean." *Slavery & Abolition* 38, no. 3 (2016): 1–24.

Bourke, Joanna. *Dismembering the Male: Men's Bodies, Britain and the Great War*. Chicago, IL: University of Chicago Press, 1996.

Bourne, Stephen. *Black Poppies: Britain's Black Community and the Great War*. Stroud, Gloucestershire: The History Press, 2014.

Brereton, Bridget. *A History of Modern Trinidad: 1783–1962*. Heinemann Educational Books, 1981.

———. Introduction to C. L. R. James, *The Life of Captain Cipriani: An Account of British Government in the West Indies*. Durham, NC: Duke University Press, 2014.

———. *Race Relations in Colonial Trinidad, 1870–1900*. Cambridge: Cambridge University Press, 1979.

———. "The White Elite of Trinidad, 1838–1950." In *The White Minority in the Caribbean*, edited by Howard Johnson and Karl Watson, 32–70. Kingston, Jamaica: Ian Randle Publishers, 1998.

Brereton, Bridget, and Kevin A. Yelvington, eds. *The Colonial Caribbean in Transition: Essays on Postemancipation Social and Cultural History*. Gainesville: University Press of Florida, 1999.

BIBLIOGRAPHY

Bressey, Caroline. "Looking for Work: The Black Presence in Britain, 1860–1920." *Immigrants and Minorities* 28, nos. 2–3 (2010): 164–82.

Brizan, George I. *Brave Young Grenadians-Loyal British Subjects: Our People In The First and Second World Wars*. San Juan, Trinidad and Tobago: Paria Pub., 2002.

———. *The Grenadian Peasantry and Social Revolution 1930–1951*. Kingston, Jamaica: Institute of Social and Economic Research, 1979.

Brodber, Erna. "Afro-Jamaica Women at the Turn of the Century." *Social and Economic Studies* 35 (1986): 23–50.

Brody, Eugene. *Sex, Contraception, and Motherhood in Jamaica*. Cambridge, MA: Harvard University Press, 1981.

Brown, Aggrey. *Colour, Class and Politics in Jamaica*. Edison, NJ: Transaction, 1979.

Brown, Vincent. *The Reaper's Garden: Death and Power in the World of Atlantic Slavery*. Cambridge, MA: Harvard University Press, 2008.

———. *Tacky's Revolt: The Story of an Atlantic Slave War*. Cambridge, MA: Harvard University Press, 2020.

Browne, David V. C. *Race, Class, Politics and the Struggle for Empowerment in Barbados, 1914–1937*. Kingston, Jamaica: Ian Randle Publishers, 2012.

Bryan, Patrick E. *The Jamaican People 1880–1902: Race, Class and Social Control*. London: Macmillan Education, 1991.

Buckley, Roger Norman. *Slaves in Red Coats: The British West India Regiments, 1795–1815*. New Haven: Yale University Press, 1979.

Burk, James. *Handbook of the Sociology of the Military*. Ed. Giuseppe Caforio. New York: Springer, 2003.

Burnett, Carla. "'Unity Is Strength': Labor, Race, Garveyism, and the 1920 Panama Canal Strike." *The Global South* 6, no. 2 (2013): 39–64.

Buxton, Hilary R. "'Crutches as Weapons': Reading Blackness and the Disabled Soldier Body in the First World War." In *Men and Masculinities in Modern Britain: A History for the Present*, edited by Matt Houlbrook, Katie Jones, and Ben Mechen., 88–110. Manchester: Manchester University Press, 2024.

———. "Disabled Empire: Race, Rehabilitation, and the Politics of Healing Non-White Colonial Soldiers, 1914–1940." PhD diss., Rutgers, The State University of New Jersey, 2018.

Campbell, Horace. *Rasta and Resistance: From Marcus Garvey to Walter Rodney*. Trenton, NJ: Africa World Press, 1985.

Campt, Tina. *Image Matters: Archive, Photography, and the African Diaspora in Europe*. Durham, NC: Duke University Press, 2012.

Carpenter, Daniel. *Democracy by Petition: Popular Politics in Transformation, 1790–1870*. Cambridge, MA: Harvard University Press, 2021.

Carr, Barry. "Identity, Class, and Nation: Black Immigrant Workers, Cuban Communism, and the Sugar Insurgency, 1925–1934." *Hispanic American Historical Review* 78, no. 1 (1998): 83–116.

Chamberlain, Mary, ed. *Caribbean Migration: Globalised Identities*. London: Routledge, 1998.

Chambers, Glenn A. *From the Banana Zones to the Big Easy: West Indian and Central American Immigration to New Orleans, 1910–1940*. Baton Rouge: Louisiana State University Press, 2019.

Casimir, J. R. Ralph. *Africa Arise: (and Other Poems)*. Roseau, Dominica: Casimir, 1967.

Chevannes, Barry. *Learning to Be a Man: Culture, Socialization, and Gender Identity in Five Caribbean Communities*. Kingston: University of West Indies Press, 2002.

Chomsky, Aviva. "Afro-Jamaican Traditions and Labor Organizing on United Fruit Company Plantations in Costa Rica, 1910." *Journal of Social History* 28, no. 4 (1995): 837–55.

Cohen, Deborah. *The War Come Home: Disabled Veterans in Britain and Germany, 1914–1939*. Berkeley: University of California Press, 2001.

Colby, Jason M. *The Business of Empire: United Fruit, Race, and U.S. Expansion in Central America*. Ithaca, NY: Cornell University Press, 2011.

Cole, Laurence, and Daniel L. Unowsky. *The Limits of Loyalty: Imperial Symbolism, Popular Allegiances, and State Patriotism in the late Habsburg Monarchy*. New York: Berghahn Books, 2007.

Conniff, Michael L. *Black Labor on a White Canal: Panama, 1904–1981*. Pittsburgh, PA: University of Pittsburgh Press, 1985.

Cormack, Michael J. *Ideology*. Ann Arbor: University of Michigan Press, 1992.

Corns, Cathryn, and John Hughes-Wilson. *Blindfold and Alone: British Military Executions in the Great War*. London: Cassell, 2001.

Costello, Ray. *Black Tommies: British Soldiers of African Descent in the First World War*. Liverpool: Liverpool University Press, 2015.

Cowley, John. *Carnival, Canboulay and Calypso: Traditions in the Making*. Cambridge: Cambridge University Press, 1996.

Cox, Edward L. "William Galwey Donovan and the Struggle for Political Change in Grenada, 1883–1920." *Small Axe* 11, no. 1 (2007): 17–38.

Crichlow, Michaeline A. *Negotiating Caribbean Freedom: Peasants and the State in Development*. Lanham, MD: Lexington Books, 2005.

Cumper, G. E. "Population Movements in Jamaica, 1830–1950." *Social and Economic Studies* 5 (1956): 261–80.

Daly, Samuel Fury Childs. "War as Work: Labor and Soldiering in History—Review Essay." *International Labor and Working-Class History* 103 (2023): 375–80.

Darrow, Margaret. *French Women and the First World War: War Stories of the Home Front*. New York: Berg, 2000.

Das, Santanu. *The Cambridge Companion to the Poetry of the First World War*. New York: Cambridge University Press, 2013.

De Barros, Juanita. *Reproducing the British Caribbean: Sex, Gender, and Population Politics after Slavery*. Chapel Hill: University of North Carolina Press, 2014.

De la Fuente, Alejandro. "Two Dangers, One Solution: Immigration, Race, and Labor in Cuba, 1900–1930." *International Labor and Working-Class History* 51 (1997): 7–29.

Dendooven, Dominiek. *The British West Indies Regiment: Race and Colour on the Western Front*. Yorkshire, England: Pen & Sword Military, 2023.

Downes, Aviston D. "Boys of the Empire: Elite Education and the Construction of Hegemonic Masculinity in Barbados, 1875–1920." In *Interrogating Caribbean Masculinities: Theoretical and Empirical Analyses*, edited by Rhoda Reddock, 105–136. Kingston, Jamaica: University of the West Indies Press, 2004.

Duke, Eric D. *Building a Nation: Caribbean Federation in the Black Diaspora*. Gainesville: University Press of Florida, 2016.

———. "The Diasporic Dimensions of British Caribbean Federation in the Early Twentieth Century." *New West Indian Guide/Nieuwe West-Indische Gids* 83, no. 3–4 (2009): 219–48.

Duncan, Natanya. *An Efficient Womanhood: Women and the Making of the Universal Negro Improvement Association*. Chapel Hill: University of North Carolina Press, 2025.

Edwards, Brent. *The Practice of Diaspora: Literature, Translation, and the Rise of Black Internationalism*. Cambridge, MA: Harvard University Press, 2003.

Eichenberg, Julia, and John Paul Newman, ed., *The Great War and Veterans' Internationalism*. New York: Palgrave Macmillan, 2013.

Eisner, Gisela. *Jamaica, 1830–1930: A Study of Economic Growth*. Manchester: Manchester University Press, 1961.

Eller, Anne. *We Dream Together: Dominican Independence, Haiti, and the Fight for Caribbean Freedom*. Durham, NC: Duke University Press, 2016.

Ellis, A. B. *The History of the First West India Regiment*. London: Chapman and Hall, 1885.

Elkins, Caroline. *Legacy of Violence: A History of the British Empire*. New York: Alfred A. Knopf, 2022.

Elkins, W. F. "Black Power in the British West Indies: The Trinidad Longshoremen's Strike of 1919." *Science and Society* 33, no.1 (1969): 71–5.

———. "Hercules and the Society of Peoples of African Origin." *Caribbean Studies* 11, no. 4 (1972): 47–59.

———. "A Source of Black Nationalism in the Caribbean: The Revolt of the British West Indies Regiment at Taranto, Italy." *Science and Society* 34, no. 1 (1970): 99–103.

———. "Suppression of the *Negro World* in the British West Indies." *Science and Society* 35, no. 3 (1971): 344–47.

Emmanuel, Patrick. *Crown Colony Politics in Grenada, 1917–1951*. Cave Hill, Barbados: Institute of Social and Economic Research, 1978.

Ewing, Adam. *The Age of Garvey: How a Jamaican Activist Created a Mass Movement and Changed Global Black Politics*. Princeton, NJ: Princeton University Press, 2014.

———. "Caribbean Labour Politics in the Age of Garvey, 1918–1938." *Race & Class* 55, no. 1 (2013): 23–45.

Featherstone, David. "Politicizing In/Security, Transnational Resistance, and the 1919 Riots in Cardiff and Liverpool." *Small Axe* 22, no. 3 (2018): 56–67.

Ferrer, Ada. *Insurgent Cuba: Race, Nation, and Revolution, 1868–1898*. Chapel Hill: University of North Carolina Press, 2005.

Flores-Villalobos, Joan. *The Silver Women: How Black Women's Labor Made the Panama Canal*. Philadelphia: University of Pennsylvania Press, 2023.

Fogarty, Richard S. "Race and Sex, Fear and Loathing in France during the Great War." *Historical Reflections/Réflexions Historiques* 34, no. 1 (2008): 50–72.

———. *Race and War in France: Colonial Subjects in the French Army, 1914–1918*. Baltimore, MD: Johns Hopkins University Press, 2012.

BIBLIOGRAPHY [337]

Foote, Nicola. "British Caribbean Women Migrants and Domestic Service in Latin America, 1850–1950s: Race, Gender and Colonial Legacies." In *Colonization and Domestic Service: Historical and Contemporary Perspectives*, edited by Victoria K. Haskins and Claire Lowrie, 289–308. New York: Routledge, 2015.

———. "Rethinking Race, Gender and Citizenship: Black West Indian Women in Costa Rica, c. 1920–1940." *Bulletin of Latin American Research* 23, no. 2 (2004): 198–212.

Foote, Nicola, and René D. Harder Horst, eds., *Military Struggle and Identity Formation in Latin America: Race, Nation, and Community During the Liberal Period*. Gainesville: University Press of Florida, 2013.

Ford-Smith, Honor. "Unruly Virtues of the Spectacular: Performing Engendered Nationalism in the UNIA in Jamaica." *Interventions* 6, no. 1 (2004): 18–44.

Fraser, Cary. "The Twilight of Colonial Rule in the British West Indies: Nationalist Assertion vs. Imperial Hubris in the 1930s." *Journal of Caribbean History* 30, nos. 1 & 2 (1996): 1–27.

Fryar, Christienna D. "Imperfect Models: The Kingston Lunatic Asylum Scandal and the Problem of Postemancipation Imperialism." *Journal of British Studies* 55 (2016): 709–27.

Fryer, Peter. *Aspects of British Black History*. London: Index Books, 1993.

———. *Staying Power: The History of Black People in Britain*. London: Pluto Press, 1984.

García Muñiz, Humberto, and Jorge L. Giovannetti, "Garveyismo y racismo en el Caribe: El caso de la población cocola en la República Dominicana." *Caribbean Studies* 31, no. 1 (2003): 139–211.

Gerber, David A. "Disabled Veterans, the State, and the Experience of Disability in Western Societies, 1914–1950." *Journal of Social History* 36, no. 4 (2003): 899–916.

Gibbs, Archibald Robertson. *British Honduras: An Historical and Descriptive Account of the Colony from its Settlement, 1670*. London: Sampson Low, Marston, Searle & Rivington, 1883.

Gills, John R., ed. *Commemorations*. Princeton, NJ: Princeton University Press, 1994.

Giovannetti, Jorge L. *Black British Migrants in Cuba: Race, Labor, and Empire in the Twentieth-Century Caribbean, 1898–1948*. New York: Cambridge University Press, 2018.

———. "Caribbean Studies as Practice: Insights from Border-Crossing Histories and Research." *Small Axe* 17, no. 2 (2013): 74–87.

Giovannetti, Jorge L., and Reinaldo L Román, eds. Special issue: Garveyism and the Universal Negro Association in the Hispanic Caribbean. *Caribbean Studies/Estudios del Caribe/Etudes des Caraïbes* 31, no. 1 (2003): 7–259.

Glymph, Thavolia. *The Women's Fight: The Civil War's Battles for Home, Freedom, and Nation*. Chapel Hill: University of North Carolina Press, 2020.

Goldthree, Reena N. "'A Greater Enterprise Than the Panama Canal': Migrant Labor and Military Recruitment in the World War I-Era Circum-Caribbean." *Labor: Studies in Working-Class History of the Americas* 13, no. 3–4 (2016): 57–82.

———. "Shifting Loyalties: War and the Gendered Politics of Patriotism in the British Caribbean." PhD diss., Duke University, 2011.

[338] BIBLIOGRAPHY

——. "'Vive La France!': Afro-Caribbean soldiers and Interracial Intimacies on the Western Front, 1915–19." *Journal of Colonialism and Colonial History* 7, no. 3 (2016), doi:10.1353/cch.2016.0040.

——. "Writing War and Empire: Poetry, Patriotism, and Public Claims-Making in the British Caribbean." In *Caribbean Military Encounters*, edited by Shalini Puri and Lara Putnam, 49–69. New York: Palgrave MacMillian, 2017.

Goldthree, Reena N. and Natanya Duncan. "Feminist Histories of the Interwar Caribbean: Anti-colonialism, Popular Protest, and the Gendered Struggle for Rights." *Caribbean Review of Gender Studies* 12 (2018): 1–30.

Goodman, Marc and V. Rushton. "A Jamaica Past, being a Glimpse into History's Last Surviving Bloodiest Battlefields - A Visit with Jamaica's Last Surviving World War I Veteran." *Jamaican Historical Society Bulletin* 11, no. 3 (1999/2000): 52–57.

Gordon, Kevin. *Seaford and Eastbourne in the Great War*. Barnsley, England: Pen & Sword Military, 2014.

Graham, Tracey E. "Jamaican Migration to Cuba, 1912–1940." PhD diss., University of Chicago, 2013.

Grayzell, Susan. *Women's Identities at War: Gender, Motherhood, and Politics in Britain and France during the First World War*. Chapel Hill: University of North Carolina Press, 1999.

Green, Jeffrey. *Black Edwardians: Black People in Britain, 1901–1914*. New York: Cass Publishers, 1998.

Greene, Julie. *Box 25: Archival Secrets, Caribbean Workers, and the Panama Canal*. Chapel Hill: University of North Carolina Press, 2025.

——. *The Canal Builders: Making America's Empire at the Panama Canal*. New York: Penguin Press, 2009.

——. "Entangled in Empires: British Antillean Migrations in the World of the Panama Canal." In *Crossing Empires: Taking U.S. History Into Transimperial Terrain*, edited by Kristin L. Hoganson and Jay Sexton, 222–40. Durham, NC: Duke University Press, 2020.

Greenfield, Sidney M. "Barbadians in the Brazilian Amazon." *Luso-Brazilian Review* 20, no. 1 (1983): 44–64.

Gullace, Nicoletta F. *"The Blood of Our Sons:" Men, Women, and the Renegotiation of British Citizenship During the Great War*. Houndmills, Basingstroke: Palgrave Macmillan, 2002.

——. "White Feathers and Wounded Men: Female Patriotism and the Memory of the Great War," *Journal of British Studies* 36, no. 2 (1997): 178–206.

Guoqi, Xu. *Strangers on the Western Front: Chinese Workers in the Great War*. Cambridge: Harvard University Press, 2011.

Guridy, Frank. "'Enemies of the White Race': The Machadista State and the UNIA in Cuba," *Caribbean Studies* 31, no. 1 (2003): 107–37.

Hacker, Barton C. "White Man's War, Coloured Man's Labour: Working for the British Army on the Western Front." *Itinerario* 38, no. 3 (2014): 27–44.

Hall, Catherine. *Civilising Subjects: Metropole and Colony in the English Imagination, 1830–1867*. Chicago: University of Chicago Press, 2002.

BIBLIOGRAPHY [339]

Hall, Douglas. *A Brief History of the West India Committee*. St. Lawrence: Caribbean Universities Press, 1971.

Hall, Stuart. "C. L. R. James: A Portrait." In *C. L. R. James's Caribbean*, edited by Paget Henry and Paul Buhle, 3–16. Durham, NC: Duke University Press, 1992.

———. "Cultural Identity and Diaspora." In *Identity: Community, Culture, and Difference*, edited by Jonathan Rutherford, 222–37. London: Lawrence and Wishart, 1990.

———. "Negotiating Caribbean Identities." In *New Caribbean Thought: A Reader*, edited by Brian Meeks and Folke Lindahl, 24–39. Kingston, Jamaica: University of the West Indies Press, 2001.

Hankey, Lord. *The Supreme Command, 1914–1918*, vol. 1. London: George Allen and Unwin, 1961.

Hanna, Martha. "A Republic of Letters: The Epistolary Tradition in France During World War I." *American Historical Review* 108, no. 5 (2003): 1338–61.

Harpelle, Ronald. "Cross Currents in the Western Caribbean: Marcus Garvey and the UNIA in Central America," *Caribbean Studies* 31, no. 1 (2003): 35–73.

———. *The West Indians of Costa Rica: Race, Class, and the Integration of an Ethnic Minority*. Montreal: McGill-Queen's University Press, 2001.

Hastings, Paula. "Territorial Spoils, Transnational Black Resistance, and Canada's Evolving Autonomy during the First World War." *Histoire Sociale/Social History* 47, no. 94 (2014): 443–70.

Heuring, Darcy Hughes. "'In the Cheapest Way Possible . . .': Responsibility and the Failure of Improvement at the Kingston Lunatic Asylum, 1914–1945." *Journal of Colonialism and Colonial History* 12, no. 3 (2011), http://muse.jhu.edu/article /463344.

Hewitson, Mark. *Conclusion to What Is a Nation?: Europe 1789–1914*. Ed. Timothy Baycroft and Mark Hewitson. New York: Oxford University Press, 2006.

Higate, Paul R, ed. *Military Masculinities: Identity and the State*. Westport, CT: Praeger, 2003.

Higman, B. W. "Domestic Service in Jamaica since 1750." In *Muchachas No More: Household Workers in Latin America and the Caribbean*, edited by Elsa M. Chaney and Mary Garcia Castro, 37–82. Philadelphia: Temple University Press, 1989.

Hill, Errol G. "Calypso and War," *Black American Literature Forum* 23, no.1 (1989): 61–88.

Hill, Kimloan. "Sacrifices, Sex, Race: Vietnamese Experiences in the First World War." In *Race, Empire and First World War Writing*, edited by Santanu Das, 53–69. New York: Cambridge University Press, 2011.

Hill, Robert A. "'Comradeship of the More Advanced Races': Marcus Garvey and the Brotherhood Movement in Britain, 1913–14." *Small Axe* 17, no. 1 (2013): 50–70.

Hoganson, Kristin L. *Fighting for American Manhood: How Gender Politics Provoked the Spanish American and Philippine-American Wars*. New Haven, CT: Yale University Press, 1998.

Høgsbjerg, Christian. *C. L. R. James in Imperial Britain*. Durham, NC: Duke University Press, 2014.

———. "'Whenever Society Is in Travail Liberty Is Born': The Mass Strike of 1919 in Colonial Trinidad." In *The Internationalisation of the Labour Question*, edited by Stefano Bellucci and Holger Weiss, 215–34. Cham: Palgrave Macmillan, 2020.

Holt, Thomas. *The Problem of Freedom: Race, Labor, and Politics in Jamaica and Britain, 1832–1938*. Baltimore, MD: Johns Hopkins University Press, 1992.

Horne, Gerald. *Negro Comrades of the Crown: African Americans and the British Empire Fight the U.S. Before Emancipation*. New York, NY: NYU Press, 2013.

Horne, John. "Immigrant Workers in France during World War I." *French Historical Studies* 14, no. 1 (1985): 57–88.

Howard, Phillip A. *Black Labor, White Sugar: Caribbean Braceros and Their Struggle for Power in the Cuban Sugar Industry*. Baton Rouge: Louisiana State University Press, 2015.

Howe, Glenford D. "In the Crucible of Race: Race, Power, and Military Socialization of West Indian Recruits during the First World War." *Journal of Caribbean Studies* 10 (1995): 163–81.

———. "Military-Civilian Intercourse, Prostitution and Venereal Disease Among Black West Indian Soldiers During World War I." *Journal of Caribbean History* 31, nos. 1–2 (1997): 88–102.

———. *Race, War and Nationalism: A Social History of West Indians in the First World War*. Kingston, Jamaica: Ian Randle Publishers, 2002.

———. "West Indian Blacks and the Struggle for Participation in the First World War." *Journal of Caribbean History* 28, no.1 (1994): 27–62.

Hughes, Matthew. *Allenby and British Strategy in the Middle East, 1917–1919*. London: Frank Cass, 1999.

———. "Allenby, Edmund Henry Hynman, first Viscount Allenby of Megiddo (1861–1936)." In *Oxford Dictionary of National Biography*. Oxford University Press, 2004; online ed., May 2008, http://www.oxforddnb.com/view/article/30392.

Hume, Yanique. "Death and the Construction of Social Space: Land, Kinship, and Identity in the Jamaican Mortuary Cycle." In *Passages and Afterworlds: Anthropological Perspectives on Death in the Caribbean*, ed. Maarit Forde and Yanique Hume, 109–38. Durham, NC: Duke University Press, 2018.

Imy, Kate. *Faithful Fighters: Identity and Power in the British Indian Army*. Palo Alto: Stanford University Press, 2019.

Jackson, Ashley, and James E. Kitchen. "The British Empire and the First World War: Paradoxes and New Questions." In *The British Empire and the First World War*, ed. Ashley Jackson, 1–30. New York: Routledge, 2016.

Jacobs, W. Richard, ed. *Butler versus the King: Riots and Sedition in 1937*. Port of Spain, Trinidad: Key Caribbean Publications, 1976.

———. "Butler: A Life of Struggle," in *In the Spirit of Butler: Trade Unionism in Free Grenada*. St. George's Grenada: Fedon Publishers, 1982.

James, C. L. R. *Beyond a Boundary*. Kingston, Jamaica: Sangster's Books and Hutchinson, 1963.

———. *The Black Jacobins: Toussaint L'Ouverture and the San Domingo Revolution*. New York: Vintage, 1989 [1963c].

James, Pearl, ed. *Picture This: World War I Posters and Visual Culture*. Lincoln: University of Nebraska Press, 2009.

James, Winston. "The Black Experience in Twentieth-Century Britain." In *Black Experience and the Empire*, edited by Phillip D. Morgan and Sean Hawkins, 347–86. New York: Oxford University Press, 2006.

———. *Claude McKay: The Making of a Black Bolshevik*. New York: Columbia University Press, 2022.

———. "Explaining Afro-Caribbean Social Mobility in the United States: Beyond the Sowell Thesis." *Comparative Studies in Society and History* 44, no. 2 (2002): 232–34.

———. *A Fierce Hatred of Injustice: Claude McKay's Jamaica and His Poetry of Rebellion*. Kingston, Jamaica: Ian Randle, 2001.

———. *Holding Aloft the Banner of Ethiopia: Caribbean Radicalism in Early Twentieth Century America*. London: Verso, 1998.

———. "Letters from London in Black and Red: Claude McKay, Marcus Garvey and the Negro World." *History Workshop Journal* 85 (2018): 290.

Jeffery, Keith. *The British Army and the Crisis of Empire, 1918–22*. Dover, NH: Manchester University Press, 1984.

Jenkinson, Jacqueline. "'All in the Same Uniform'? The Participation of Black Colonial Residents in the British Armed Forces in the First World War." *The Journal of Imperial and Commonwealth History* 40, no.2 (2012): 207–30.

———. *Black 1919: Riots, Racism and Resistance in Imperial Britain*. Liverpool: Liverpool University Press, 2009.

Jennings, Eric T. "Monuments to Frenchness? The Memory of the Great War and the Politics of Guadeloupe's Identity, 1914–1945." *French Historical Studies* 21, no.4 (1998): 561–92.

Johnson, Howard. "Barbadian Migrants in the Putumayo District of the Amazon, 1904–11." In *Caribbean Migration: Globalized Identities*, edited by Mary Chamberlain, 182–93. New York: Routledge, 2002.

———. "The British Caribbean from demobilization to constitutional decolonization." In *The Oxford History of the British Empire: The Twentieth Century*, edited by Judith Brown and William Roger Louis, 597–622. Oxford: Oxford University Press, 1999.

Johnson, Howard, and Karl Watson, eds. *The White Minority in the Caribbean*. Kingston, Jamaica: Ian Randle Publishers, 1998.

Johnson, Rashauna. *Slavery's Metropolis: Unfree Labor in New Orleans During the Age of Revolutions*. New York: Cambridge University Press, 2016.

Jones, Margaret. *Public Health in Jamaica, 1850–1940: Neglect, Philanthropy and Development*. Kingston, Jamaica: University of the West Indies Press, 2013.

Joseph, Cedric L. "The British West Indies Regiment, 1914–1918." *Journal of Caribbean History* 2 (1971): 94–124.

Joseph, Michael. "Beyond the Nation: Anticolonialism in the British and French Caribbean after the First World War (1913–1939)." PhD diss., University of Oxford, 2019.

———. "Black Women, Separation Allowances and Citizenship in the French Caribbean during the First World War." *French History* 35, no. 4 (2021): 431–48.

———. "First World War veterans and the state in the French and British Caribbean, 1919–1939." *First World War Studies* 10, no. 1 (2019): 1–18.

Kamugisha, Aaron. *Beyond Coloniality: Citizenship and Freedom in the Caribbean Intellectual Tradition.* Bloomington: Indiana University Press, 2022.

Kaushik, Roy. "Race and Recruitment in the Indian Army, 1880–1918." *Modern Asian Studies* 47, no. 4 (2013): 1310–47.

Killingray, David. "'A Good West Indian, a Good African, and, in Short, a Good Britisher': Black and British in a Colour-Conscious Empire, 1760–1950." *The Journal of Imperial and Commonwealth History* 36, no. 3 (2008): 363–81.

———. "All the King's Men?: Blacks in the British Army in the First World War." In *Under the Imperial Carpet: Essays in Black History, 1780–1950*, edited by Rainer Lotz and Ian Pegg, 164–81. Crawley, England: Rabbit Press, 1986.

———. "Race and Rank in the British Army in the Twentieth Century." *Ethnic and Racial Studies* 10, no. 3 (1987): 276–90.

Killingray, David, and James Matthews. "Beasts of Burden: British West African Carriers in the First World War." *Canadian Journal of African Studies/La Revue Canadienne des Études Africaines* 13, no. 1–2 (1979): 5–23.

Kilson, Robin Wallace. "Calling Up the Empire: The British Military Use of Non-White Labor in France, 1916–1920." PhD diss., Harvard University, 1990.

Knight, Franklin W. "Jamaican Migrants and the Cuban Sugar Industry, 1900–1934." In *Between Slavery and Free Labor: The Spanish-Speaking Caribbean in the Nineteenth Century*, edited by Manuel Moreno Fraginals, Frank Moya Pons, and Stanley L. Engerman, 94–114. Baltimore, MD: Johns Hopkins University Press, 1985.

Kowalsky, Meaghan. "'This Honourable Obligation': The King's National Roll Scheme for Disabled Ex-Servicemen 1915–1944." *European Review of History [Revue européenne d'Histoire]*14, no. 4 (2007): 567–84.

Lambert, David. "'[A] Mere Cloak for their Proud Contempt and Antipathy towards the African Race': Imagining Britain's West India Regiments in the Caribbean, 1795–1838." *The Journal of Imperial and Commonwealth History* 46, no. 4 (2018): 627–50.

——— . *Soldiers of Uncertain Rank: The West India Regiments in British Imperial Culture.* New York: Cambridge University Press, 2024.

———. *White Creole Culture, Politics and Identity During the Age of Abolition.* Cambridge: Cambridge University Press, 2005.

Lasso, Marixa. *Erased: The Untold Story of the Panama Canal.* Cambridge, MA: Harvard University Press, 2019.

———. "Nationalism and Immigrant Labor in a Tropical Enclave: The West Indians of Colón City, 1850–1936." *Citizenship Studies* 17, no. 5 (2013): 551–65.

Leach, Christopher. "Uniforms and Commercial Culture: Constructing a Vision of Warfare in Pre-Great War Britain." *Cultural History* 10, no. 1 (2021): 31–60.

Leeds, Asia. "Toward the 'Higher Type of Womanhood': The Gendered Contours of Garveyism and the Making of Redemptive Geographies in Costa Rica, 1922–1941." *Palimpsest: A Journal on Women, Gender, and the Black International* 2, no. 1 (2013): 1–27.

Lentz-Smith, Adriane. *Freedom Struggles: African Americans and World War I.* Cambridge, MA: Harvard University Press, 2009.

Levine, Philippa. "Battle Colors: Race, Sex, and Colonial Soldiery in World War I." *Journal of Women's History* 9, no. 4 (1998): 104–30.

BIBLIOGRAPHY [343]

Levy, Andrea. "Uriah's War." In *Six Stories and an Essay*, by Andrea Levy, 113–27. London: Tinder Press, 2014.

Levy, Michèle. Introduction to *The Man Who Ran Away and Other Stories of Trinidad in the 1920s and 1930s*, by Alfred Mendes. Kingston, Jamaica: University of the West Indies Press, 2006.

Lewis, Gordon K. *Growth of the Modern West Indies*. New York: Monthly Review Press, 1968.

———. *Main Currents in Caribbean Thought: The Historical Evolution of Caribbean Society in Its Ideological Aspects, 1492–1900*. Baltimore, MD: Johns Hopkins University Press, 1983.

Lewis, Lancelot S. *The West Indian in Panama, 1850–1914*. Washington, DC: University Press of America, 1980.

Lewis, Linden, ed. *The Culture of Gender and Sexuality in the Caribbean*. Gainesville: University Press of Florida, 2003.

Lewis, Linden. "Nationalism and Caribbean Masculinity." In *Gender Ironies of Nationalism: Sexing the Nation*, edited by Tamar Mayer, 261–82. New York: Routledge, 2000.

Lewis, Rupert. *Garvey: Africa, Europe, the Americas*. Kingston, Jamaica: Institute of Social and Economic Research, University of the West Indies, 1986.

———. *Marcus Garvey: Anti-Colonial Champion*. Trenton, NJ: Africa World Press, 1988.

Lewis, Rupert, and Patrick Bryan, eds. *Garvey, His Work and Impact*. Trenton, NJ: Africa World Press, 1991.

Lobdell, Richard A. "Women in the Jamaican Labour Force, 1881–1921." *Social and Economic Studies* 37, no. 1–2 (1988): 203–40.

Lockley, Tim. *Military Medicine and the Making of Race: Life and Death in the West India Regiments, 1795–1874*. New York: Cambridge University Press, 2020.

Look Lai, Walton. "C. L. R. James and Trinidadian Nationalism." In *C. L. R. James's Caribbean*, edited by Paget Henry and Paul Buhle, 174–209. Durham, NC: Duke University Press, 1992.

———. *Indentured labor, Caribbean Sugar: Chinese and Indian Migrants to the British West Indies, 1838–1918*. Baltimore, MD: Johns Hopkins University Press, 1993.

Loughran. Tracey. "Shell Shock, Trauma and the First World War: The Making of a Diagnosis and Its Histories." *Journal of the History of Medicine and Allied Sciences* 67, no. 1 (2010): 94–119.

Lowe, Lisa. *The Intimacies of Four Continents*. Durham, NC: Duke University Press, 2015.

Lunn, Joe. "'Les Races Guerrières': Racial Preconceptions in the French Military about West African Soldiers during the First World War." *Journal of Contemporary History* 34, no. 4 (1999): 517–36.

Macpherson, Anne S. *From Colony to Nation: Women Activists and the Gendering of Politics in Belize, 1912–1982*. Lincoln: University of Nebraska Press, 2007.

Maddox, Tyesha. *A Home Away from Home: Mutual Aid, Political Activism, and Caribbean American Identity*. Philadelphia: University of Pennsylvania Press, 2024.

Maguire, Anna. *Contact Zones of the First World War: Cultural Encounters Across the British Empire*. Cambridge: Cambridge University Press, 2021.

———. "'I felt like a man': West Indian Troops under Fire during the First World War." *Slavery & Abolition* 39, no. 3 (2018): 602–21.

———. "'A pageant of empire?': Untangling Colonial Encounters in Military Camps." In *Colonial Encounters in a Time of Global Conflict, 1914–1918*, edited by Santanu Das, Anna Maguire, and Daniel Steinbach, 37–56. London: Routledge, 2021.

Mallison, W. T. "The Balfour Declaration: An Appraisal." In *The Transformation of Palestine: Essays on the Origin and Development of the Arab-Israeli Conflict*, edited by Ibrahim Abu-Lughod, 66–95. Evanston, IL: Northwestern University Press, 1987.

Makalani, Minkah. "Diaspora and the Localities of Race." *Social Text* 27, no.1 (2009): 1–9.

———. *In the Cause of Freedom: Radical Black Internationalism from Harlem to London, 1917–1939*. Chapel Hill: University of North Carolina Press, 2011.

Maloney, Gerardo. *El Canal de Panamá y los trabajadores antillanos: Panamá 1920, cronología de una lucha*. Panama City: Universidad de Panamá, 1989.

Man, Simeon. *Soldiering through Empire: Race and the Making of the Decolonizing Pacific*. Oakland: University of California Press, 2018.

Manley, Norman. "The Autobiography of Norman Washington Manley." *Jamaica Journal* 7, no.1 (1973): 4–19.

Mann, Gregory. *Native Sons: West African Veterans and France in the Twentieth Century*. Durham, NC: Duke University Press, 2006.

Marshall, Dawn. "The History of West Indian Migrations: The Case of the West Indies." *Caribbean Review* 11, no. 1 (1982): 15–31.

Martin, Gregory. "The Influence of Racial Attitudes on British Policy Towards India During the First World War." *The Journal of Imperial and Commonwealth History* 14, no. 2 (1986): 91–113.

Martin, Tony. "Marcus Garvey and Trinidad, 1912–1947." In *The Pan-African Connection: From Slavery to Garvey and Beyond*, edited by Tony Martin, 63–94. Dover, MA: Majority Press, 1984.

———. *Race First: The Ideological and Organizational Struggles of Marcus Garvey and the Universal Negro Improvement Association*. Westport, CT: Greenwood Press, 1976.

———. "Revolutionary Upheaval in Trinidad, 1919: Views from British and American Sources." *The Journal of Negro History* 58, no. 3 (1973): 313–26.

Matera, Marc. *Black London: The Imperial Metropolis and Decolonization in the Twentieth Century*. Oakland: University of California Press, 2015.

Mathieu, Sarah-Jane (Saje). "L'Union Fait La Force: Black Soldiers in the Great War." *First World War Studies* 9, no. 2 (2018): 230–44.

Mathurin, O.C. *Henry Sylvester Williams and the Origins of the Pan-African Movement, 1869–1911*. Westport, CT: Greenwood Press, 1976.

Matthews, James K. "World War I and the Rise of African Nationalism: Nigerian Veterans as Catalysts of Change." *The Journal of Modern African Studies* 20, no. 3 (1982): 493–502.

Mawani, Renisa. *Colonial Proximities: Crossracial Encounters and Juridical Truths in British Columbia, 1871–1921*. Vancouver: University of British Columbia Press, 2009.

Mawby, Spencer. *Ordering Independence: The End of Empire in the Anglophone Caribbean, 1947–69*. New York: Palgrave Macmillan, 2012.

Mayo, James M. *War Memorials as Political Landscape: The American Experience and Beyond*. Westport, CT: Praeger, 1988.

McLeod, Marc C. "'Sin dejar de ser cubanos': Cuban Blacks and the Challenges of Garveyism in Cuba." *Caribbean Studies* 31, no. 1 (2003): 75–105.

———. "Undesirable Aliens: Race, Ethnicity, and Nationalism in the Comparison of Haitian and British West Indian Immigrant Workers in Cuba, 1912–1939." *Journal of Social History* 31, no. 3 (1998): 599–623.

McNish Weiss, John. *The Merikens: Free Black American Settlers in Trinidad 1815–16*. London: McNish & Weiss, 2002.

Meeks, Brian. *Narratives of Resistance: Jamaica, Trinidad, The Caribbean*. Kingston, Jamaica: University of the West Indies Press, 2000.

Melman, Billie, ed. *Borderlines: Genders and Identities in War and Peace, 1870–1930*. London: Routledge, 1998.

Melzer, Annabelle. "Spectacles and Sexualities: The 'Mise-en-Scène' of the 'Tirailleur Sénégalais' on the Western Front." In *Borderlines: Genders and Identities in War and Peace 1870–1930*, edited by Billie Melman, 213–45. London: Routledge, 1998.

Mendes, Alfred H. *The Autobiography of Alfred H. Mendes, 1897–1991*. Kingston, Jamaica: University of the West Indies Press, 2002.

Merritt, Brittany J. "Developing Little England: Public Health, Popular Protest, and Colonial Policy in Barbados, 1918–1940." PhD diss., University of South Florida, 2016.

Metzgen, Humphrey, and John Graham. *Caribbean Wars Untold: A Salute to the British West Indies*. Kingston, Jamaica: University of the West Indies Press, 2007.

Mintz, Sidney W. *Caribbean Transformations*. New York: Columbia University Press, 1989.

Mohammed, Patricia, ed. *Gendered Realities: Essays in Caribbean Feminist Thought*. Kingston, Jamaica: University of the West Indies Press, 2002.

———. "Taking Possession: Symbols of Empire and Nationhood." *Small Axe* 6, no. 1 (2002): 31–58.

Momsen, Janet Henshall, eds. *Women and Change in the Caribbean: A Pan-Caribbean Perspective*. Bloomington: Indiana University Press, 1993.

Moore, Brian L. *Cultural Power, Resistance, and Pluralism: Colonial Guyana, 1838–1900*. Barbados: University of the West Indies Press, 1995.

———. "'Married but not Parsoned': Attitudes to Conjugality in Jamaica, 1865–1920." In *Contesting Freedom: Control and Resistance in the Post-Emancipation Caribbean*, edited by Gad Heuman and David Trotman, 197–214. London, Macmillan, 2004.

Moore, Brian L., and Michele A. Johnson. *Neither Led Nor Driven: Contesting British Cultural Imperialism in Jamaica, 1865–1920*. Kingston, Jamaica: University of the West Indies Press, 2004.

——. *"They Do as They Please": The Jamaican Struggle for Cultural Freedom After Morant Bay*. Kingston, Jamaica: University of the West Indies Press, 2011.

Morrow, John H. *The Great War: An Imperial History*. New York: Routledge, 2004.

Moyd, Michelle. "Centring a Sideshow: Local Experiences of the First World War in Africa." *First World War Studies* 7 (2016): 111–30.

——. "Color Lines, Front Lines: The First World War from the South." *Radical History Review* 131 (2018): 13–35.

——. "Radical Potentials, Conservative Realities: African Veterans of the German Colonial Army in Post-World War I Tanganyika." *First World War Studies* 10, no. 1 (2019): 88–107.

——. *Violent Intermediaries: African Soldiers, Conquest, and Everyday Colonialism in German East Africa*. Athens, OH: Ohio University Press, 2014.

Munroe, Trevor. *The Politics of Constitutional Decolonization: Jamaica, 1944–62*. Jamaica: Institute of Social and Economic Research, University of the West Indies, 1972.

Murphy, David. "Race and the Legacy of the First World War in French Anti-Colonial Politics of the 1920s." In *Minorities and the First World War: From War to Peace*, ed. Hannah Ewence and Tim Grady, 201–26. London: Palgrave Macmillan, 2017.

Neiberg, Michael S. "Toward a Transnational History of World War I." *Canadian Military History* 17, no. 3 (2008): 31–37.

Neptune, Harvey. *Caliban and the Yankees: Trinidad and the United States Occupation*. Chapel Hill: University of North Carolina Press, 2007.

——. "Manly Rivalries and Mopsies: Gender, Nationality, and Sexuality in United States-Occupied Trinidad." *Radical History Review* 87 (2003): 78–95.

Newbury, Colin. "Milner, Alfred, Viscount Milner (1854–1925)." In *Oxford Dictionary of National Biography*. Oxford University Press, 2004; online ed., Oct 2008, http://www.oxforddnb.com/view/article/35037.

Newton, Velma. *The Silver Men: West Indian Labour Migration to Panama, 1850–1914*. Kingston, Jamaica: Ian Randle Publishers, 2004.

Obika, Nyahuma. *An Introduction to the Life and Times of T.U.B. Butler, the Father of the Nation*. Trinidad: Caribbean Historical Society, 1983.

O'Brien, Derek. "The Commonwealth Caribbean and the Westminster Model." In *The Oxford Handbook of Caribbean Constitutions*, ed. Derek O'Brien, Richard Albert, and Se-shauna Wheatle, 131–61. Oxford, England: Oxford University Press, 2020.

Omissi, David E, ed. *Indian Voices of the Great War: Soldiers' Letters, 1914–1918*. London: MacMillan, 1999.

Oxaal, Ivar. *Black Intellectuals and the Dilemmas of Race and Class in Trinidad*. Cambridge, MA: Schenkman Publishing, 1982.

Öztabak-Avcı, Elif. "Andrea Levy's 'World-Themed' Fiction: Curating the World Wars in *Small Island* and "Uriah's War." *Ariel: A Review of International English Literature* 53, no. 1–2, (2022): 139–65.

Page, Melvin E., ed. *Africa and the First World War*. New York: St. Martin's Press, 1987.

Palmer, Colin A. *Freedom's Children: The 1938 Labor Rebellion and the Birth of Modern Jamaica*. Chapel Hill: University of North Carolina Press, 2014.

——. *Inward Yearnings: Jamaica's Journey to Nationhood*. Kingston, Jamaica: The University of the West Indies Press, 2016.

BIBLIOGRAPHY [347]

Parker, Jason C. *Brother's Keeper: The United States, Race, and Empire in the British Caribbean, 1937–1962*. New York: Oxford University Press, 2008.

Parker, Jeffrey W. "Sex at a Crossroads: The Gender Politics of Racial Uplift and Afro-Caribbean Activism in Panama, 1918–32." *Women, Gender, and Families of Color* 4, no. 2 (2016): 196–221.

Paton, Diana. *No Bond But the Law: Punishment, Race, and Gender in Jamaican State Formation, 1780–1870*. Durham, NC: Duke University Press, 2004.

Perez, Louis A. "Armies of the Caribbean: Historical Perspectives, Historiographical Trends." *Latin American Perspectives* 14, no.4 (1987): 490–507.

Pérez-Fernández, Irene. "From over the Seven Seas the Empire's Sons Came": Addressing Historical Oblivion in Andrea Levy's "Uriah's War." *Journal of Postcolonial Writing* 53, no. 5 (2017): 518–29.

Perry, Kennetta Hammond. *London Is the Place for Me: Black Britons, Citizenship and the Politics of Race*. New York: Oxford University Press, 2016.

Petras, Elizabeth McLean. *Jamaican Labor Migration: White Capital and Black Labor, 1850–1930*. Boulder, CO: Westview Press, 1988.

Phillips, Anthony De V. "Go Ahead England, Barbados is Behind You: Barbadian Responses to the Outbreak of the Great War." In *Before and After 1865: Education, Politics and Regionalism in the Caribbean*, edited by Brian Moore and Swithin Wilmot, 342–50. Kingston, Jamaica: Ian Randle, 1998.

Polk, Khary Oronde. *Contagions of Empire: Scientific Racism, Sexuality, and Black Military Workers Abroad, 1898–1948*. Chapel Hill: University of North Carolina Press, 2020.

Post, Ken. *Arise Ye Starvelings: The Jamaican Labour Rebellion of 1938 and its Aftermath*. The Hague: Nijhoff, 1978.

———. *Strike the Iron: A Colony at War: Jamaica, 1939–1945*. Atlantic Highlands, NJ: Humanities Press, 1981.

Pradhan, S. D. "Indian Army and the First World War." In *India and World War I*, edited by Dewitt C. Ellinwood and S. D. Pradhan, 46–67. New Delhi: Manohar, 1978.

Pratt, Mary Louise. *Imperial Eyes: Travel Writing and Transculturation*. New York: Routledge, 1992.

Prochnow, Kyle. "'Saving an extraordinary expense to the nation': African recruitment for the West India Regiments in the British Atlantic world," *Atlantic Studies* 18, no. 2 (2021): 149–71.

Puri, Shalini. *The Caribbean Postcolonial: Social Equality, Post-Nationalism, and Cultural Hybridity*. New York: Palgrave MacMillan, 2004.

Puri, Shalini, and Lara Putnam, eds. *Caribbean Military Encounters*. New York: Palgrave Macmillan, 2017.

Putkowski Julian, and Julian Sykes. *Shot at Dawn: Executions in World War One by Authority of the British Army Act*. London: Leo Cooper, 1992.

Putnam, Lara. "Borderlands and Border Crossers: Migrants and Boundaries in the Greater Caribbean, 1840–1940." *Small Axe* 43, no. 1 (2014): 7–21.

———. "Circum-Atlantic Print Circuits and Internationalism from the Peripheries in the Interwar Era." In *Print Culture Histories Beyond the Metropolis*, edited by James Connolly, 215–40. Toronto: University of Toronto Press, 2016.

——. "Citizenship from the Margins: Vernacular Theories of Rights and the State from the Interwar Caribbean." *Journal of British Studies* 53, no. 1 (2014): 162–91.

——. *The Company They Kept: Migrants and the Politics of Gender in Caribbean Costa Rica, 1870–1960*. Chapel Hill: University of North Carolina Press, 2002.

——. "Eventually Alien: The Multigenerational Saga of British West Indians in Central America and Beyond, 1880–1940." In *Blacks and Blackness in Central America: Between Race and Place*, edited by Lowell Gudmundson and Justin Wolfe, 278–306. Durham, NC: Duke University Press, 2010.

——. "Nothing Matters but Color: Transnational Circuits, the Interwar Caribbean, and the Black International." In *From Toussaint to Tupac: The Black International Since the Age of Revolution*, edited by Michael O. West, William G. Martin, and Fanon Che Wilkins, 107–30. Chapel Hill: University of North Carolina Press, 2009.

——. "Provincializing Harlem: The 'Negro Metropolis' as Northern Frontier of a Connected Caribbean." *Modernism/Modernity* 20, no. 3 (2013): 469–84.

——. *Radical Moves: Caribbean Migrants and the Politics of Race in the Jazz Age*. Chapel Hill: University of North Carolina Press, 2013.

——. "Undone by Desire: Migration, Sex across Boundaries, and Collective Destinies in the Greater Caribbean, 1840–1940." In *Connecting Seas and Connected Ocean Rims: Indian, Atlantic, and Pacific Oceans and China Seas Migrations from the 1830s to the 1930s*, edited by Dirk Hoerder and Donna Gabaccia, 302–37. Leiden: Brill, 2011.

Queeley, Andrea J. *Rescuing Our Roots: The African Anglo-Caribbean Diaspora in Contemporary Cuba*. Gainesville: University Press of Florida, 2015.

Ramdin, Ron. *Arising from Bondage: A History of the Indo-Caribbean People*. New York: New York University Press, 2000.

——. *The Making of the Black Working Class in Britain*. Brookfield, VT: Gower, 1987.

Reddock, Rhoda. *Elma Francois: The NWCSA and the Workers Struggle for Change in the Caribbean in the 1930s*. London: New Beacon Books, 1988.

——. "Men as Gendered Beings: The Emergence of Masculinity Studies in the Anglophone Caribbean." *Social and Economic Studies* 52, no. 3, (2003): 89–117.

——. *Women, Labour & Politics in Trinidad & Tobago: A History*. London: Zed Books, 1994.

Reddock, Rhoda E., ed. *Interrogating Caribbean Masculinities: Theoretical and Empirical Analyses*. Jamaica: University Press of the West Indies, 2004.

Reid, Christopher. *Islands at War: The British West Indian Experience of the First World War, 1914–1927*. PhD diss., Memorial University of Newfoundland, 2021.

Renfrew, Barry. *Britain's Black Regiments: Fighting for Empire and Equality*. Cheltenham, England: The History Press, 2020.

Reyes Rivas, Eyra Marcela. *El trabajo de las mujeres en la historia de la construcción del Canal de Panamá, 1881–1914*. Panama City: Universidad de Panamá, Instituto de la Mujer, 2000.

Richards, Glen. "Friendly Societies and Labour Organisation in the Leeward Islands, 1912–19." In *Before and After 1865: Education, Politics and Regionalism in the Caribbean*, edited by Brian Moore and Swithin Wilmot, 136–49. Kingston, Jamaica: Ian Randle, 1998.

BIBLIOGRAPHY [349]

———. "Race, Class and Labour Politics in Colonial Jamaica, 1900–1934." In *Jamaica in Slavery and Freedom: History, Heritage and Culture*, edited by Kathleen E.A. Monteith and Glen Richards, 340–62. Kingston, Jamaica: University of the West Indies Press, 2002.

Richardson, Bonham C. "Caribbean Migrations, 1838–1985." In *The Modern Caribbean*, edited by Franklin W. Knight and Colin A. Palmer, 203–28. Chapel Hill: University of North Carolina Press, 1989.

———. *Panama Money in Barbados, 1900–1920*. Knoxville: University of Tennessee Press, 1985.

Robb, George. *British Culture and the First World War*. Houndmills, Basingstoke, Hampshire: Palgrave, 2002.

Rocha, Elaine P., and Frederick Alleyne. "'*Millie Gone to Brazil*': Barbadian Migration to Brazil in the Early 20th Century." *Journal of the Barbados Museum and Historical Society* 58 (2012): 1–42.

Rodney, Walter. *A History of the Guyanese Working People, 1881–1905*. Baltimore, MD: The Johns Hopkins University Press, 1981.

Rogers, Simon. "There Were No Parades for Us." *The Guardian*, November 6, 2002. http://www.guardian.co.uk/uk/2002/nov/06/britishidentity.military.

Rossum, Deborah J. "'A Vision of Black Englishness': Black Intellectuals in London, 1910–1940." *Stanford Electronic Humanities Review* 5, no. 2 (1997): http://www.stanford.edu/group/SHR/5-2/rossum.html

Rubinstein, William D. "The Secret of Leopold Amery." *Historical Research* 73, no. 181 (2000): 176, 184–85.

Rush, Anne Spry. *Bonds of Empire: West Indians and Britishness from Victoria to Decolonization*. New York: Oxford University Press, 2011.

Ryan, Selwyn D. *Race and Nationalism in Trinidad and Tobago: A Study of Decolonization in a Multiracial Society*. Toronto: University of Toronto Press, 1972.

Saltman, Julian Thiesfeldt. "'Odds and Sods': Minorities in the British Empire's Campaign for Palestine, 1916–1919." PhD dissertation, University of California, Berkeley, 2013.

Samaroo, Brinsley. "Cyrus Prudhomme David: A Case Study in the Emergence of the Black Man in Trinidad Politics," *Journal of Caribbean History* 3 (1971): 77–78.

Samaroo, Brinsley, and Cherita Girvan. "The Trinidad Workingmen's Association and the Origins of Popular Protest in a Crown Colony." *Social and Economic Studies* 21, no. 2 (1972): 205–22.

Sammons, Jeffrey T., and John H. Morrow. *Harlem's Rattlers and the Great War: The Undaunted 369th Regiment and the African American Quest for Equality*. Lawrence: University Press of Kansas, 2014.

Saunders, Gail. *Race and Class in the Colonial Bahamas, 1880–1960*. Gainesville: University Press of Florida, 2016.

Scott, James C. *Domination and the Arts of Resistance: Hidden Transcripts*. New Haven: Yale University Press, 1990.

Senior, Olive. *Dying to Better Themselves: West Indians and the Building of the Panama Canal*. Kingston, Jamaica: University of the West Indies Press, 2014.

Shah, Nayan. *Stranger Intimacy: Contesting Race, Sexuality and the Law in the North American West*. Berkeley: University of California Press, 2011.

Sharpley-Whiting, T. Denean. *Negritude Women*. Minneapolis: University of Minnesota Press, 2002.

Sheller, Mimi. *Citizenship from Below: Erotic Agency and Caribbean Freedom*. Durham, NC: Duke University Press, 2012.

———. *Democracy after Slavery: Black Publics and Peasant Radicalism in Haiti and Jamaica*. Gainesville: University Press of Florida, 2000.

Shepherd, Anthony. *The Postal Censorship in Barbados During the First and Second World Wars*. London: British West Indies Study Circle, 1984.

Shepherd, Verene, Bridget Brereton, and Barbara Bailey, eds. *Engendering History: Caribbean Women in Historical Perspective*. New York: St. Martin's Press, 1995.

Sherlock, Phillip. *Norman Manley: A Biography*. London: Macmillan, 1980.

Sherwood, Marika. *Origins of Pan-Africanism: Henry Sylvester Williams, Africa, and the African Diaspora*. New York: Routledge, 2011.

Shesko, Elizabeth. "Constructing Roads, Washing Feet, and Cutting Cane for the *Patria*: Building Bolivia with Military Labor, 1900–1975." *International Labor and Working-Class History* 80 (2011): 6–28.

Singh, Kelvin. *Race and Class Struggles in a Colonial State: Trinidad 1917–1945*. Calgary: University of Calgary Press, 1994.

Singha, Radhika. *The Coolie's Great War: Indian Labour in a Global Conflict, 1914–1921*. New York: Oxford University Press, 2020.

Smith, Faith. *Strolling in the Ruins: The Caribbean's Non-Sovereign Modern in the Early 20th Century*. Durham, NC: Duke University Press, 2023.

Smith, Leonard. "Caribbean Bedlam: The Development of the Lunatic Asylum System in Britain's West Indian Colonies, 1838–1914." *Journal of Caribbean History* 44, no. 1 (2010): 1–47.

———. *Insanity, Race and Colonialism: Managing Mental Disorder in the Post-Emancipation British Caribbean, 1838–1914*. Basingstoke: Palgrave Macmillan, 2014.

Smith, Raymond T. *Kinship and Class in the West Indies: A Genealogical Study of Jamaica and Guyana*. Cambridge: Cambridge University Press, 1988.

Smith, Richard. "'The Black Peril': Race, Masculinity and Migration During the First World War." In *Gendering Migration: Masculinity, Femininity and Ethnicity in Post-War Britain*, edited by Louise Ryan and Wendy Webster, 19–34. Aldershot: Ashgate, 2008.

———. "British West Indian Memories of World War One: From Militarized Citizenship to Conscientious Objection." In *Caribbean Military Encounters*, edited by Shalini Puri and Lara Putnam, 39–47. New York: Palgrave Macmillan, 2017.

———. "'Heaven Grant You Strength to Fight the Battle for Your Race': Nationalism, Pan-Africanism and the First World War in Jamaican memory." In *Race, Empire and First War Writing*, edited by Santanu Das, 265–82. New York: Cambridge University Press, 2011.

———. *Jamaican Volunteers in the First World War: Race, Masculinity, and the Development of National Consciousness*. Manchester: Manchester University Press, 2004.

———. "Loss and Longing: Emotional Responses to West Indian Soldiers during the First World War." *Roundtable: The Commonwealth Journal of International Affairs* 103, no. 2, (2014): 243–52.

BIBLIOGRAPHY [351]

———. "World War I and the Permanent West Indian Soldier." In *Empires in World War I: Shifting Frontiers and Imperial Dynamics in a Global Conflict*, edited by Andrew Tait Jarboe and Richard S. Fogarty, 303–27. New York: I.B. Tauris, 2014.

Snape, Michael Francis. *God and the British Soldier: Religion and the British Army in the First and Second World Wars*. London: Routledge, 2005.

Starling, John and Ivor Lee. *No Labour, No Battle: Military Labour during the First World War*. Stroud: Spellmount, 2009.

Stapleton, Timothy. "Visual Symbols and Military Culture in Britain's West African Colonial Army (c.1900–60)." *International Journal of Military History and Historiography* 41, no. 1 (2020): 42–73.

Steinbach, Daniel. "Between Intimacy and Violence: Imperial Encounters in East Africa during the First World War." In *Colonial Encounters in a Time of Global Conflict, 1914–1918*, edited by Santanu Das, Anna Maguire and Daniel Steinbach, 98–122. New York: Routledge, 2022.

Stephens, Michelle Ann. *Black Empire: The Masculine Global Imaginary of Caribbean Intellectuals in the United States, 1914–1962*. Durham, NC: Duke University Press, 2005.

Stephens, Ronald J., and Adam Ewing, eds. *Global Garveyism*. Gainesville: University Press of Florida, 2019.

Stevens, Margaret. *Red International and Black Caribbean: Communists in New York City, Mexico and the West Indies, 1919–1939*. London: Pluto Press, 2017.

Stoddart, Brian. "Cricket and Colonialism in the English-speaking Caribbean to 1914: Towards a Cultural Analysis." In *Pleasure, Profit, Proselytism: British Culture and Sport at Home and Abroad*, edited by J. A. Mangan, 231–57. Totowa, NJ: Frank Cass, 1988.

Stolar, Ann Laura. "Colonial Archives and the Arts of Governance." *Archival Science* 2 (2002): 87–109.

Stovall, Tyler. "The Color Line behind the Lines: Racial Violence in France during the Great War." *American Historical Review* 103, no.3 (1998): 737–69.

———. "Colour-Blind France? Colonial Workers during the First World War." *Race & Class* 35, no. 2 (1993): 35–55.

———. "Love, Labor, and Race: Colonial Men and White Women in France during the Great War." In *French Civilization and its Discontents: Nationalism, Colonialism, Race*, edited by Tyler Stovall and Georges Van den Abbeele, 297–323. Lanham, MD: Lexington Books, 2003.

Streets, Heather. *Martial Races: The Military, Race and Masculinity in British Imperial Culture, 1857–1914*. New York: Manchester University Press, 2004.

Sullivan, Frances Peace. "'Forging Ahead' in Banes, Cuba: Garveyism in a United Fruit Company Town." *New West Indian Guide* 88, no. 3–4 (2014): 231–61.

Tabili, Laura. *'We Ask For British Justice': Workers and Racial Difference in Late Imperial Britain*. Ithaca, NY: Cornell University Press, 1994.

Taylor, Christopher. *Empire of Neglect: The West Indies in the Wake of British Liberalism*. Durham, NC: Duke University Press, 2018.

Teelucksingh, Jerome. *Caribbean Liberators: Bold, Brilliant and Black Personalities and Organizations*. Palo Alto, CA: Academica Press, 2013.

[352] BIBLIOGRAPHY

———. *Ideology, Politics, and Radicalism of the Afro-Caribbean*. New York: Palgrave Macmillan, 2016.

———. *Labour and the Decolonization Struggle in Trinidad and Tobago*. New York: Palgrave Macmillan, 2015.

Thame, Maziki. "Racial Hierarchy and the Elevation of Brownness in Creole Nationalism." *Small Axe* 21, no. 3 (2017): 111–23.

Thomas, Deborah A. *Modern Blackness: Nationalism, Globalization, and the Politics of Culture in Jamaica*. Durham, NC: Duke University Press, 2004.

Thomas-Hope, Elizabeth M. "The Establishment of a Migration Tradition: British West Indian Movements to the Hispanic Caribbean in the Century after Emancipation." *International Migration* 24 (1986): 559–71.

Thompson, Krista. *An Eye for the Tropics: Tourism, Photography, and Framing the Caribbean Picturesque*. Durham, NC: Duke University Press, 2007.

Trouillot, Michel-Rolph. *Silencing the Past: Power and the Production of History*. Boston, MA: Beacon Press, 1995.

Tynan, Jane. *British Army Uniform and the First World War: Men in Khaki*. New York: Palgrave Macmillan, 2014.

Van Galen Last, Dirk, with Ralf Futselaar. *Black Shame: African Soldiers in Europe, 1914-1922*, translated by Marjolijn de Jager. New York: Bloomsbury Academic, 2015.

Varnava, Andrekos, and Michael Walsh. "Colonial Volunteerism and Recruitment in the British Empire during the Great War." *Itinerario* 38, no. 3 (2014): 19–26.

Watkins-Owens, Irma. *Blood Relations: Caribbean Immigrants and the Harlem Community, 1900-1930*. Bloomington: Indiana University Press, 1996.

Way, Peter. "Black Service . . . White Money: The Peculiar Institution of Military Labor in the British Army during the Seven Years' War." In *Workers Across the Americas: The Transnational Turn in Labor History*, edited by Leon Fink, 57–80. New York: Oxford University Press, 2011.

Westerman, George W. *Los inmigrantes antillanos en Panamá*. Panamá: Impresora de la Nacion, 1980.

Whalan, Mark. *The Great War and the Culture of the New Negro*. Gainesville: University Press of Florida, 2008.

———. "'The Only Real White Democracy' and the Language of Liberation: The Great War, France, and African American Culture in the 1920s." In *Paris, Capital of the Black Atlantic: Literature, Modernity, and Diaspora*, edited by Jeremy Braddock and Jonathan P. Eburne, 52–77. Baltimore, MD: Johns Hopkins University Press, 2013.

Whitney, Robert, and Graciela Chailloux Laffita. *Subjects or Citizens: British Caribbean Workers in Cuba, 1900-1960*. Gainesville: University Press of Florida, 2013.

Williams, Chad L. "A Mobilized Diaspora: The First World War and Black Soldiers as New Negroes." In *Escape from New York: The New Negro Renaissance Beyond Harlem*, edited by Davarian L. Baldwin and Minkah Makalani, 247–69. Minneapolis: University of Minnesota Press, 2013.

———. *Torchbearers of Democracy: African American Soldiers in the World War I Era*. Chapel Hill: University of North Carolina Press, 2010.

———. *The Wounded World: W. E. B. Du Bois and the First World War*. New York: Farrar, Straus and Giroux, 2023.

Williams, Eric. *From Columbus to Castro: The History of the Caribbean, 1492–1969*. New York: Vintage, 1984.

Wilson, Peter J. *Crab Antics: A Caribbean Study of the Conflict Between Reputation and Respectability*. Prospect Heights, IL: Waveland Press, 1995.

Wilson, Ross. "The Burial of the Dead: The British Army on the Western Front, 1914–18." *War & Society* 31, no. 1 (2012): 22–41.

Winter, Jay Murray. *Remembering War: The Great War Between Memory and History in the Twentieth Century*. Yale University Press, 2006.

———. *Sites of Memory, Sites of Mourning: The Great War in European Cultural History*. Cambridge: Cambridge University Press, 1998.

Wood, Donald. *Trinidad in Transition: The Years After Slavery*. London: Oxford University Press, 1968.

Woodfin, Edward C. *Camp and Combat on the Sinai and Palestine Front*. New York: Palgrave Macmillan, 2012.

Woodward, David R. *Hell in the Holy Land: World War I in the Middle East*. Lexington: University Press of Kentucky, 2006.

Wright, Winthrop. *Café con Leche: Race, Class, and National Image in Venezuela*. Austin: University of Texas Press, 1990.

Vassell, Linnette. "The Movement for the Vote for Women 1918–1919." *Jamaican Historical Review* 18 (1993): 40–54.

Zenger, Robin Elizabeth. "West Indians in Panama: Diversity and Activism, 1910s–1940s." PhD diss., University of Arizona, 2015.

Zumoff, Jacob. "Black Caribbean Labor Radicalism in Panama, 1914–1921." *Journal of Social History* 47, no. 2 (2013): 429–57.

Zürcher, Erik-Jan. *Fighting for a Living: A Comparative Study of Military Labour 1500–2000*. Amsterdam: Amsterdam University Press, 2013.

INDEX

Italic page numbers refer to figures.

abuse, 104, 112, 126, 130, 137–40, 165, 172, 219, 231
accommodations, 4, 84, 112–14, 120–23, 148
activism, 2, 6, 9, 12, 22, 118, 139, 180, 249, 251; and demobilization, 177, 179–80, 190; and recruitment, 47, 49; and veterans' politics, 200, 206, 208, 221, 226, 234
advancement, 23, 48–49, 149–50, 152, 156, 160, 162
Africa, 4–6, 9, 12–15, *35–36*, 42, 48, 72, 93–94, 104, 179–80; and black transnationalism, 48; and colonial subjects, 19, 130, 133, 135, 144, 244; and discrimination, 147, 152, 166; East Africa, 32, 107, 109, 125, 213; North Africa, 14, 113; and slavery, 23, 242; Togoland, 69; West Africa, 10, 28–29, 69, 74, 118, 136, 171, 221; West African Frontier Force, 39, 147
African Blood Brotherhood, 182
African diaspora, 9, 12–13, 15, 23, 146
African Methodist Episcopal Church, 182
Allardyce, William, 178–79
Allen, H. T., 168–69
Allenby, Edmund, 138, 145–46, 153, 296n32
Allies, 1, 5, 41, 73, 125, 152, 213, 227, 244; and troops, 116, 126–27, 259n9
Amery, L. S., 153
Ancient Order of Foresters, 122, 161
Anderson, Samuel, 79
Anglicanism, 114
Anglo-Ashanti Wars, 28, 221
anti-colonialism, 143, 160, 163–64
Antigua, 66, *80*, 103, 176
Anti-Slavery and Aborigines' Protection Society, 20
anti-whiteness, 166, 218–19
Armistice, 15, 139, 152–55, 159, 175, 177, 180–81, 241–42, 301n97
Army Council, London, 145, 170, 220; and imperial belonging, 29–30, 38–39, 45; and recruitment, 54–55, 60, 81
Army Order No. 1 (1918), 138, 140, 143–53, 156, 165–67, 169–72, 178, 295n21, 295n26, 304n147

Army Service Corps, 43
Army Veterinary Corps, 43
Ashdown, Peter, 197, 311n113
Ashwood, Amy, 48
Asian communities, 5, 95, 130, 133, 180. *See also* Chinese people
Aspinall, Algernon, 44, 148
Australia, *35–36*, 59, 144, 259n9; Australian and New Zealand Army Corps (ANZAC), 110, 147
authority, military, 13, 74, 111, 141, 156, 158, 193–94, 199, 225. *See also* military authorities

Bahamas, 7, 25, 107, 119, 165, 262n32, 303n135; and demobilization, 178–79; First Bahamas Contingent, 83–84; and military labor, 114, 125, 131, 134; Nassau, 83, 108–9; and recruitment, 59, 69–71, 79–80
Balfour, Arthur, 20
Balfour Declaration (1917), 166
banana industry, 26, 184, 186
Barbados, 7, 11, 15, 102, 109, 221, 246, 250, 262n32, 303n135; Barbados Citizens' Contingent, 102; Barbados House of Assembly, 10, 150, 167; Barbados Legislative Council, 87, 148, 150; Bridgetown, 62, 87–88, 113; Combermere School, 83; and demobilization, 176–78, 181–82, 184, 186; and discrimination, 138, 141, 149–52, 154, 167; First Barbados Contingent, 83; and imperial belonging, 28, 31, 34, 36, 39–41, 44; Old Comrades' Association, 207; and recruitment, 53–54, 57–58, 73, *80*, 83, 87–88, 97, 103; St. Michael's, 82, 93
Barber, Karin, 7
Barchard, A. E., 121, 163
Battle of Poelcappelle, 101
Bean, Dalea, 13, 65
Belgium, 12, 41, 109, 127, 130; Flanders, 101; Ypres, *5*
benefits, soldiers', 7, 56, 67, 139, 143–47, 152–53, 156–57, 167–70, 185; and

[355]

benefits, soldiers' (*continued*)
veterans' politics, 179, 183, 185, 206,
208, 214, 235–36. *See also* Army Order
No. 1 (1918); compensation; wages
Bermuda, 115, 168
Billouin, Emanuel, 119, 121, 226
Blackden, L. S., 61, 116
Blackman, George, 250–51
black nationalism, 6, 19, 48, 180
blackness, 49, 74, 118–19, 122, 126, 131–33,
136, 161
black servicemen, 6–7, 12–15, 179, 212,
242, 244, 248, 250; and Caribbean
League, 162, 164; and discrimination,
138, 141, 144, 146–47, 149, 151, 153–54,
156–57, 168; and Europe, 118, 127,
132–33, 136; and recruitment, 28,
31, 38, 50, 55, 73–74, 81–82, 84, 93.
See also black West Indians
black transnationalism, 11–13, 15, 48
black West Indians, 4, 12–15, 133, 202,
239–42, 244, 250; black West Indian
women, 25, 31, 67, 181; and Caribbean
League, 161–62; and commemoration, 242, 244; and demobilization,
175–76, 179, 183, 185–86, 189–90; and
discrimination, 146, 169–72, 294n12;
and imperial belonging, 19–33, 36–43,
45–47; and racism, 111, 122, 169, 234;
and recruitment, 53, 58, 61, 72, 75,
85–86, 92–94, 96–99, 101, 103; and
reform, 49–50, 73; and uprisings, 187,
195, 197, 216–18; and veterans' politics,
216–17, 219, 221–23, 226–29. *See also*
black servicemen
Boer War. *See* South Africa: Second South
African War (Boer War)
Bolland, Nigel, 80
Bowen, A. S., 97, 99–100
bravery, 13, 40, 57, 72–73, 102–3, 113,
233
Brazil, 11, 48
Breeders' and Trainers' Association, Trinidad, 22
Briscoe, A. E., 66, 94
British Admiralty, 113, 115–16
British Army, 3–4, 8, 114, 250, 301n102;
Army Chemical Warfare Department,
156; British Army Act, 147; County of
London Regiment, 42; and demobilization, 177, 183, 189; and discrimination,
138–40, 143–45, 149, 151, 156–60, 167,
169–70, 177; Eleventh Battalion, Dev-
onshire Regiment, 42; General Headquarters, 138, 156; and imperial belong-

ing, 26–30, 32–33, 36–38, 40, 43–45;
Manual of Military Law, 26–27; Nineteenth London Regiment, 43; and racism, 14, 111–12, 125–26, 135–36, 147, 149,
151, 162, 244; and recruitment, 52–53,
55–56, 60, 77–78, 80–81, 84, 93, 96–102;
Royal Garrison Artillery, 43, 304n139;
Third Royal Berkshire Regiment, 176;
and veterans' politics, 180, 214–15, 220;
Worcestershire Regiment, 156, 160
British Crown, 10, 41, 47–48, 92, 111, 179,
181, 185, 191, 262n32; and veterans'
politics, 206, 211–12, 214, 218, 229, 233,
236. *See also* colonial governments
British Empire, 3–5, 7, 9, 11, 13, 240–44,
248; and blackness, 118, 131–33, 170;
and Caribbean League, 161–62, 165;
and commemoration, 241–42, 244;
and demobilization, 175, 184, 189; and
discrimination, 140–41, 143, 146, 149,
151–53, 156–57, 166–67, 169; and imperial belonging, 19–21, 23–25, 35–37,
44–46, 50; and military labor, 109–10,
117, 122; and racism, 112, 135–36, 169;
and recruitment, 52, 54–55, 58–60,
69, 72, 74, 76, 90, 93–95, 181; and
reform, 179, 182, 191; and veterans'
politics, 189, 203, 205–6, 209–10, 213,
224, 229–30, 238. *See also* colonial
governments; England; Great Britain;
United Kingdom
British Empire Workers and Citizens
Home Rule Party, 2
British Expeditionary Force, 171
British Guiana, 7, 11, 39, 148, 165, 178–82,
190, 303n135; and BWIR training,
120–21; Combined Court of British
Guiana, 58; Demerara, 28, 73, 86, 176;
First British Guiana Contingent, 83;
New Amsterdam, 92; and recruitment,
57–58, 60–61, 67–68, 79–80, 84, 96
British Honduras, *14*, 41, 47, 49, 165, 217,
246, 309n60; Belize Prison, 195, 202;
Belize Town, 7, 62, 187, 189–90, 192,
194, 196–99, 201–4; British Honduras
Contingent Committee (BHCC), 62,
198–202; British Honduras Employment Committee, 192, 198; British
Honduras Legislative Council, 187,
192; British Honduras Supreme
Court, 201; British Honduras Territorial Force, 195–97; Corozal, 181; and
demobilization, 177, 182, 185, 187–92,
200; and discrimination, 135, 141–*142*,
147; and recruitment, 53, 59, 62, 66,

INDEX [357]

79–80, 93, 97; Returned Soldiers Welfare Committee, 187, 195; and veterans' politics, 201–2, 210, 219

British Raj, 131

British servicemen, 5, 55, 110–11, 119, 130, 197, 250; and discrimination, 126, 135–39, 143, 149–50, 154, 156, 159, 163, 166–68, 171; and imperial belonging, 19–20, 26, 29, 32, 37, 46, 50; and veterans' politics, 214, 216, 220, 225, 235–36

British subjecthood, 3–4, 6–12, 96, 146, 162; and BWIR, 110–11, 115, 117–18, 122, 126–27, 130–31, 133–34; and discrimination, 139, 141, 143, 145, 156, 168; and imperial belonging, 19, 23, 26–27, 31, 34, 41, 46; and recruitment, 61, 69, 72, 74–77, 79, 86, 90, 92–93, 95, 103; and reform, 179, 181, 191; and veterans' politics, 206, 229, 242, 244

British Treasury, 147, 168

British West Indies Regiment (BWIR), 1–9, 11–15, 279n103, 104, 279n106, 107, 279n109, 280n110, 280n118, 286n18, 289n86, 290n111, 291n129, 297n45, 298n64; and Army Order No.1, 137–59, 166–72; British Honduras Contingent, 187, 193, 201–2; and Caribbean League, 160–65; and commemoration, 244–50; and demobilization, 175–84, 186–89, 191–93, 196–98, 201–2, 308n46; Eight Battalion, 155, 158, 162, 215; Eleventh Battalion, 155, 158, 163; Fifth Battalion, 144, 291n120; First Battalion, 138–39, 144, 148, 153, 215, 299n68, 299n77; Fourth Battalion, 155, 158, 163, 250, 269n59; and imperial belonging, 23, 30, 43, 45–46, 49; Jamaican Contingent, 91, 241–42, 249; and military labor, 107, 109–25, 127–35; Ninth Battalion, 154–55, 157–58, 163–65, 300n83; and recruitment, 51–61, 63–67, 69–71, 73–86, 89–94, 96–104; Second Battalion, 139, 144, 215, 299n68, 299n77; Seventh Battalion, 155, 158, 163; Sixth Battalion, 155, 163; Taranto mutiny, 140–41, 143, 152–60, 163–65, 171, 177, 300n79, 80; Tenth Battalion, 155, 158, 161–64; Third Battalion, 155, 160–61, 163, 299n77; and veterans' politics, 207–11, 213–16, 219–28, 231, 233–40

Brown, Bernard, 122, 164

Brown, Vincent, 53

brown people, 15, 93, 101, 132. *See also* colored West Indians

Bryan, Herbert, 241

Burkett, Algernon, 221–36, 238–39

Butcher, John, 152

Butler, F. G. A., 100

Butler, Tubal Uriah "Buz," 1–3, *8*, 206

Buxton, Travers, 20

cadets, 49, 83, 149–50

Cain, Hubert Hill, 49, 191

Cameroon, 39

Campbell, Joseph, 85–86

Canada, 11–12, *35*, 48, 59, 77, 92, 126, 144, 259n9; Canadian Expeditionary Force, 79, 147; Halifax, Nova Scotia, 115–17, 247; Kinmel Park Camp, 159; Militia of Canada, 36; and servicemen, 110, 115–16, 119, 159. *See also* Newfoundland

Caribbean League, 160–65, 171, 177–78, 182, 215, 302n114, 302n119

Carnival, 62–63

Cary-Barnard, Cyril Darcy Vivien, 171–72, 245, 300n79

Cavell, Edith, 66

censorship, 138, 182, 289n86

Central America, 75–79, 177, 238, 294n14. *See also individual countries*

Central Powers, 4

Chancellor, John, 138, 153, 209, 232–36, 238–39, 246

Channel Islands, 144–45

children, 5, 210, 216, 242; black children, 25–26, 48–49; and demobilization, 190, 194, 200, 203; and interracial encounters, 117, 119; and recruitment, 53–54, 64–65, 67–68, 78, 89; white children, 218. *See also* youth

China, 5, 95

Chinese Labour Corps, 130

Chinese people, 126–27, 130, 147; Chinese Caribbean people, 4, 15–16, 95, 120

Christianity, 37, 110–11, 147, 154

Cipriani, Arthur Andrew, 2–3, 20–24, 30, 34, 36, 46, 236, 245; and military labor, 113–14, 122; and recruitment, 59, 62–65, 82, 85, 96–98, 100, 221; and veterans' politics, 224–26, 228, 235–36, 239–40, 247–48

civilians, 2–5, 7, 12–13, 107, 152, 171, 245, 248; and BWIR, 110–12, 115–16, 118–19, 121–22, 126–27, 130–32, 135; and Caribbean League, 160–61; and demobilization, 176–77, 179, 185, 187–89, 194; and imperial belonging, 23, 29, 31–33, 36; and labor, 155, 163;

civilians (*continued*)
and racism, 136, 138–39, 146, 148, 245–46; and recruitment, 53–54, 57, 64–66, 69, 73–74, 77, 79–80, 87–88, 90; and uprisings, 193–97, 200, 203; and veterans' politics, 148, 208–10, 212, 216–17, 221–22, 225–26, 228, 231, 236, 249. *See also* labor, civilian
Clarke, Eugent Augustus, 74–75, 250–51, 325n29
Clarke, F. J., 167
class, 4, 23, 46, 242; and BWIR, 118, 145, 149–50, 157; and demobilization, 176, 184–85, 187; and discrimination, 150, 154; and veterans' politics, 214, 217–19. *See also* elite classes; middle classes; upper classes; working classes
clergymen, 53, 119, 122, 130
climates, geographic, 37–40, 115–17, 120–23, 125, 127, 130, 154
clothing, 53, 66, 114–16, 130, 148, 190, 194, 198, 237. *See also* military uniforms
Cobham, Cecil, 223
cocoa industry, 20, 36, 211
Collman, Herbert C., 160–61, 164
Colombia, 12
colonial authorities, 1–2, 15, 33–34, 95, 116–17, 167; and Caribbean League, 162–66; and commemoration, 241, 244; and demobilization, 175–80, 182–87, 189–90; and discrimination, 138–39, 141, 143, 148, 150–53, 156–58, 160, 163, 170–72, 194; and imperial belonging, 26, 33–34, 36–37, 39–41; and racial conflict, 214–15, 217, 219; and recruitment, 53–59, 61–63, 76–77, 79, 81, 84, 88, 90–97, 99–100, 103; and uprisings, 196–200, 202–4; and veterans' politics, 205–9, 211, 213, 220–22, 224–40, 245, 248, 250. *See also* colonial governments; Colonial Office, London
colonial governments, 1–3, 6–7, 9–11, 15, 248; and demobilization, 177, 185; and imperial belonging, 20, 30, 47; and racial conflict, 214, 217–18; and recruitment, 56–57, 59, 62–63, 72, 76, 86, 88, 94, 101; and reform, 164, 179, 181, 191; and uprisings, 197, 202; and veterans' politics, 180, 187, 205, 208, 213, 221–27, 229–35, 237–38, 246. *See also* British Crown; colonial authorities
Colonial Office, London, 10, 219, 239; and Caribbean League, 164–67; and demobilization, 168–70, 176–77, 186;

and discrimination, 141, 148, 152, 158, 167–70; and imperial belonging, 20, 24, 26–30, 37–40, 42–45; and recruitment, 54–61, 94, 97, 99–100, 103
color divisions, 5, 12, 29, 40, 51, 103, 127, 131, 133, 176; and discrimination, 144, 152, 154, 168–70; and veterans' politics, 217–18, 220, 228
colored West Indians, 12, 15, 44, 48, 244, 250; and BWIR, 4–5, 151, 248, 250; and demobilization, 176, 179, 183–85; and discrimination, 138, 141, 144, 146–47, 149, 151–54, 156–57, 164, 167–69, 171–72; and imperial belonging, 23–24, 26–27, 29–30, 32–33, 36–40, 42–47; and racism, 108–9, 111, 118, 169; and recruitment, 53, 55–58, 61–62, 73–74, 81–82, 84, 92–93, 96–97, 102–3; and reform, 48–50, 73; and veterans' politics, 186, 194, 197–98, 219, 223, 233, 236, 244. *See also* brown people
combat, 4, 12, 14, 50, 126, 133; and BWIR, 77, 109, 112, 126–27, 130, 133, 137–39, 151, 153–54, 219–20; 299n68; and imperial belonging, 24, 27, 31–32, 34, 39, 43–45
commanding officers, 104, 112, 121, 162–63, 172, 188; and discrimination, 138, 144–45, 154, 157
commemoration, 241–47, 249
commissions, 140, 143, 149–50, 156, 226, 298n64
compensation, 245, 248; and veterans' politics, 206, 208, 210, 213, 221, 223, 225, 231, 233, 235–39. *See also* Army Order No. 1 (1918); benefits, soldiers'; pensions; wages; war gratuities
complexion, skin, 15, 41, 43, 51–52, 74, 81, 97
conscription, 4, 52, 58, 92–95, 143, 181, 191, 259n9
Cordova, Michael de, 61
Corns, Cathryn, 159
Costa Rica, 11, 42, 76, 186
court-martialing, 7, 164, 199, 225
Cousturier, Lucie, 136
Cran, James, 187, 192–94, 196–97
Creole people, 22–24, 42, 61–62, 66, 100, 103, 146, 190, 219
criminalization, 88, 199, 201–2, 220, 222, 225
Crowe, J. H. V., 155–56
Cuba, 12, 186, 247
Cuban American Sugar Company, 186
Cubitt, B. B., 29, 55, 60, 146, 170, 304n150

INDEX [359]

Cunningham, Jacob Stanislaus, 123–25
Curaçao, 31

Dadd, G. J., 119, 122
Dale, Archibald "Arch," 35
Darnley, E. R., 29, 165, 169–70, 304n139
Darrow, Margaret, 133
Davis, J. A. Shaw, 77
Davis, Vernon, 216, 220
death, 100, 113–15, 133, 138, 152–53, 159, 213, 242, 248
de la Hire, Marie, 133
de Lisser, Herbert G., 24, 65, 81, 83, 116
demobilization, military, 6, 12, 15, 74, 152, 154, 159–65, 168–72, 208; and BWIR, 175–78, 181–89, 196, 206–11, 230, 235, 238, 245, 308n46
democracy, 2, 6–7, 14–15, 50–52, 112, 179–82, 191; and veterans' politics, 205–6, 214, 229, 240, 244
Diamond Jubilee, 179
disabled veterans, 116, 125, 185, 209, 239, 246–47; and disability pensions, 56, 117, 209–10
discharge, 1, 12, 31, 61, 87, 89–90, 101, 116–17, 121–22, 152, 169, 205; and Discharged Soldiers Central Authority (DSCA), 206, 208–14, 218, 223, 227, 231, 233. *See also* rejection, military
discipline, 1, 13, 27–28, 49, 97, 120–21, 139, 184, 193, 232; and discrimination, 155, 158, 165
discrimination, 4, 6, 14, 190; and British Army, 135, 137, 139–41, 149–50, 152, 156–57, 177, 215, 238, 248; and BWIR, 111–12, 126; and demobilization, 162, 165–66, 168, 171–72, 190; and imperial belonging, 26, 29, 42, 47; and recruitment, 52, 73, 81, 104. *See also* equality; oppression; racism
Distinguished Conduct Medal, 149
Domingo, W. A., 181, 197
Dominica, 30, 40, 69, *80*, 103, 141, 150, 176, 186
Douglas, Annie, 65–66
du Cros, Arthur, 20–21, 63
Dumas, Alexandre, 108
Dundonald, Douglas Mackinnon Baillie Hamilton Cochrane, 36, 38–39, 44
Dupuch, Etienne, 107–9, 111–14, 125–27, 130–31, 134–35, 291n120

East African Military Labour Corps, 144
East Indian people, 15–16, 24, 33, 61, 95–96, 98. *See also* Indo-Caribbean men

Eccleston, A. G., 72
economics, 6–7, 9–11, 158, 165, 240; and imperial belonging, 23, 31–32, 34–35, 37, 40; and recruitment, 52–57, 61, 67, 74, 78; and veterans, 181, 185–86, 190–91, 197–98, 201–3, 251; and veterans' politics, 207–13, 215, 220–21, 225–26, 228–31, 233, 235–38, 247
education, 65, 101, 103, 117–18, 162, 248; and BWIR, 145–46, 149, 157, 185; and recruitment, 47, 49, 51, 53, 83–84, 89, 96; and veterans' politics, 217, 238
Egypt, 37–39, 44, 72, 107, 109, 140–41, 144, 149; Alexandria, 112, 125; and BWIR, 111, 126, 152–53, 155, 194, 224–25; Egyptian Expeditionary Force, 138, 145
elite classes, 6, 9, 13, 23–25, 27, 29–30, 33–34, 49, 171, 210; and demobilization, 175–76, 184; and recruitment, 52–53, 60–62, 64–65, 69, 82, 94, 96–99, 102–3; white elites, 116, 166, 179, 195, 197, 209, 213, 218–19. *See also* planters; privilege; upper classes
Ellis, A. B., 28, 228
emancipation, 35, 48, 242
emigration, 11, 177, 186–87, 211. *See also* migration
Empire Day, 45, 203
employment, 2, 31, 37, 39, 44, 77, 96, 234; and demobilization, 180, 184–90; and interracial encounters, 107, 117–18, 133, 165; and veterans, 192, 198–99, 202, 225, 245, 247; and veterans' politics, 209–11, 214, 231–32, 234–38
England, 6–7, 14, 19, 126, *129*, 137, 279n109, 286n18; Birmingham, 32; Brighton, 121; Bristol, 118; and BWIR, 109, 111–12, 114–19, 147, 151–53, 165; General Federation of Trade Unions, 143; and imperial belonging, 28, *35*–37, 41–44; Liverpool, 118, 123; Newhaven, 121; North Camp, 119–23, 125; Officer Training Corps, 42–43; Plymouth, 113, 117, 119, 123, 145; and recruitment, 55–56, 61, 69, 72, 75, 78, 80, 92, 100–101; Seaford, 94, 118–20, 122–25, 290n111; Surrey Convalescent Home, Seaford, 123–24, 290n112; and veterans' politics, 182, 189, 215–16, 229, 235, 239, 244, 249–50; Withnoe Camp, 119, 123, 125, 296n37. *See also* London, England
English language, 11, 23, 49, 77, 89, 134, 179; and BWIR, 8, 61, 75, 81, 122, 127, 132, 147, 291n129, 294n14

INDEX

enlistment, 3–4, 8, 11, 13, 194, 201, 279n107, 280n110; and discrimination, 143–44, 150–51, 154, 156, 167, 169; and elitism, 97–102; and imperial belonging, 21, 23, 26, 28, 33, 36–38, 42–46; and military labor, 107, 109, 111–12, 117, 122, 130–31; and recruitment, 51–53, 57–58, 60–61, 64, 66–68, 70–71, 75–94; and veterans' politics, 209–11, 219, 221, 225, 227, 231, 235, 237–39, 244–45, 250

equality, 74, 81, 94, 141, 151, 153; and British Army, 160, 170, 176, 180, 191; racial equality, 4–6, 9, 15, 47–48, 135, 143, 146, 240; and veterans' politics, 208, 210, 229, 240, 244, 250

ethnicity, 16, 22, 27, 74

Europe, 5–6, 9, 14, 152, 179, 181, 210, 250; and demobilization, 176, 179–81, 189; and discrimination, 141, 144, 150, 152, 158; and imperial belonging, 19, 23–25, 27–32, 34, 36–40, 45, 47, 49; and interracial encounters, 125, 127, 132–35, 217; and recruitment, 51, 56, 74, 76, 93–94, 100, 103–4; and travel, 113, 118, 125, 154–55

Europeans, 4, 15, 42–43, 56, 62, 81, 132–35, 158–59; and veterans' politics, 189, 199, 203–4, 215

families, 7, 13, 22, 26, 149, 184, 186–88, 274n8; and BWIR, 222, 241; and interracial encounters, 107–8, 119, 134; and recruitment, 54–56, 61, 69, 79, 94–96, 101; and veterans' politics, 202–3, 210–12, 221, 229, 236–37. *See also* children; mothers; sons; wives

Fiddes, G. V., 38

Fiji, 148, 155, 168; Fijian Labour Corps, 126, 304n139

finances. *See* economics; fundraising

fitness, military, 13, 49, 120; and imperial belonging, 24, 27–28, 30–31, 39; and recruitment, 52, 58, 60–61, 74, 84–86, 89. *See also* medical exams

Fleming, Francis, 167, 303n135

Flowers, Annie, 202

Fogarty, Richard, 133

France, 5, 12, 19, 27, 43, 74, 92, 109, 259n9, 267n33; Abbeville, 100; Arras, 127; Boulogne, 126–27; and BWIR, 107, 109, 111–12, 125–36, 154–56, 189, 213, 219, 250–51; and colonialism, 58, 76, 135, 213; Dijon, 134; Fréjus, 136; Jura Mountains, 126; Marseille, 126–27, 155; Meuse, 136; Paris, 13, 126;

Rouen, 127; St. Martin's Rest Camp, Boulogne, 126; and troops, 38, 40, 43, 58, 76, 92, 131–32, 135–36, 159; and women, 133–35; Ypres, 44. *See also* French language; French Revolution

Fraser, Percy, 176, 217

freedom, 10, 46, 74, 94, 111, 157, 160–62, 182, 187, 242

French language, 49, 132, 134

French Revolution, 23, 28

fundraising, 25, 44–46, 116, 188, 191, 221; and recruitment, 53, 62, 64, 76–77, 97, 99–100, 102

Garvey, Marcus, 1, 19–23, 47–48, 51, 69, 118, 177, 180–81

gender, 4, 13, 23, 49, 127, 160, 184, 221; and patriotism, 66, 133–34, 146; and recruitment, 69, 86, 104, 247. *See also* masculinity; women

George, Percy, 192–93, 195, 201

George V (King), 19–20, 36, 41, 44–46, 64, 69, 73, 139, 294n12; and commemoration, 241, 244–45; and demobilization, 184–85, 189; and recruitment, 74, 76, 86, 90, 93–94, 98, 103; and veterans' politics, 227, 233

Germany, 6, 24–25, 37, 39, 49–50, 94, 182, 203; and World War I, 32, 40–43, 69, 72–75, 77, 90–91, 115, 152, 163, 250

Glymph, Thavolia, 9

Gordon, William G., 97, 219–20, 229

Graham, J. A., 120, 123

Graham, Thomas, 192, 194

Grant, J. H., 194, 198

Great Britain, 9, 16, 127, 259n9; British House of Commons, 143; British House of Lords, 143; British Independent Order of Good Samaritans and Daughters of Samaria, 45; British Navy, 36, 72, 88, 115, 178, 202; British Parliament, 20, 229; and demobilization, 175, 177, 181; and discrimination, 141, 144, 148, 151–53, 156, 162, 165, 167; and imperial belonging, 20, 23–28, 30–31, 35, 37, 41–42, 46, 49; and recruitment, 58, 66, 72–73, 82, 86, 93; and veterans' politics, 208, 215, 225, 231, 233, 236, 242, 244, 250. *See also* British Army; British Empire; British subjecthood; England; United Kingdom

Grenada, 3, 7, 11, 141, 190, 289n86; Grenada Legislative Council, 88, 92; Grenada Representative Government Movement, 2; Grenada Union of

INDEX [361]

Returned Soldiers, 1–2, 206, 208; and imperial belonging, 36, 41–43, 46–47, 50; and recruitment, 59, 62, 69, 73, 79–*80*, 92, 102; St. George's, 1–2, 49, 83, 113, 206, 208
Grindle, Gilbert, 27, 29, 38, *56–57*, 99–100, 158, 165, 167, 169, 175
Guadeloupe, 31
Guatemala, 182
Gullace, Nicoletta, 66

Haddon-Smith, George, 57, 62, 153
Haitian Revolution, 23
Hall, Rufus, 194, 197, 201
Hamilton, Patrick, 195, 197–99
Hankey, Maurice, 175–76
Harcourt, Lewis, 19–20, 33, 37–39, 42, 44–45, 55
Harper, Edwin, 212–13
Harris, Arthur, 216, 220
Havelock, E. W., 25
Hayes-Saddler, James, 167, 303n135
Haynes, Samuel, 187, 196–204, 240, 247
Hercules, F. E. M., 118
Hitchens, Leslie W., 77
HMS *Constance*, 187, 197
HMS *Dartmouth*, 216, 220
HMS *Magdalena*, 113–14
HMS *Verdala*, 112–13, 115–17, 249
HMS *Veronej*, 187
Hoar, William, 195, 202
Hodge, Samuel, 31, 269n59
Hodgeon, Frederic M., 167, 303n135
Hoganson, Kristin, 23
Homfray, J. R. H., 175–79, 305n14
Hope, J. C., 83, 149
Horner, Alfred, 110, 119, 126–27, 130–32, 134
hospitality, 119, 131–32, 135
hospitals, 88, 114–16, 123–24, 127, 133–34, 137, 144–45, 171, 216
Howard University, 48
Howe, Glenford, 88, 134, 150
Huggins, George F., 97–100, 209, 218
Hughes-Wilson, John, 159
Hulse, George, 194
Hulse, Greville, 197–98
humiliation, 6, 48, 63, 90, 107, 111, 149, 197
Hutson, Eyre, 187–90, 195–99, 202–3, 217, 314n162

illness, 39, 89, 114–15, 123–25, 137, 154, 171. *See also* medical ailments

imperial belonging, 10, 15, 20, 23, 34–35, 117–18, 241, 244
imperial patriotism, 7, 9–10, 13, 15, 20, 23, 30, 37, 50; and BWIR, 95, 123, 156; and demobilization, 177, 180, 182, 184, 189; and recruitment, 52, 93–94; and veterans' politics, 206, 229, 242, 245, 247. *See also* patriotism
imperial troops, 139, 147–49, 159, 170, 191, 214, 233, 236
impressment, 4, 23, 92
imprisonment, 2–3, 90, 94, 111, 158–59, 201–3, 220, 232, 245–46
India, 5, *35*, 59, 259n9; Indian Army, 27–28, 40, 110, 144, 267n33; Indian soldiers, 60, 125–26, 130–31, 144. *See also* East Indian people; Indo-Caribbean men
Indigenous peoples, 60, 67–*68*, 88, 126, 133
Indo-Caribbean men, 4, 60–61, 79, 89, 95, 218–19, 240. *See also* East Indian people
infantry troops, 127, 131, 136, 147, 156, 171, 177
interracialism, 4, 14, 46, 116, 177, 244; and BWIR, 127, 130–34, 217; and discrimination, 112, 139, 143, 149, 162, 166, 170, 172, 244; and recruitment, 52, 55, 64, 76, 81, 86, 91, 93, 97–98, 103–4
Irish people, 110, 119, 126, 203
Isle of Man, 144–45
Israel, 145
Italy, 107, 109, *129*, 213, 250; Cimino Camp, 154–55, 158; Italian Labour Corps, 155; Taranto, 139–43, 154–60, 162–65, 171–72, 175–77, 194, 215, 245–46, 300n79

Jamaica, 6–7, 10–11, 15, 48, 94, 303n135; Billy Dunn Estate, Half Way Tree, 32; and BWIR, 114–17, 120, 123, 131–32; and Caribbean League, 162–65; Central Supplementary Allowance Committee (CSAC), 185–86; Christiana, 26; Claremont, 42; and commemoration, 241–*43*, 244; Constabulary Force, 83; and demobilization, 176–78, 180–82, 184–85, 190, 192; and discrimination, 148, 154–55, 160, 162–65, 168; Duan Vale, 72; Gayle, 92; and imperial belonging, 20, 22, 24, 28, 30–34, 39, 41–43; Irish Town, 65–66; Jamaica Defence Force (JDF), 250; Jamaica Ex-Service Men Association, 207; Jamaica Federation of Labour (JFL), 184; Jamaica Legion, 251; Jamaica Legislative Council, 88, 94–95, 185; Jamaica Military

Jamaica (*continued*)

Headquarters, 183; Jamaica Military Museum, 250; Jamaican Gleaner Company, 69; Jamaica Old Comrades' Association, 246; Jamaica Patriotic League, 47–48; Jamaica War Contingent, 81–82, 86; Linstead, 103; Manchester, 48; National Club, 181; Ocho Rios, 69; Point Hill, 64; Port Antonio, 45, 161; Port Henderson, 85; and recruitment, 51–54, 57–62, 65–66, 69, 72, 74–85, 87–91, 94; Retreat, 102; St. Andrew, 87; St. Ann's Comrades of the War Association, 207; St. Elizabeth, 83, 184; St. Mary, 83; Up Park Camp, 32, 75, 86, 89, 92, 250; and veterans' politics, 206–7, 209, 217, 230, 238, 242–51; War Contingent Committee, 61; Whitfield Town, 26. *See also* Kingston, Jamaica

James, C. L. R., 1, 42, 51–52, 84, 101–2

James, Winston, 146

Johnson, Jack, 223–24

Johnson, S. A. G., 89

Jones, A. P., 160, 164

journalism, 2, 6, 9, 22, 46, 49, 118, 133, 181, 221, 230; and recruitment, 61, 65, 81, 93

Julien, W. E., 138–39, 149

justice, 6, 11, 19, 30, 46, 94, 114, 251; and demobilization, 180, 187, 199; and discrimination, 130, 147, 151, 156–57, 160, 162, 167, 169–70; and veterans' politics, 206, 233, 240, 242, 245

Kelley, Robin D. G., 10

Kennedy, E. C., 197

King's Royal Rifle Corps, 100, 144

Kingston, Jamaica, 11, 19, 25, 32–33, 46–47, 109, 161, 207; Chee Kung Tong Society, Kingston, 95; and commemoration, 242, 246–47, 250; and demobilization, 180, 183–85, 187; Kingston Public Hospital, 88; Memorial Square, 241; and recruitment, 67, 74, 83, 87, 91, 95

Kipling, Rudyard, 157

Kitchener, Herbert, 4, 28, 32, 42, 45

labor, civilian, 5, 11–12, 133, 219, 240, 248; and demobilization, 180, 183–86, 188, 190, 192; and discrimination, 147, 154–55, 163; and imperial belonging, 26, 31, 36, 45; and recruitment, 52–53, 65, 75, 77, 80, 84–85, 89, 92, 94–96, 103; and veterans' politics, 209–11, 221, 232, 234, 236; and Western Front, 126, 130–31, 133–35. *See also* labor movements; working classes; working conditions

labor, military, 4–5, 9, 133; and BWIR, 109–11, 126–27, 133, 137, 140, 147, 179, 213; and discrimination, 144, 154, 156–58, 171; and imperial belonging, 23, 32, 34, 37, 46, 49; and recruitment, 74, 93

labor and migration studies, 9

labor movements, 206, 208, 218–19, 221, 226, 234–35, 240, 248. *See also* labor, civilian

Laurence, Stephen, 233

Law, Bonar, 55–56, 96, 99–100, 143–44

laws, colonial, 2, 62, 74, 83, 88, 90, 94–95, 147, 151; and veterans' politics, 179, 197–98, 200, 217–18, 222–24, 230, 232

Lazare, Emanuel M'Zumbo, 179–80

League of the Empire, 83

Leeward Islands, 15, 26, 30, 59, 79, 178, 303n135; Leeward Island Contingent, 88, 150

Le Hunte, George, 20, 34, 58, 100, 148, 167, 275n22, 303n135

Lentz-Smith, Adriane, 15

Lewis, Gordon K., 9

literacy, 8, 53, 80–81, 83, 88–89, 103; and BWIR, 127, 141, 221, 291n129, 294n14

Llewelyn, R. B., 167, 303n135

local authorities, 167, 245; and demobilization, 178, 185–87, 195; and recruitment, 57, 59, 61–63, 74, 81, 90, 99–100; and veterans' politics, 200, 202, 205–6, 214, 217, 219, 225, 228–31, 233, 239

London, England, 6, 10, 13, 20–21, 26, 245; County of London Regiment, 42; and discrimination, 141, 148, 172; and imperial belonging, 34, 36, 40, 43; and interracial encounters, 118, 125; and recruitment, 54, 57, 92, 95, 99; and veterans' politics, 231, 245; West India Committee, 25, 33, 44, 96, 247; West Indian Contingent Committee, 120, 148, 166–67, 188, 297n47, 304n151. *See also* Colonial Office, London; War Cabinet, London; War Office, London

Long, Walter, 151–52, 156, 165

Louise, Princess Marie, 148

loyalty, 2, 7, 9–11, 117, 244; and demobilization, 176–85, 191, 199; and discrimination, 139, 143, 146, 156, 162, 168–69, 171; and imperial belonging, 19–21, 23–25, 30–31, 34–35, 37–39, 41, 45, 47; and interracial encounters, 111, 113, 117; and recruitment, 63, 69, 75,

94, 103; and veterans' politics, 196–97,
199, 201–4, 206, 219, 230, 242
Lynch, J. Challenor, 87–88, 148–52

Macpherson, Anne, 66
Mair, Ernest, 244–45
Mallet, Claude, 77–78
Malta, 155
Manley, Norman and Roy, 43–44
Mann, Gregory, 10, 74, 171
Manning, William, 20, 24, 31–33, 42–43,
57–59, 62, 94, 161, 275n22
Māori Pioneer Battalion, 126
marches, 67, 90–91, 120, 124–25 134, 155;
and demobilization, 184, 189, 193–96;
and veterans' politics, 207, 215–16, 219,
232–33, 245–47. *See also* parades
Marryshow, T. A., 2, 47, 49, 206
Martinique, 12, 31, 58
martial races theory, 27, 60
Mary of Teck (Queen), 189
masculinity, 4, 9, 13, 49, 101, 107–8, 139;
and imperial belonging, 21, 23–24, 27,
34–35, 42; and recruitment, 53, 66–67,
72–74, 85–86, 91, 93
May, G. H., 216–17
McDonald, Frederick, 193–94, 196–97,
199, 201–2
McKay, Claude, 6, 175, 180
medical ailments, 85–89, 91, 116, 209, 221,
247; mental illness, 209, 247. *See also*
fitness, military; illness
medical exams, 7, 33, 51, 53, 80, 83–87, 92
medical treatment, 83, 87–88, 114, 124–25.
See also nurses; physicians
Meilke, Louis, 47–49
Mendes, Alfred Hubert, 100–101
Mesopotamia, 107, 109, 140–41, 194, 201,
213
methodology of book, 3, 7–13
middle classes, 13, 47, 49, 108, 118, 149,
184, 190; and recruitment, 62, 65, 84,
95, 97, 101–3
Middle East, 5, 9, 12, 14, 104, 109, 125, 219,
224, 250, 299n68, 299n77; and discrimination, 138, 140, 150, 154
migration, 11–13, 20, 31, 48, 95, 109, 154,
211, 263n41; and demobilization,
186–87, 189, 199; and recruitment,
51–53, 60, 64, 75–76, 79. *See also*
emigration
militancy, 6–7, 136, 141, 161, 164, 171; and
veterans' politics, 176–77, 180–81, 187,
194, 198, 201, 203, 208, 234, 244
military authorities, 7, 29, 95, 101, 112, 116,
130; and Caribbean League, 162–63,

166; and demobilization, 176, 183;
and discrimination, 138–39, 148, 151,
156, 158–59, 170–71; and recruitment,
53–56, 60–62, 66, 76, 84, 86, 90, 92
military barracks, 75, 80, 85–87, 89, 92,
104, 119, 127, 131, 232
military boosters, 23, 30, 32, 36, 40, 46;
and recruitment, 54, 57, 60, 62, 64, 72,
77, 81, 85, 88
Military Medal, 101
Military Service Bill, Jamaica, 94–95
military training, 14, 22, 27–28, 32–33,
37–40, 42, 49, 59, 100, 178; and BWIR,
53, 59, 82, 85, 87, 89–90, 94, 119–24;
and discrimination, 137, 139, 161
military uniforms, 25, 33, *35*, 42, *142*,
249; and BWIR training, 102–3,
107, 115, 119, 121, 124; and interracial
encounters, 107, 115, 121–22, 125–26,
131; and recruitment, 57, 67, 74–75,
81, 87, 90–91; and uprisings, 193, 196,
198; and veterans' politics, 209, 216,
219–20, 231, 250
militias, 28, 32–33, 36, 65, 83, 96, 121,
178–79, 187, 196, 227
Milner, Alfred, 165–67, 169–70, 176, 178,
184, 246, 308n44
Mitchell, W. H. Steele, 36, 42, 44
mobilization, military, 3, 11–12, 99, 109,
126, 133, 221, 247; and discrimination, 140, 143, 152, 162; and imperial
belonging, 20, 23–24, 27, 31, 33, 45;
and recruitment, 52–53, 57, 59–61,
63, 65, 67, 76, 79, 82–85, 96. *See also*
demobilization, military
Montserrat, *80*, 150
Moore, W. A., 19, 36
Morales, Eduardo, 6
morality, 48, 65–67, 88, 90, 133, 170, 225,
228, 248
mothers, 26, 54, 66–67, 69, 84, 133–34
Moulton, Charles, 31–32
murder, 133, 136, 159, 203–4
mutinies, 137–43, 154–60, 163–65, 171,
176–77, 245–46
mutual obligation, 30, 46, 52, 94, 139, 143,
156, 180, 188, 235, 246
Myers, A. A., 40–41

Napoleonic Wars, 23, 25, 28
Nardal, Jane, 12
Nathan, Alonzo, 43
nationalism, 9–10, 48–49, 100, 135, 143,
160; black, 6, 19, 48, 180. *See also*
patriotism
Negro World, 6, 180–82, 203, 244

Newfoundland, 59, 144; Royal Newfoundland Regiment, 147
New Zealand, *35–36*, 59, 92, 126, 144, 259n9; Australian and New Zealand Army Corps (ANZAC), 110, 147
Nicaragua, 11; Bluefields, 76
noncombatant duties, 4–5, 14, 24, 126–27; and BWIR, 77, 109, 112, 130, 137, 153, 219–20; and Non-Combatant Corps, 144
nonwhite colonial troops, 27, 46, 127, 133, 141, 146, 149, 179, 244. *See also* British West Indies Regiment (BWIR)
nurses, 53, 63, 66, 123–24, 133–34

obedience, 13, 111, 120, 158, 194
O'Brien, Charles, 138–39, 150–52, 167, 176, 178, 184, 246
Olivier, Sydney, 148, 167, 303n135
oppression, 4, 6, 69, 131, 191, 244–45
Oxford University, 43, 149

Padmore, George, 6, 51
Palestine, 137–38, 140, 219, 299n68; Gaza, 145, 296n32
Pan African Association, 179
Panama, 6–7, 12, 14, 154, 161, 209, 279n107; Bocas del Toro, 75, 77, 89; Canal Zone, 32, 37, 52–53, 76, 181, 211, 269n60; Friendly Societies War Contingent Committee, 89; Isthmian Canal Commission, 11, 31, 48, 269n60; Panama City, 75, 77, 79; and recruitment, 32, 64, 78–79, *79–80*
parades, *3*, 65, 90, 120–25, 160, 184, 187, 215–16, 219–20, 224. *See also* marches
patriotism, 4, 11, 13, 113, 245, 248; and discrimination, 139, 156; and gender, 133–34; and imperial belonging, 19–20, 24–25, 30, 34, 48; and recruitment, 62, 64–66, 69, 75, 83, 90, 93, 103; and veterans' politics, 181, 191–92, 201, 212, 222, 224. *See also* imperial patriotism; nationalism
Peace Day, 184, 215, 217, 220–21
pensions, 7, 55, 180, 185, 229, 250–51; disability pensions, 56, 117, 209–10
physicians, 13, 42, 60–61, 84–85, 87–88, 114, 233
planters, 13, 20–22, 25, 29–30, 36, 42, 44, 149, 209, 219; and recruitment, 62, 64, 96–102
poetry, 9, 13, 72, 89, 101, 112, 123–25, 157, 180, 212–13, 244
Poincaré, Raymond, 19

policing, 7, 37, 44, 62, 65, 83, 90, 99, 159, 164; and demobilization, 178, 182, 189, 195–97, 202; and veterans' politics, 200, 209, 220, 222, 224, 232, 239
politics, 2–3, 5, 7, 9–13, 15, 161, 163, 166; and demobilization, 176–77, 179, 185; and discrimination, 139, 141, 150, 152, 161, 163, 166–71; and imperial belonging, 19, 23, 25, 28–29, 35, 38–39, 44–45, 47; and recruitment, 52, 63, *68*, 73–74, 77, 95, 99; and reform, 48–50, 118, 180–82, 190–92; and veterans, 201–2, 206, 208–9, 223–24, 228, 240, 242, 245–49
Port of Spain, Trinidad, 10, 20, 25, 46, 48, 112–13, 138, 248; and demobilization, 179, 187, 190; and discrimination, 137–38; Queen's Park Savannah, 215–16, 219, 221; and recruitment, 51, 57–58, 63–*65*, 67, 83, 87, 89–93, 98; Red House, 214, 235; and veterans' politics, 205–7, 224, 226–27, 230–32, 234–36; Woodford Square, 223, 234
Pouchet, Leon, 161–64, 302n114
Prada, Enrique, 97
Pratt, Mary Louise, 127
press coverage, 3–4, 6–7, 9, 12, 133; and BWIR discrimination, 137, 141, 246, 289n86; and BWIR travel, 116, 120; and commemoration, 242, 244–45; and demobilization, 183, 186, 190; and imperial belonging, 20, 24–25, 30–33, 35, 40–42, 46–48; and labor movements, 234–35; and recruitment, 54, 57–60, 62–69, 72–75, 77–78, 85–86, 89–94, 98, 102–3; and reform, 49, 179–82, 191; and veterans' politics, 192, 205, 209–10, 212–20, 223, 226–27, 230–32, 236–37, 239
privilege, 10, 23, 27, 33, 50, 60, 191, 214; and BWIR, 111, 127, 138, 179; and discrimination, 145–46, 149, 156, 158; and imperial belonging, 27, 33; and recruitment, 74, 77–78, 102. *See also* elite classes
Probyn, Leslie, 34, 40, 62, 103, 165, 176, 182, 186, 230
proficiency pay, 4, 55–56, 143, 145
propaganda, 37, 41, 133
property ownership, 96, 154, 180, 270n68; and veterans, 185–86, 192, 198, 211, 213–14, 236, 245, 247; and veterans' politics, 212, 218, 223–25, 231, 233
protest, 2, 7, 28, 47, 93, 162, 248; and demobilization, 170–71, 177, 183,

193–98, 201, 203; and discrimination, 136, 139–41, 148, 150, 153–56, 159, 167; and veterans' politics, 207, 217–18, 229, 231, 233–34, 239. *See also* uprisings

Putnam, Lara, 11

race, 4–6, 9, 12–13, 15–16, 175, 182, 244, 247; and British Army, 125–26, 187; and discrimination, 140, 144, 146, 161, 166–72; and imperial belonging, 22–24, 27–30, 33, 37, 40–43, 45–50; and interracial encounters, 127–*128*, 130–36; and recruitment, 52–53, 56, 60, 65, 69, 72–76, 82–86, 94, 96–103; and uprisings, 195, 201, 216–17; and veterans' politics, 215–21, 223, 228–29, 234, 242. *See also* equality; interracialism

racism, 4, 6, 13, 41, 48, 122, 161, 244, 250; and British Army, 151, 157, 159, 169–70, 172, 176–77; and BWIR, 118, 141, 146, 150, 300n79; and military labor, 111–12, 118, 135–36; and recruitment, 51–53, 81, 94, 98. *See also* color divisions; white superiority

radicalization, 6, 130, 159, 164, 175, 204, 217, 219, 234

rallies, 13, 53, 63–66, 69, 72, 80, 89, 95, 103

Ratepayers Association, 179

rations, 61, 113, 120, 130

recreation, 4, 14, 88, 111, 120–22, 127, 134, 171, 187, 189. *See also* social life

recruitment, 3–4, 13–14, 113, 120, 127, 138, 141, 148, 259n9; and demobilization, 178, 196, 199; and discrimination, 138, 141, 148–51, 153–54, 156, 163; and imperial belonging, 20, 30–32, 37, 39–41, 46–47; and martial masculinity, 63–87, 89–103; and veterans' politics, 213, 221, 225–28; and West Indies, 51–55, 57–62. *See also* military boosters

Red Cross Society, 53, 63, 66, 116, 124

Reddock, Rhoda, 184

reformism, 7, 9, 118, 164, 198, 248; and demobilization, 177, 179–80, 183, 190–92; and imperial belonging, 20, 23, 46–47, 49–50; and recruitment, 54, 62, 73; and veterans' politics, 202–3, 240

rejection, military, 36–37, 42–45, 51–52, 56, 61, 84–89, 101, 109. *See also* discharge

religion, 2, 4, 19, 64, 111, 122, 146–47, 182; and recruitment, 53, 64, 69, 76, 96. *See also* Anglicanism; Christianity

Renwick, C. F. P., 49, 62

respectability, 13, 107, 140–41, 145–46, 171, 246

Returned Soldiers' and Sailors' Council (RSSC), 205–8, 221–39

rights, political, 2, 6, 10, 23–24, 26, 30, 41, 244, 248, 251; and demobilization, 185, 191, 200; and discrimination, 146, 151, 167, 171; and interracial encounters, 111, 118, 121; and recruitment, 54, 57, 65, 73–74, 86; and veterans' politics, 206, 227, 234

riots, 2, 159, 165, 169–70, 195–97, 201–4. *See also* uprisings

Roberts, Charles, 139–39, 294n7

Roberts, Frederick, 27

Ross, James Ernest, 43

Royal Army Medical Corps, 42

Royal Field Artillery, 32, 43

Royal Flying Corps, 43

Royal Horse Artillery, 32

Royal Mail Steam Packet Company, 44, 113

Royal Marine Artillery, 175

Royal Marines, 176

Royal Warwickshire Fusiliers, 20

rural recruits, 83, 87, 94, 154

Rushdie-Gray, G. O., 43

Russian Revolution, 176, 182

sacrifice, 1, 4, 6, 35, 46, 67, 76, 119, 133, 154; and demobilization, 177, 179–81, 188, 191; and veterans' politics, 212–13, 223, 225, 231, 233, 235, 238, 241, 245–46

Samoa, 186

Sands, James Osborne "Doc," 107

Scott, James, 10

Scottish people, 92, 126, 203

sedition, 2, 164–65, 178, 182, 218

segregation, 48, 51, 171, 300n79

self-government, 47–50, 59, 73, 144, 161–62, 206

separation allowances, 55–56, 67–68, 144–45, 147–48, 156, 198, 274n8

sex, 133–35, 216–17

sexuality, 13, 66, 74

sex workers, 87, 134

Sierra Leone, 32, 38

Simpson, H. A. L., 94, 245

Singh, Kelvin, 208, 228

slavery, 20, 23, 28, 47, 72, 78, 181–82, 231, 242, 244

Smith, Claude, 200

Smith, Faith, 10–11

Smith, Maxwell, 162, 215

Smith, Richard, 133, 270n68

socialism, 180–82, 217

social life, 3, 5, 7, 9–10, 161, 221, 234, 251; and BWIR, 111, 113, 120, 157, 220; and discrimination, 141, 146, 152; and imperial belonging, 22–23, 35, 47–48; and interracial encounters, 126, 130–32; and recruitment, 52–54, 61, 64, 73–74, 78, 94; and reform, 50, 118, 181. *See also* recreation

social mobility, 53, 146, 210

Soldiers and Sailors Union (SSU), 206, 226, 233, 235

solidarity, 116, 150, 157, 203, 221, 234, 242

songs, 13, 72–73, 91, 132–33, 224

sons, 79, 84, 96, 99–100, 208, 213, 245

South Africa, 110, 126, 168, 295n26; Second South African War (Boer War), 25, 166; South African Native Labour Corps, 144; South African Overseas Contingent, 166; South African War, 29, 145; Witwatersrand, 178

South Pacific, 148, 186. *See also individual countries*

Spanish language, 11, 49

Stamfordham, Lord, 44–45

stereotypes, 13, 28, 118, 122, 132, 135–36, 225

St. Kitts and Nevis, *80*, 150, 176, 182

St. Lucia, 79–*80*, 141, 176, 186, 190

Stovall, Tyler, 135

Streets, Heather, 74

strikes, 111, 121, 159, 162–64, 178, 186, 208, 211, 231, 234–35

St. Vincent, 11, 79–*80*, 113, 164, 186

sugar industry, 12, 67, 96, 186

surveillance, 2, 7–8, 162, 164–65, 239

Sutherland, Charles, 194

Thomas, Herbert, 176, 182, 184, 217

Thullier, Henry, 156, 163–64

Thurn, Everard im, 148, 170

Toraille, Felix, 112, 115, 117, 119

Transvaal Town Police, 178

travel, 12, 44, 48, 186; and discrimination, 154–55, 159, 162; and interracial encounters, 100, 109, 111–18, 121, 125; and recruitment, 51, 56, 75–80; and veterans' politics, 181, 186, 191, 201, 211, 228

Treaty of Versailles, 215

trench warfare, 89, 101, 109

Trinidad and Tobago, 2–4, 6–7, 11, 15, 49, 245–46, 250, 286n19, 303n135,

324n21; Archer Coaling Company, 234; and BWIR, 90, 111–14, 118–19, 121–22; and Caribbean League, 161, 165; City Police Court, 62; and demobilization, 176–79, 181–82, 184, 190; and discrimination, 137–38, 141, 148, 153; and elitism, 96–102; Government House, 232–33; Greyfriars Hall, 225–26; and imperial belonging, 20–22, 25, 30, 34, 36, 39, 42, 46–47; Legislative Council, 10, 180, 209, 219, 233, 248; Merchants' and Planters' Contingent, 97–102, 233; Queen's Royal College, 51–52, 101–2; and recruitment, 52–54, 57–64, 67, 72–73, 75, 77–*80*, 82, 85, 87–93; Returned Soldiers' and Sailors' Council (RSSC), 205–8, 221–40; San Fernando, 190, 234; Soldiers and Sailors Union (SSU), 206, 226, 233, 235; St. John's Hall, 228; Trinidad Artillery Corps, 121; Trinidad Electric Company, 238; Trinidad Executive Council, 233; Trinidad Land and Finance Company, 234; Trinidad War Fund, 62; Trinidad Workingmen's Association (TWA), 2, 226, 234–35, 242, 244, 248; and veterans' politics, 205–40. *See also* Port of Spain, Trinidad

Trinidad Workingmen's Association (TWA), 2, 226, 234–35, 242, 244, 248

troopships, 109, 112–17, 123, 125

Union Jack, 23, 36–37, 67, 93, 114, 144, 161, 189, 241

United Fruit Company, 11, 42, 77, 186

United Kingdom, 20, 44, 144–45, 153. *See also* British Army; British Empire; British subjecthood; England; Great Britain

United States, 5, 7, 11–12, 111, 169–70, 203, 248; African American soldiers, 126, 132, 135; British West Indies World War Veterans' Association, 207–8, 246; Harlem, 180, 182, 208, 246; and imperial belonging, 31, 35, 48–49; New York, 13, 79, 181, 207–8, 211; and recruitment, 73, 76–77, 79, 259n9; U.S. Public Health Service, 48

Universal Negro Improvement Association and African Communities League (UNIA), 19–20, 23, 47–48, 69, 177, 180–81, 203

upper classes, 61, 97, 101–2, 150. *See also* elite classes

uprisings, 7, 28, 157, 159, 177–79, 187, 192–203, 217, 219, 223. *See also* protest; riots
urban recruits, 83, 87, 89

venereal disease, 13, 87–88
Venezuela, 11–12, 211
Vernon, H. H. H., 62, 189, 193–94, 198
veterans, 15, 69, 83, 165, 171, 244, 247, 249; black veterans, 1–3, 6–9, 12, 15, 175, 177–79, 198, 206, 210, 231–32; British veterans, 208; colored veterans, 176, 185, 198; and commemoration, 245–46; and demobilization, 176, 178, 180, 184–88; disabled veterans, 116–17, 125, 185, 209, 239, 246–247; and discrimination, 145, 148, 161, 165, 167, 171; and employment, 189–90, 202; and imperial belonging, 31–32, 36–37; and politics, 180–84, 191, 205–21, 248, 250; and supports, 1–2, 6, 185–86; and uprisings, 192–93, 195–204; veterans' organizations, 1–2, 198–200, 202–3, 205–8, 223–40; 246; white veterans, 198
veterinarians, 42–43
Victoria Cross, 31
Victoria I (Queen), 179, 294n12
violence, 7, 15, 43, 159, 162–65, 223, 240; and interracial encounters, 123, 127, 132–33, 135–36, 216, 220; and protest, 139, 143, 155–56, 172, 177–78, 182, 187, 195, 201, 217, 231; and recruitment, 52, 69, 93
volunteerism, 3–4, 8, 11, 13, 181, 244, 246, 250; and demobilization, 175–76, 179, 196; and discrimination, 138, 143, 150, 167–69; and elitism, 95–103; and imperial belonging, 23–24, 26–27, 29–34, 36–40, 42–43, 46; and interracial encounters, 109, 133–35, 138; and recruitment, 51–58, 60–61, 63–64, 66–67, 69, 73, 75–79, 81–92; and veterans' politics, 201, 213, 226
voting, 2, 10, 185, 248

wages, 2, 4, 6, 11, 33, 36, 121, 248, 295n21, 295n23, 297n45, 304n147; and Caribbean League, 162, 165–66; and discrimination, 138, 140–41, 143–45, 147–50, 152–53, 156–57, 162, 167–68, 170; and labor, 130, 211, 234; and recruitment, 55–56, 67; and veterans' politics, 180, 183–84, 186, 188, 190–92, 215, 220–22, 225, 230, 234–35. *See also* Army Order No. 1 (1918); benefits,

soldiers'; compensation; pensions; proficiency pay; war gratuities
Wales, 92, 126; Cardiff, 44
Walter, Robert, 182
War Cabinet, London, 27, 38, 153, 267n33
War Contingent Fund, 45
War Council, London, 175
war gratuities, 170, 183, 188–89, 229, 236–38, 245
War of 1812, 212
War Office, London, 13, 125, 229, 298n64; and Caribbean League, 164–66; and demobilization, 175–77; and discrimination, 138–39, 141, 145–50, 152–53, 155–59, 168–70; and imperial belonging, 24, 26, 29–30, 33–36, 38–45, 50; and recruitment, 54–57, 59–61, 63, 77, 79, 82, 104. *See also* Army Council, London
warships, 177–78, 182–83, 197, 202
Watterson, G. F., 145–46
wealth, 23, 44, 62, 96–97, 103, 134, 245
Western Front, 40–41, 44–45, 77, 100–101, 109; and BWIR, 112, 126–27, 130–31, 133, 145
West Ham Police Court, 44
West India Regiment (WIR), 28, 31–32, 34, 37, 39, 43, 221, 250; and demobilization, 179, 183, 187; and recruitment, 55–56, 92, 97; Second Battalion, 32
West Indies, 3–4, 6, 9, 23, 170, 246; and BWIR, 120, 122–24, 250; and Caribbean League, 160–62, 164; and demobilization, 176–77, 186–87; and discrimination, 137–39, 141, 146–51, 153–54, 156, 158, 160, 166–72; and imperial belonging, 20–21, 24–31, 33, 35–42, 44–45, 47–50; and interracial encounters, 127–36; and recruitment, 52, 54–55, 57, 59, 73–81, 90–93; and reform, 179, 181; and transatlantic travel, 107, 109, 111–12, 115–19; and veterans' politics, 211, 221; West Indian Federation Committee, 49. *See also* black West Indians; white West Indians
white men, 13, 15, 133, 170, 176, 180, 202–3; and BWIR, 110, 149; and Caribbean League, 161–62; and imperial belonging, 20, 22–25, 29–33, 42, 46, 50; and racism, 111–12, 126, 146; and recruitment, 36, 52–54, 61, 64, 82, 93–94, 96–99, 101–3; and veterans' politics, 206, 218. *See also* white servicemen; white superiority

white people, 14, 41, 46, 74, 143, 162, 175, 182, 187, 199; white civilians, 112, 118, 122, 133, 135, 155; white elites, 82, 98, 116, 166, 179, 195–97, 209, 213, 218–19, 227–28; white women, 65, 119, 133–35, 176, 216–18. *See also* white men; white servicemen; white superiority; white West Indians

white servicemen, 4–8, 13, 54, 150–51, 162, 179, 189, 198, 242; and discrimination, 101–3, 111–12, 126, 135, 154–56, 158–59, 161–62, 172, 244; and imperial belonging, 37–38, 42; and recruitment, 56, 61, 67, 74, 81, 85, 97; and veterans' politics, 215–16, 218–20, 224, 226–28, 233. *See also* British servicemen; white superiority

white superiority, 50, 52, 73, 146. *See also* racism

white West Indians, 110, 149, 154, 179, 185, 189, 195–97, 218–19, 239; and demobilization, 175, 179, 185, 187, 189, 195–97, 201, 203; and imperial belonging, 20–24, 29–33; and recruitment, 64, 82, 96, 98

Wickham, Clennell Wilsden, 109–11, 245

widows, 56, 183–84

Wilhelm II (Kaiser), 50

Williams, Chad, 12

Williams, Henry Sylvester, 118

Willis, Reginald E., 154–55, 157, 165

Wilson, William, 61, 167, 303n135

Windward Islands, 57–59, 84, 153, 178, 303n135

Wiseman, R. A., 27–29, 38, 60–61, 99

wives, 54, 56, 66–69, 87, 99, 117, 135–36, 202, 210

women, 5, 11, 13, 47–48, 53, 146–47, 246, 309n60; black West Indian women, 25, 31, 67, 180–81; and BWIR, 110, 119, 121–22, 131, 134–35; and Caribbean League, 160–61; and labor, 133, 148, 184; and recruitment, 64–68, 72, 88, 90, 93, 95; and veterans' politics, 183, 185, 190–91, 194, 200–203, 207, 223; white women, 65, 119, 133–35, 176, 216–18; Women's Recruiting Committee, 66

Wood-Hill, Charles, 107, 114, 125, 138, 153–54, 159

Woods, Phillip, 192

working classes, 2, 10–11, 13, 25–26, 44–45, 154, 184–85, 190, 234; and recruitment, 53, 62–63, 66, 75, 83–85, 94, 96–97, 100, 103; and uprisings, 200–201; and veterans' politics, 206, 208, 214, 217, 221, 234. *See also* labor, civilian

working conditions, 2, 139, 154, 251. *See also* labor, civilian

World War I, 1, 3–4, 6–7, 9–15, 101, 166; and BWIR, 109, 111, 118, 126, *129–130*, 133, 157; and commemoration, 241–42, 244, 246, 249–50; and demobilization, 175–76, 181, 183, 186, 188; and imperial belonging, 19–20, 23–27, 34, 43; and recruitment, 51–53, 58–59, 62, 69, 74; and veterans, 205–6; and veterans' politics, 213, 221, 239

World War II, 3, 12, 249–50

Wyatt, Robert, 189, 195–96, 202, 314n162

youth, 48, 51, 64, 90, 102, 109, 200, 210. *See also* children